Mastering
Theology

Palgrave Master Series

Accounting
Accounting Skills
Advanced English Language
Advanced English Literature
Advanced Pure Mathematics
Arabic
Basic Management
Biology
British Politics
Business Communication
Business Environment
C Programming
C++ Programming
Chemistry
COBOL Programming
Communication
Computing
Counselling Skills
Customer Relations
Database Design
Delphi Programming
Desktop Publishing
Economic and Social History
Economics
Electrical Engineering
Electronic and Electrical Calculations
Electronics
Employee Development
English Grammar
English Language
English Literature
Fashion Buying and Merchandising
    Management
Fashion Styling
French

Geography
German
Global Information Systems
Human Resource Management
Information Technology
Internet
Italian
Java
Management Skills
Marketing Management
Mathematics
Microsoft Office
Microsoft Windows, Novell
    NetWare and UNIX
Modern British History
Modern European History
Modern United States History
Modern World History
Networks
Organisational Behaviour
Pascal and Delphi Programming
Philosophy
Physics
Practical Criticism
Psychology
Shakespeare
Social Welfare
Sociology
Spanish
Statistics
Strategic Management
Systems Analysis and Design
Theology
Visual Basic
World Religions

www.palgravemasterseries.com

Palgrave Master Series
Series Standing Order ISBN 0–333–69343–4
(outside North America only)

You can receive future titles in this series as they are published by placing a standing order. Please contact your bookseller or, in case of difficulty, write to us at the address below with your name and address, the title of the series and the ISBN quoted above.

Customer Services Department, Macmillan Distribution Ltd.
Houndmills, Basingstoke, Hampshire RG21 6XS, England

Mastering
Theology

Michaela Davey

palgrave

First published 2002 by
PALGRAVE
Houndmills, Basingstoke, Hampshire RG21 6XS and
175 Fifth Avenue, New York, N.Y. 10010
Companies and representatives throughout the world

PALGRAVE is the new global academic imprint of
St. Martin's Press LLC Scholarly and Reference Division and
Palgrave Publishers Ltd (formerly Macmillan Press Ltd).

ISBN 0–333–61172–1

This book is printed on paper suitable for recycling and
made from fully managed and sustained forest sources.

A catalogue record for this book is available
from the British Library.

Library of Congress cataloging-in-publication data has been applied for.

10   9   8   7   6   5   4   3   2   1
11 10 09 08 07 06 05 04 03 02

Printed and bound in Great Britain by
Creative Print and Design (Wales), Ebbw Vale

Contents

Preface

Mastering Theology brings together in one book an introduction to the main themes in Christian theology. It is aimed at a wide readership, including theology undergraduates, and those training for the ministry at theological colleges of all denominations throughout the English-speaking world. It should also be helpful for those studying towards examinations for the lay ministry.

The book provides a simplified view of basic issues in the Christian faith. It introduces the Hebrew Scriptures and the New Testament, as well as surveying the development of Christianity from its infancy right through to major themes in ethics and modern theology.

Theology can be a daunting subject to approach because of the vast array of theological tomes that intimidate us by their size and language. This informative, wide-ranging book will give the newcomer a manageable overview, and will stimulate interest to pursue further study. Theology can be a very exciting subject, and learning about it helps to deepen our understanding of the Christian faith.

This book assumes no previous knowledge of theology, and all the major issues are presented in a readable format to help those with an interest to find their way around the subject. Anyone who reads this useful introduction will gain a greater awareness of Christianity, and will be left with the desire to find out more about it.

This book started off as a joint venture with the Reverend Joanna Penberthy, but owing to Joanna's work commitments it became a single project. I am very grateful for her substantial input to Chapters 1, 2, 3 and 11.

Finally, I must also mention my husband Charles Davey. When I first started writing this book, Charles paid little attention to my venture. However, as time went by, he became increasingly interested in the subject and started to research various points that we had discussed, or argued over! Many of the chapters owe much to his contributions.

Michaela Davey

Acknowledgements

The authors and publishers wish to thank the following for permission to use copyright material:

Penguin Books Ltd for figure, 'Number of Abbeys of Cistercian Monks, 1098–1500' from R W Southern, *The Pelican History of the Church: Western Society and the Church in the Middle Ages*, Penguin Books (1970) p. 254. Copyright © R W Western, 1970.

Every effort has been made to trace the copyright holders but if any have been inadvertently overlooked the publishers will be pleased to make the necessary arrangement at the first opportunity.

I would especially like to express my appreciation to Suzannah Tipple, Publisher, for her constructive comments, and professional advice.

I am also grateful for the anonymous publishers' reviewers for their helpful criticism and encouragement.

Maps

■ ⋎ ▮ The history of the Jewish people in the biblical period

1.1 Definitions

The term 'Israel' has been shown to refer to at least ten different entities in biblical literature. A definition of 'Jewish' is equally problematic; it derives from the Greek version of Judaeans and strictly speaking refers to those coming from the small southern state centred on Jerusalem. Josephus who, in the first century, wrote a history of the Jewish people from Adam to Nehemiah, said the term derived from those who had returned from Babylon to Palestine after the exile. As with 'Israel', whenever the term is used, whether in the biblical literature or in modern studies, it is necessary to ask oneself: which Israel? which Jewish people?

The term seems originally to have referred to the tribes that lived in the hill country of Ephraim and later the northern kingdom. This is how we shall normally use the term, although our interest covers the forebears of all those who later felt themselves to belong to Israel.

BOX 1.1

From the work of A.R. Hurst and H. Hayes, ten meanings for Israel have been identified:

1. the name of the ancestor Jacob;
2. a name for the descendants of Jacob/Israel;
3. the name of a sacral league of tribes;
4. a pre-monarchic tribal grouping in Ephraim;
5. the name of a united kingdom at Jerusalem;
6. the name of one of the kingdoms into which that kingdom was later divided, i.e. the northern kingdom;
7. after 722, another name for Judah;
8. after the exile, the name for the socio-religious community within the province of Yehud;
9. the name of a group within this community, the laity as opposed to the clergy, known as Aaron;
10. adherents of various forms of Hebrew and Old Testament religion.

Scholars are divided in what they see as the task of the historian of the biblical period. The 'biblical period' normally means the time span that the Hebrew Bible describes or purports to describe. Some regard the narratives as fundamentally truthful. They see the role of the historian as being that of fleshing out with extra-biblical evidence the essential historicity of the biblical account. Others see the whole of the Hebrew Bible story as being a construct of the faith and beliefs of those who wrote and preserved the biblical documents, who constructed a past to justify a present reality or future hope. Scholars disagree about the dating of the final redaction of the first five books of the Hebrew Bible, known as the Penta-teuch, and the historical books. Some would place this writing of the past at the time of the exile in the mid-sixth century BCE. Others date it as late as the Hasmonaean state in the second century BCE. If the books of the Hebrew Bible are regarded as a construction from a much later period, then the historian's task is to see what if anything can be known of those who inhabited Palestine from the late Bronze Age (*c.* **1550–1200**) to the rule of the Hasmonaeans. Some even preclude using the Bible as evidence and on that basis discount the existence of the united monarchy under David, since there is no external evidence to verify it.

Few scholars, however, would argue that the biblical narratives were made up entirely of material that had been newly written for the purpose. It is generally agreed that they are made up of several layers, some of which probably originated in an oral form. While an early date does not prove historicity, the inclusion of ancient traditions does give the Hebrew Bible some evidential authority.

1.2 Sources

The Hebrew Bible

The main source for the history of Ancient Israel is obviously the various biblical narratives themselves. Even the historical books (Joshua, Judges, I Samuel, II Samuel, I Kings, II Kings, I Chronicles, II Chronicles, Ezra and Nehemiah), how-ever, cannot be regarded as dispassionate accounts of what actually happened. Rather they are attempts to explain the experiences of the people from a particu-lar theological standpoint. However old the tradition which they contain (and few would deny the existence of old material within the biblical corpus), each book of the Hebrew Bible was put together at a particular time, by a particular individual or group looking at the traditions they received from the stance of their own faith.

All written history is interpretation, even the historical books of the Bible. The oral form of the tradition would also have been moulded by the faith and prac-tice of those who preserved and passed them on. To use the Hebrew Bible as a source for the history of the people who lived in Palestine, we must appreciate that the faith, outlook and preconceptions of those who formed the books and those who had transmitted the traditions they contain affected the way this story was told.

The biblical books are useful for the background detail they contain. Their accounts of contemporary customs, geography or political realities make them invaluable for the historian even though the stories they tell cannot be taken simply at face value. Whilst it is not always easy to tell which period they reflect, assistance can be derived from extra-biblical evidence.

Extra-biblical sources

(i) Documents

These include secular documents such as administrative records, accounts of military campaigns, records of trade and religious documents describing wisdom or myth from nations surrounding Israel. Pseudepigraphal or apocryphal books, which were books that sections of the Jewish community revered but which the Rabbis later excluded from the canon, may also contain early traditions.

The first mention of Israel in ancient documents is in a triumphal hymn inscribed on a black basalt stela from the fifth year of Pharaoh Mernephtah's reign. It speaks of their defeat alongside Philistine cities and means that their occupation of parts of Canaan must have preceded this date, thought to have been about **1207 BCE**. 'Documents' range from scrolls and papyri, to large stone monuments and clay tablets. Some of the ancient civilisations that surrounded Israel kept libraries or annals and parts of these have been discovered by archaeologists. Israel and Judah kept annals of the reigns of their kings (see, for example, in II Kings 12: 8) but unfortunately none of them survive.

(ii) Remains

As well as discovering documents of varying types, archaeologists have studied the way in which people lived at differing periods within the region. Much has been learnt from the rubbish that settlements have left behind, such as broken pottery, as well as from buildings and ruins which survive. Even the land itself shows traces of ancient farming practices. Such testimony is mute, however, and such traces can tell us little about the self-consciousness of the people who left them.

1.3   Beginnings

The victory stela of Pharaoh Mernephtah provides us with a fixed point. 'Israel' (whatever that encompassed at the time) was in Canaan in sufficient numbers for Pharaoh to consider his victory over them worth mentioning. The start of Mernephtah's reign is dated anywhere from **1238** to **1213**. So the late thirteenth century BCE provides the dividing line between the history of 'Israel's' settlement of Canaan and its prehistory which the Bible records in the Pentateuchal narratives. What, if anything, can be known of this earlier period?

1.3.1   The ancestral period

Biblical sources: Genesis 12: 1 – 50: 26

Those who assembled the Pentateuch (the first five books of the Hebrew Bible, also known as the Torah) saw the roots of their people's history not in David's monarchy or the settlement of Canaan by the 'children of Israel' but in the stories of Abraham, Hagar, Sarah, Isaac, Rebecca, Jacob, Leah, Rachel and Esau. They saw the growth of the two kingdoms, of Israel and Judah, as fulfilling the promises to the ancestors that their descendants would inherit the land of Canaan through which the ancestors had wandered. Were these stories passed down from one generation to the next from an historical ancestral age? Some scholars feel the stories reflect later hopes and aspirations projected back into the past, while others feel that disparate traditions from the various groups that came to form Israel and Judah have been merged into something more cohesive.

Were there ever historical people called Abraham, Isaac, Jacob or Joseph, or does any vestige of historical veracity that lies in the stories adhere to tribal movements rather than to individuals? Perhaps the truth lies in-between. Stories such as the rape of Dinah and Simeon and Levi's response in Gen 34, or Tamar's begetting of children at all costs in Gen 38, are usually thought to represent tribal or clan traditions. On the other hand, accounts of God appearing to an ancestor at a particular place are thought to be drawn from the traditions which were used to legitimate a particular shrine, for example, Abraham at Mamre/Hebron in Gen 12 or Jacob at Bethel in Gen 28: 10ff. The narratives also legitimise customs in the same way, for example, circumcision in Gen 17 or the ban on human sacrifice from Gen 22. Stories that are used to legitimise or explain the origin of something are called aetiological. At one time scholars believed that the patriarchal figures were the memories of tribal gods but few if any would defend that idea now.

It is impossible to be certain about the origins of these stories. Some scholars believe that the ancestral stories have no basis in history whatsoever but are an attempt to give legitimacy to a situation that existed, or was hoped for, at the time when the Pentateuch was written. Ancient stories that promised the land to Israel's ancestors would keep national sympathies alive at times of crisis. There were still some scholars, however, who though recognising the tribal background to some stories and the aetiological nature of others, maintained that such figures as Abraham, Isaac and Jacob probably did exist even if not as father, son and grandson, and were ancestors to at least some of those who later became 'Israel'.

As to dating, some scholars consider that the pentateuchal stories best reflect the milieu of the court of the united monarchy, whence one of the strands of the Pentateuch noted by Wellhausen (for more details see Chapter 2) was once thought to have derived. They therefore maintain that the search for an 'ancestral age' in Israel's prehistory is nonsense. Others, agreeing that the narratives tell us nothing about an 'ancestral age', would argue that the Pentateuch reflects later periods such as the exile, the time of Nehemiah or of the Maccabees (who liberated Judaea from Seleucid rule).

Those who believe in the basic historicity of the ancestral narratives hailed the discovery of tablets from Mari and Nuzi as bearing this out. Mari was the centre of a kingdom which developed as the Sumerian kingdom centred on Ur declined. It held sway as far as Haran before it was itself destroyed in **1697 BCE** by Hammurabi of Babylon. Archaeologists have found over twenty thousand cuneiform tablets from the site and many of the names which we know from the ancestral narratives are there. Tablets from the fifteenth century BCE found at Nuzi show similarity with ancestral customs mirrored in the Pentateuch. For example, slave adoption was practised by childless men, hence Abram's fear that only Eliezer would inherit from him; likewise allowed in these texts is the practice of a childless wife giving her slave girl to her husband to bear children. In such cases, the rights of the woman and any children she bore were protected, which gives a context to Abram's concern for Ishmael and Hagar. Such congruence does not, of course, demonstrate the historicity of the Genesis stories. How texts which some scholars believe derive from after the exile or later came to reflect the legal code of late bronze age Nuzi rather than 'Israel's' own legal codes is something which, nevertheless, has to be explained. Some argue that these customs are more widely spread than was once thought and that their occurrence in the ancestral narratives does not help us to define an ancestral age.

Scholars used to feel that the wanderings of the Patriarchs in Genesis reflect the tribal movements of the West Semitic/Amorite peoples and that, therefore, if any historicity attaches to the stories at all, the period c. 1700–1300 BCE can best be termed the 'Ancestral' or 'Patriarchal Age'. But the theory of large-scale Amorite invasions at this time has now largely been discounted. Archaeologists have noticed a decline in urban centres at this time but do not think it necessarily implies large-scale migrations.

Most scholars would now see the patriarchal narratives as reflecting the concerns of those who told the stories or wrote them down rather than of any specific ancestral age. The stories were told about local heroes or ancestor figures who may or may not have existed. Opinion is divided about where these traditions come from. Although Hebron and Beersheba appear particularly in the Abraham and Isaac stories, some scholars feel that the original site of these stories was in the hill country of Ephraim and Benjamin, and that the southern emphasis comes from a later period when Judah was in political ascendancy. Genesis 13 preserves a tradition that Abraham lived further north. Jacob-el occurs as a place name in lists of enemies conquered by Pharaohs, firstly in the reign of Thutmosis III, c. 1483–50 BCE and finally in Ramesses III's reign, 1198–66. It is thought to have been near Beth-Shean. The origins of Israel seem to be in this area.

The precursors of Israel were small farmers and pastoralists who would have had to move their flocks around to get the best pasture, and who would have seen themselves as distinct from the city dwellers. Whether this distinction is enough to account for the sense of foreignness to be found in the ancestral stories is debatable. Later Israel definitely saw their origins as doubly outside the land: the land was 'conquered' by those who had been foreigners in Egypt and the ancestral figures, tied to shrines and sites in Canaan, were described as coming from outside, from even beyond the river Euphrates. Some see the word 'Hebrew' as deriving from the word 'eber', meaning 'beyond'.

1.3.2 Ancestral religion

Although the name YHWH appears in the Genesis stories as a name for the god who appeared to the ancestors (Gen 15: 2; 21: 1; 22: 14), the story of Moses at the burning bush (Ex 3) says that the name YHWH was introduced by Moses to a community which had previously worshipped the God/Shield of Abraham, the God/Fear/Kinsman of Isaac and the God/Mighty One of Israel/Jacob: the God of the/your fathers. Whether or not there was a group in Egypt worshipping the God of the Fathers who had prior links with Canaan, later Israel depicted its earliest forebears as worshipping a god who had revealed himself to their ancestors at particular places or by a particular designation. The God of Abraham was associated with Hebron and the Mighty One of Jacob at Bethel, and El Roi with Hagar at Beerlahairoi. In Gen 17: 1 God revealed himself to Abraham as 'El Shaddai', God Almighty. El was the name for the Canaanite High God who was worshipped at different shrines throughout Palestine under different appellations reflecting different manifestations of the same god.

BOX 1.3.2

YHWH – pronounced Yahweh. At that time Hebrew had no vowels. Now vowels are represented by a system of dots.

In the ancestral narratives of Genesis, the manifestation of the deity was not tied to a particular shrine but to a particular person, i.e. Abraham or Jacob who subsequently became linked to a certain pre-existing El shrine. Although those scholars who see no historical setting from which the ancestral stories derived would deny the validity of any attempt to isolate the characteristics of the religion of the patriarchs, it seems clear that the Pentateuch does bear witness to a memory that YHWHism was introduced at some stage to groups who worshipped the god of the fathers.

As will be apparent from the above, the origins of later Israel are impossible to recover but the end of the late Bronze age (*c.* **1200**) is a likely setting for the emergence of new tribes and peoples in Canaan, whether their stories bore any relation to the patriarchal narratives or not. It was at this period that Egypt's control over her Empire in Canaan was weakening, the Hittite Empire in northern Syria had fragmented into warring city states and the Dorian invasion of Greece had given rise to the migration of the Sea Peoples into the Near East. One of these Sea Peoples was the Philistines who, in turn, pushed the existing inhabitants into central Canaan, an area sparsely populated. It is to this area and time that we will return after we have considered the Exodus narratives.

1.3.3 The Egypt, exodus and wilderness traditions

Biblical sources: Exodus, Leviticus, Numbers and Deuteronomy

Genesis ends with a group of Abraham's descendants going to live in Egypt because of famine in Canaan. The remainder of the Pentateuch tells of their stay in Egypt, their escape and their journey to Canaan. As with the ancestral narratives, opinion is divided as to whether any credence can be given to these accounts. Some see them as reflecting more of the theology of the final redactors than the experiences of some ancient peoples and maintain that to look for historical parallels in Egypt and Canaan of the late bronze age is to misunderstand the nature of the texts. Others argue that comparison with other sources shows that these texts contain at least enough consistent memories of the period which they purport to describe to merit granting them some status as an historical source.

A tablet dating from the reign of Sethos II (*c.* **1200/1190**) has been found containing a report from the Egyptian border on the east of the Nile delta detailing how a group of Semitic nomads had been allowed through the border to pasture their flocks on Egyptian land beyond. Whilst it comes from a period later than most scholars would want to date the exodus, it does show that the biblical conception of nomads being allowed to graze within Egyptian borders in the eastern delta, as Jacob's descendants were said to have done, is credible.

It has been conjectured that the Pharaoh under whom Joseph is said to have risen to prominence was himself a Semite. From about **1674–1565 BCE** a group known as the Hyskos dominated Egypt; their name is the Greek version of their Egyptian name which means 'foreign lords' and they are thought to have been Semitic in origin. For those seeking a correlation between the biblical account and 'history', this could give a neat 400 years (the biblical time span, see Gen 15: 3; Ex 12: 40) between the arrival of Jacob's family in Egypt and a date of *c.* **1230** for the exodus! However, the correlation with the Hyskos remains only an hypothesis.

Most scholars would agree that the Joseph stories at the end of Genesis (chapters 39–50) are different from the rest of the book in that they form a coherent whole and bear the hallmarks of a novella. The story is accurate in many of its details such as the price given for Joseph by the slave traders, 20 shekels of silver – the going rate in the late seventeenth and early eighteenth century according to the stele of Hammurabi (**1728–1686**). The price had dropped by the thirteenth century to 10 shekels according to the Ras Shamra texts from Ugarit. That the names of the Egyptians in the story are common in the tenth century BCE will counsel against any easy conclusions, however.

Pharaoh Mernephtah's victory against the 'men of Israel' was recorded towards the end of the thirteenth century BCE. For those scholars who see the Bible enshrining a memory of historical events, this fits in well with the interpretation of Exodus 1: 11 and 2: 23 as reflecting the time of the 19th dynasty (*c.* **1310–1200**) agreed by most scholars. To fit the Exodus in before Israel is mentioned on Mernephtah's stela, the Pharaoh of the exodus narratives would have to be his predecessor, Ramesses II, or the Pharaoh who died 'after a long time' (Ex 2: 23), Sethos I. However, since it is Ramesses II who reigned for about 70 years, it is more likely to be his death which the Bible records. That this points to a group in Canaan already known to Pharaoh Mernephtah as Israel at about the same period as the Exodus fits in with the perception in Genesis that the name Israel was one that was added, rather than native to the ancestral traditions (Gen 35: 9). Few Old Testament scholars would defend the assertion that the ancestors of all those who later felt themselves to be Israel had experienced the stay in Egypt and the Exodus.

Genesis records how Joseph's family came to Egypt, while Exodus tells how a Pharaoh arose 'who did not know Joseph' (Ex 1: 80) and who put the people to forced labour 'and they built for the Pharaoh store-cities Pithom and Raamses' (Ex 1: 12). Extra-biblical sources from the thirteenth century show that the Pharaohs used forced labour and built on a large scale in the eastern delta in this period. Moses is an Egyptian name (from the same root as the pharaonic names, Thutmoses and Ramesses), as are Phinehas (Num 25: 7), Hophni (I Sam 1: 3) and Hur (Ex 17: 10), which points to knowledge of an Egyptian connection if nothing else.

What, if anything, can be known about the events that gave rise to the accounts in Ex 1–15? Has the story grown around the Passover festival (which on this understanding would have been, originally, a spring festival, which was to mark the change from winter to summer pasturage or the birth of lambs) as a way of explaining its origins? If this were the case, the birth of these stories would have to be fairly late, as in II Kings 23: 22 it is clear that Josiah's holding of the Passover festival marked the first of any note since the time of the judges, although II Chronicles speaks of a renewal of the Passover in the reign of Hezekiah. In Ezra 6: 19, the returning exiles and those who had separated themselves from the people of the land celebrated the Passover and by the time of Jesus, the Passover was celebrated on a large scale. A good case could be made for seeing the narrative in Exodus as providing an ancient rationale for a later festival. However this ignores such features in the description of how the Passover was celebrated as the lack of sanctuary and priesthood in the Exodus 12 account, which imply an earlier origin.

The event of plagues, escape of forced labourers and the destruction of Egyptian soldiers while in pursuit are not mentioned in any extra-biblical text, and many of the places in the wilderness narratives are unknown to us. Yet, to say that no evidence has survived is not the same as saying something did not happen; the stance that a scholar takes about the historicity of the text is therefore often a matter of hermeneutics, a question of how he interprets the text. For example, the majority of biblical scholars accept that the book of Jonah is a story, a parable, and therefore to look at a point in the history of Nineveh at which Jonah's ministry is taking place is to misread the point of the text (although the prophet Jonah, son of Amittai mentioned in II Kings 14: 25 was prophesying during the reign of Jeroboam II and hence when Assyria was in its ascendancy!). Thus scholars who see the Pentateuch as being composed to answer a theological need of its redactors will not be as impressed with historical congruences as scholars who see the texts as historical documents, albeit ones that need careful handling. The former will not expect any thirteenth century extra-biblical evidence to back up the biblical account, while the latter will continue to assess the text historically without it; but both treatments will be driven by the prior decision that the scholar has made about the nature of the biblical text.

What is generally agreed to be among the earliest material in the bible, the Song of Deliverance (Ex 15: 1–18) has been placed in Exodus as a commentary on the events of the flight from Egypt and the failure of the Egyptian pursuers. While the earliest date for the poem as a whole must be after the settlement of Jerusalem (verse 17), some commentators think that the first couplet, repeated at verse 21 as Miriam's song, is much older and perhaps even derives from the event itself. A leather scroll, dated from the 5th year of Ramesses II's reign, records the feast day of a certain goddess which was a holiday for the conscripted labourers, and a tablet found in Thebes records how labourers were idle on certain days because they had gone to make offerings to their gods. Against this background, Moses' plea in Ex 5: 25–9 sounds more plausible.

Much scholarly effort has gone into finding the place where the crossing of the Red Sea might have occurred. The Hebrew 'Yam Suf' has been retranslated as Reed Sea, but more recent scholarship has concluded that the traditional translation of Red Sea is correct. In the case of the Exodus narratives this refers to the Gulf of Suez (it is also used elsewhere for the Gulf of Aqaba), which it is thought extended further north in the thirteenth century BCE, but quite what experience lies behind the text is impossible to know.

The same uncertainty clouds the wanderings in the wilderness. Not all of the places mentioned have been located, not even Sinai/Horeb, the mountain of God. One thing that is clear throughout the people's history is the memory that YHWH came from the south; he was not a God native to Palestine but the God which the people brought with them into the land.

BOX 1.3.3

Where does YHWH come from?

Ex 3: 1	Moses at the burning bush on Mt Horeb in the wilderness and part of the range of the priest of Midian's pasturage
Ex 17: 6	Rock of Horeb linked with Massah and Meribah, near Kadesh Barnea
Ex 19	God spoke to the people through Moses at Sinai
Deut 1: 6	God spoke to the people through Moses at Horeb
Deut 1: 2	Horeb is 11 days' journey from Kadesh Barnea by way of Mt Seir
Deut 33: 2	Sinai, Seir, Mt Paran
Judges 5: 4–5	Seir, Edom, Sinai
I Kings 19: 8	Elijah sought God at Horeb, forty days and forty nights into the wilderness from Beersheba
Habb 3: 3	Teman, Mt Paran

In Exodus, YHWH is seen as revealing himself to Moses on the holy mountain in the land of Midian. But where is Midian? Some scholars believe it to be in north-west Arabia, although the Midianites are mentioned in connection with many different parts of Palestine also. It is interesting that Jethro, priest of Midian, with whom Moses took refuge after his first flight from Egypt when he had his encounter with YHWH at the burning bush, according to Ex 2–3, is mentioned again at the point in Exodus when the people are at the rock of Horeb near Massah and Meribah. Could Midian have been here? The tradition persists later on. Elijah who lived, according to I Kings 17: 1*ff*, in the reign of Ahab (*c.* 875–53), went south from Beersheba into the wilderness to meet with YHWH on Mt Horeb.

While there is doubt about where the mountain is, it seems clear that YHWH was a mountain and storm god. Few accept that the account of the wanderings in the wilderness describes a real journey of all the ancestors of those who became Israel. While some scholars feel little credence can be given to the accounts at all, others think that memories of various groups have been merged. However, it is clear from the wilderness stories that it was during their time in the wilderness that the people were bonded to YHWH, who then led them into the promised land where they merged with existing groups. So strong were the Horeb/Sinai traditions that they became dominant. What if anything can be learned about the Sinai/Horeb encounter?

In the final redaction of the Pentateuch, Sinai becomes synonymous with YHWH giving the law to Moses, but some scholars see evidence of earlier accounts particularly in Ex 24. Despite the prohibition in Ex 24: 2 on the elders coming near

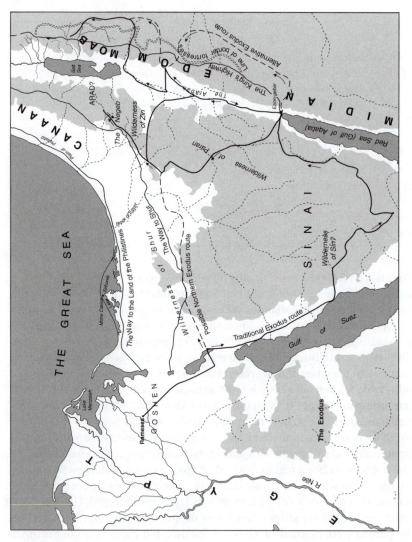

Map 1 The Exodus

to worship, in verses 9–11 we have an account of how all the elders saw 'the God of Israel' and ate and drank before him unharmed. Some feel this is the kernel of the Sinai 'event', the original cultic ceremony, which has become overlaid subsequently by the account of the receiving of the Mosaic law and the making of the covenant. Some scholars would argue that the Decalogue belongs originally in Deuteronomy and was later inserted at the relevant point of the story in Exodus.

The idea of law being delivered by a god is ancient. The stele of Hammurabi, which has a legal collection written on it, includes a depiction of the god Shamash giving the law to the king and dates back to *c*. **1792–1750 BCE**. Moses, of course, was not the king. Did the 'Mosaic' law originate with pronouncements of the king, as some scholars think, or can its origins be traced back into pre-monarchic times? It is unlikely to date from a period of wandering, as most of the laws imply a settled existence. This does not in itself preclude a pre-Canaan period, as the tradition includes a long stay in the wilderness outside Canaan. The pre-monarchic source for Israel's law is likely to have been the pronouncements of the Levites. The earliest role for priests in Israel, if the account in Judges can be given any historical credence, is that of delivering the decision of YHWH about a particular problem. The answer may have been arrived at using the Urim and Thummin, probably a way of arriving at YHWH's decision by lot and mentioned at Num 27: 21. Even if these became entwined with royal laws at a later stage, it is true that throughout its history, Israel remained conscious that YHWH, not the king or priesthood, was the ultimate source and sanctioner of its legal code.

In Exodus 25: 10 to 27: 21, there are elaborate instructions about the building of the ark, table, sacrificial vessels, a lamp-stand, curtains and a tent. Although the account looks straightforward, it presents a number of problems. Scholars have doubted that such an elaborate shrine could possibly have been carried around by nomads or that whichever tribes comprised Israel at the time could have possessed the skills required to make it, since years later, when making the Temple in Jerusalem, Solomon had to draw on the skills of the kingdom of Tyre. Some scholars have pointed to the portable shrines of the Bedu as evidence for the possibility that the tribes did indeed have a shrine which they carried with them before they entered the land. There is a certain confusion within the Pentateuch itself: some stories refer to a tent which was outside the camp, Ex 33: 7, the 'tent of meeting', to which YHWH would descend in a pillar of cloud when Moses went in; others describe the 'tabernacle of Testimony' surrounded by the Levites, Num 1: 52–3, or by all the tribes in order, Num 2: 1*ff*, in which YHWH dwelt in the middle of the camp, Num 5: 3.

There is confusion also about the ark. What did it contain? Deuteronomy 10: 2 says it held the two tablets of stone upon which YHWH had written his laws and statutes; Exodus and Numbers concur but in Exodus the two tablets are joined by a jar of Manna, 16: 40, while in Numbers it is Aaron's rod, 17: 10.

Various other cultic objects are also mentioned in the Pentateuch. The golden bulls are mentioned with horror (Ex 32) and the bronze serpent (perhaps this is the aetiology for the bronze serpent which Hezekiah had removed from the Temple, II Kings 18: 4*f*) simply in passing (Num 21: 4–9); the Ephod and Urim and Thummim (Lev 8: 8) have become part of the High Priestly vestments. Some think that sacred items from differing groups have been combined in the Pentateuchal traditions.

As with the ancestral narratives, it is difficult to discover the truth about any events which may lie behind the narratives in Exodus and Numbers. While it is easy to see how the story of YHWH wandering with his people towards the promised land with neither King nor Temple was important for those in exile in Babylon, people do not usually derive strength from a story they know to have been recently made up. While its later centrality may come from the use it was put to at the time of the exile, it would seem most likely that the story does ultimately go back to a group which came to be part of Israel, who did experience oppression in Egypt and saw their entry to Canaan as their deliverance.

1.4   Settlement

Biblical sources: Joshua and Judges

The original scholarly view of the settlement of Canaan was that Joshua led the tribes over the Jordan and they fought their way through to conquest, each tribe routing the Canaanites in the area which had been assigned to them.

This is the impression that the narrative of Joshua wished to portray but archaeology reveals a different picture. There was indeed a large infiltration of population into the hill country of Ephraim and Benjamin *c.* **1200 BCE**, a proliferation of small unfortified settlements over the area which were settled from north-west to south-east. Between Shechem and Hebron, archaeologists have found over a hundred new settlements which date from this period. However there is little evidence of the clashes described in the book of Joshua. There is no archaeological evidence that Jericho was a walled city between *c.* **1400** and **1200**; it was occupied briefly *c.* **1325** but at this time was uninhabited and was only inhabited again about **1200** as a village. The burnt rubble there has been dated to a conflict *c.* **2400**. At the site that is thought to be Chephirah, there are no thirteenth century remains nor is there any trace of occupation in this period at Arad, Heshbon, Hormah or Jarmuth. Hazor, Lachish and Debir were destroyed around or before **1230** although archaeology can give no clues as to the identify of its assailants. Alt's theory of a gradual peaceful settlement is now generally accepted and it fits in better with the picture we are given in Judges 1 where the limits of Israel's occupation are freely acknowledged.

The conflict of the Joshua account is thought by some to fit more naturally in the milieu of the United Monarchy when Israel was developing as a state and extending her control over the land. No account of ancient history can ever be definitive, however, and who knows when new evidence will compel a reassessment!

1.5   Pre-monarchic Israel

Biblical sources: Judges; I Sam 1–7; I Chron 1–2

Scholars like Martin Noth once thought that Israel's existence before the monarchy could best be understood by analogy to the cultic groupings of ancient Greece, where city states, under allegiance to a common shrine, became an alliance. He felt that in a similar way, the twelve tribes of Israel formed an alliance under common allegiance to YHWH. Scholars now feel that the twelve tribe structure was a product of the United Monarchy rather than its forerunner and that the original tribal grouping of Israel was smaller. This is borne out by the evidence of Judges where small groups of tribes acted together against a common enemy.

The largest grouping of the tribes of Israel to act together was under the leadership of Deborah. In the prose account of the battle against Jabin, king of Hazor, only the tribes of Naphtali and Zebulun fight, but in the poem six tribes are mentioned: Ephraim, Benjamin, Machir, Zebulun, Issacher and Naphtali. There is also a perceived link with Reuben, Gilead, Asher and Dan because they are reproved for not coming to fight. In the account of the Ammonites crossing the Jordan to attack, Judah is counted as Israel along with Benjamin and Ephraim, and is included in the muster at Mizpah to avenge the murder of the concubine by the Benjaminites in Gibeah in Judges 19. Whether their inclusion is original to the tradition or inserted after the United Monarchy is a matter for debate.

Israel had no formal constituency at this time. Individual charismatic leaders gained authority as they gave leadership against external threats; their forces depended on which of the tribes would rally to them. They were linked by their worship of YHWH but they would probably not have seen worship of YHWH as precluding worship of the other gods of the land in quite the way that the writers of the Hebrew Bible did; for example, accounts of Micah making an image with silver which his mother had consecrated to YHWH and given to Micah to make an image (Judges 17: 3) and Gideon making an ephod (Judges 8: 27 which seems also to have been an image of some kind rather than part of the high priestly regalia as it is presented in Exodus and Leviticus). These stories do not square with the imageless worship of YHWH enjoined in the Ten Commandments.

The importance of the Levitical priesthood (Judges 17: 13), one of whose functions was to 'inquire of YHWH' (Judges 18: 5) and who seem to be able to function anywhere, comes across very strongly in the book of Judges (see 17: 13). This contrasts strongly with their position as Temple servants in the centralised Jerusalem cult. Perhaps the high places that the kings were commended for destroying or rebuked for leaving were not always shrines to Baal but old YHWHist sanctuaries (see I Chron 16: 39).

However, because we lack any corroboratory evidence, there are scholars who would say that the Bible is not able to supply us with any material which we can use to reconstruct the experience of Israel in the early Iron Age; we simply know too little to be able to separate reliable evidence from the casing of later preconceptions.

1.6 Saul

Biblical sources: I Sam 9–31; I Chron 8: 33 – 10: 4

Saul's career began in the same way as previous judges; on hearing of an attack on Jabesh-Gilead by the Ammonites he is seized by the spirit of YHWH and summons Israel to fight (I Sam 11: 6; compare Judges 11: 29). After his victory he is anointed by Samuel at Gilgal 'before YHWH'. The more literary account of his becoming king in chapters 9–11 is probably a later tradition and it emphasises how in choosing to have a king, Israel was rejecting the rule of YHWH (I Sam 8: 7). The events hinted at in chapter 11 show that Israel felt threatened by her neighbours and needed a king to defend her interests. Although Saul is usually credited with being the first king of Israel, Abimelech, Gideon's son, ruled Israel from Shechem for three years (Judges 9: 16, 22).

Saul's power base was the tribes in the hill country of Ephraim and Benjamin and his main enemies the Philistines, who had arrived in Palestine after the Israelites and whose power base lay in the coastal plain. They had the five cities of Ashdod, Gaza, Gath, Ekron and Ashkelon from which they controlled the surrounding villages. Judah, Israel and the Philistines jostled for territory and influence during the reigns of Saul, Ishbosheth and David until later in David's reign an equilibrium was attained.

Saul is recorded as fighting the Ammonites, the Philistines, the Amalekites, Moab, Edom and the Kings of Zobah (I Sam 14: 47–8). He seems to have secured the hill country for Israel but was vulnerable when fighting on the plains, partly because the Philistines were far better equipped; iron implements were rare in Israel and I Sam 13: 19 states that the Philistines kept the technology of iron to themselves. Excavations in Saul's territory of Ephraim, Benjamin and Gilead for the eleventh century BCE reveal a network of farms, small villages and cultic high places compared to the flourishing urban civilisation of the Philistines. The small farms and villages which we call Israel reveal nothing of the self-understanding of their inhabitants, making it difficult to know to what extent these tribes-people would recognise themselves in the biblical history, dating as it does from about seven hundred years after the time of Saul.

Despite being YHWH's first 'anointed' (messiah in Hebrew), Saul's kingship belongs to the past. He had no capital and although there are hints in the narrative of a standing army (I Sam 13: 2; 14: 52) he still relied on the muster of the tribes for his forces. He was king over people, the tribes of Israel. Whilst it is not certain which tribes that included at the time, his kingship probably did not extend to Judah, even though he may well have had some influence there, as Judah is shown fighting alongside Israel in I Sam 17: 1. He was king of the tribes of Israel, rather than of a definite territory, with all its inhabitants whatever their ethnic origin or religious allegiance. David, on the other hand, had developed his own power base before the tribes approached him to be king and, in choosing and developing Jerusalem as a capital after his coming to power, he retained his independence. Jerusalem became the capital of a state which, after the rebellion of Sheba (II Sam 20: 1*ff*) was able to compel the Israelite tribes to remain in a union they had entered voluntarily.

Saul's reign came to an end at the battle of Mt Gilboa. His son Jonathan was killed with him and his rule passed to his son Ishbosheth who used Mahanaim, east of the Jordan, as his base. He was unable to consolidate his position and his commander, Abner, entered into negotiations with David who had already been made king over Judah. The story is told in II Sam 2: 8 – 4: 12 and culminates in the assassination of Ishbosheth and the tribes of Israel offering allegiance to David.

1.7 The United Kingdom

Biblical sources: II Sam 5–11; Kings 2: 12; I Chron 10: 1 – 29: 30

The narratives of the books of Samuel and Kings read as if they were history. The difficulty for a modern historian evaluating their reliability is the almost complete lack of corroboratory extra-biblical evidence. There are small tantalising glimpses for a few of the later kings, which we shall mention as we come to them. For David, however, we have no extra-biblical evidence at all. This lack has led one commentator to ignore him in building up a picture of what we actually know of Israel in what is known as the biblical period. Such a position, however, ignores the existence of Jerusalem, central to Jewish hopes even today.

The problem with using the biblical material about David to build up some kind of historical picture is that we cannot be sure whether the 'Davidology' we see in parts of the psalms, for example, has developed from his kingship or from a later attempt to glorify the past. We have no means of checking whether the traditions about the Davidic kingdom in the histories or psalms have developed from an historical present or from a later attempt to provide a rationale from the past for a nationalism among the 'traditions' compilers. To what extent is the Davidic kingdom an invention of the writers of Samuel and Kings?

Given the lack of any other evidence, our assessment of David will rest on the assumptions we make about the nature of the biblical text, as we discussed earlier. To give credence to the biblical data is not simply a leap of faith. Because evidence has not been found or survived does not mean it never existed. Not only were the capitals of what became the southern and the northern kingdoms sacked but they were sacked by forces who were themselves in turn invaded, hardly conditions suitable for the survival of state archives! In the discussion of the monarchies which follow, it must be remembered that it is the biblical picture that is being discussed and the extent to which historical reality underlies the account is something that is difficult to decide and is pursued in the suggested reading.

David

The account in Samuel shows David's rise to prominence as one of Saul's fighting men. Animosity develops between them and David eventually seeks sanctuary among the Philistines; the king of Gath offers him Ziglag which becomes his head-quarters. During his time of hiding from Saul in Israel, he had attracted a personal following from among those who were disaffected in some way (I Sam 22: 2) and this he consolidates. According to Samuel, he is able to remain a loyal ally of Achish, king of Gath, while building up support in Judah. On the death of Saul and Jonathan in the battle at Mt Gilboa, Judah anoints him king at Hebron, while Ishbosheth becomes King over 'all Israel' at Mahanaim (II Sam 2: 9*f*). There is confusion in the sources since David is said to have reigned for seven years as king in Judah while Ishbosheth only for two before David is approached by 'Israel and the whole house of Benjamin' (II Sam 3: 19) to become their king. Did his kingship in Hebron over Judah overlap with Saul's? Ishbosheth remains in the Mahanaiam in the Transjordan and loses the faith of his commander, Abner, who makes approaches to David.

After his anointing, he conquers Jerusalem, makes it his capital and continues to establish a power base that does not depend entirely upon tribal support. In the account in II Samuel, one of the first things he does is to bring the ark into Jerusalem. The tabernacle shrine of Moses with the altar of burnt offering seems to have remained at the high place in Gibeon (II Chron 1: 3–4). In the time of Eli, the ark had been kept at Shiloh and then captured by the Philistines and returned to Kiriath-Jearim to 'the house of Abinadab on the hill' from where David took it to Jerusalem and erected a tent sanctuary especially for it. His priests there were Abiathar, the son of the priest Ahimelech (who gave David and his men the bread from the table before the Lord at Nob and was subsequently massacred along with his family at Saul's behest after being accused of plotting against the king), and Zadok whom some scholars believe to have been from the pre-Davidic Jebusite priesthood because of the similarity of his name to Melchizedek, king of Salem, mentioned in Genesis. It is his descendants who became the priesthood of Jerusalem, relegating the Levites, the traditional YHWHist priesthood, to the status of Temple servants.

II Sam 9: 15f outlines the skeleton of an administration to which some scholars have seen parallels in the Egyptian system. David had two commanders, one of his army and one of the 'Cherithites and Pelethites', which are taken to refer to a mercenary force. His civil officials were a recorder, a secretary and the priests. It is the beginnings of a centralised state but it would be effective as a power base, independent of the tribes, only as long as David was in control in Jerusalem. After Absalom's revolt, during which time Absalom reigns from Jerusalem, it is the tribe of Judah who bring David back to his capital. This burgeoning of bureaucracy continues with Solomon.

David is also concerned with expansion of his territories and control. The books of Samuel tell of conquest and alliances which spread David's sphere of influence from the Negev in the south almost to Damascus in the north. The weakness of Egypt in this period and the decline of Hittite power in the north, leaving a number of small city states to struggle for ascendancy, is the ideal background for an expanding Judah–Israel kingdom.

The ease with which the United Kingdom falls apart after the death of Solomon underlines the fact that the kingdom was united only in so far as it shared the same king and God. Despite the attempts of David and Solomon to develop the structures of the state, the union of the tribe of Judah with the tribes of Israel remains a personal union dependent upon the person of the king.

Solomon

Biblical sources: II Kings 2: 12 – 11: 43; II Chron 1: 1 – 9: 31
Extra-biblical sources: the Gezer Calendar

I Kings 4: 21 says that Solomon ruled over all the land west of the Euphrates to the borders of Egypt. While this is pious exaggeration, the narrative in I Kings does show Solomon developing the structure of the state internally and his kingdom's role in trade internationally. His list of officials in I Kings 4: 1f is more extensive than the equivalent in the account of David's rule and includes the office of 'king's friend', someone in charge of the palace, someone in charge of the officers and someone in charge of the forced labour. The account in II Kings describes the division of the land into twelve, each division supplying the palace for a month.

The accounts of Solomon's reign in both Kings and Chronicles describe a great building programme and this has been borne out by archaeology to the extent that buildings in similar style have been found in Hazor, Megiddo and Gezer dating from the assumed period of Solomon's reign, but unfortunately there is no epigraphical evidence to link them specifically with Solomon. Tradition links Solomon particularly with the building of the Temple. Two biblical accounts of Solomon's Temple survive, in I Kings (5–9) and II Chronicles (2–8) and both are influenced by the attitude of the writers to the monarchy and the Temple cult. Kings is usually hostile, regarding the sins of the kings as the cause of Jerusalem's eventual destruction. Its account of Solomon's Temple differs from the account given by the Chronicler whose attitude is more positive. The Kings' account links the building programme with forced labour while the Chronicles' account says the programme was limited to the aliens resident in Israel. Both accounts recognise the high price paid for Solomon's endeavours. As well as the Temple, the Kings' account describes the palace, hall of judgement and the house which Solomon built for Pharaoh's daughter, whom he married as a token of an alliance between the two countries which lasted until the accession of Pharaoh Shishak.

A shift in culture is discernible in archaeological remains from the tenth century. The ceramics are better quality and small precious objects are more widely found. The earliest document extant in Hebrew, the Gezer Calendar, an account of the agricultural year, month by month, dates from this period. The archaeological evidence is meagre but the picture in the Hebrew Bible of a kingdom growing by the fruits of trade is credible, given the strategic position of Judah and Israel across many of the ancient trade routes and the weakness of the power blocks to the north and south in this period. Solomon equipped his army with Egyptian chariots and Cilician horses which he also traded.

Solomon is also clearly linked in the tradition with wisdom. I Kings 4: 29–34 describes the wise men of the past whom he is said to have outshone, and describes his proverbs, songs and sayings about natural lore. The Queen of Sheba (Assyrian texts mention a state of Sheba in Northern Arabia, while some archaeologists prefer a Transjordanian site) is said to have come to hear his wisdom (I Kings 10: 1*f*) which encompasses far more than simply sage advice. The Book of Proverbs is attributed to him.

The union of the two kingdoms rested partly on the personal strength and shrewdness of the king and partly on there being more to be gained for Israel staying in the union than opting out. Israel had borne the brunt of supplying labour and supplies for the Kingdom and once Solomon was dead, was prepared to do so no longer. In the reign of Solomon's son Rehoboam the kingdoms split.

1.8   The two kingdoms: the northern kingdom

Jeroboam's dynasty, *c.* 921–909

Biblical sources: I Kings 11: 26–40; 12: 1–20; 15: 25–31; II Chron 10: 1–19; 13: 3–21; 16: 1–6
Extra-biblical evidence: the Karnak Temple Inscription of Pharaoh Shishak

According to the account in II Kings 12: 1f, Rehoboam went to Shechem so that the northern tribes could acclaim him king. Accession to the throne in Jerusalem was obviously not considered guarantee enough. Jeroboam had fled to Egypt, according to the Old Testament, after being designated king of Israel by the prophet Abijah during Solomon's reign; the dissatisfaction in the north pre-dated the rule of Rehoboam. According to one tradition, Jeroboam is said to have led the delegation at Shechem which agreed to remain under Davidic control if the tax burdens were lifted. When Rehoboam refused to compromise, the familiar cry was heard: 'To your tents O Israel'. Jeroboam was made king at Shechem instead.

BOX 1.8			
Kingdom of Judah 921–586 BCE		Kingdom of Israel 921–722/1 BCE *(Grouped in dynasties)*	
Rehoboam	921–913	Jereboam I	921–910
Abijam/Abijah	913–911	Nadab	910–909
Asa	911–869	Baasha	909–886
		Elah	886–885
		Zimri	885
		Omri	885–874
Jehoshaphat	872–848	Ahab	874–853
		Ahaziah	853–852
J(eh)oram	854–841	J(eh)oram	852–841
Amaziah	841		
Athaliah	841–835	Jehu	841–814
J(eh)oash	835–796	Jehoahaz	814–798
Amaziah	796–790	Joash	798–782
Uzziah/Azariah	790–739	Jereboam II	793–753
Jotiam	750–731	Zachariah	753–752
		Shallum	752
		Menahem	752–742
		Pekahiah	742–740
(Jeho)ahaz	735–715	Pekah	740–732
Hezekiah	729–686	Hoshea	732–723/2
Manasseh	696–641		
Amon	641–639		
Josiah	639–608		
Jehoahaz	608		
Jehoiakim	608–598		
Jehoiachin	598–597		
Zedekiah	597–586		

It is important to remember that the sources we have for the reigns of the kings of Israel are theological and not historical. It is clear throughout that the writers of Kings and Chronicles were dependent upon other writings, including first-hand sources such as 'the Book of the Chronicles of the Kings of Israel' (II Kings 14: 19). Events have been selected to serve the theological purpose of the writer or writers. Some think that the books of Samuel and Kings have gone through a number of different revisions. The final redaction must have taken place in Judah, which was a hostile state for large stretches of Israel's history.

This is a complicating factor if we are interested in the events, if any, which lie behind the texts of the Hebrew Bible.

Jeroboam's first capital was at Tirzah and was involved in conflict with Rehoboam and his successor, Abijam: the border was constantly disputed. Areas over which Solomon had influence took advantage of the Israel/Judah split to reassert themselves, but that Israel still controlled part of Transjordan is shown by Jeroboam moving his capital to Penuel. Although the Hebrew Bible does not mention it, Egyptian evidence from the account of Shishak's campaigns in the Temple at Karnak shows that Pharaoh attacked Israel as well as Judah, and archaelogical excavations at the known sites on Pharaoh Shishak's route have borne out his claims.

Jeroboam enhanced sanctuaries at Bethel and Dan as alternatives to the Jerusalem Temple. In them YHWH was worshipped as a bull, a common image for El, the Canaanite High God, or as a calf, a common way of representing the god Baal against whose worship the prophets fulminate. This is not an innovation, as a cult site has been excavated in Samaria which reveals that YHWH was being worshipped as a bull in the twelfth century BCE. This accounts for the tenacity of the custom shown by the occurrence of the proper name, Egelyau, meaning YHWH is a calf, or the calf of YHWH on one of the eighth century Samaritan ostraca (a piece of ceramic). Despite the probable antiquity of the practice, it is Jeroboam upon whom the opprobrium of the prophets falls. Like many of his successors, he starts his reign being named by a prophet and ends being blackened in the biblical accounts.

Other changes instigated by Jeroboam include the celebrating of festivals in the eighth month instead of Judah's seventh, and the following of the Egyptian rather than the Judaean dating system. He started the year in the spring rather than the autumn. The ancient world knew no division between politics and religion. To assert his political independence from Judah, Jeroboam needed to assert his independence from the Jerusalem shrine. He seems also to have opposed the native Levitical priesthood, which he is said to have ousted from their shrines in favour of his own nominees (I Kings 13: 33–4; II Chron 11: 13–15).

Jeroboam was succeeded by his son, Nadab, who was assassinated shortly after by Baasha (c. **909–886**). He too was involved in fighting Judah to the south and Benhadad of Damascus to the north. He was succeeded by his son, Elah, who was assassinated by Zimri who reigned for seven days before the throne was seized by Omri, an army commander who was acclaimed by his troops when they heard of Elah's assassination. He survived a challenge from a faction led by Tibni, who some scholars think was only finally defeated in **880**. For the next century, Israel was known in Assyrian records as the house of Omri.

Omri's dynasty, c. 885–841

Biblical sources: I Kings 16: 21 – 22: 40; 22: 47–53; II Kings 1: 1 – 8: 15; 9: 1 – 10: 11; II Chron 18: 1–34; 20: 35–7; 22: 2–9
Extra-biblical sources: the Moabite Stone, the Kurkh stele

Omri secured peace with the king of Tyre to the north and subdued Moab to the west. Unlike his predecessors, Omri kept peace with Judah, presumably after a border between them had been agreed. His successors continued this policy and Ahab gave his daughter Athaliah to Joram (or Jehoram), son of Jehosaphat, king of Judah.

Like David, Omri set up a capital on land that had not previously belonged to the tribes of Israel; he bought a hill on which he built his new capital, Samaria, which remained the capital until its sack in **722 BCE**. Ahab was able to build on the foundation Omri had laid and Israel seems to have gained prosperity; Ahab is said to have had an ivory palace, and ivory has indeed been found in excavations of Samaria which dated from this period. Evidence of building during these years has been found at Hazor and Megiddo also. In the Assyrian document, the Kurkh stele, which records the battle between Syrian states, including Israel, and the Assyrians under Shalmaneser at Kharkar in **853 BCE**, Ahab is listed as supplying the largest company of chariots, 2000 out of 3940.

The Hebrew Bible makes much of the clash between YHWHists and Baal worshippers under Ahab in the stories of Elijah and Elisha, and presents it purely as a matter of conflicting religious loyalties. The kings of Israel might have seen religious toleration as vital for holding power in a state which included native Canaanites alongside Israelites, inevitable now that they were kings of a territory rather than a group of tribes. The religious pluralism of the period reflects political realities, particularly Omri's and Ahab's close links with Phoenicia, symbolised by Ahab's marriage to Jezebel, daughter of the king of Tyre, a woman who served as the focus for the prophets' vitriol.

Ahab died in battle against the Syrians, his former allies, and was succeeded by his sons, Ahaziah and Joram in turn. Joram, together with Ahaziah, king of Judah, were assassinated by Jehu while they were both waging war against Syria. Just as Omri had assassinated the king and founded a new dynasty, so his grandson was assassinated by the founder of a new ruling dynasty, Jehu, whose great-great-grandson was in his turn killed by a new king. This differing pattern can be seen in the monarchies of the two kingdoms; the house of David retains power (even after a king is assassinated) until the fall of Jerusalem to the Babylonians in **587**, whereas dynasty replaces dynasty in the north. A northern king could never be sure that a prophet had not already anointed his successor.

Jehu's dynasty, c. 841–752

Biblical sources: II Kings 9: 1–36; 13: 1–25; 14: 8–16, 23–9; 15: 8–12; II Chron 25: 17–24; Amos; Hosea; Micah
Extra-biblical sources: Black Obelisk of Shalmaneser (*c.* **841**), the account of Adad-Nirari's expedition to Syria and Palestine (*c.* **803**) on the Nimrud slab inscription, the Samaritan Ostraca

According to II Kings 9: 6, one of 'the sons of the prophets', sent by Elisha, anointed Jehu king over Israel and provoked a revolt which put Jehu's family on the throne of Israel for almost a century. Jehu is credited with eradicating Baal worship, although the frequent occurrence of names compounded with the name of the god Baal (for example, Abibaal meaning 'Baal is my father' and Baalmeoni) on ostraca found in Samaria and dating from the eighth century seems to undermine this claim. He did not destroy the sanctuaries of Dan or

Bethel where YHWH was worshipped as a bull, however, and so is still criticised by the writers of the Hebrew Bible histories. Whether the YHWHists of his own time would have been so critical is a matter of debate. When Amos preached during the reign of Jehu's great-grandson he criticised the sanctuaries of the north, including Bethel, but does not mention the calves; his criticism is levelled at those who offer sacrifice without living rightly.

Jehu and his successors paid tribute to the Assyrians. Jehu's submission is not mentioned in the Hebrew Bible but we have both a written and pictorial record left to us on the Black Obelisk of Shalmaneser III.

The main struggle of these years was with Syria; Jehoahaz, Jehu's successor, lost territory to them and had his forces much depleted. He is recorded on the Nimrud pavement slab as paying tribute to Assyria whose attacks on Damascus in **803 BCE** and **796 BCE** would have been in Israel's interest, in the short-term at least. His son Joash regained territory previously lost to the Syrians as did his son Jeroboam, whose influence is said to have reached almost as far as the United Monarchy, Judah excepted. He took Damascus in and ruled as far as Lebo-Hamath, possible because of the policy of remaining at peace with a weakened Assyria. With the kingdom of Uratu on Lake Van putting pressure on Assyria's northern borders, it was in their interests to encourage a strong Israel to counterbalance the Syrian states which might otherwise have threatened their southern borders. The peace with Judah, however, which had continued through the Omride dynasty, came to an end with Israel's forces under Joash breaching the walls of Jerusalem and taking vessels from the Temple.

After the defeats inflicted by the Syrians in Jehoahaz's reign, Israel's fortunes rose under his successors. The preaching of both Amos and Hosea, who prophesied in the reign of Jeroboam II, implies a society in which the rich maintain their position at the expense of the poor. Their main complaints were the perversion of justice, complacency and the worship of foreign gods which would follow allegiance to Assyria. The years of stability ended, as Amos and Hosea said they would, with the assassination of Jeroboam's son, Zachariah.

The last kings of Israel, c. 752–722

Biblical sources: II Kings 15: 10–31, 37; 16: 5–9; 17: 1–41; 18: 9–12; II Chron 28: 5–15
Extra-biblical sources: Annals of Tiglath-Pilaser III 150–7, Nimrud tablet, Annals of Sargon II 10–18, Nimrud Prism iv 25–41, display inscription, Khorsabad Pavement Inscription, Annals 23–57, Annals Khorsabad (Room XIV) 11–15

Zachariah was killed by Shallum who only reigned for a month before being assassinated in his turn by Menahem who reigned for ten years. He is said in II Kings to have bought Assyria off, and Tiglath-Pilaser III mentions him among a list of those who bring him tribute. However, this did not help him secure his northern borders and he lost territories to Syria. His son Pekahiah succeeded him but was assassinated by Pekah who reigned for eight years. He turned Menahem's policy around and allied with the Syrian states against Assyria. They attacked Judah to try to force it into a league against Assyria but this had the opposite effect. Judah called upon the help of Tiglath-Pilaser who attacked Damascus and seized Galilee and Gilead, deporting the local population to Mesopotamia.

Prior to Tiglath-Pilaser, Assyrian monarchs ruled their subject territories through vassal kings but he changed this policy and transformed the puppet states into directly ruled provinces. Pekah's rebellion provided the pretext for making much of Israel into Assyrian provinces. A rump state was left centred on Samaria under Hoshea, who had either seized the throne (according to the Hebrew Bible) or was made king after Pekah was deposed (according to Assyrian records). He was an Assyrian puppet but conspired with Egypt during the troubles surrounding the accession of Shalmaneser V in **726 BCE**. Samaria was captured after a three-year siege, most of its people deported (27,290 according to the Assyrian annals), and it was made into an Assyrian province. After its restoration, it was re-populated by subject peoples from elsewhere.

Sargon II claims to be the conqueror of Samaria in his annals, but the list of Assyrian kings says the siege took place in Shalmaneser V's reign, **725–3 BCE**. The Hebrew Bible records the conqueror of Samaria simply as 'the king of Assyria'. Some scholars think that Shalmaneser took the city and that Sargon II, his successor, claims to have conquered the city because he put down a later rebellion in Palestine in **720 BCE**.

1.9   The two kingdoms: the southern kingdom

Biblical sources: I Kings 12: 1–24; 14: 21 – 15: 24; 22: 1–33; 41–50; II Kings 3: 5–27; 8: 16–29; 9: 16–29; 11: 1 – 12: 21; 14: 1–14, 17–22; 15: 1–7; 15: 32 – 16: 20; 18: 1 – 25: 30; II Chron 10: 1 – 36: 23; Isaiah 1–39; Micah; Amos; Zephaniah; Jeremiah; Lamentations
Extra-biblical sources: Karnak Temple Inscription, Nimrud South-east Palace inscription rev 6–16, Broken Prism, Taylor Prism, Siloam Inscription, Bull Inscription, Nineveh (Nebi Yunus) Slab Inscription, Annals of Assyria, British Museum Tablet No. 21946 1–18, rev 11–3, the Lachish Letters

I Kings depicts the ignominious beginning to Rehoboam's reign as he flees for his life from Shechem where the tribes of Israel had acclaimed Jeroboam king. Benjamin remains with Judah. Both I Kings and II Chronicles record how Rehoboam is dissuaded from his first impulse to fight to retain Israel but the summary of his reign in II Chronicles says he and Jeroboam were continually at war. Accordingly the first peace cannot have lasted long. Only II Chronicles records that he created a buffer of fortified cities between Israel and Judah and strengthened his control over his own territories. Both accounts, however, tell of Pharaoh Shishak's campaign against Judah which culminated in his army even despoiling the Temple, and both see it as a judgement by God. Only the Kings' account explains what they saw as occasioning it: the people had built sanctuaries, 'high places', set up pillars and goddesses known as Asherah and allowed male cult prostitution. II Chronicles is a little more circumspect, saying that after three years' walking in the way of David and Solomon, he 'forsook the law of the Lord' (II Chron 12: 1 RSV).

Rehoboam's son Abijah/Abijam succeeded him; we learn from I Kings that he continued his father's religious policy, but from the II Chronicles' account that he won a major battle against Jeroboam from which the king of Israel never recovered; it implies that Abijah outlived him, whereas we learn from I Kings that Jeroboam was still king when Asa, Abijah's son, succeeded to the throne.

About Asa, the writer of Kings has initially nothing but good to report: he was a zealous religious reformer and his affairs prospered accordingly. Late in his reign he was threatened by Israel, now ruled by Baasha, and made an alliance with Syria to attack Israel from the north. He is criticised by the writers of Kings for this lack of trust. The border disputes between Israel and Judah continued until later in the reign of Asa's son, Jehoshaphat, when he married his son to Ahab's daughter and joined in Ahab's campaign against Ahab's former allies, the Syrians. After Ahab's death he continued his support for Israel, fighting with them against Moab. During his reign, Israel and Judah attempted a trading expedition to Tarshish by sea from Ezion-Geber, but the ships were wrecked and it does not seem to have been attempted again. Ezion-Geber had been the port of the United Monarchy under Solomon.

Internally, Jehoshaphat continued the religious reforms. He sent Levites around Judah and even into the hill country of Ephraim according to II Chron 19: 4, teaching the Law of the Lord, and set up judges in the cities in Judah. As we have seen, religious reform is inextricably linked with political strength and this pattern recurs throughout Judah's history. The two kings particularly noted for their religious purity are Hezekiah and Josiah. Both were also concerned for Judah's independence: Hezekiah took a stand against Assyrian domination while Josiah, a century later, extended Judah's borders to Galilee.

In the reign of Joram (sometimes spelt Jehoram), Jehoshaphat's successor, there were unsuccessful campaigns against the Philistines in the west and the Arabs to the south, the only routes of expansion for Judah possible since alliance with Israel under Ahab. During this time Edom regained its independence. The death of Joram's son, Ahaziah, at Megiddo in Jehu's coup after less than a year on the throne, prompted an Israelite-style coup in Jerusalem. Ahaziah's mother, Athaliah (Ahab's daughter), seized the throne and killed all Ahaziah's sons with the exception of Joash who was hidden in the Temple by Joram's daughter Jehoshabeath and her husband Jehoiada, a priest. After six years they challenged Athaliah, and the restoration of a son of David to the throne in Jerusalem was accompanied by religious reformation. II Chronicles records that he allowed the worship of other gods towards the end of his reign and had the prophet Zechariah, Jehoiada's son, killed after he had rebuked him for it. This is given as the reason for the attack on Jerusalem by the Syrians which Joash was forced to buy off. This religious pluralism is shown vividly by the remains of a shrine discovered at Kuntillet 'Arjud in the Negev. Evidence of the worship of YHWH, YHWH's consort, El and Baal have been found in one centre dating from the late ninth or early eighth century. However, a recent study of epigraphical remains in Israel and Judah from monarchic times support the dominant position of YHWHism.

Joash's assassination quickly followed the Syrian attack on Jerusalem. So strong was the dynastic principle in Judah, that the assassins did not usurp the throne but installed Joash's son, Amaziah, in his place, as they did six years later when Amaziah was himself assassinated and replaced by his son Azariah/Uzziah. Amaziah regained Edom but was captured in a battle he seems to have provoked against Israel, and was ignominiously returned to Jerusalem by his captors who broke through the walls of the city and seized some of the Temple treasures before returning to Samaria. This, together with the religious pluralism he is said to have fostered, caused enough dissatisfaction to provoke his assassination.

His son Uzziah reigned for fifty years, co-reigning with his son Jotham for the last ten because of his leprosy. Uzziah continued the policy of expanding Judah's borders southward, stationing troops at Elath on the Red Sea and 'building towers in the wilderness', remains of which have been found. Forts with work dating from around this period have been found at Kadesh Barnea, Arad Rabbah and Ezion-Geber. Uzziah fought successful campaigns with his well-equipped army against the Arabs, Philistines and Edomites. His reign seems to have been a time of prosperity.

Hostilities with Israel began again in Jotham's reign; he defeated the coalition of Pekah of Israel and Rezin of Damascus and continued his father's policy of fortifying the south. The Ammonites paid him tribute. In the reign of his son Ahaz (Jehoahaz in the Assyrian documents), who had been co-regent since 735, the threat from Damascus and Israel strengthened and Ahaz became an Assyrian vassal to counter them. This vassal status was accompanied by an increase in the worship of foreign gods; he set up an Assyrian stele in the Temple to replace the Solomonic one. His vassal status is mentioned in the Nimrud, South-east Palace, Slab inscription (rev 6–16).

Ahaz followed recent practice and made his son, Hezekiah, co-regent in 729 and they reigned together for fourteen years before Ahaz's death in 715. Hezekiah's reign is among the best documented in the Old Testament. He undertook the strengthening of Jerusalem's defences and built the famous Siloam tunnel to ensure a water supply within the city walls.

The writers of Kings and Chronicles praise his religious reformation. He purged Jerusalem of its other gods, some there as symbols of foreign domination and others because of the people's attachment to them, as Jeremiah realised a century later when he noted the people's attachment to the Queen of Heaven. But he also took action against the shrines of YHWH in the former kingdom of Israel and the high places outside Jerusalem. He made attempts to secure the allegiance of YHWHists in Israel and kept the Passover in a way not seen since Solomon's time (II Chron 30: 26). The early chapters of Isaiah (1–39), some of which stem from the preaching of Isaiah in Hezekiah's reign, however do not seem so favourable. Just as Isaiah had rebuked Ahaz for seeking Assyrian protection, so he rebuked Hezekiah for rebelling because he saw the disaster for the people that sprang from both policies.

Hezekiah remained a quiet vassal of Assyria through the last days of Israel but took advantage of the turmoil created by Sargon II's death in 705 to revolt in alliance with Merodach-baladan of Babylon and Egypt, much to Isaiah's disgust.

Sennacherib first defeated Merodach-baladan and his allies in the east and then campaigned in Palestine. Several Assyrian inscriptions which report Hezekiah's submission have survived.

All the land which had been gained under Uzziah had been lost by Ahaz and Hezekiah until, during Sennacherib's siege of Jerusalem, all the fortified cities of Judah had been taken and Hezekiah remained in Jerusalem, stuck 'like a caged bird'. Sennacherib did not take Jerusalem, either because he felt he had made his point and went home, or because of disaster in the Assyrian camp (II Chron 32: 21; II Kings 19: 35; Isaiah 37: 36), or because of rumours of trouble at home (II Kings 19: 7). The siege is thought to have taken place in 701 but because of the mention of Tirhakah, who became king in 690/89 and the speed with which the account mentions the death of Sennacherib, some have inferred a later siege which is not mentioned in the Assyrian annals. Few think this case has been satisfactorily demonstrated.

Hezekiah was succeeded by his son Manasseh, co-regent since 696, who is reviled as an idolater and murderer in Kings and a seducer of the people in Chronicles. The Chronicler explains how such a man could reign for fifty years by telling how he repents, and reforms worship in Jerusalem and beyond after he has been brought to book by the Assyrians and he turns to YHWH for help. As an Assyrian vassal, he supplied timber to Assyria for Esarhaddon's palace and then troops for Ashurbanipal's campaign against Egypt.

Judah's position became easier once the Arabs, Tyre and some other western states had been crushed after siding with Ashurbanipal's brother in an abortive rebellion. Judah was allowed by Assyria to rebuild fortresses, once Manasseh had renounced all treaties with Tyre (and hence renounced their gods) and resumed control over the southern trade routes.

Amon succeeded his father but was assassinated after only two years, and his son Josiah was put on the throne by popular acclaim as well as by the nobles. During his reign the Assyrian empire declined and finally collapsed. He took advantage of the power vacuum in the region to follow a policy of national renewal. The accounts in the Hebrew Bible describe his religious reforms but his policy also entailed territorial expansion. He took control of Ephraim and as far north as Naphtali, including Galilee and the valley of Jezreel, and in the south he fortified Arad and En-gedi.

His religious programme included, as Hezekiah's had done, not only the removal of foreign gods but the centralisation of YHWHism in Jerusalem. Archaeology has produced evidence which may substantiate the reforms: remains of the temple at Arad, built in the tenth century, show it was destroyed in the seventh; while on the eastern slope of Mt Ophel in Jerusalem, many deliberately broken cultic figures have been found which could date either from the reign of Hezekiah or Josiah. The success of these reformations may be shown by the fact that none of the names in the Lachish Letters, which date from just before the fall of Jerusalem to Nebuchadnezzer, are compounded with any divine name apart from YHWH, in marked contrast to the names found on the eighth century Samaritan ostraca. The account of Josiah's reign in II Kings and II Chronicles includes details of the finding of 'the book of the law of the Lord given by Moses' in the Temple during rebuilding work there. Some scholars have linked this with the book of Deuteronomy. Like Hezekiah, he is said to have held a magnificent Passover, the like of which had not been seen since the time of the Judges. Some scholars feel that some of the early material in the biblical books, such as the original prophecies of Isaiah, were edited at this time. However, as with the reforms of Hezekiah, the books of II Kings and II Chronicles seem more positive than the contemporary writings of the prophet Jeremiah, some of whose words may indeed be critical, e.g. Jer 7: 4 and 8: 8.

Josiah was killed at Megiddo in **608** while attempting to prevent Pharaoh Neco going to the aid of the remains of the Assyrian empire, settled on Haran (Nineveh had been destroyed in **612**), when it was under attack by the Babylonians. Jehoahaz succeeded his father and followed his pro-Babylonian policy but after only three months he was captured by Pharaoh Neco and sent to Egypt. Neco installed Jehoiakim (also known as Eliakim), Jehoahaz's elder brother, in his place. He remained an Egyptian vassal until **605** when Nebuchadnezzer, the then Crown Prince, defeated Egypt. Jehoiakim became a vassal of Babylon until he switched sides again in **601** after a battle between Babylon and Egypt in which both sides suffered substantial losses. It took the Babylonian forces a year to recover. Nebuchadnezzer besieged Jerusalem in **598** and Jehoiakim died during the siege. His son, Jehoiachin, surrendered the city on the 15/16th March **587 BCE** and was taken into exile, where he remained under house arrest until he was released and brought to court by Nebuchadnezzer's son, Evil-merodach, in **561/0 BCE**.

Documents have been found in Babylon which refer to the food ration of Jehoiachin and his entourage. Craftsmen and members of the nobility were exiled with him and his family. Nebuchadnezzer put his uncle, Mattaniah, on the throne and changed his name to Zedekiah but Jehoiachin was still regarded as the legitimate king and events dated by his captivity.

Zedekiah remained loyal until the planning of the rebellion which brought about the final destruction of the kingdom of Judah. He tried to form a coalition with Edom, Ammon, Moab, Tyre and Sidon, but Nebuchadnezzer moved swiftly and besieged the city from 15th January **588 BCE** to its fall on 19th July **586 BCE**. Zedekiah escaped but was captured at Jericho and brought to Nebuchadnezzer at Riblah. His sons were killed in front of him and his eyes put out before he was taken to Babylon. The fire that destroyed Jerusalem raged for three days from the 15th to the 18th of August and the book of Lamentations is a vivid evocation of the time.

BOX 1.9

The enemy has stretched out his hands over all Jerusalem's precious things; yea, she has seen the nations invade her sanctuary, those whom Thou didst forbid to enter the congregation. All her people groan as they search for bread; they trade their treasures for food to revive their strength. 'Look, O Lord, and behold for I am despised.'

Lam 1: 10–11

Bibliography

Bernhard W. Anderson, *The Living World of the Old Testament*, Longman (1988)

Philip R. Davies, *In Search of Ancient Israel*, Sheffield Academic Press (1995)

Magus Magnuson, *The Archaeology of the Bible Lands*, Bodley Head, London (1977)

Hershel Shanks (Ed.), *Ancient Israel: A Short History from Abraham to the Roman Destruction of the Temple*, SPCK, London (1999)

D. Winton Thomas, *Documents from Old Testament Times*, Harper Torch Books, New York (1961)

■⋎ 2   The Old Testament

2.1   What is the Old Testament?

The books that the Christian Church calls the Old Testament are also the scriptures of the Jewish people. For that reason many scholars now refer to them as the 'Hebrew Bible'. However, whilst the Old Testament of the Protestant churches corresponds to the Hebrew Bible, this is not true of the Orthodox, Roman Catholic and non-Chalcedonian Eastern churches, nor indeed of the Anglican churches. They have always accepted a larger number of sacred books than the Rabbis.

The group of accepted books is called the 'canon' from the Greek word for 'rule' or 'standard'. The Hebrew canon is in three parts: the Law, the Prophets and the Writings. While it is generally thought that the Law and the Prophets were fixed in the second century BCE, what constituted the Writings was not formalised until after the time of Jesus. Those Jews who became the early Church accepted, as scripture, books that were later not accepted by rabbinic Judaism. It was only the Christian Church that preserved these books. One book, that of Enoch, revered by at least some Jews in Jesus' day (it is quoted and alluded to in the letters of Jude and 2 Peter), was preserved only by the Ethiopian church. Ethiopia had been evangelised by missionaries from the Syriac church, who presumably had taken it with them. This book was 'rediscovered' by the West in the nineteenth century when the Bible of the Ethiopian church was translated into English and found to contain extra books. Portions of the book had been known previously in Greek, but findings of Aramaic fragments at Qumran revealed a Palestinian original behind the Greek and Ethiopian texts.

BOX 2.1

x = included; 0 = not included

	Roman Catholic	Ortho- doxy	Anglican Commu- nion	Syrian Non- Chalc	Slavonic Orthodoxy	Ethiopian
I Esdras/III Esdras	x	0	0	0	0	0
II Esdras	x	x	0	0	0	0
Tobit	0	0	0	0	0	0
Judith	0	0	0	0	0	0

BOX 2.1 (Continued)						
Additions to Esther	0	0	0	0	0	0
Wisdom of Solomon	0	0	0	0	0	0
Wisdom of ben Sirac	0	0	0	0	0	0
Baruch	0	0	0	0	0	0
Letter of Jeremiah	0	0	0	0	0	0
Additions to Daniel	0	0	0	0	0	0
I Maccabees	0	0	0	0	0	0
II Maccabees	0	0	0	0	0	0
III Maccabees	×	0	×	0	0	0
I Enoch	×	×	×	×	×	0
Jubilees	×	×	×	×	×	0
Ps 151	×	0	×	0	0	0
Prayer of Manasseh	×	0	0	0	0	0
IV Maccabees	×	×	×	0	0	0

Jerome was one of the first Christians to doubt the standing of these extra books when he came to translate the Greek scriptures into Latin for the Western church, at a time when Greek was no longer easily understood in the West. He was unhappy because he knew that these books were not in the Hebrew Bible. Theologians have argued about the status of the books ever since. At the Synod of Trullo (692), the Eastern church accepted the longer list of Old Testament books while noting the reservations of those who disputed them. At the Reformation, Protestant reformers like Calvin rejected the books altogether, whilst others like Cranmer accepted them as useful, but denied that they could be used as a source for doctrine. The Council of Trent officially accepted the longer canon and used the title 'Deutero-canonical' of the books not found in the Hebrew Bible. Some have later interpreted this to imply a lower status but this was not intended at the time; it simply denoted those books whose canonicity was only formalised later.

2.1.1 The Septuagint

The confusion arose in the first place because the Church used the Greek translation of the Hebrew Bible known as the Septuagint, generally referred to as the LXX, the Roman numeral for 70. This was translated in the third century BCE in Alexandria. Its name derives from the legend that 70 or 72 scholars were locked in separate rooms and all produced the same version. A translation demands a fixed canon and the canon that they worked from was the one to which the early church stuck. It is important to remember that despite its popularity with the early church and its later disavowal by the rabbinic authorities, the LXX was originally translated to serve a Jewish constituency, albeit a Greek-speaking one. Why did the Rabbis, who later fixed the Hebrew text, exclude books which the translators of the LXX had thought important? It is now being recognised that Judaism was never the monolithic whole it was once thought to have been – perhaps those who later came to dominate **post-70 CE** Judaism belonged to a tradition which had always been narrower in its definition of what was and was not scripture. We cannot exclude the possibility, however, that the translation and its canon was rejected by later Rabbis precisely because of its popularity among Christians. Scholars differ on what they think the first translation of the LXX contained; some believe the first version contained only the Pentateuch.

The LXX not only differs from what became the Hebrew Bible, the Masoretic text (MT), in the number of books it contained, but also in the texts of the books they had in common. This was originally attributed entirely to scribal error. However the presence at Qumran of Aramaic manuscripts which follow both the MT and the LXX textual traditions shows that the differences between the two later versions preceded the Greek translation.

2.1.2 The Samaritan Pentateuch

A third manuscript tradition for the Hebrew scriptures has survived in the Samaritan Pentateuch. The Samaritans that we are familiar with from the pages of the New Testament still survive to this day. They believe that the proper place to worship God is not Jerusalem but Mt Gerizim, where they had a Temple in the intertestamental period. They are a conservative Jewish group who follow the Sabbath regulations and food laws very strictly. They only recognise the authority of the Pentateuch, the first five books of the Hebrew Bible also known as the 'Torah' (the Law). Their text of the Torah differs from the MT in about 6000 places and the LXX agrees with about 1900 of these. Many of these differences are of little theological significance but it is important to remember that the Hebrew text of the MT does not have the automatic right to be considered the purest text.

2.1.3 The Masoretic text (MT)

The MT takes its name from the scholars, the Masoretes, who passed the text on from one generation to the next, adding a system of vowel points to preserve the correct reading and making notes to show textual variants. It is still the text used by the Jewish community. The Masoretes began *c.* **600 CE** but the earliest manuscripts still extant date from the late ninth century CE. It is clear from comparing these medieval texts with some fragments found at Qumran that there was a careful scribal tradition that preserved the text as far as possible. The pre-Masoretic text had no vowels, which could have led to serious misunderstanding without the careful handling of the Masoretes and their rabbinic forerunners.

The present chapter will focus on the Masoretic text since it provides the Old Testament for most Bibles produced today in English. Those books which were valued and preserved by the first Christians, the Apocrypha (books in the LXX which Jerome was not sure about) and Pseudepigrapha (the generic term for all other intertestamental literature), will be discussed in the next chapter.

2.2 What does the Hebrew Bible include?

The Old Testament is as much a library as a book. Each book is like a photograph of the religious ideas and beliefs of the group or person which produced it; it represents a stage in the developing traditions. The Hebrew Bible has traditionally been divided into the Law, the Prophets and the Writings. *The Law* or Torah comprises the books Genesis, Exodus, Leviticus, Numbers and Deuteronomy, which were believed (and are still so believed by sections of Orthodox Jewry and Christian Fundamentalists) to have been dictated by God to Moses. These books start with accounts of creation and primal history and chart the relationship of YHWH and his chosen people from Abram's call to the death of Moses. *The Prophets* in the Hebrew Bible are divided into the earlier prophets, i.e. Joshua, Judges, I and II Samuel and I and II Kings, and the later prophets, namely Isaiah, Jeremiah, Ezekiel and the twelve minor prophets. The former prophets chart the story of the chosen people from their entry into Canaan until the release of Jehoiachin from imprisonment by Nebuchadnezzer's son, Evil-merodach. *The Writings* encompass all the rest of the books included in the Protestant Old Testament. It is a varied selection ranging from history to theology and from hymns and proverbs to love songs and lamentations. It includes Daniel, Ruth and the books of I and II Chronicles, as well as Ezra and Nehemiah, which in Christian Bibles are placed among the minor prophets, between Judges and I Kings and after II Kings respectively.

The Hebrew Bible has been through a succession of collections and editings. The last normative one was undertaken by the Pharisees and finalised after the fall of Jerusalem. It was precipitated not only by the need for Judaism to have a normative base but also for it to define itself in relation to Christianity, the other Judaism to survive **70 CE**. It is from this revision that the differences between the Hebrew Bible and the Old Testament of the early church spring. Previous crises had bred previous revisions. The followers of Judas Maccabees, resisting what they saw as the Hellenism of the Jerusalem priesthood, both collected existing scriptures and wrote new ones such as Esther and Daniel, kept in both the subsequent Christian and Jewish canons, and I Maccabees, kept only by the early church. According to II Maccabees 2: 13, Nehemiah gathered a library of sacred writings. Before this, there were those who produced the Pentateuch and those who produced Deuteronomy and the Deuteronomic histories, the trace of whose pen is seen by some scholars upon the book of Jeremiah. Those who preserved the prophecies of Isaiah drew other prophetic writings into a larger Isaianic corpus which we know as the book of Isaiah. Even those prophets who may have escaped editing and addition were still preserved only because those who followed saw in their writings the word of God. We will never know what writings have not been preserved but the existence of the apocrypha and pseudepigrapha, preserved by the church, sheds light on what might have happened at earlier stages.

2.3 The Pentateuch

The first five books of the Hebrew Bible, Genesis, Exodus, Leviticus, Numbers and Deuteronomy, have always been grouped together as the Torah. Some scholars have felt that the sources that have been detected in the Torah can also be seen in the book of Joshua and therefore have described a Hexateuch (six books). Other scholars have thought that the distinct nature of the book of Deuteronomy means that we should see the first four rather than the first five books as an entity, the Tetrateuch (four books). Whatever the strengths of these arguments, most scholars prefer to regard the Pentateuch as a coherent unit.

The Pentateuch covers the story of God's dealing with His people from creation to just before the crossing of the Jordan. *Genesis* covers creation, primal history and the stories of the ancestors, sometimes called the Patriarchs. However, the generic term 'Ancestors' is probably to be preferred, since the stories include the wives and concubines of the men, God indeed appearing to Hagar separately, and promising to make her a great nation (Gen 16: 7–15; 2: 15–21). The stories of creation and primal history provide the context for all that follows; it was not any god who called Abram, but God, maker of heaven and earth and all that is in them and the God in whose image all people are created. The inclusion of Gen 1–11: 9 reflects what some scholars see as an exilic insight that their god YHWH is the only true God.

The stories of the ancestors start with God, the God of Abraham, the Shield of Abraham as he is also known, calling Abraham (or Abram as he then was) 'to leave your kindred and your Father's house and go to a land that I will show you. There I will make of you a great nation'. 'He' is an accurate reflection of the perception of God as male which persisted throughout the time of the Bible's writing, which occurred in a world of gods and goddesses. There are a collection of stories about Abraham, Isaac, Jacob, also called Israel, and Joseph, and Genesis ends with Jacob's family seeking refuge in Egypt from a famine in Canaan. The narrative is based around God's promise and its fulfilment, and follows Abram and his family from Haran to sites in what was to become Israel and Judah. The final chapters of Genesis are a novella about Joseph and explain how the people of Israel, nomads in a land they have been promised, come to be in Egypt.

Exodus covers the change in the people's fortunes – from honoured guests to aliens put to hard labour – and describes the appearance of the one chosen by God to rescue them. It narrates the birth of Moses, his adoption by the Egyptian princess, his flight, his call, and subsequent return and confrontation with Pharaoh. It follows the fortunes of the people from the celebration of the first Passover, the exodus and journey to Sinai, and includes laws and cultic instructions. It finishes with the account of the erecting of the portable sanctuary called the tabernacle or tent of meeting which was built to hold the ark, reputed to have held the two tablets of stone on which God had written the law and sometimes, also, a jar of manna and Aaron's rod.

Leviticus covers laws, sacrifices, and the ordinations of Aaron and his sons as priests. The story of the people's wandering in the wilderness is continued in

Numbers which takes the story up to the people camping on the far banks of the Jordan and some last-minute instructions. *Deuteronomy*, thought by some scholars to have been the book of the law which is discovered in Josiah's renewal of the Temple in **621 BCE**, is a recapitulation of the wilderness experience and purports to be the final speeches of Moses and a reiteration of the law and demands of the covenant. Although it has always stood as the fifth book of the Pentateuch, it is obviously linked with the histories of Joshua to II Kings, which follow it. Some scholars share the opinion of Martin Noth that Deuteronomy was originally written as an introduction to the historical books, known as the Deuteronomic or Deutero-nomistic histories because of their similarity in style with Deuteronomy. They argue that when the P revision (see below) took place, either during or after the exile, Deuteronomy became detached from the histories and was combined with other accounts of Israel's prehistory.

Critical study of the Pentateuch began with Julius Wellhausen (**1844–1918**). He drew on the work of Henning Bernhard Wilter who in 1711 was the first to use the different names for God found in the Pentateuch as a means of identifying differ-ent strands within it. From the time of the Reformation, the Pentateuch was thought to have been the work of Moses. This began to be questioned in the seventeenth and eighteenth centuries but Wellhausen's work was the first to command serious attention. He identified four strands within the Pentateuch, namely: (i) the Yahwist, known as J; (ii) the Elohist, known as E; (iii) a combination of E with J material by a later editor, known as JE; and (iv) P, being the final redac-tion of the Pentateuch. This was said to date from the time of the exile and return and to reflect priestly concerns. They were identified by their different uses of YHWH and Elohim for God. A study of Deuteronomy led Wellhausen to think that the Deuteronomist (D) was familiar with JE but not P, the final editing of the Pentateuch. He considered that J was the oldest strand, dating from the ninth century, that the Elohist (E) dated from the eighth century and that these were combined by an editor in the seventh century, producing JE. JE then becomes itself the basis for a later redaction by D, the Deuteronomist, in the sixth century when it was combined with a pre-existent Deuteronomy.

This, in turn, is added to and becomes the basis for a final redaction by P, which Wellhausen thought occurred in the exile. It is a complicated theory because even if the outline is correct and does explain why the Pentateuch is in the form we have it today, it cannot be assumed that all E is later than J, all D later still and all P the most recent, because the later redactors may well have had access to older material that was simply not included in earlier works because it derives from a different geographical area or group. Wellhausen's theory was known as the Documentary theory and has provided the basis for almost all Christian Pentateuch research ever since. Later scholars felt that not all of the Pentateuchal sources need have been written documents and so criticism that derives from Wellhausen's method became known as source criticism.

Alongside Wellhausen's theories, those of Herman Gunkel (**1852–1932**) have also been influential. He was interested in the oral prehistory of the sources; if JEDP did exist, in whatever form, from where did they get their material? Instead of dividing a passage between its various sources, he studied each story as an entity. Where did this story come from? What is its 'Sitz im Leben' (situation in life)? What was the setting which would have given rise to the telling of this story? This school of criticism is known as 'form criticism' and most Pentateuchal scholars in the first half of this century worked with a combination of both source and form criticism. Different scholars identified different types of 'Sitz im Leben' or forms.

BOX 2.3

Type of form	Examples
Aetiological (to explain the origin of a shrine or custom)	(a) of circumcision, Gen 17: 1–14
	(b) of place, Gen 16: 1–14
	(c) of Levites, Ex 33: 25–9
	(d) of the bronze serpent, Num 21: 4–9 (see also II Kings 18: 4–5)
Miracle story	Ex 15: 22, water from the rock
Background to a saying(s)	(a) Ex 19–20, the Ten Commandments
	(b) Ex 14: 15–30, the crossing of the Red Sea as a background to Miriam's song, Ex 15: 21
Background to the festivals	Ex 7: 8 – 12: 49, the Passover

One of the main forms is aetiological. A story is told, not only to advance the narrative but also to explain the existence of a particular custom or shrine. Akin to this are the stories told to explain festivals or specific ordinances. Scholars such as Sigmund Mowinckel and Gerhard von Rad felt that many of the Pentateuchal stories originated in cultic festivals.

The existence of JEDP remained largely unchallenged until the **1970s**. Some began to doubt the existence of previously independent accounts of the pre-history of Israel/Judah lying behind the Pentateuch. Some commentators felt that form criticism could explain the shape of the Pentateuch so completely that source criticism was unnecessary. The paucity of any references to the ancestral stories, however, in the definitely pre-exilic biblical texts was felt by some to undermine the case for ancient oral sources, whether as coherent narrative or as individual units. The consensus has vanished.

Both source criticism and form criticism are interested in how the text as we have it came into existence, vital questions if the Pentateuch is to be assessed as an historical source for the history of people who became Israel and Judah. In the eyes of many modern commentators, however, they are not so vital for a theological understanding of the text. In the opinion of Bernard Childs, the text as it is, rather than anything that might lie behind the text, is the proper object of theological reflection. His approach is known as 'canonical criticism' and driven by the theological importance he attaches to the received text, the canon of scripture. The same conclusion is reached for different reasons by proponents of the 'New Criticism', in which the text is viewed as a closed system. These scholars applied to biblical text the insights of modern literary criticism (e.g. Russian formalism, French structuralism and deconstructionism), in which a text is interpreted without recourse to its historical setting or to the history of what it intends to describe, a synchronic rather than a diachronic process. A 'synchronic' study analyses how the text works as text; how does it work as a narrative, what response does it try to evoke in its implied reader, how does the writer's style achieve his ends? 'Diachronic' describes the traditional methods of analysis in which the processes that might have brought the text into being are also studied. The New Criticism has re-established the text as the proper object of study for the biblical scholar, but few have dispensed with traditional methods entirely. Ignoring the historical context or contexts is no less misleading than forgetting the text among a welter of supposition.

Pentateuchal criticism has seen not only new critical methods but also new techniques; what were held to be the different sources in Genesis have been analysed by computers to see whether the differences held up under such scrutiny. Within each source, the text was analysed according to varying functions, such as narrative, God's speech and human speech. J and E were found to be almost impossible to differentiate and the narrative material in all strands was found to be different in style from speech, both divine and human, in all strands. There were definite breaks in style detected between chapters 2–11, the quasi-mythical material, chapters 12–36, the semi-heroic and 37–50, the fully human material, which seemed to override the previous differences observed between JEDP.

Whatever the results of future scholarship as to how the Pentateuch was put together, it seems clear that it was put together in the exilic or post-exilic period to provide a firm foundation upon which the chosen people could live, learning from God's dealings with them in the past. They had lost their independence, but they did not wish to lose their covenant status.

2.4   The Deuteronomic histories

Martin Noth was the first to point out the similarity of phrases and themes between the books of Joshua, Judges, I and II Samuel and I and II Kings. The books are an account of Israel and Judah's experience from the crossing of Jordan under Joshua, to the exile of Jehoiachin, king of Judah. Although they are one of the two main sources we have for Israel/Judah's history in this period, it becomes clearer in the latter books that they are not written as if they were a straightforward historical account. Throughout I and II Kings, reference is made to books in which the reader will find fuller accounts of the kings' reigns (e.g. I Kings 11: 41; 14: 19; 15: 7; 16: 5; 22: 39; II Kings 1: 18; 10: 34; 12: 19; 15: 6; 21: 17; 23: 28; 24: 5).

As well as noting the similarities between these books, Noth also noted their similarity to the book of Deuteronomy. It was his contention that Deuteronomy represented the theological programme of those responsible for the histories. As early as 1805, W.M.L. de Wette recognised that the author(s) of II Kings intended 'the book of the law', which had been found in the house of the Lord, to be identified as some form of Deuteronomy. While, like the Pentateuch, the histories are not the original works of one person but seem to be the result of a compiling and editing of pre-existent sources, the theological thrust of the books' framework is in line with the theology of Deuteronomy.

The promised land will be enjoyed by the chosen people only so long as they keep to their covenant with YHWH. The demands of the covenant were twofold:

living in YHWH's commands and worshipping YHWH alone, in the prescribed way, i.e. in the one legitimate sanctuary in Jerusalem. Jerusalem is never mentioned in Deuteronomy but is implied by the phrase 'the place which YHWH your God will choose'.

Since de Wette's work, Deuteronomy has been dated to around the time of the Josianic reformation, *c.* **622 BCE**, and the Deuteronomic histories to soon after the last event it describes, the release from prison of Jehoiachin, king of Judah, by Evil-merodach, king of Babylon in **561 BCE**. This does not mean that the books originated at this date but that this date marks the earliest point at which the final redaction took place.

Some scholars hold to a 'dual recension' theory; they believe the histories were first put together, perhaps from older sources, at the time of the Josianic reformation. It had been a time of hope; the state's borders under Josiah were almost the same as under the United Monarchy, Assyria was approaching its decline and Josiah had taken advantage of this weakness to reassert Judah's position. He had not only rid Jerusalem of Assyrian religious symbols but Canaanite ones as well, and had attempted not only to be faithful to YHWH but also to the centralist policy of the Deuteronomists. By rights, his rule should have been unshakeable and he should have 'slept with his fathers' at a ripe old age, instead of which he was killed at the battle of Megiddo in **609 BCE** and within twenty-two years the Temple had been destroyed. The books from Deuteronomy to II Kings represent the attempt of one group to make sense of this.

2.4.1 Joshua

The book of Joshua consists of two sections of core material that probably represents traditions available to the editors, within an editorial framework (chapters 1 and 23). Chapter 24 represents a later editorial addition. Chapters 2–12 are stories about the settlement under Joshua and are mainly aetiological units in form and explain the existence of certain place names or features. They are mostly located in one region, the area of the tribe of Benjamin around Gilgal, but include a northern and southern campaign.

Chapters 13–21 concern the division of the land and include both tribal boundaries and city lists, as well as units of tradition concerning individual groups such as the Calebites.

The area covered by the city lists is the tribal area of Judah. Some of the cities have been discovered by archaeologists to have been founded in Iron Age II and so this list probably represents the divisions of the kingdom of Judah from the reign of Jehoshaphat onward. It is difficult to know whether the tribal divisions of chapters 13–19 represent a pre-monarchic division of the land, which some tribes settled and some did not, or represents a later theological construct. The boundaries given here do fit with what can be adduced from the Samaritan ostraca of the eighth century BCE. The 'labels' attached to these jars, found in the palace in Samaria, probably represent supplies sent in from one of the districts into which Israel was divided administratively. All the names of towns fit with the names of the tribe of Manasseh given in the book of Chronicles, and those places which are able to be located with certainty fall within the tribal district of that tribe, as given in Joshua.

Map 2 The Kingdoms of Israel and Judah

The editorial framework of Joshua implies a military campaign that extended throughout Israel and Judah and which involved an extermination of all Israel's enemies, those who worshipped other gods. However, the campaigns described cover only a small area so it is likely that the total strategy described derived more from theology than history.

The Deuteronomists who edited Joshua believed that total obedience to YHWH was only possible when no compromise was made with other groups and this belief they projected back into their account of the settlement of the land of Canaan by the tribes of Israel. The book of Deuteronomy presents a covenant made by Moses, and in Joshua this covenant is renewed at Shechem. It is in the light of these covenants that the subsequent history of the people is written.

2.4.2 Judges

The book of Judges is more realistic in its account of relations between Israel and the Canaanites. Judges chapter 1 includes a list of those cities which had not been captured and chapter 2 a theology to explain it. The book is no less an editorial creation however. It mentions twelve judges, some of whom remain only names while others are shown as the means by which God delivers his people. The time span of the book is far too long for the judges to have followed each other. It is more likely that they were operating within their own tribal areas and consequently overlapped. These stories of local heroes have been moulded into a framework of apostasy, punishment, repentance and restoration to make the point that the chosen people can only rest secure within their settlements if they keep to their covenant with YHWH. Judges tells not only of the tribes of Israel fighting those who do not worship YHWH but also of campaigns among themselves; in 12: 1–6 Jephthah fights the Ephraimites and in 20: 1 Benjamin is pitted against 'all Israel'.

BOX 2.4.2: *Tribal activity in the book of Judges*

Tribal group	Activity
Judah, Simeon, Calebites, Kenites	(a) defeated Adonibezek at Bezek
	(b) took Jerusalem but did not oust the Jebusites
	(c) fought in Negev, at Hebron and at Debir
	(d) took Zephath, Gaza, Askelon and Ekron
	(e) took possession of hill country, not the plain as the inhabitants had chariots of iron
Calebites, Kenites	inhabited Hebron, Debir and Arad in the Negev
Joseph	Bethel
Othniel, the Kenite	fought against Cushan-rishathaim, king of Mesopotamia
Ehud, the Benjaminite	defeated Moab who were in coalition with the Ammonites and Amalekites
(a) *Prose account*: Deborah from Ephraim and Barak from Naphtali with men from Zebulun	won battle against Sisera, commander of the army of Jabin, king of Hazor
(b) *Poetic account*: Deborah and Barak with Ephraim, Benjamin, Machir, Zebulun, Issacher and Naphtali. Reuben, Gilead, Dan and Asher rebuked for not coming	defeated the armies of Jabin, king of Hazor under Sisera

---

Gideon with men from Manesseh, Asher, Zebulun, Naphtali and Ephraim after the battle	defeated the Midianites
Abimelech, son of Gideon the Abiezerite	ruled Shechem for a short time as king
Judah, Benjamin and Ephraim	called Israel in Judges 10: 9
Jephthah the Gileadite	defeated the Ammonites and then the Ephraimites in civil war
Dan	the tribe moved from Zorah and Eshtaol to Laish north of Lake Huleh

Whilst the books of Samuel and Kings have a definite anti-monarchical flavour, the opposite is true in Judges and this perhaps strengthens the case for a dual redaction, one in the time of Josiah and one after the destruction of Jerusalem. The positive references to the king in Judges as the guarantor of stability and the rule of law would be the work of the first redactor. See for example, Judges 17: 6; 18: 1; 19: 1; 21: 25.

2.4.3   The books of Samuel and Kings

Although Samuel and Kings are each split into two in the English versions of the Old Testament, in the original Hebrew text the books are a unity. The narrative of these books covers Israel's transition from a loose network of tribes that recognised common bonds to a nation state, and the later dissolution of the united monarchy and the final destruction of both capitals. As with all written history, the editors of these books do not intend, even if it were possible, to write an account of everything that happened but to write a history that explains why things turned out as they did.

This methodology is not so far removed from that of modern historians. Those who believe that the acts of great men and women mould events write of prime ministers, monarchs, industrialists and reformers. Those who follow process method write of social and economic trends. Modern minds find it somewhat harder to accept the Deuteronomist's premise that it is God who moulds events – they write the history of their people from the perspective of the covenant with YHWH, the breaking of which led inevitably to disaster.

Their theology is not entirely systematic. Judges implies that the hope for Israel's peace is a king. Deuteronomy sees kingship as an inevitable consequence of a settled life and hopes for a king who will rule according to YHWH's law (see Deuteronomy 17: 14, 15, 18, 19). This positive outlook is repudiated in I Samuel.

The beginning of I Samuel has the same flavour as the book of Judges and the narrative moves in the same way, around the figures of the central characters. The main character in the early chapters is Samuel but his emergence is prepared for by the account of Eli and his sons. Eli is the priest of the House of

YHWH at Shiloh where the Ark of the Lord is, although there is no explanation as to how it arrived there from Bethel, where it was at the end of Judges, 20: 27. The pattern in the book of Judges of disobedience to YHWH's law bringing punishment, is highlighted in the experience of one family; Eli has been serving as a priest, presumably faithfully since no ill is spoken of him, but his sons are abusing their trust and judgement is prophesied against them. The story of the conception and birth of Samuel is told alongside the collapse of Eli's family so that he takes over the priestly function when the promised judgement comes about. He is also described as a judge, a man of God and a prophet. His sons also prove unworthy and the people ask for a king.

Three separate traditions about how Saul becomes king are included: 11: 1–14 shows Saul acting as the judges had done and in the face of an external threat is raised by the Spirit of God to leadership. He rescues the Jabesh-Gilead from Nahash the Ammonite with the support of the mustered tribes and in response to his victory the tribes and Samuel make Saul king and renew the covenant at Gilgal. I Sam 9: 1 – 10: 14 tells how Saul meets Samuel while searching for his father's asses and is anointed by Samuel in secret, while I Sam 10: 17–27 has the dramatic account of Saul being chosen by lot. Despite the triumphant shouts of 'Long live the King', 12: 11–18 underlines the mistake Israel has made.

BOX 2.4.3

Now therefore stand still and see this great thing which the Lord will do before your eyes. Is it not the wheat harvest today? I will call upon the Lord that he may send thunder and rain; and you shall know that your wickedness is great, which you have done in the sight of the Lord in asking for yourselves a king.

I Sam 12: 16–18

Saul disobeys God and the kingship is given to David by secret anointing. His kingship is the benchmark against which all others are measured. The Deuteronomist says of Hezekiah:

And he did what was right in the eyes of the Lord according to all that his father David had done.

David was not regarded as a person without faults or sins but he reacts to them with genuine repentance and piety. The seeds for the kingdom's eventual split are seen as lying in the worship of other gods that Solomon allows in Jerusalem because of his marriages to foreign princesses. Realpolitik might have demanded such shrines as signs of alliances but this did not change the opinion of the Deuteronomists: such behaviour was against Israel's covenant with YHWH and would bring punishment, I Kings 11: 29–40. The reigns of David and Solomon are told in such a way as to legitimate the centralisation of the worship of YHWH in the Temple in Jerusalem. The consecration of the Temple marks the high point of this section of the story. Loyalty to this shrine becomes another mark of the one who walks in the way of God's commandments. Uzziah or Amaziah, the king of Judah in the year of whose death the prophet Isaiah received his call, is commended by the Deuteronomists for doing what was right in God's sight except that he continued to allow YHWH to be worshipped at high places and shrines outside Jerusalem; leprosy is the result.

After the split of the kingdoms under Solomon's son Rehoboam, the narrative of I and II Kings concentrates on the northern state until the fall of Samaria when Jerusalem becomes the focus. Before that the southern kings are only mentioned inasmuch as they have dealings with Israel. It is this section of the work which justifies its place in the Hebrew Bible under the title of 'The Former Prophets' because, after the death of Solomon, the next major heroes are not kings but the prophets Elijah and Elisha who are seen as the defenders of YHWHism against monarchs who allow the worship of other gods and the subverting of Israel law. As with the other parts of the work, the overriding aim of the Deuteronomists is to tell their story in such a way as to explain what subsequently happened. The northern tribes were sent into exile because their kings had failed to prevent, had even encouraged, the people of Israel in their worship of other gods or their false worship of YHWH. The kings of Judah mostly failed to learn from the fate of Israel. Manesseh and his son Amon so provoked God by their unfaithfulness that even the righteousness of Josiah could not prevent Jerusalem's fall and the destruction of the Temple.

2.4.4 Conclusion

The simple message that only obedience to YHWH will guarantee prosperity and security in the promised land is stressed on every possible occasion throughout these books. When Samaria and then Jerusalem fell, the faith of the Deuteronomists in YHWH was unshaken. YHWH cannot have been beaten by the gods of the Assyrians and Babylonians, therefore Samaria and Jerusalem, with its sanctuary and its Davidic king, must have been given by YHWH into the power of their enemies. This way of explaining a people's defeat was not confined to Israel/Judah: it can be seen in the Moabite stone where Mesha, king of Moab, accounts for his father's defeats at Israel's hands by saying that Chemosh their god was displeased with them. The Deuteronomists also provide the reason for YHWH's displeasure; he is shown as acting in accordance with the covenants made by Moses, Joshua and Samuel and therefore even in the midst of disaster, he can be approached as faithful and trustworthy because he is a God who keeps his promises, whether to bless or to curse. The unfolding of Israel's history in this light takes up a major proportion of the Hebrew Bible and there are those who think that the editorial hand of the Deuteronomists stretches even further. They may even have redacted the prophecies of Jeremiah to prove their case.

It was long assumed that the Hebrew Bible was a product of a homogeneous theological outlook. While it remains true that to have survived and reached canonical status, the books of the Hebrew Bible must have been largely seen as sympathetic to the theology of those who were in control of truth and orthodoxy, nevertheless the occasional discordant note is sometimes heard. The Deuteronomists were not the only ones seeking to explain the catastrophes of **721 BCE** (see page 21) and **587 BCE** (the surrender of Jerusalem, see page 26).

2.5   I, II Chronicles, Ezra and Nehemiah

In English copies of the Old Testament, unlike the Hebrew Bible where they are placed in the third section of the scriptures, the Writings, these books are placed after the Deuteronomic histories. Scholars cannot agree whether Chronicles, Ezra and Nehemiah were ever one work; details of style and emphasis can be used to argue both ways. The books are thought to date from the fourth century BCE. The last datable event in II Chronicles takes place in **559 BCE** and in Nehemiah *c.* **430 BCE**, which puts the author(s) close enough to the events of the restored community to make the use of memoirs from those involved possible.

2.5.1   The books of Chronicles

Its Greek title means 'the things left out', implying that its translators viewed it as filling in the gaps left by the Deuteronomists. Chronicles, however, has its own purpose and themes. It begins with Adam, showing, as does the Pentateuch, that YHWH is not just the God of Israel but the God of all peoples and places. The first nine chapters are a series of genealogies which the author intends to be taken very seriously. Sometimes he mentions his sources; in I Chron 4: 41 he mentions some Simeonites who went from the 'entrance to Gedor' to Seir, stressing that they had been registered in Hezekiah's day and were still there. When he discusses the potters who lived at Netaim and Gederah, 4: 22–3, he emphasises how ancient are their genealogical records. In 5: 23*f* he mentions the clan names of those deported to Halah, Habor, Hara and the river Gozan from Gilead and Galilee by Tiglath-Pilaser after Pekah's rebellion. He says they are still there in his own day. The genealogy of David in chapter 3, he takes to six or seven generations from Jehoiachin which is almost the generation of the Chronicler. Whether we can or cannot give these genealogies any credence as source for historical research today does not alter the seriousness of the Chronicler's enterprise. To the returning Jews, descent was everything. With a genealogy came proof of continuity with what went before, proof of standing within YHWH's covenant community. If the Deuteronomist was providing an understanding of the past, the Chronicler was providing a base for the future, a base with known roots.

After the nine chapters of genealogy, the Chronicler moves straight on to Saul's defeat at Mt Gilboa. He tells how 'all' Israel came to David at Hebron and entered into a covenant with him to make him king. When he next tells of how Jerusalem was taken from the Jebusites to become David's royal residence, the background to the story is complete and the narration of the royal house in Jerusalem starts. He follows the fortunes of the Jerusalem monarchy until Cyrus' decree to enable exiles to return to Jerusalem to begin rebuilding the Temple.

His account of David's reign begins with his intent to bring the Ark of the Covenant from Kiriath-jearim to Jerusalem. Like the Deuteronomic histories, Chronicles is mainly interested in Israel's religious history, particularly the history of how YHWH was worshipped: the cult. The account of David's reign moves selectively from one significant event to another, background details of

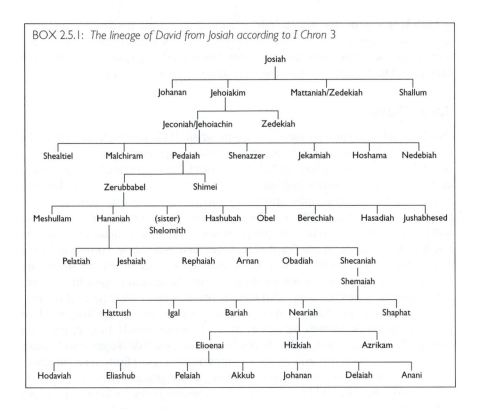

BOX 2.5.1: *The lineage of David from Josiah according to I Chron 3*

Josiah

Johanan   Jehoiakim   Mattaniah/Zedekiah   Shallum

Jeconiah/Jehoiachin   Zedekiah

Shealtiel   Malchiram   Pedaiah   Shenazzer   Jekamiah   Hoshama   Nedebiah

Zerubbabel   Shimei

Meshullam   Hananiah   (sister)   Hashubah   Obel   Berechiah   Hasadiah   Jushabhesed
Shelomith

Pelatiah   Jeshaiah   Rephaiah   Arnan   Obadiah   Shecaniah

Shemaiah

Hattush   Igal   Bariah   Neariah   Shaphat

Elioenai   Hizkiah   Azrikam

Hodaviah   Eliashub   Pelaiah   Akkub   Johanan   Delaiah   Anani

how David added to the borders of Israel (chapters 18–20) being added only to show how YHWH was blessing the king of his choice. David's mistakes are told only so far as they impinge on the Chronicler's theme: we are told of David's decision to take a census of Israel because out of it comes the knowledge of where God wants the Temple built. David is not allowed to build the Temple but we are told in detail of his plans and then the focus shifts to Solomon who was allowed to build the Temple. The Chronicler's account of the dedication of the Temple differs from that of the Deuteronomic histories in one significant respect: the Deuteronomic histories make no mention of the music used in worship; the Chronicler even includes the text of some psalms.

Because his major concern is the Davidic dynasty and the worship of YHWH in Jerusalem, the Chronicler regards the split of the kingdoms as rebellion against the house of David (II Chron 10: 19). Five verses earlier, he makes it clear that he is aware of YHWH's word to Jeroboam but he does not dwell on it. Like the Deuteronomic historian, the Chronicler distinguishes between good kings and bad kings. He too is concerned about the high places (e.g. II Chron 20: 33) and assumes the YHWH will bless good kings and punish bad ones. He also emphasises the reforms of Hezekiah and Josiah, and is troubled by the long reign of the bad king Manasseh which he explains by telling how Manasseh repented once god brought him back to Jerusalem after he had been summoned to the king of Assyria to give an account of himself. The Chronicler describes the disobedience of both king and people under Zedekiah and their refusal to listen to the warnings of the prophets. The sack of Jerusalem and destruction of the Temple are seen as the inevitable result but the Chronicler ends the story not with Jerusalem in ruins but with Cyrus' decree which promises hope for the future.

2.5.2 Ezra

This book raises several problems. It begins where II Chronicles leaves off, at the decree of Cyrus, but scholars have not been able to agree whether or not the two works (together with the book of Nehemiah) came from the same hand. Some see similarities of style, others see differences of emphasis. Emphasis is laid in the book of Ezra on the chosen people, who were clearly marked out from others by their proven descent, recreating themselves as a people. They were to build the Temple and uphold pure worship in it, keeping themselves separate from other peoples by not intermarrying and by keeping the law. Whether or not Ezra was produced by the same writer(s) as Chronicles, most scholars date the book to the fourth century BCE. It uses a variety of sources: royal edicts (now thought to be genuine by most scholars because of similarities with documents relating to other parts of the Persian empire that have come to light), memoirs written both in the first and third person from Ezra's mission, as well as the writer's own words. In both Ezra and Nehemiah it is clear that not all of those who worshipped YHWH agreed with Ezra's insistence on racial purity and that the community that grew from the amalgam of the survivors and the returnees was not without its disagreements.

Ezra starts with Mithredath, Cyrus' treasurer, handing over the Temple treasures to Sheshbazzar, prince of Judah and a return to Jerusalem under Zerubbabel to rebuild the Temple. This is eventually accomplished, the Temple dedicated and the Passover celebrated. The book breaks off and resumes the narrative with Ezra's mission to Jerusalem in the seventh year of Artaxerxes, king of Persia. He is charged to ensure the proper running of the cult of the 'God of Heaven' in the Jerusalem Temple and to set up a legal system to enforce God's law. The remainder of the book tells of his work in Jerusalem. The historical background and problems of Ezra's mission have been discussed earlier. Like all the historical books of the Hebrew Bible, the writer is not concerned simply with the recording of events that happened but with the story of how God's will was fulfilled. As with I and II Chronicles, the emphasis is on the Temple cult but there is also a stress on the right keeping of the Law. In the recording of the decrees of the kings, God is called 'the God of Heaven' but Ezra uses the titles familiar from the rest of the Hebrew Bible: YHWH our God, and YHWH, God of our Fathers.

2.5.3 Nehemiah

The book of Nehemiah has the same variety of sources as Ezra. It includes royal decrees, first-person memoirs as well as the writer's own words. It tells how Nehemiah, a Jew in the service of Artaxerxes, king of Persia (perhaps a eunuch because he serves in the presence of the Queen, which would account for his reluctance to flee to the Temple when under pressure from his enemies 6: 11–12), asks permission to go to Judah to rebuild the walls of Jerusalem. He is allowed to go and given a grant and an escort. The book shows how he completes the task despite opposition from neighbouring provinces. The concern in Ezra about mixed marriages is here also, as is concern over keeping the Sabbath. Other, more political and economic concerns surface in Nehemiah, such as the complaints against the nobles from the ordinary people who are so stretched having to pay tax that they are forced to mortgage their land to the wealthy to pay it and keep their families fed. To pay the interest they then accrue they are forced to sell themselves or their families into slavery.

Like Ezra and I and II Chronicles, Nehemiah includes genealogies which shows the interest in continuity and pedigree among the community for whom these books were written, as well as the communities who kept them in the time prior to their inclusion here.

2.6 The prophets

In the Hebrew Bible, the major prophets, Isaiah, Jeremiah and Ezekiel, and the minor prophets are together under the title of the Later Prophets. They provide insight into the history of Israel and Judah and to the religious priorities of those who gave and cherished these words. We shall look at them in chronological order but it would be misleading to think that this gives us an account of the development of Judaism in the relevant periods because the shape of the prophetic books, as we have them, may owe as much to their editors as to the prophets.

2.6.1 Amos and Hosea

Amos is the earliest of the 'Writing' prophets, as those prophets with books named after them are sometimes known, to distinguish them from the prophets whom we know of from descriptions in the histories, such as Elijah and Elisha. The dating in the book itself is quite specific: during the reigns of Uzziah and Jeroboam II, two years before the earthquake. These reigns span the first half of the eighth century but scholars have traditionally dated Amos' mission to *c.* **760–50**. However, because of the lack of any clear reference to Assyria, some scholars would now put his ministry earlier in the century. Unfortunately we do not know when the earthquake took place. Amos is from Tekoa in the southern state of Judah but sent by God to preach in the north. He tells us that he was not from a family of prophets but was following the flocks when he received his commission.

Although his style is more like Hebrew prose than his near contemporary Hosea, it is highly rhythmic and is sometimes known as 'prophetic oratory'. His message is addressed to the north but builds up to this in chapters 1 and 2. Each of the surrounding nations is first rebuked in turn for particular sins and punishment promised. One can imagine the books' readers cheering the prophet on until Israel too is rebuked. Although Judah is rebuked for idolatry, Amos' main charge against Israel is their corruption of justice and oppression of the poor. He denounces their shrines and sacrifices, not because God would prefer they take place at Jerusalem but because they are abhorrent coming from those who exploit people weaker than themselves. Judgement is inevitable because Israel has failed to take notice of

God's warnings and the priests and king have rejected the prophet's message. These themes of justice and social justice pervade the book of Amos.

Several influences can be seen in the book. Amos refers to the people being brought by YHWH out of Egypt and 'the Amorite' driven out before them after forty years in the wilderness. His knowledge is derived from a slightly different tradition from that which has survived in the Pentateuch, because he takes for granted that those he addresses would know that sacrifice was not offered there, 5: 25–6. He mentions the plagues in Egypt and the destruction of Sodom and Gomorrah. He refers to the shrines of Isaac and the people of Isaac, in parallel with the shrines and people of Israel but without any mention of Abraham. From the more recent past he mentions David in connection with the making of new instruments. There is a clear connection with what we know as wisdom in 3: 7; 4: 13; 5: 8–9; 9: 5–6, where God's creative and destructive power is stressed. Amos has a vision of the God of Israel as the God who created the heavens and the earth. What is taken by some to be an insight almost forced on a people who found their God still with them in the strange land of Babylon, is found here in the earliest of the prophets. The title, YHWH of Hosts or YHWH, God of Hosts is frequent and refers to the idea of YHWH as leader of the host of heaven.

Although much of his prophecy is negative and stresses the anger of God at the behaviour of his people and their refusal to repent, like Hosea after him, Amos does not see judgement as the end but foresees the restoration of Israel in peace.

Hosea is set in the mid eighth century BCE and probably extends beyond the reign of Jeroboam II because of the rapid switching of kings to which the prophet alludes in 7: 7 and 8: 4. The book is based around the allegory of an unfaithful wife representing YHWH and Israel, which Hosea is told to act out by marrying an 'unchaste' woman and having children with her. What happened between Hosea and Gomer is only slightly alluded to as the main focus is on YHWH and Israel. The emotions a husband would feel on being betrayed, feelings which Hosea's audience could well imagine and which the prophet was made to experience, are evoked to portray the feelings that YHWH has towards the people he brought up from Egypt. When Hosea buys Gomer (presumably it is the mother of his children to which the text refers when Hosea is told to 'Go again and bestow your love on a woman, loved by another man, an adulteress', rather than a second woman) and brings her back to live in his house, this time faithfully, it is likened to the time that Israel will live 'without king or leader, without sacrifice or sacred pillar, without ephod or teraphim', 3: 4. It is a verse which surveys the culture of Hosea's day and is worth studying. The king or leader is contrasted with 'David their king' in 3: 5. The period of time when they are to be deprived of all they hold dear is to bring them back to their true allegiance, to the Davidic line, just as Hosea hopes to win back his wife. The sacred pillar referred to could be a reference to the sacred poles used as symbols of the goddess Asherah, but it more probably refers to the pillar in YHWH's Temple. We know there were sacred pillars in the Jerusalem Temple (I Kings 7: 15; II Chronicles 3: 15–17) and it is probable that Jeroboam's Temple followed a similar pattern as Solomon's design as it was not unique. Several similar structures have been found in middle to late bronze age sites in Syria. According to Leviticus, the ephod was part of the High Priestly vestments, whereas in Judges it seems to be some sort of image connected with the worship of YHWH; in both cases it seems to have some sort of oracular function. Teraphim were also images; in Genesis, they seem to be household gods, as Rachel steals them from her father.

Hosea has three main accusations to make: God's people are worshipping Baal and idols that they have made with their own hands; they seek political alliances with major powers to bring them stability and protection; and they have lost any sense of justice in the way they treat each other. Unlike Amos, Hosea specifically criticises the calf idols which Jeroboam I had set up. Hosea sees 'want of know-ledge', which Amos prophesies would take place, as being the root cause of their sins (4: 6) for which he blames the prophet and the priest. It is a vicious circle; their 'want of knowledge' leads them into sin and 'the spirit of immorality which is in them' bars them from knowing the Lord, 5: 4.

But Hosea's prophecy is not only a reflection on what Israel has done but on God's reaction and the struggle between his righteous anger and a sense of betrayal, on the one hand, and tenderness, pity and love, on the other. It is in the prophetic books of the Hebrew Bible that the contrast between the unmoved 'God of the Philosophers' who crept into early Christian doctrine, and the God of Israel is at its most marked. The book of Hosea ends on a note of hope: repentance and restoration are possible because while the anger of God is assuaged by punish-ment, the love and faithfulness of God last forever.

Despite the occasional mention of Judah, most of Hosea's prophecy is directed to Israel. Of the stories in the Pentateuch, Hosea refers to Jacob and Esau struggling in the womb for supremacy, Jacob struggling with God and God, YHWH, the God of Hosts meeting Jacob at Bethel. He also mentions Jacob fleeing to Aram to get a wife and tending sheep to win her. He also knows of God rescuing the people from Egypt, and how the people were fed in the wilderness and worshipped God at the Tent of Meeting. We cannot be sure whether he believed this worship to be with sacrifice as described in the Pentateuch, or without as related in Amos. He does not mention Moses by name, saying that YHWH brought Israel out of Egypt and tended them by a prophet. He also refers to the people asking YHWH for a king and being given one 'in . . . anger'. Despite the importance of the covenant theme, there is no mention of Sinai/Horeb traditions.

The text of Hosea is a difficult one. Poetic style in most languages is usually harder to understand than prose, so scholars differ on how pure they believe the text to be: are the difficulties because of a corrupt text or Hosea's style? This is a question that is almost impossible to answer but it serves to remind us that what we know about Israelite religion is always provisional.

2.6.2 Micah

The prophet Micah was from the Judean foothills and roughly contemporary with Isaiah, preaching in the reigns of Jotham, Ahaz and Hezekiah, according to 1: 1. While scholars argue about the authenticity of some verses (2: 12–13; 4: 1–11; 5: 7–9; 7: 8–20), few would doubt that most of the book can be ascribed to Micah himself. The prophecy is addressed to both Israel and Judah. There is some con-demnation for idolatry, 1: 7, but the main complaints levelled against YHWH's people are concerned with the way they treat one another and the way they worship

YHWH. Injustice and exploitation are roundly condemned, as are those who manipulate religion to give people what they want to hear regardless of authenticity or truth. The most famous verse in the book comes after the prophet has stressed, just as Amos (Amos 5: 21*f*) and Hosea (Hos 8: 13*f*) did, how sacrifice in itself pleases God not at all:

> *He* [the Lord] *has shown you what is good; and what does the Lord require of you but to do justice, to love kindness and to walk humbly with your God.*

As Hosea and Amos do, he reflects on YHWH's care shown to Israel in their rescue from Egpyt. In 6: 4 he mentions Moses by name, the earliest mention we have of him. Aaron and Miriam are mentioned along with Moses as those whom YHWH sent to lead his people. Perhaps there was a broader tradition about Miriam than has survived into the Pentateuch. In common with all the prophetic books, is the message that YHWH is not indifferent to the way his people behave and that his anger with them is experienced not through prophetic words but through events which YHWH allows or causes.

2.6.3 Isaiah

The book of Isaiah has been recognised as a composite work since the sixteenth century, with J.C. Doerderlein arguing that chapters 40–66 were written later than chapters 1–39. There is a wide range of opinion on which parts of the book hail from which period, some scholars dating parts of Isaiah as late as the second century BCE. The debate is further confused by the appearance of themes which run throughout the material, such as the centrality of Jerusalem, the promise of a Davidic ruler and the idea of YHWH as the 'Holy One of Israel'.

The book is named after the prophet whose prophecies form its core, Isaiah, son of Amoz. His work was kept and reinterpreted during the reign of Josiah; the failure of Sennacherib to capture Jerusalem in Hezekiah's reign was seen almost as a mark of Zion's invincibility. This in turn had to be reinterpreted after the disaster of **587**. Reinterpretation meant resetting the old oracles and adding new prophetic words. Each new phase in Israel/Judah's history demanded a representation of old truths. Most scholars feel that the book of Isaiah had reached its present form by the fourth century but others see its evolution continuing until the period of the successful Maccabean revolt against the Seleucids in the second century BCE.

The original Isaiah was from Jerusalem and was familiar with court and Temple ritual. His famous call narrative tells of his vision of YHWH of Hosts, the king, seated on a throne filling the Temple with the hem of his robe. Like the other eighth century prophets, he is concerned to see behind the events of the day to the will of YHWH. He too sees a lack of knowledge of YHWH as the root of the problem. He castigates the rulers and the rich for their failure to ensure justice and for their seeking alliances with secular powers to provide the security Judah should have found in obeying God. The kernel of Isaiah's prophecy concerns the Syro-Ephraimite war when Pekah, king of Israel and Rezin, king of Aram, marched on Jerusalem to force Ahaz into an alliance with them against Assyria and later, Hezekiah's relations with Assyria, culminating with the siege of Jerusalem by

Sennacherib. Isaiah urges both kings to stand firm and trust YHWH but in both cases alliances are made: Ahaz with the Assyrians, and Hezekiah first with Egypt and then with Babylon. Hezekiah is even rebuked for fortifying the wall of Jerusalem and ensuring a water supply within the city walls; such measures are pointless without looking to YHWH, the final source of Jerusalem's security (22: 9–11).

Isaiah's prophecies are also directed to the neighbouring peoples and are not always negative (19: 19*f*). Although he knows God as the Holy One of Israel, he is aware that YHWH's concern reaches beyond his chosen people. The thought world of some of these oracles, whether to his own or foreign peoples, is akin to apocalyptic works (see 5: 25; 13: 13; 34: 4). Some of the prophet's images are familiar to us from the pages of the Hebrew bible. In 1: 9–10 and 3: 9 he mentions Sodom and Gomorrah; in 5: 24 the Law; in 10: 24 the oppression in Egypt and the battle at the rock of Oreb against the Midianites. The exodus from Egypt is mentioned in 11: 6 and Abraham in 29: 22. However much of Isaiah's religious imagery sits uncomfortably with what we assume to be YHWHistic orthodoxy. Rahab and Leviathan, the sea beasts of chaos whom God defeated to bring forth creation are here; 27: 1, 30: 7 and 24: 21 include a clear reference to the fallen angels who brought disobedience to mankind in the enochic myths, perhaps echoed in 34: 5. The lament over the fall of the prince of Tyre in chapter 14 is couched in imagery that is unlike anything else in the Hebrew Bible apart from apocalyptic. Some scholars have therefore begun to look for the roots of later Jewish apocalypticism, not in the thought worlds of neighbouring cultures but in Israel's first Temple period.

It used to be thought that chapters 1–39 came from Isaiah, son of Amoz. Most scholars would see the hand of later editors here too, but editors from which later period and in which specific chapters and verses is a matter for debate.

Chapters 40–55 have been commonly known as Second or Deutero-Isaiah and have a distinctive and homogeneous flavour. They are addressed to the exiled community in Babylon and are full of hope. The prophet stresses both God's power in creation and his continuing care of his people even after their exile. The exodus from Egypt is re-worked to give hope in this new exile. Idols are mocked as the position of YHWH as the only God (El) is stressed. In 41: 6, 21 YHWH is addressed as 'king', his title in the Jerusalem cult (6: 5). These chapters have been very important to Christians because of the 'Suffering Servant Songs' which have been seen by many as messianic prophecy which Jesus fulfilled. The theme of Zion and Jerusalem which was so important to First Isaiah is stressed here also.

The theme which runs throughout this section and ties in with Isaiah's account of his call in chapter 6, is that of true prophecy springing from the true God. Idols and false prophets are denounced because they did not announce what came to pass, they cannot provide an understanding for it which will help people to reflect on their experiences, and they cannot give any advice or hope for the future.

This provides a rationale for the book as a whole, reflecting on fulfilled prophecy from the past and giving insights which illuminate both the present and the future (e.g. Isaiah 41: 21; 42: 9; 43: 9; 44: 7, 25–6; 45: 21; 46: 10; 48: 5, 13). Allied to this is the depiction of idols, the host of heaven and disobedient people as being blind and deaf. Only YHWH and those who follow him can see and hear but, as in 42: 19, they do not always choose to.

These chapters use images which we see in wisdom and apocalyptic literature, as at 40: 10, 12, 22; 42: 13; 44: 24; 45: 18; 48: 13; 51: 6, 12.

Of the Pentateuchal stories, Abraham and Sarah are referred to, as is Noah, while Eden is held up as a symbol of fruitfulness. God's victory in drowning the Egyptians in the Red Sea is allied with his primeval defeat of the sea monster Rahab and pointed to as the basis for hope in God's victory for Israel in the future. God is seen as the God of history who will use Cyrus to restore Jerusalem just as he used the Babylonians to destroy it. These chapters resound with confidence and hope.

The final section of the book, sometimes known as Third Isaiah, is said to reflect the experience of Judah after the return of the exiles. Despite the great hopes of the middle section, the actual experience of rebuilding a community proves to be difficult. The leaders of the restored community are accused of the blindness that has been such an important theme of the book, 56: 10, idol worship is still practised despite everything, 57: 3–13, and the righteous' only hope for peace lies in death, 57: 1–2. The community is rebuked for substituting religious observance and sacrifice for justice and righteousness. The only specifically religious commandment which has the approval of the prophet is the observance of the Sabbath. In complete opposition to the practice of Ezra and Nehemiah, the prophet regards obedience to God as the only way in which a person can be seen as in or out of the covenant community. Both eunuch and foreigner have a place of honour on God's holy hill if they are obedient and holy. There are definite signs of a clash over this point:

> This is the word of the Lord, who gathers those driven out of Israel: I shall add to those already gathered.
>
> Is 56: 8

'Israel' is normally used of people and not place and perhaps refers to those YHWHists whom the returnees did not regard as Israel. Chapters 63: 11*f* and 66 may also refer to a split within Israel.

Along with many of the prophets, Third Isaiah has a vision of YHWH the warrior who comes in judgement (59: 17 and 63). Hope has not disappeared, however, and the prophet looks forward to a time when God will establish Jerusalem in justice and peace. There are few references to Israel's religious tradition; the exodus and Moses are both mentioned in 63: 11–12, while the style of some verses such as 66: 1–2 owes something to the wisdom tradition. Still, the events of the more recent past provide enough ground for reflection.

2.6.4   Zephaniah, Nahum, Habbakkuk and Obadiah

Zephaniah's ministry is dated to Josiah's reign, 640–609; either his preaching took place before Josiah's reform in 621 or the prophet was extremely unimpressed. This contrast between the attitude of contemporary prophets and the Deuteronomic historians to events which they record as religious reforms can also be see in Isaiah's lack of praise for Hezekiah's reforms. Zephaniah preaches against foreign influence and foreign gods, and envisages a judgement upon all who seek to put themselves beyond accountability to God, be they of Israel or not. The only mention of any Pentateuchal themes comes at 2: 9 where the judgement to come upon Moab is likened to that upon Sodom and Gomorrah. However Zephaniah does use the first Temple title of 'king' for God in 3: 13. Despite being so sure of the inevitability of God's judgement, Zephaniah still has hope for Zion beyond.

Nahum also speaks words of judgement but not upon his own people. He prophesies the fall of Nineveh and so would have preached in the years leading up to its demise in 612. He draws a vivid picture of YHWH the warrior requiting the enemies of his people. While the alternatives to Assyria proved worse, this oracle stood as proof that YHWH will judge those who stand against his chosen.

Habbakkuk prophesied in the reign of Jehoiakim and was therefore a contemporary of Jeremiah. In this book we have the fullest picture of YHWH the warrior. Habbakkuk begins by bewailing the lack of justice he sees around him and is promised that God's judgement will come in the shape of the Babylonians; the prophet is still not satisfied since the Babylonians do not acknowledge God and are no more righteous than those whom they have been used to punish. But the prophet will not give up and waits for God's answer. This comes in the shape of a vision in which Habbakkuk is promised that however long it takes, judgement will always come to those who build their security and wealth by exploiting others. Chapter 3 is a psalm attributed to Habbakkuk in which he describes YHWH the warrior coming to save his people.

Unlike other prophets, Habbakkuk does not try to warn his contemporaries about God's impending judgement. The situation is irretrievable; the prophet seeks not to avert but to understand and thus to provide a basis for continuing to hope in YHWH beyond the destruction of nation, capital, temple and king.

Obadiah, of whom nothing is known, prophesied after the fall of Jerusalem but probably before the return of the exiles because his hopes for a return of the exiles of Israel and Judah are unblemished. Like Deutero-Isaiah, Obadiah could hope for a better future rather than having to come to terms with a restoration confused by the conflicts and disappointments of reality as Third Isaiah did. Obadiah proclaims judgement against Edom for their behaviour when Judah and Jerusalem were captured. There is no mention in either II Kings or II Chronicles of what he might mean, but other biblical passages reflect anger against Edom, e.g. Ps 137: 7, Lam 4: 21, Joel 3: 19 and Mal 1: 4. Judgement is proclaimed against Edom but with a promise of a re-established kingdom for Jerusalem.

2.6.5 Jeremiah

Jeremiah is not a well-organised account of the ministry of the prophet. It has no coherent chronology; chapter 21 deals with events of the final siege of Jerusalem while chapter 26 refers to events twenty years earlier. Incidents are repeated, for example Jeremiah's sermon in the Temple occurs both in chapter 7 and chapter 26. This is not to say that the book is without arrangement. Passages are gathered around themes: 3: 1 – 4: 4, for example, dealing with the infidelity and adultery of

God's people. The book is a mixture of poetry and prose. There is no doubt that its final shape has been dictated by editorial activity, perhaps more than once, but few scholars doubt that much of the book can be traced back to the ministry of Jeremiah himself.

According to the introduction, Jeremiah prophesied from **627** to **587** but the book does record prophecy after the fall of Jerusalem also. Many think that the poetic oracles in chapters 1–25 are Jeremiah and perhaps represent the collection which Jehoiakim burnt in **604** and which Jeremiah dictated afresh to Baruch. Also original are the poetic reflections on the prophetic ministry and its cost; they are the only such personal accounts in the Hebrew Bible. The book of consolation, chapters 30, 31 and 33, is also thought to contain material which originates with Jeremiah. The biographical detail about the prophet describes events mainly in the final days of Jerusalem and its aftermath and, while it is therefore not possible to write an account of Jeremiah's life on the basis of it, there is little reason to doubt its accuracy.

The oracles against foreign powers in chapters 46–51 are thought by some to have existed as a separate unit which may or may not have originated with Jeremiah. However, foreign oracles are a standard part of the prophetic books that we have and there is no reason to doubt that they were also a part of Jeremiah's ministry. In some of the prose passages which link the poetic oracles, there are those who have seen the hand of the Deuteronomists because of a similarity in thought and style, and therefore believe them to be a product of the exile. Others believe these sermons and speeches do originate either with Jeremiah himself, his scribe Baruch or a contemporary editor because of the rhetorical prose style which some scholars think derives from Jeremiah's period.

Unlike his predecessors, Jeremiah's main concern is against idolatry. The leaders are rebuked for their exploitation of the poor but the majority of the complaints laid against the people and their rulers concern the worship of idols. He censures the rulers, priests and prophets for leading the population astray. Like Amos, Jeremiah knows of traditions in which no sacrifices were offered in the wilderness and points out how sacrifice without obedience is anathema to YHWH. What God wants is obedience to the covenant symbolised in keeping the Sabbath and the circumcision of the heart. He makes clear, like Ezekiel after him, that God punishes no one for his father's sins, everyone's actions will be put only to their own account. This was not an idea popular with the Deuteronomists who put Jerusalem's punishment down to the offences of their kings, particularly Manasseh (see II Kings 24: 3), a theology that finds a place in the book of Jeremiah also at 15: 4. To stress personal responsibility not only means that one will not be punished for the sin of another, it also, equally unpopularly, means that only the individual's righteousness can save him. It is no use sheltering under the inviolability of Jerusalem. The inhabitants of Jerusalem can and will be punished despite the presence of the sanctuary.

Of the Pentateuchal traditions, the rescue from Egypt is the one that gives the prophet most food for reflection. Moses and Samuel are mentioned to point out that even their intercession would not move YHWH to pity, so much has Jerusalem sinned. Sodom and Gomorrah are mentioned as exemplars of judgement. Varying influences are evident in the book; the idea of the prophet standing in YHWH's council to hear his word is elaborated. True prophecy comes from an encounter with God. We see traces of the wisdom and apocalyptic ideas that God has been in control since creation, 10: 12–13, and that his judgement can be seen in creation itself, 4: 23–4. Idolatry is not only wrong because it breaks YHWH's covenant but ludicrous because YHWH alone is and has ever been God, 10: 14–16. Jeremiah sometimes uses the title 'king' by which some think YHWH was worshipped in the first Temple cult.

Jeremiah has hope initially that he can engender much repentance, and that disaster will be averted. When such hope has vanished, he still has hope in the long-term commitment of YHWH to his people; God will punish those who punished Israel and bring them back to their own land, 50: 18–19. This time God will make it possible for the people to keep their side of the covenant by putting it upon their hearts, 31: 31–4, an idea echoed in Ezekiel and picked up by the early church.

2.6.6 Ezekiel

Ezekiel is contemporary with Jeremiah's later ministry. He is among those exiled from Jerusalem with Jehoiachin/Jeconiah in **598** and receives his prophetic call while in exile. It is clear from the book that he has dealings both with the exiles from Judah and from Israel. He dated his oracles from the year that the king went into exile. The book is concerned with dating and chronology. His last oracle, 29: 17, can be dated to **571**.

Ezekiel uses a wide range of forms to express YHWH's word, from descriptions of his own visionary experiences to complex allegories. The complex visions of God's glory that he had became the centre of a type of Jewish mysticism, known as Merkavah or Chariot mysticism, and few were advised to meditate upon these passages. Like Jeremiah, Ezekiel's main concern is with idolatry, the rebellion against YHWH's covenant, which he sees in visions happening even within the Temple itself. He sees that the very sin which caused the destruction of both kingdoms has not been rooted out of the community, which still practises idolatry in exile. Like Jeremiah, he promises that God will change his people from the inside to enable them to remain faithful to their God. Like most of the prophets, he draws on the rescue from Egypt motif but he is unable to look back and see a golden age in which the people were faithful. He looks back and sees them caught in idolatry from the beginning and that the only real hope is for this radical remaking by God. Here lies his hope for the future: the people, renewed by God, are brought back to their own land. The settlement is to happen afresh but this time foreigners who are obedient to God are to be welcomed into His community and given their own stake in the land. The Temple is to be rebuilt and more care is to be taken over protecting it from the impurity of life. The glory of God which Ezekiel had seen depart from the Temple before its sack will return to the new Temple.

There are a number of places in which Ezekiel gives us a glimpse into religious practice as he knew it. In chapter 44, Ezekiel lays down the distinction between the Levitical priests and the Zadokite priests; only the Zadokites are to come near the altar. This is an arrangement we know from regulations elsewhere in the Hebrew Bible, which implies this is how it was from the beginning of organised sacrifice. But if this were the case in the first temple, Ezekiel would have had no need to stress the point. It is presented as a change, as a punishment because of their leading the Israelites into idolatry. In this light, parts of the Pentateuch, of the Deuteronomic histories and of Chronicles may be underwriting current practice rather than describing former ways.

Like Hosea and Isaiah, Ezekiel not only delivers the Lord's message in words but acts it out; Isaiah was required to go around barefooted and naked while Ezekiel was to lie on his side, one side after the other, to symbolise Israel and Judah receiving the Lord's punishment. Hosea was to marry a woman of no reputation while Ezekiel was forbidden to show any signs of mourning for his wife as a sign to the exiles that when news of the Temple's desecration came, they were to remember that it was the Lord's doing.

Ezekiel's hope is that after his anger, God will restore for himself a people who are able to be a sign and a channel of his holiness; he has a vision of a restored Temple, a place of pure ritual from which water flows out for cleansing and healing even of the sea. It is a vision for ultimate harmony which survives into the hope of the early church.

2.6.7   Haggai and Zechariah

Both prophets began their ministry in **520**, the second year of Darius, king of Persia. Haggai prophesied over three months while Zechariah's dated visions carried on for two years. Haggai contends that the poverty of the resettled Judean community springs from their sloth in rebuilding the Temple. He also criticised the offerings that they did make, presumably at the altar which had been set up early in Zerubbabel's governorship. Along with censure comes the radical challenge to trust YHWH, to put money into rebuilding the Temple and to see how God would provide for them as a result. The Governor, Zerubbabel, grandson of Jehoiachin, becomes the centre of messianic hopes; YHWH has chosen him and promised that the glory of the house that he shall build will be greater than the glory of the previous Temple.

Zechariah receives the word of the Lord in the form of visions; in his visions what he sees is explained to him by an angel but he is also spoken to directly by YHWH of Hosts. These visions are recounted in the first eight chapters and then the style changes into poetic and prose oracles. Some scholars consider that in the same way as in the book of Isaiah in which the original prophecies were re-interpreted and built upon in different circumstances, so the later chapters of Zechariah come from different prophets who saw themselves as preaching in his tradition.

Zechariah himself stands in the prophetic tradition which saw legitimate words from YHWH springing from the prophets' being privy to the unfolding events of YHWH's heavenly council. He puts social and political concerns at the centre of YHWH's complaint against his people but along with complaint comes promise; promise that YHWH will once again choose Jerusalem and punish those who sacked it and exiled the people. He calls upon the exiles to return and promises that God will be with the renewed community as he was with their ancestors in the wilderness. He promises that Zerubbabel will complete the building of the

Temple and that God has cleansed the High Priest Joshua to serve there. There is evidence of messianic hope centred around the 'Branch'. Controversy surrounds the crowning of Joshua the High Priest in chapter 6; verse 13 states that there will be a priest beside the throne of the one who has assumed royal dignity, but if the original passage did refer to Joshua this seems an unnecessary addition since Joshua himself is a priest. This has led some scholars to suppose that the original referent of this prophecy was Zerubbabel. The idea of twin messiahs, one priestly and one from the house of David, is important later in the Qumran community.

The messianic hope centred on the house of David and Jerusalem is stressed in the later chapters. Further battles over Jerusalem are foretold and while it is promised that the city will be taken and half the population exiled, it is promised that YHWH will continue to fight for his city and in the process become 'king over all the earth' and make Jerusalem, as Ezekiel also promised, a source of water to east and west.

The book of Zechariah has often been pointed to as marking a transition from classical prophecy to later apocalyptic but this is to overlook the 'apocalyptic' features of earlier prophets. Certainly his visionary experience and how he expresses it is akin to that of Revelation but his prophetic method is not limited to the telling of visions; chapters 7 and 8 include non-visionary words of the Lord, just as eighth-century Amos includes visions. Elisha, likewise, in II Kings, chapter 6, is credited with visionary experience. The early church included both visionaries and prophets. The interrelationship between apocalyptic and prophecy is more complex than is sometimes made out.

2.6.8 Malachi and Joel

The book of Malachi is usually dated in the Persian period after the completion of the Temple in 512 BCE but before the ministries of Ezra and Nehemiah. As some parts of the books may imply a difference of opinion with the views of Ezra as we know them from the biblical book named after him, they may even be contemporary. The book begins with an oracle for Edom and expresses the same anger that we see in Obadiah. After stating that God's greatness stretches beyond Israel, the prophet launches into an attack on the way worship is conducted in the Temple. People are despising God by offering animals that are infirm or sickly. In chapter 2, Malachi criticises priests for negating YHWH's covenant with the Levites and for leading people astray by their teaching. This seems in direct contradiction with the word spoken through Ezekiel: that God himself had revoked his covenant with the Levites for their worshipping of idols and with the practice of Tabernacle and Temple worship described in Exodus and Chronicles, in which the priests alone approached the altar while Levites performed other duties. It confirms what can be gleaned from Judges and parts of the Pentateuch that the Levites were the original priesthood of Israel. After this, Malachi rebukes those who divorce 'the wife of your youth', which seems significant in that both Ezra and Nehemiah enjoined divorce for those who have married foreign women. Then Malachi promises that God will suddenly intervene and send a messenger to purify the Levites so that they will once more be fit to offer sacrifice to YHWH.

Malachi ends with a promise of judgement which will spell disaster to the disobedient but hope for the faithful. Disobedience to the covenant is measured both by cult, in offering blemished animals or neglecting tithes, and practically, in exploiting those who have no one to protect them. God's concern is for all areas of life. Malachi ends with the promise of Elijah's return before 'the great and terrible day of the Lord comes'. It is this great promise which ends English versions of the Old Testament. Nothing is known about Malachi. The name means 'my Messenger' and therefore may not be a proper name at all.

Joel is thought to date from about fifty to a hundred years later than Malachi and is also concerned with correct worship in the Temple. A plague of locusts and a failure of the crops is blamed upon a neglect of YHWH's offerings. The prophet promises judgement and calls for repentance, which he promises will be effective because of YHWH's great love for his people. He elaborates on the theme of judgement and it becomes judgement upon the nations which have despoiled Israel. He promises that water will well up from the Lord's house to water Judah and that Jerusalem will be holy, the dwelling place of God.

2.6.9 Conclusion

Despite the four centuries which separate Amos from Joel, there are a number of themes which can be seen running throughout the prophets.

Throughout the prophetic corpus, the name most commonly used of God is YHWH of Hosts. The name implies the setting which we see referred to through-out, the heavenly council in which the true prophet is admitted to hear the word of YHWH (Jer 23: 22; I Kings 22: 19; Is 6: 1ff). Because of verses such as Ps 82: 1 and Deut 32: 8–9, there are those who think that the council was originally the council of El, or God Most High, in which YHWH was one of the members, one of the sons of El. The opening of Job would support this view where the Hebrew of 1: 6 is as likely to read 'set themselves against YHWH' (as it does in Ps 2: 2) as 'present themselves before'. Thus, although YHWH becomes Lord of the Host, taking the place of or merging with El, he was first thought of as one of the Host. YHWH of Hosts and the angels who surround him are just as real in the prophecy of Zechariah after the exile as they were to Micaiah, the prophet, in Ahab's reign in the first half of the ninth century.

As well as sharing this heavenly context, the Prophets also share the assumption that human behaviour matters to God. God cares about the righteousness of his people; it matters to him whether the rich and the powerful oppress the poor and the powerless, it matters whether they are faithful to him. He will not just stand by and watch. As he rescued his people from Egypt and made a nation out of them, so he will listen to the cry of the oppressed today. His first response is then to communicate to his people through the prophets, and this assumption provides the rationale for the whole prophetic task. The prophets can declare the word of the Lord because YHWH is a God who communicates. That he acts within the historical process is another shared assumption but he does not do so without explanation. What people do moves him to activity but not without him first communicating his purpose, giving time for response and repentance (Amos 3: 7).

2.7 Wisdom literature

The remainder of the books in the Hebrew Bible are found in the third section, the Writings. This section includes I and II Chronicles, Ezra and Nehemiah, which are found in English Bibles after II Kings, Ruth, which in English Bibles is found after Judges, Lamentations, which is found after Jeremiah, and Daniel, which is found among the minor prophets. The Writings are not linked by any one common theme but only by their not being in either of the other sections, the Law or the Prophets.

Three of the books, Job, Proverbs and Ecclesiastes, are seen, at least in modern minds, as belonging to a common genre, Wisdom, of which there are also two examples in the Apocrypha: the Wisdom of Solomon and the Wisdom of ben Sirach. As with all labels, it is important to remember that they may mean more to the later scholar than to those who produced the works and their first audience.

Solomon was the hero figure of Israelite wisdom; both the Deuteronomic histories and the Chronicler emphasise the famed yet God-given nature of his wisdom while two of the wisdom books we have are attributed to him: Proverbs and the Wisdom of Solomon. Many of the allusions to wisdom in the Hebrew text are unsatisfactory in translation, because they are translated using different words – the English word 'wisdom' is much narrower in scope than the Hebrew word that it is used to translate. For example, the II Chronicles' account of Solomon's reign mentions how he was given his wisdom and stresses how the fame of his wisdom spread but, unlike the Deuteronomic histories, seems to give no account of it in practice in the English translation. However behind English words like 'skilful' lies the Hebrew word for wisdom. Skill to build and create was the result of wisdom. Solomon asks King Huram of Tyre for a skilled craftsman in English, but in Hebrew for a wise man able to work in wood or gold or violet yarn. The primary result of Solomon's wisdom for the Chronicler is his building of the Temple. The Pentateuchal accounts of the building of the Tent of Meeting are also full of men and woman whose wisdom enabled them to work in gold or wood or with cloth. The contents of the canonical wisdom books perhaps do not give us a true picture of the scope of Israelite wisdom. It is instructive to compare the contents of Proverbs, Ecclesiastes and Job with other verses that describe the nature of wisdom. Two such references, one from a canonical and one from an apocryphal wisdom text, are given in Box 2.7.

BOX 2.7

God gave Solomon deep wisdom and understanding as wide as the sand on the sea-shore so that Solomon's wisdom surpassed that of all the men of the East and of all Egypt. For he was wiser than any man, wiser than Ethan the Ezrahite, and Heman, Calcol and Darda, the sons of Mahol; his fame spread among all the surrounding nations. He propounded three thousand proverbs and his songs numbered a thousand and five. He discoursed of trees, from the cedar of Lebanon to the marjoram that grows out of the wall, of beasts and birds, of reptiles and fish.

I Kings 4: 29–33

(Continued)

BOX 2.7 (Continued)

God grant that I may speak according to his will and that my own thoughts may be worthy of his gifts, for even wisdom is under God's direction and he corrects the wise; we and our words, prudence and knowledge and craftsmanship, are all in his hand. He it was who gave me true understanding of things as they are: a knowledge of the structure of the world and the operation of the elements; the beginning and end of epochs and their middle course; the alternating solstices and changing seasons; the cycles of the year and the constellations; the nature of living creatures and behaviour of wild beasts; the violent force of winds and human thoughts; the varieties of plants and the virtues of roots. I learnt it all, hidden or manifest, for I was taught by wisdom, by her whose skill made all things.

Wisdom of Solomon 7: 15–22

Solomon is supposed to have uttered three thousand proverbs, according to I Kings. The word used in the Greek Bible, the Septuagint, to translate the Hebrew word for 'proverb' here is the same word which the New Testament writers used to describe the stories of Jesus, namely 'parable' and not the word used as the title of the book of Proverbs.

This difference between what we have been left of Israelite wisdom and what it might once have entailed is highlighted in many other references. The English translation frequently hides the use of the Hebrew word for wisdom (or one of its derivatives) and the range of biblical activities attributed to wisdom. See, for example, Ex 28: 3; 35: 26, 31; 36: 1; I Kings 4: 29–34; Proverbs 9: 10; 30: 3; Isaiah 40: 20; Jer 10: 9; Ezek 27: 8–9; Dan 1: 4, 17–18; Wisdom of Solomon 7: 15–22.

It is important to bear this breadth in mind when reading the wisdom literature in the Bible; it prompts the question of what has happened to the rest as well as how we interpret what we have.

2.7.1 Proverbs

The book is attributed to Solomon who was well known for his wisdom. God favoured him because when asked what he wished God to give him, he asked for the wisdom to rule well. I Kings has stories of how he used his wisdom and how far his fame spread but it is doubtful whether any of the book of Proverbs derives from his teaching. Scholars have identified six sections in the book:

(a) proverbs of Solomon, 1: 1 – 9: 18, probably post-exilic;
(b) a second collection also attributed to Solomon and probably earlier than the first collection, 10: 1 – 22: 16;
(c) 'words of the wise', 22: 17 – 24: 22, probably post-exilic;
(d) 'these are also the words of the wise', 24: 23–34;
(e) 'proverbs of Solomon that the officials of King Hezekiah of Judah copied', 25: 1 – 29: 27; the collection is dated to Hezekiah's reign and may include earlier material;
(f) 30: 1 – 31: 31, the concluding chapters which some think are the works of the editors and are therefore post-exilic.

Commentators often speak of the integration of the religious and secular in Proverbs, implying that they were previously separate. It is only in more modern times that such a divide has arisen. It would not have occurred to any of the writers of the Hebrew Bible that YHWH was lord over some parts of his people's life and not others. Many differing accounts of the books of Proverbs have been given by modern commentators: the one thing that unites these varying opinions is that the book is unlikely to represent fully the pre-exilic wisdom tradition.

Proverbs makes plain that 'the fear of YHWH is the beginning of wisdom' and for most of the book sketches out maxims, precepts and principles which if followed would lead to right living. The advice is aimed at individuals but includes a concern for justice and fairness through the advice offered to judges and the wealthy. The implied setting of the book is a rural monarchy.

Scholars have noted a lack of 'theology' and mythology. There is no mention of the traditions which the Pentateuch claim are fundamental to Israelite self-consciousness. Some have put this down to the international nature of wisdom; wisdom emerged in the royal courts and the thought processes of those who guided monarchs had more in common with each other than with their own individual cultures. Others think this lack of self-conscious Israelite world-view is best accounted for by a heavy editing of the text; there was religion and mythology in the texts originally but it was unacceptable to those who preserved the texts and was therefore edited out.

The material in Proverbs chapters 1–9 differs from the rest of the book; some of the units of thought are longer and there is a discernible progression of thought. The chapters include warnings against adulterous women that are standard in the later chapters, but the warnings in the early chapters are at some length and some scholars see underneath them dissension among the Jewish community of the time. Proverbs chapter 8 provides the personified picture of Wisdom which proved so fruitful to the New Testament writers. That the book provokes such scholarly discussion reminds us that we know far less than was once thought about the Old Testament with which we are so familiar.

2.7.2 Job

The book is very difficult to date; estimates have ranged from the seventh to the second centuries BCE. Job is mentioned in Ezekiel 14: 14, 20 but as some scholars believe he was an ancient folk-hero it is impossible to prove that Ezekiel knew of Job from the book of his name and that therefore the book is pre-exilic. It used to be thought that the prose introduction and epilogue to the book once existed independently of the poetic core but most scholars now see the book as a whole. The prose introduction gives the context to what follows and because we, the reader, know, as the characters in the book do not, what led up to Job's predicament, we are given a particular stance toward the various views expressed by the characters.

The book opens by describing the righteous man Job; the scene then shifts to the heavenly court where Satan is given leave to test Job's righteousness, first by decimating his family and possessions and secondly by disease. When challenged by his wife to 'curse God and die', Job replies that as one accepts good at God's hand so should one accept evil. His friends approach to be with him in his suffering and then the poetic debate begins with Job cursing not God but the day of his birth. Job does not doubt that God is the source of his problems and, as the book progresses, he demands that God explain himself; the traditional explanations of his friends have proved less than adequate both to him and to the readers. The readers are spared the task of assessing each speech on its merits because they know why Job is suffering. God finally comes to Job but does not provide him with any explanation whatsoever. His angry words are contrasted with the creative wisdom of God who brought all things forth and who sustains their continued existence. He is shown the narrowness of his perspective and rebuked for not acknowledging the limits of his own capacity to understand, but his righteousness before his friends is upheld.

The book provides the happy ending; Job is restored to health, wealth and happiness but none of the characters within the story are given any explanation as to why Job, the righteous man, was allowed to suffer. They were left with the paucity of their own understanding in the face of God. In not allowing the events of the prologue to intrude upon the events of the dialogue, the explanation of Job's suffering, given only to the readers, was not raised into an all encompassing theodicy. The readers also, when looking beyond the experiences of Job to the real world, are also simply left to acknowledge the limits of their own reasoning:

> *Who is this who dares to cloud my design with ignorant words?*
> Job 38: 1

2.7.3 Ecclesiastes or Qohelet/Qoheleth

The Hebrew title for this book is a form of the verb meaning to assemble, the Assembler. It is in the form of a didactic treatise and shares with Job the sense of the limitedness of human reason or wisdom. The first half of the book is a discussion of the seeming pointlessness of life and the second half is a reflection on how to live in the light of such a philosophical position. It draws not on revealed truth but on experience. The conclusion the Speaker draws is that it is best to live moderately and to make the most of opportunities as they are offered since death will one day rob the individual of all of them. Scholars are unable to agree on whether the book is a single or composite work. It is thought to date from the third century BCE.

2.8 The Psalms

2.8.1 Introduction

The Psalter, known in Hebrew as the 'Book of Praises' is a collection of material which spans over a thousand years. Its text in the MT is among the most corrupt in the Hebrew Bible and scholars argue whether or not the LXX textual traditions should be given priority. The LXX can throw light on the text that may lie behind the MT but is itself not always accurate. The book has been divided into five collections by the insertion of doxologies at Ps 41: 13, Ps 72: 18–19, Ps 89: 52, Ps 106: 48 and Ps 150: 6. As it is now, the book dates from somewhere between the sixth and fifth centuries BCE and **200 BCE**, but most scholars feel that it consists of earlier collections which may contain some material that pre-dates the monarchy.

2.8.2   The Psalms and form criticism

Hermann Gunkel (**1862–1932**) was the first to use modern critical techniques to understand Psalms, and his work continues to provide the basis of most contemporary scholarship. He showed how form critical analysis can increase our understanding of the psalms and their purpose:

(I) The first form he drew attention to was the *hymn*, which begins on a joyful note with a call to worship, sometimes addressed by the psalmist to his own soul, sometimes to a community. The reasons for worship usually concern YHWH's creative activity or his saving acts. The hymns can be further subdivided around similar themes, for example –
(a) the songs of Zion: Pss 46, 48, 84, 87 and 122
   praise is centred on Jerusalem as the place of the divine dwelling and the invincibility of Zion, and
(b) the enthronement/acclamation of YHWH: Pss 47, 93 and 95–9.

(II) Gunkel noted *thanksgiving psalms* as a second independent form, although more recently this form has been seen as a part of the hymn type. They begin like the hymns of praise but concentrate on YHWH as rescuer. They are offerings of thanks for YHWH's deliverance out of distress or suffering and include Pss 18, 30, 40, 66, 116 and 118.

(III) *Laments* begin with a cry for help, followed by a description of the person's suffering or plight: sin, sickness, death, false accusation, enemies. YHWH's love and faithfulness are appealed to, more probably because of his election of Zion and the Davidic house rather than the Sinai covenant which is only mentioned in two psalms: Ps 78: 10 and Ps 50: 16. Apart from Ps 88, laments include an assertion that God has heard and will answer prayer. Some feel that this springs from a movement in the liturgy, when after the problem had been aired and YHWH called upon, some form of oracular response would have been forthcoming from an officiant in the Temple, a word of comfort or of hope which led the petitioner on to express faith and hope in God. Although no such oracle has been retained, there are hints of such a process in Pss 12: 5, 35: 3, 85: 8 and 91: 14–16. Some oracles have been retained in the Psalter in the Royal psalms. Presumably only those oracles given to the king were worth preserving. This form includes national as well as individual laments.

(IV) *The Royal psalms*, Pss 2, 18, 20, 21, 45, 72, 89, 101, 110, 132 and 144, have been the subject of hot debate. Some are obviously enthronement psalms (Pss 2, 72, 101 and 110), but do they imply an annual enthronement ceremony? Some scholars have also seen an annual ceremony of enthronement for YHWH in the psalms that acclaim YHWH as king, but more recent scholarship has stressed the eternal nature of YHWH's kingship as seen in the psalms. Because of the lack of any cultic instructions in the Psalter, scholars looked to near eastern parallels and found such annual ceremonies both for king and God, but most scholars now feel that such a cycle cannot be discerned in the Hebrew Bible, either for YHWH or his anointed. Prophetic oracles, hinted at elsewhere, are recorded in these psalms: Ps 2: 6–7, Ps 110: 1 and Ps 89: 19*f.*

(V) Scholars used to speak of *wisdom or didactic psalms* but most now prefer to see the influence of wisdom across the spectrum of the psalms rather than it being confined to one form.

(VI) Some psalms are also classified as *liturgical* because of their liturgical format, e.g. Pss 14 and 23. In some sense all the psalms are liturgical because they originated in Temple worship.

2.8.3 Date of the Psalms

It is impossible to date many psalms with certainty. In this account of the book of Psalms, I have followed the work of Hans-Joachim Kraus who believes that the earliest psalm is probably Ps 29, which he would date as preceding the monarchy. He would also date Ps 68 to the twelfth century BCE and Ps 18 to the eleventh. He would do so because of their archaic language, unpolished style and the prominence of Canaanite themes, but scholars differ as to whether they think archaic language is genuinely early or deliberate archaism. One person's early Canaanite myth is another's late syncretism. Kraus believes that the Royal psalms date from the period of the monarchy, Ps 110 being the earliest and Ps 89 the latest. Others have thought they originated at the time of the Hasmonaen monarchy in the second century BCE but Kraus believes that the Psalter was complete by then. Certain psalms that refer to the king are also thought by Kraus to originate from the monarchy itself, as do some songs of Zion and some laments and hymns. He feels that most of the community laments are exilic. For the provenance of each psalm it is wise to consult a commentary and to remember that it is almost impossible to tell a psalm that genuinely springs from the 'Sitz im Leben' it purports to reflect and a psalm which has used an inherited conventional form. How can we know whether a lament has sprung from Temple worship or whether it is a beautiful but late composition using a conventional setting?

2.8.4 The setting of the Psalter

Whether pre-exilic or post-exilic, scholars agree that the Psalter is a product of the Jerusalem Temple cult. Traces of the northern state are looked for, and in Kraus's view only Ps 68 can be definitely said to originate in the north (although it has obviously been re-worked in the Jerusalem Temple). Some scholars believe that Ps 45 was composed for the wedding of a northern king. The titles for the psalms, added in Hellenistic times, give directions for tunes and instruments. Although the account in I Kings omits any mention of music in Temple worship, the Psalter seems to back the picture given in Chronicles of music and song. An interesting reference in Ezekiel (33: 32) perhaps shows that cult prophets gave their words to music. For the setting of the individual lament psalms, Kraus envisages the cult prophet taking the concerns of the individual and giving them form and perhaps giving an oracle in reply. Evidence from Asia Minor shows how individuals brought their concerns to the Temple and wrote them down on stelae together with the deliverance, promised or accomplished, a custom some think is perhaps hinted at in Ps 40: 7. Together with individual psalms, whether of lament or praise, there are community psalms and some of the individual psalms were later used in community cultic settings, e.g. Ps 30, which Kraus thinks was originally an individual hymn of thanksgiving but which was sung at the dedication of the Temple.

2.8.5 Poetry and theology in the Psalms

Scholars argue over the existence or otherwise of metre in Hebrew poetry. All agree, however, that the main poetic device is parallelism by which the second clause repeats in different words the thought of the first clause. Sometimes the second clause states the opposite of the first clause, or carries the first thought forward rather than just a straight repetition, but in some way the second clause is always a response to the first. This device is so common that the occurrence of a single clause brings with it the suspicion of a corrupt text! Psalms 111 and 112 are the only psalms not to use parallelism but they are acrostics in which each clause begins with a consecutive letter of the alphabet.

One of the themes running through the psalms is the election of Jerusalem and the Davidic king, akin to which is the inviolability of Jerusalem which some scholars think may be a re-working of the mythology of the pre-Israelite 'Most High God' shrine.

Bibliography

Margaret Barker, *The Gate of Heaven*, SCM, London (1991)
Margaret Barker, *The Great Angel*, SCM, London (1992)
Margaret Barker, *The Lost Prophet*, SCM, London (1988)
Margaret Barker, *The Older Testament*, SCM, London (1987)
Joseph Blenkinsopp, *The Pentateuch*, SCM, London (1992)
R.E. Clements, *Deuteronomy*, Old Testament Guides, JSOT Press (1989)
'Genesis: An Authorship Study and Current Hal Pentateuchal Criticism', in *Journal for the Study of the Old Testament*, No. 42, Oct. 1988
R.P. Gordon, *I & II Samuel*, Old Testament Guides, Sheffield Academic Press (1993)
A.D.H. Mayes, *Judges*, Old Testament Guides, JSOT Press (1985)
W. McKane, *Prophets and Wise Men*, SCM, London (1983)
Bruce M. Metzger and I.D. Michael Coogan, *The Oxford Companion to the Bible*, OUP, Oxford (1993)
Gerhard von Rad, *Commentary on Genesis*, SCM, London (1972)
G. von Rad, *Wisdom in Israel*, Abingdon, New York (1973)
Y.T. Radney, H. Shore and D. Wickman, *Genesis: An Authorship Study in Computer Assisted Statistical Linguistics*, Analecta Biblica 103, Rome Biblical Institute Press (1985)
C. Rowland, *The Open Heaven*, SPCK, London (1982)
Morton Smith, *Palestinian Parties and Politics that Shaped the Old Testament*, SCM, London (1987)
H.G.M. Williams, *Ezra and Nehemiah*, Old Testament Guides, JSOT Press (1987)
R.N. Whybray, *Wisdom in Proverbs*, SCM, London (1965)

◼ ☑ **3** Intertestamental literature

Despite the above title, some of the works discussed in this chapter were written before others that were later included within the more restricted canons of the Old Testament. Similarly, the later works may have been written after the earliest New Testament literature.

3.1 **The Apocrypha**

BOX 3.1

The most comprehensive of the modern texts of the Apocrypha in English is in the NRSV in *The Oxford Annotated Bible with Apocrypha, an Ecumenical Study Bible*, OUP, 1991 which includes the standard Roman Catholic Apocrypha plus I Esdras, the Prayer of Manasseh, Psalm 151, III Maccabees, II Esdras and IV Maccabees.

When the literature that has become known as the Pseudepigrapha and Apocrypha was written, the canon had not been agreed by all Jews. Some writings, such as the Pentateuch and the Prophetic books, both the Former and Later Prophets (i.e. the prophets and the histories), were beyond dispute but the third section of the Jewish scriptures, the Writings, were regarded differently by the various groups. The Samaritans and Sadducees, who could not be much further apart in most things, nevertheless agreed that only the Pentateuch should be regarded as authoritative. The Pharisees, however, revered the Pentateuch, the Prophetic books and those books in the Writings which later came to comprise the Hebrew Bible and the Protestant Old Testament. They also revered the oral law, which survives in the Mishnah and Talmud. During the Persian and Hasmonaeon period, other books were regarded highly, as is shown by their inclusion in the Septuagint (LXX), a translation of the Hebrew scriptures for the Greek-speaking Jew and which remained the Old Testament of the church until the Reformation. Those books included in the LXX are now known as the Apocrypha, and other books from the period are called the Pseudepigrapha. Together they are referred to 110 times in the New Testament. The fact that they were all preserved by the church shows their importance for the ancient Christian communities.

The word 'apocrypha' was coined by Jerome who translated the Old Testament into Latin and was suspicious of the books he did not find in Hebrew. The word means 'hidden things', although why Jerome thought that was an appropriate name is not known. Pseudepigrapha comes from the Greek words for 'false' and 'to write' because some of these books purport to have been written by figures from the past, a feature found also in canonical books.

There is disagreement as to which books constitute the Apocrypha. Accordingly we begin by examining the books which the Roman Catholic Church includes since their total is the smallest and includes only books accepted by other pre-Reformation churches.

3.1.1 The novella

Tobit and Judith are both examples of the novella, a story or folk-tale, a form of writing which has a long provenance and occurs in the Masoretic text (MT) in the story of Joseph in Genesis. Tobit was written between *c.* **225 BCE** and **175 BCE** and shows why the title 'intertestamental' is misleading, since Tobit pre-dates the canonical Daniel. Judith is later, dating from *c.* **135–105 BCE**. In both cases, the dates refer to the written version since the stories themselves may be older. Both books had been preserved only in Greek, by the Christian community. The discovery of the Dead Sea Scrolls proved the Hebrew origin of Tobit, as pieces of it from one Hebrew and four Aramaic manuscripts were discovered at Qumran. Scholars are in little doubt as to Judith's Hebrew origin because of the number of Hebraisms in the text.

Both stories show how God blesses the efforts of the righteous: Tobit has become blind and poor as a result of his piously burying an executed man; but he recovers both his sight and his fortune through the efforts of his son, Tobias, who also gains Sarah as his wife with the help of the angel Raphael. In a story laden with irony, Judith, a beautiful and wealthy widow, saves her home town by entrancing and then killing the commanding officer of the Assyrian forces besieging the town.

3.1.2 Additions to the canonical texts

Esther and Daniel are significantly bigger in the LXX than in the Masoretic text, Greek Esther having 107 more verses than its Hebrew counterpart, while Greek Daniel includes three additional sections, one of which, the Song of the Three Young Men, fits within the narrative of the canonical text, while the other two are independent units. The additions to Daniel and Esther are of two distinct types. The verses in Esther were added to alter an existing text. However, the presence of Daniel material at Qumran, which is found neither in the MT nor in the LXX, is further evidence that the Daniel tradition of ancient times was far greater than has survived. Some scholars think that the original focus for the Daniel material was not the exilic hero but a mythic wise man, perhaps the figure Ezekiel refers to in 14: 14, 20, although none of the material that remains has a pre-exilic setting.

The verses added to Esther seem to have been put in to make the book more suitably religious; the Hebrew text of Esther does not mention God at all, while the additions are either prayers or references to God or good Jewish practices.

The Song of the Three Young Men, which consists of psalm-type prayers and laments, is inserted at 3: 23 of the Hebrew text of Daniel. They have become part of the liturgies of the Church and can still be found in use today as the Benedict thanksgiving after mass. Susanna, on the other hand, is a folk-tale in which a woman's honour in impugned because of jealousy, but cleared because of Daniel's skilful advocacy by which he uncovers the truth. Daniel's cleverness is to the fore in Bel and the Dragon, two tales in which he exposes the fraudulent claims of the Persian priesthood for their gods. Though framed as stories, they were written as vehicles to demonstrate the foolishness of idol worship.

The additions reveal a complex textual tradition, four out of the six additions showing signs of a Hebrew original. It is likely that the book went through at least three stages:

(i) the Hebrew original, preserved by the Masoretes;
(ii) the original plus four Hebrew additions;
(iii) the expanded book translated into Greek plus two more additions which appear to have been composed in Greek.

To complicate matters further, there is another Greek text, which seems to rest on a different Hebrew original.

The additions to the book of Daniel date from the second century BCE, not long after the canonical book was written. The short text of Esther could date from as early as the fifth century, with the various additions therefore dating from any time after the original was written down to just before the text arrived in Egypt, 'in the fourth year of the reign of Ptolemy and Cleopatra' in about **114 BCE**.

3.1.3 Wisdom

There are three examples of this genre in the Apocrypha: the Wisdom of ben Sirach (also known as Ecclesiasticus), the Wisdom of Solomon and the middle section of Baruch.

Ben Sirach and the middle section of Baruch show considerable similarities with the canonical wisdom texts except that Wisdom is linked with the Torah (Ecc 24: 23; Baruch 4: 1). These texts include proverb material common to many ancient systems but also, as in the canonical proverbs, reflections on the nature of wisdom itself. Wisdom is called 'the word spoken by the Most High' and linked to the worship of YHWH in Jerusalem (Ecc 24). The Wisdom of Jesus, ben Sirach, was probably written about **180 BCE** and translated into Greek by his grandson in **132 BCE**. The Hebrew work was published in Jerusalem and pre-dates Daniel. There is evidence that it was used in the ancient synagogue services; there are clear echoes of this work in the New Testament, 10: 24, even in Jesus' words, 28: 2–3. The Pharisees probably did not include it in the canon because of its traditional beliefs about death. There is no hint of any hope beyond death; the dead descend to Sheol from which no praise of God emerges, 17: 27–8.

The Wisdom of Solomon does not include traditional wisdom proverb material and shows familiarity with Greek philosophy but it does have clear links with canonical wisdom. As in Proverbs, Wisdom is personified as a woman, envisaged as sitting on God's throne and her role in creation is described. Although his name is never mentioned, the book is written as if by Solomon who is looking back on his prayer for wisdom (I Kings 3: 3–14).

As in the description of what wisdom entails in I Kings 4: 32–3, the Wisdom of Solomon demonstrates that the wisdom literature which survives in the canon is not necessarily a fair reflection of what Israelite wisdom was. The subjects referred to in the Wisdom of Solomon are even wider than in I Kings 4: 22–3 and include topics seen in apocalyptic literature, leading some scholars to suspect that apocalyptic literature derived from wisdom rather than from prophecy, as was originally thought.

The Wisdom of Solomon was written in Greek and dates from *c.* **100 BCE** to *c.* **100 CE**. It is a polished work which is written in the style of an exhortation. As the church fathers were to do later for Christianity, it couches Jewish teaching in a sophisticated form suitable for an Hellenistic audience. Its teaching about life after death is at variance with that of the traditional views found in Ecclesiasticus. There is a clear belief in a judgement after death and a promise that whatever the experience of the righteous on earth, their souls are safe with God. Unlike the canonical wisdom texts, the historical experience of God's people is important to the writer, especially their salvation from Egypt. There are many similarities with New Testament passages, although whether the writers knew the book or were drawing on a common tradition is not known; but the number of references to apocryphal works and quotations from the LXX (of which the apocrypha was a part) version of books also found in the Masoretic text, makes it most probable that at least some of the New Testament writers were familiar with these works.

BOX 3.1.3

Apocryphal passage	New Testament allusion
Baruch 4: 7	I Cor 10: 20
Baruch 4: 35	Rev 18: 2
Judith 11: 19	Mark 6: 34
ben Sirach 1: 8	Rev 6: 16
ben Sirach 25: 23	Heb 12: 12
ben Sirach 5: 11	James 1: 19
ben Sirach 11: 19	Luke 12: 19–20
Wisdom of Solomon 6: 18	John 14: 15
Wisdom of Solomon 5: 18	Eph 6: 14

The pre-existence of souls, a view later embraced by Origen, is mentioned by the writer at 8: 19–20.

3.1.4 Historical books

Despite the suggestion of progression in their titles, I and II Maccabees are independent works. Both are histories told from a particular standpoint. This is true of all historical works but is easier to see in a work written a long time ago. I Maccabees tells the story of the Hasmonaeons from the uprising of Mattathias soon after the erection of an altar to Zeus in the Holy of Holies in **164 BCE**, to the death of Simon and accession of his son, John Hyrcanus in **134 BCE**. There is clear evidence that the author had access to contemporary sources (I Macc 8: 23–32; 11: 30–7; 14: 27, 48–9; 16: 24) and earlier histories (I Macc 9: 22), and his account is often backed up by Greek historians such as Polybius.

For all his accuracy, he was not aiming to be dispassionate. The book is an unashamed manifesto for the Hasmonaean family and a defence of their assumption of the High Priesthood even though they were not of the High Priestly line. Some, who had supported their campaign for political independence, found their use of the High Priesthood hard to take. The book was probably written in Hebrew during the reign of John Hyrcanus (**134–104 BCE**) but only survives in Greek. II Maccabees is also an account of the rise of the Hasmonaeons but the emphasis is not on the family but on what they did, how they 'regained possession of the Temple famous throughout the world, and liberated the city and re-established the laws that were about to be abolished, while the Lord with great kindness became gracious to them . . . ', 2 Macc 2: 22.

I Maccabees sets the scene for the Maccabean uprising (Maccabees is properly only the nickname for Judas, Mattathias' son, but has been used to describe the whole family) by describing the desecration of the Temple and the persecution of those trying to live in obedience to the Law. II Maccabees expands the picture to include incidents of God protecting his sanctuary whether by angelic intervention or by the piety of his people; the Maccabeans were God's agents but they are seen in II Maccabees as part of a wider picture. The author says his work is a paraphrase of a five-volume work by Jason of Cyrene. No fragment of this work has survived and this is the only mention of it. Claiming the authority of a previous work, whether it existed or not, was a literary convention of the ancient world which the author may have been following. His style of writing shows his familiarity with Greek historians such as Heroditus and Thucydides. Like them, he comments on events through the speeches of important characters. He includes accounts of miraculous events but is as concerned as the author of I Maccabees to use the contemporary sources, whether they were included in the work of Jason he paraphrased or discovered by him. Scholars see evidence of access to the Temple archive at 1: 1–2, 18 and 11: 16–38, and a Seleucid source at other places, e.g. 4: 21–2, 30–1; 9: 1; 10: 11–13.

It is thought that Jason wrote his work in the mid–late second century BCE while II Maccabees was composed between **124 BCE** and **63 BCE**. Just as Esther was used to explain the significance of the feast of Purim, the letters at the beginning of II Maccabees imply that the book was intended to be used in a similar way for the feast of the Purification of the Temple, celebrated on the 25th December to mark the re-dedication of the Temple by Judas Maccabeus in **164** after it had been used for pagan sacrifices by Antiochus IV. Despite its connection with a festival still celebrated today, the book did not find its way into the Jewish canon. It shows the range of religious practices in the Judaism of its time, including sacrifice on behalf of the dead (II Macc 12: 39–45), thought necessary because of the belief in the resurrection of the dead. The early Christians practised baptism of the dead for similar reasons (I Cor 15: 29).

3.1.5 Prophecy

Baruch purports to have been written by Jeremiah's scribe, Baruch, at the time of the Babylonian exile. In fact it is not a unified composition and was probably written in Hebrew or Aramaic, by Palestinian Jews in the late second or early first century BCE. It is in three sections; as we saw earlier, the middle section is like ben Sirach and traditional Jewish wisdom literature while the first and third are in the style of biblical prophecy. All of the book is closely based on biblical passages such as Dan 9: 4–19 and Isaiah 51. It includes a confession of the sins of the Jewish people to be used by those still living in Jerusalem while they offer sacrifice on behalf of the exiles. In some manuscripts the Letter of Jeremiah is included with Baruch. The letter is written as if from Jeremiah to the exiles in Babylon and is an exhortation against Babylonian religion. It has been dated from as early as **300 BCE** to early in the second century and therefore pre-dates Baruch. It is a polemic against idol worship.

These books make up the Deutero-canonical books of the Roman Catholic Church but other churches accept a wider list.

3.2 Other Deutero-canonical works

BOX 3.2

The word 'Deutero-canonical' comes from the Greek words second and rule. It does not imply that these books were of second-class canonical status, but rather that their canonicity was formally recognised later.

As well as the books above recognised by all of the pre-Reformation churches, there are a number of books included in the Canon of at least some of them.

3.2.1 Historical books

I Esdras also known as III Ezra

This is an alternative version of the Book of Ezra, also included in the LXX alongside the version which tallies with what we have in the Masoretic text. It has quite a divergent text, includes parts of the book of Chronicles and omits the figure of Nehemiah altogether even though it shows knowledge of the book of Nehemiah. It includes the story of the three guardsmen not found elsewhere. Some argue that the book is a mutilated version of Ezra/Chron. Scholars are divided, although the view that it is all that remains of an earlier Greek translation of Ezra joined with material about Ezra from Nehemiah is the most plausible. Some biblical books did exist in variant forms and perhaps this represents an alternative collection of Ezra material. The existence of this book confirms the mystery surrounding the post-exilic period. The Greek version of I Esdras is probably not later than **100 BCE**. Although this book has not been accepted as canonical by the Roman Catholic Church since the Council of Trent (**1545–63**), it appeared in the Vulgate (the Latin translation of the Bible, accepted as authoritative by the Roman Catholic Church) in an appendix after the New Testament.

III Maccabees

This book recounts a miraculous saving of Jews condemned for not apostatising under the rule of Ptolemy IV Philopator (**221–203 BCE**). Despite its name, the action described is set about half a century before the Maccabees and was known to Eusebius as 'Ptolemaica'. Although some of the historical details are correct, such as the name of the High Priest in office at the time of Ptolemy's attempt to enter the Holy of Holies, most scholars think it is an historical tale drawn from stock motifs. Josephus, the Jewish historian, describes the elephant story as happening in the reign of Ptolemy VIII Physcon (**145–116 BCE**). The text shows the author was familiar with the Greek translation of Esther which was written *c.* **114 BCE**. III Maccabees dates from between the first century BCE and the first century CE and was written in Alexandria to encourage the Alexandrian Jews to stand firm in one of the many crises they faced about their status in the city. The Jewish community was traditionally allowed to live in Alexandria, ruled by their own elders. It was a Greek city in which native Egyptians were not allowed to live, and the privileges of the Jews were always subject to revision.

3.2.2   Devotional works

Like I Esdras, the prayer of Manasseh appeared after the Council of Trent in the appendix to the Vulgate. It still has Deutero-canonical status in other pre-Reformation churches although it was never part of the LXX. It purports to be a prayer of repentance uttered by King Manasseh after his captivity in Babylon. II Kings knows nothing of this episode but it is mentioned in II Chronicles 33: 11–13. Scholars consider that it was inserted by the Chronicler to account for the long reign of a king who is depicted as being at such odds with orthodoxy. The Deuteronomists account for it by blaming Manasseh for the subsequent fall of Jerusalem (II Kings 21: 10–14). Manasseh was a test case. Does God's mercy outweigh his wrath? Can even Manasseh be forgiven? The prayer is a classic plea for forgiveness and is filled with the assurance that God has answered the prayer. The Greek version dates from the second century BCE and was probably used as a canticle by the early church. It may have been written originally in Hebrew. The Episcopal Church of the United States uses it as a canticle in its alternative prayer book.

Those churches who derive their psalter from the LXX have a psalter slightly bigger than the 150-psalm version of the Masoretic text and and in a modified order. The Syriac church, for example, has 155. Psalm 151 is the one most commonly accepted by those churches that do recognise psalms beyond 150. Until the discovery of the Dead Sea Scrolls, none of the extra psalms rested on a Hebrew original but in Qumran cave 11 a manuscript was discovered containing the last 40 of the MT psalms (not in the same order as the canonical text), Ps 151 from the LXX and Pss 151, 154 and 155 from the Syriac Psalter as well as four psalms not otherwise extant. Comparison between the Hebrew and LXX texts of Ps 151 shows that the LXX text is a conflation of two originally separate psalms, one about David's anointing by Samuel and one about his victory over Goliath.

3.2.3 Treatises

The author of IV Maccabees takes the story of a family accepting torture and martyrdom one by one rather than disobey the Torah, their ancestral law, and makes it the centre of an apologetic for Judaism and the epitome of how reason can be the mistress of the soul, enabling a person to stick to his/her purpose whatever the cost. The discourse was perhaps designed to be delivered on the anniversary of death of the Maccabean martyrs. It was written sometime after II Maccabees and before the fall of Jerusalem in **70 CE.**

The account derives from the description of the martyrdom of Eleazar and his family in II Maccabees 6: 12 – 7: 42 and concentrates on how reason can control the emotions. The author shares with the Stoics an acceptance of the four cardinal virtues – patience, courage, justice and self-control – and shows how reason can be used to control the emotions which are at war with these virtues.

The acceptance of martyrdom rather than eating pork by Eleazar, his seven sons and finally his wife, is seen as proof that even in the face of the fiercest torments reason can be sufficient defence against the emotions that might have led them to give in to their tormentors. Eleazar's wife receives special credit as she has watched the torment of her husband and seven sons. She is able to encourage them to stand firm rather than save themselves and finally accepts martyrdom herself. She is praised as a daughter of Abraham. In II Maccabees, the martyrs put their sufferings down to God's anger with their people but express a firm hope that God will be reconciled to his people, and in the youngest brother's speech (II Macc 7: 38) there is a hint of the atonement theology which is more fully drawn out in IV Maccabees.

BOX 3.2.3

You know, O God, that though I might have saved myself, I am dying in burning torments for the sake of the law. Be merciful to your people, and let our punishment suffice for them. Make my blood their purification and take my life in exchange for theirs.

IV Macc 6: 27–8 NRSV

There is a definite doctrine of substitutionary atonement; Eleanar talks of his death and sufferings in sacrificial terms.

3.2.4 Apocalypses

Apocalypses such as II Esdras make up the core of the genre known as apocalyptic literature. It is important to remember when using such terms that they are descriptions used by later scholars to help understand the parameters within which an ancient author wrote and to see which works can be usefully analysed together. They become unhelpful if they are used to develop strict definitions to decide whether or not a book falls into a certain category.

It is a complex genre, perhaps because of the number of extra-canonical apocalypses which have survived. Most scholars think that apocalyptic literature grew out of classical prophecy, its roots being seen in passages like Zechariah 9–14, Ez 38–9 and Is 24–7, while others think it has close links with wisdom and the theology of the first Temple. It shares a curiosity about how the world works and about the natural order, with descriptions of wisdom found in texts as diverse as I Kings 4: 33, Job 28: 1–27 and Wisdom of Solomon 7: 15–22. It shares also a world view in which events are shaped as much by cosmic powers, whether malign or good, as by the people who take part in them, with passages such as Deut 32: 8–9, Is 14: 12*ff*, Ez 31: 2*ff* and the many passages in the eighth-century prophets concerning the Day of the Lord. According to this view, the apocalyptic literature of the third century BCE and after is renewing an older perspective rather than developing a new one.

Whatever its origins, one of its main features is divine disclosure, usually to an exalted figure of the past. Revelation in the New Testament is the exception to this: John writes in his own name. The disclosure of heavenly secrets takes place through visions, trances, the hearing of voices, dreams or out-of-body experiences. Usually the secrets are also mediated by angels. There is a wide spectrum of what is disclosed. Sometimes it refers to the layout of heaven, the workings of the universe and the correct calendar, and sometimes it refers to an understanding of history and the heavenly realities that underlie present events. The visions are portrayed in symbolic imagery, which was probably designed to make them easily understood by those for whom they were intended. It is harder for us when we have to rebuild the understanding of the mythological framework which underlay it.

The seer was usually commanded to keep his revelations secret until the appropriate time. Again, Revelation is an exception to this. Much of this literature was written to encourage the oppressed with an understanding of what their sufferings meant, and to give an assurance that God was in control and that those who opposed him and his people would eventually be punished. Apocalyptic literature shares a common world view in which heaven and earth are closely related. Heaven is peopled with angelic beings, some of whom help and some of whom hinder the purposes of God. Earthly empires hold sway only with divine permission whether it is acknowledged or not, and all creation, both heaven and earth, is moving towards the new age from which evil will be banished and of which the present troubles are but the birth pangs. It will be finally delivered among cosmic chaos, whether political upheaval or natural disaster. The reality of judgement and resurrection are important in most texts.

With a genre which shows an interest in such diverse topics as the origin of evil and the correct days upon which to celebrate festivals, it is important to remember that no single work can be expected to feature every aspect of apocalyptic literature. Recent scholarship has shown that some works are more interested in calendrical purity than in the New Age and that eschatology, which was once thought to be the hallmark of this genre, is not always a feature of works which are otherwise at home within this group. It is important not to let the rigidity of our modern definitions blind us to relationships that do exist even when they make our categories less than tidy!

II Esdras (IV Ezra)

The central core of the book, chapters 3–14, was probably written at the close of the first century CE by a Jew. This was translated into Greek and preserved by the church. The first two and the final two chapters were added in the second to third centuries, the first two chapters being added first. The work was so popular among Christians that it was translated into at least seven languages: Syriac, Coptic, Ethiopic, Armenian, Georgian, Arabic (in two different versions) and Latin (in several versions). The main extant text is Latin. The original Hebrew or Aramaic text has not survived, and the Greek only in fragments, but enough exists of the other texts to help with the reconstruction of the Latin text where it is difficult.

It is a Jewish apocalypse with the first two chapters and last two probably Christian additions. The Jewish core is called the Ezra apocalypse and includes the hope of a peaceful Messianic age on earth before the Messiah and all humanity die, leaving the earth to return to its primeval silence for seven days before God judges the old creation and inaugurates the new. Its ancient popularity perhaps springs from the importance of the questions which Ezra raises, questions of why God allows suffering especially when it is the righteous who seem to suffer most.

The Ethiopian Orthodox church has a shorter and a longer canon, and in its longer canon accepts two more books from this genre: I Enoch which is a classic apocalypse, and Jubilees which scholars argue about how to define but which has definite affinities with apocalyptic literature. The rest of the church defines these books as pseudepigraphal.

I Enoch

This book was known in Greek fragments until a version was contained within the longer canon of the bible of the Ethiopian Orthodox church. A semitic original was always suspected and indeed was found at Qumran. The Dead Sea Scrolls did not include the Hebrew or Aramaic of all the Ethiopian text, but the parts of the text that do exist in both cohere so much that scholars are able to use the Ethiopian text to fill the gaps.

I Enoch coheres around the revelation given to Enoch, 'the seventh after Adam' of whom it is said in Genesis 'and God took him away'. It hinges on a world view common in the pseudepigraphal literature that the world was corrupted not so much by the sin of Adam but by the sin of the angels who lusted after women, mated with them and produced a race of giants with whom they led people further and further into sin by giving them heavenly knowledge that was not for people to know. Writing was one of the arts taught to people by the fallen angels. It was because of the evil of these angels and their giant offspring that God decided to flood the earth. As well as destroying the giants and the people whom they had corrupted, God's judgement was meted out to the fallen angels who were locked in a pit until the Day of Judgement. The story of the angels is alluded to in Genesis 6: 4*ff.* Scholars vary over whether they think the pseudepigraphical literature has expanded a few verses in Genesis or whether the writers of Genesis have merely alluded to a wider and well-known tradition.

I Enoch is in five parts of differing ages: The book of the Watchers (1–36), The Similitudes or Parables (37–71), The Astronomical Book (72–82), The Book of Dreams (83–90) and The Epistle of Enoch (91–107). Fragments of four parts have been found at Qumran. The Similitudes or Parables of Enoch was then thought by some to be a Christian interpolation because of the importance within it of the messianic Son of Man figure. One of the problems with this argument has always been that a Christian writer or circle would be unlikely to identify the Son of Man with Enoch. The scholarly consensus is now that the work is a Jewish work that had joined the rest of I Enoch by the end of the first century CE.

Jubilees

Until the discovery of the Qumran scrolls, the only complete text of Jubilees that survived was in the Ethiopian canon. A quarter of it existed in Latin and there were Greek and Syriac fragments. It was clear that both the Latin and the Ethiopic texts were translations of the Greek, which, with the Syriac, was the only link with the original. The fragments of Jubilees found at Qumran, including a manuscript that can be dated to **75–50 BCE**, show that Jubilees was probably written in the middle of the second century BCE, by a Jew in sympathy with those who later on, because of the Hasmonaeons' seizures of the High Priesthood, broke away and formed the Qumran community.

Jubilees is presented in the form of a revelation to Moses while on Sinai; it is a re-working of the narrative of Genesis and Exodus up to the point when Moses receives the Torah. It retells the Adam and Eve story but shares with I Enoch the understanding that the real source of evil was not man's (or woman's) disobedience but the disobedience of angelic powers and their corruption of humanity which resulted in the Flood. It is obvious that the writer is drawing upon a set of beliefs about pre-history far wider than that which survived in the MT.

Jubilees, I Enoch and the Qumranic literature share a common concern with the origin of evil, the regulation of world history by God and its division into specified times, the correct observance of the sabbaths and festivals, and hence a concern to follow the proper calendar and the restoration of God's children.

The author of Jubilees does not include any of the bizarre imagery used in the apocalypses nor a sense of an impending eschatological disaster, but he is just as keen as they to present God's will afresh in his own time.

3.3   Pseudepigrapha

This is the most difficult of all the categories to discuss as it is impossible to define. The word means '*falsely ascribed to*' or '*with a false ascription*' and derived originally from those works that are attributed to heroes of Israel's past. This title is retained even though it is not entirely accurate in that not all pseudepigraphal works are included in the Pseudepigrapha (some are in the Bible!) and not all the books in the Pseudepigrapha have a false ascription. The most comprehensive collection of Pseudepigraphal works can be found in *The Old Testament Pseud-epigrapha*, Vols I and II by James H. Charlesworth. The pseudepigrapha is not a canonical collection, and therefore what is included in any one collection will be decided by the editor, as Charlesworth writes in his introduction to Volume II of his 1985 edition.

Charlesworth identifies five characteristics of these works:

(i)   they are Jewish or Christian (the wisdom tale, Ahiqar, is the only exception to this);
(ii) they are often attributed to ideal figures in Israel's past;
(iii) they usually claim to contain God's word or message;
(iv) they frequently build on ideas and narratives from the Old Testament;
(v)   they were composed or written down in the period **200 BCE** or preserved material from that period.

The Pseudepigrapha may always be increased by further archaeological discovery or reduced by scholarship defining more exactly a text's provenance. For example, Charlesworth does not include 'The fragments of a Zadokite work' or 'Pirke Aboth' which were contained in an earlier collection, since the first is now known to be from the Qumran, and the second to be a rabbinic work.

3.3.1   Apocalypses and related works

There has been great debate in recent years on what does and does not consti-tute an apocalypse. The early definitions took the canonical apocalypses such as Daniel and Revelation as their starting points: works were apocalypses in as much as they resembled them. However as scholars began to analyse the pseudepigraphal literature, they began to realise that works which obviously shared a world view with the canonical apocalypses also had interests that were wider. I Enoch is an apocalypse by any definition, but it had an interest in the workings of the world, especially its calendar, that goes beyond anything we see in the Bible. The picture is complicated by some works that are called apo-calypses but which have little in common with the rest of apocalyptic literature, as defined by modern scholars, and others which are definitely apocalyptic yet without the title.

3.3.2   Books which are expansions of the Masoretic text

There are books which deal with the pre-history recorded or hinted at in Genesis, such as the Life of Adam and Eve, the Ladder of Jacob or those which centre on historical figures from Israel's past such as The Lives of the Prophets or the Martyrdom and Ascension of Isaiah. Books which Charlesworth has categorised in this way can also be put into separate genres; for example, the story of Joseph and Asenath is a novella and Jubilees (because it is only within the canon of the Ethiopian church, and is usually counted as pseudepigraphal, as is I Enoch) is a testament.

3.3.3 Wisdom and philosophical literature

In this category, Charlesworth includes III and IV Maccabees as well as Ahiqar which is an Assyrian work and earlier than **200 BCE** but is alluded to in Tobit and may have been known by other biblical writers. Other works in this group are Pseudo-Phocylides and the Syriac Menander, both of which are proverb collections.

3.3.4 Devotional literature

This group includes psalms (Ps 151 and those added to the Syriac psalter), prayers and prayers of penitence, including the Prayer of Manasseh. Parts of the fourth century writings called 'the Apostolic Constitutions' are now thought by some scholars to derive from synagogue worship in the Diaspora and are included here. There are two collections attributed to Solomon: the Psalms and the Odes. The psalms are from a group of Jews, horrified by the behaviour of their Hasmonaeon rulers which culminated in their inviting the Roman general Pompey into Jerusalem. They are particularly interesting as they attest to first-century BCE messianic hope. The Odes are quite different and were written by Christians at the turn of the first century CE. There are no quotations from the New Testament but there are similarities of thought:

> *'Because they became my members and I was their head.'*

> *'I have put on incorruption through his name and stripped off corruption through his grace.'*

Living water is an important theme.

3.4 Rabbinical works

All the books discussed in this chapter so far have been Jewish works preserved by Christians, but the **post-70 CE** Jewish community had its own way of preserving its heritage and ensuring its survival for future generations. The fact that none of the rabbinic works survive in a form that pre-dates the third century CE does not mean that earlier traditions are not incorporated within the works as they have been handed down. While they must be handled carefully if they are to shed any light on the period covered by the intertestamental literature, to ignore them would be foolish. The Rabbis whose teaching makes up the Mishnah saw themselves working from a tradition they had received and so within the early rabbinical works we see a snapshot of a process which goes back to the rabbinic discussions of the first century and before. Hillel, whose guidelines on how to interpret the oral law became foundational, died *c.* **10 CE**. At some points in the Gospels we can see that Jesus is drawn into rabbinic disputes, for example when he is asked his opinion on divorce he is being asked to decide between the opinions of differing rabbinic schools.

The Rabbis whose theology survives in the Talmud were Pharisees. For them, Judaism consisted in living by the Torah, both written and oral, i.e. the Pentateuch and the teaching of previous Rabbis about its application to everyday life. As important as the Temple and their national life was to them while these survived, it was the survival of Judaism as a way of life that was of paramount importance. Scholars debate how important the rabbinic schools at Yavneh were but few doubt their importance for moulding the future shape of Judaism.

The Mishnah was set in its present form by Judah ha-Nasi (Judah the Prince) about **200 CE**, but it may not have been written down until later still. Most of the Rabbis quoted in it are second century, but they would have seen themselves as inheritors of a tradition and perhaps working by the same methodology as their forbears. It is in six divisions; each division includes material gathered about a broad topic, for example agriculture, special ordinances, women and family matters, government ordinances and ways of resolving conflict, the regular sacrifices and regulations about uncleanness and purification. It is an interpretation of the instructions and commandments of the Pentateuch and its basic principle was to put a fence around the Torah so that if people followed the rabbinical teaching they would be sure not to have breached the biblical teaching. Some scholars argue, however, that far from containing echoes of the teaching of earlier rabbis, the Mishnah and its commentary, the Gemara, which together make up the Talmud, represent only the opinions of the later Rabbis who wrote it down.

The Rabbis not only engaged in discussion among themselves but also expounded the scripture in the synagogue, a custom which existed for a long time before any of their teaching was written down. Some scholars think that because of the practice of Rabbis handing teaching down to their disciples, the midrashim, as the rabbinic bible commentaries are called, may contain material older than itself. This also is a point of debate. There are two types of material in the midrashim: commentary on the legal ordinances of the Bible known as Halakah, and narrative and homiletic matters known as Aggadah. The earliest midrashim are ascribed to rabbis from the period **200 BCE** to **500 BCE**, but they may be the product of the later Rabbis who passed the teaching on. Some midrashim are verse-by-verse commentaries while others are gathered around themes.

Targums are the other type of early Jewish literature. There are two Targums still in existence, the Palestinian and the Babylonian. The text of the Mishnah is substantially the same in both, but the Babylonian Gemara is much longer and contains more complex discussion. The Mishnah forbade the writing of Targumic texts but that the preservers of the text worked in a careful tradition can be shown by the New Testament writers of the first century being familiar with Targumic interpretations not written down until considerably later. For example, the version of Psalm 68 found in Eph 4: 8 is closer to a Targum text than to the Hebrew. A Targum was a free translation of the Hebrew text into Aramaic and Targums have survived which translate the Bible into both forms of Aramaic. The Targum would have been read to interpret the Hebrew portion of scripture set for a Sabbath but is not always a literal translation. It reflects the sense of the passage as the Rabbis wished to teach it, so they are a good source for the theology of the circle that produced them. The difficulty, as with all early rabbinic literature, is deciding which group of people's theology is represented by a given work. Such decisions can only ever be provisional and therefore all early rabbinic material must be used carefully when it is being asked to yield information on anything other than itself.

3.5 The Dead Sea Scrolls

In 1947, Bedu shepherds discovered a cache of ancient manuscripts in a cave in the Judaean desert. Since that time, hundreds of Aramaic and Hebrew manuscripts of biblical, apocrypha/pseudepigraphal and sectarian documents have been discovered. Some of the manuscripts are almost complete, such as the Isaiah scroll, while others are very small fragments. The documents date from between **250 BCE** and **70 CE**. Most scholars believe these manuscripts represent the library of the sect who lived at Qumran and is therefore a deliberately chosen collection which can reveal much about the belief system of those who collected them. Others believe it is a haphazard selection of documents put there for safe keeping during the upheavals of the uprising of the **late 60s CE**.

Every biblical book is represented there, with the exception of Esther, and some of them in more than one copy. The find is evidence of the care that the Masoretes took in transmitting their text, because some of these scrolls exhibit what became the MT exactly. Some show the same consonant pattern but with different vowels, and other manuscripts are from different textual families altogether. There are manuscripts that agree with the Hebrew underlying the LXX, some that agree with the Samaritan Pentateuch and others that are independent of any other text still existing.

We have already discussed some of the apocryphal and pseudepigraphal books that were found at Qumran, some of which are the only manuscripts extant in Hebrew or Aramaic. Very important also are those documents which are presumed to explain the thinking of the group that lived at Qumran and which have widened our knowledge of Judaism in this period. The Qumran group are thought to have been a community of Essenes who withdrew into the desert after they split with the Hasmonaeons over their abuse of the High-Priesthood. Such scrolls include the Damascus Document already known from a find at Cairo in **1896**.

This outlines the rules of the community and explains the group's origins. The details of the community's daily life are outlined in the Manual of Discipline and their grievances with the Jerusalem establishment are set out in a letter written by the Teacher of Righteousness. The Temple Scroll explains the Torah according to the group's principles and the War Scroll describes the future war between the sons of darkness and the sons of light. Their own documents also include biblical commentaries called 'pesarim', meaning 'interpretations', referring to the way the discussion of a portion of scripture was introduced with the phrase 'the word is interpreted'.

The wide breadth of literature that has survived from this period has led some scholars to speak of Judaisms rather than Judaism existing at this time. Even if this is an overstatement, it is important to remember that our assessments of the past rest only on the evidence that has survived.

3.6 Other literature from the period

3.6.1 Philo

Philo lived between **15 BCE** and **50 CE** in Alexandria and was a well-respected leader of the Jewish community there. His main concern was the interpretation of scripture and his works represent the only works on scripture that have survived from the first century from someone who lived and died as a respected member of mainstream Judaism. The only other examples we have of first century hermeneutics are from Qumran and in the New Testament. Because of this, claims by scholars that Philo owes more to Greek philosophy than to his own tradition must be carefully scrutinised. The truth is that we have little with which his writing can be compared.

His writings are grouped into three works: The Allegorical Commentary, an exegesis of Genesis 1–17 in terms of the inner life; The Exposition of the Law, which contains biographies of the Patriarchs as well as an exegesis of the Decalogue and Mosaic Law; and Questions and Answers, which survives in an incomplete Armenian translation, and poses questions on the text of Genesis and Exodus which are then answered literally, figuratively and allegorically. The figure of Moses is of crucial importance; he is an ideal figure assuming the roles not only of law-giver and prophet but also of philosopher. Philo's debt to Plato and neo-Platonism in particular is clear, but since we have no other Jewish writing from the period, it is impossible to know whether Philo has derived his substance as well as his terminology from philosophy. His ability to discuss the attributes of God almost as distinct from God must affect our understanding of the way in which the Christian doctrine of the Trinity developed. Philo spoke of the Logos as being the interface between God and the world, an idea which was used creatively in the early church. Whether Philo was drawing upon a Jewish tradition of such speculation is uncertain but the respect with which he was held among his own community shows that his thought was by no means considered heterodox.

3.6.2 Josephus

Born *c.* **37 CE** in Jerusalem, Josephus lived through tumultuous times. He was charged with the defence of Galilee during the revolt against Roman rule that started in **66 CE** and culminated in the destruction of the Temple in **AD 70**. Galilee did not hold out as long. In his account of the period, Josephus puts this down to Roman might and Roman skill but contemporaries suspected treachery by Josephus and his commanders. After he surrendered to Vespasian, he won his favour by predicting that he would become Emperor. He remained as a pensioner of the Flavian family for the rest of his life. Four of his works have survived: *The Jewish War*, which described the War against Rome in which he was involved on both sides; *The Jewish Antiquities*, which aimed at explaining Judaism to the Romans among whom he lived; *Against Apion*, which noted and rebuffed the anti-semitism of his time; and finally an autobiography, *Life*.

As a young man, he spent time with the Essene community in the Desert and on his return became involved with the Pharisees, and accordingly his views on first century Judea are an invaluable resource. His writings provide a glimpse into the world in which the early church was developing.

Bibliography

James H. Charlesworth, *The Old Testament Pseudepigraphica*, Vols 1 and 2, Darton Longman & Todd, London (1985)

▪ ˇ 4 The New Testament

4.1 Judaism in the first century

The first century was a momentous era for Judaism. Not only did it see the birth and early expansion of Christianity, but also witnessed a continual struggle with Rome and the destruction in **AD 70** of the Temple in Jerusalem, which struck at the heart of Judaism. The century was characterised by increased competition between the various strands of Judaism, culminating in the second half of the century in the emergence of Rabbinic Judaism as the dominant and unifying force. The success of Rabbinic Judaism was greatly facilitated by a meeting of a council of rabbinic teachers at Jamnia in **AD 90** which introduced various provisions aimed at assuring its predominance.

At the time of the events described in the Gospels and Acts there were still a number of different groupings within Judaism. Moreover the Jews were dispersed throughout most of the Roman Empire. It is estimated that at this time the Jewish population was some six million, of whom between only two and two and a half million were living in Judaea. Elsewhere there were large Jewish populations in Babylon and Egypt, with smaller numbers scattered throughout the Mediterranean. For the most part, the Jews lived in their own communities where they maintained their own separate cultural identity. Whilst Palestine was far from detached from the influences of Greek culture, it had much greater impact on the Jews of the Dispersion, many of whom were more used to reading the Law or Torah in Greek than in Hebrew. Outside Judaea the effects of the various divisions in Judaism were less strong and had to compete with the influences of Greek religion and philosophy.

In Palestine itself the divisions were marked, with various factions such as the Pharisees, Sadducees, Essenes and Zealots. Little is known of these groupings, and what few details we do have originate from the writings of Rabbinic Judaism which so successfully rose to pre-eminence. A major source of information about this period is the Jewish historian Josephus (**AD 37–100**), the author of the *History of the Jewish War*, and of *Jewish Antiquities*. Josephus' work covers only the period up to **AD 66**. It also has to be read with some care, in particular his presentation of both the Jews and the Roman authorities: Josephus was dependent upon the Flavian emperors and came to be considerd by many Jews as a traitor.

Much about Judaism and the impact of the Roman Empire has in fact been recorded by the Christian writers of the New Testament. The accuracy and objectivity of the information, however, is sometimes questionable. Rabbinic Judaism retained some writings of its own including the Talmud, which consists of a collection of assertions of legal obligations dating from the end of the second century together with a commentary, and also the Midrash which is a discussion on the Scriptures. The difficulty with these texts is that they were not intended to record a history of the period, were not written until the second century and portray events from a rabbinic perspective. Where they do provide more authoritative information is in relation to Jewish religious thinking and the organisation of Jewish religious life.

Important knowledge of this era has been discovered at a number of archaeological sites, in particular those preserving the Dead Sea Scrolls and details of the Qumran community. These two sources have provided a wealth of information about this sect which had not previously been available.

In a work of this nature it is impossible to do more than describe these groupings in barest outline.

The Sadducees

The relatively little that is known of the Sadducees is not complimentary, which as it originates from their opponents is not particularly surprising. The high priest usually came from among the Sadducees, whose power and influence arose from their domination of the Temple, and the fact that the Sadducean party included many of high social rank. There was a bitter acrimony between this rather conservative party and the new ideas of the Pharisees, as the latter endeavoured to challenge those of the Sadducees.

The Pharisees

In contrast to the selectivity of the Sadducees, the Pharisees belonged to a movement of the laity which sought to include all Jewish people. The leaders were scribes, and by **70 BC** they had managed to enter the Sanhedrin. The Pharisees believed in strict obedience to the law. To become a Pharisee a propective member had to accept a series of regulations and serve a probationary period, before graduating as a full member. A central feature of Pharasaic outlook was its preoccupation with creating detailed regulations based on interpretations of scripture, but designed to cover a whole range of scenarios.

The Zealots

Zealots believed in a messianic age when the Jews would be freed from Roman rule. They maintained, however, that the Jewish people should themselves take the initiative by political and military opposition to the Romans. God would battle alongside them and ensure their deliverance, but they had first to take up the fight. The Zealot movement is thought to have dated from about **AD 6** to not long after the fall of Jerusalem in **AD 70**.

The Samaritans

There was a bitter enmity between the Jews and the Samaritans. The latter considered themselves to be the true Israel, having separated from the rest of Judaism many years earlier. In the first century AD Jewish pilgrims had been attacked whilst travelling through Samaria, which only served to increase Jewish hatred of them.

The Essenes and Qumran

It is thought that the inhabitants of Qumran were Essenes, a movement which is referred to by Josephus and also by Philo. The Essenes saw themselves as the inheritors of the true Israel, and longed for the coming of the messianic age. They organised themselves into twelve tribes, with some of their members being appointed clergy and having authority over the laity. Those wishing to enter into the community had to swear a covenant, and it is thought that they had to undergo a probationary training period of two years before being fully accepted into the community, at which point they would have to renounce ownership of all personal property. Celibacy was not demanded, although the evidence suggests that many opted for this. Worship revolved around the sharing of meals together.

The Essenes rejected much of Judaism and many chose a life of isolation in the desert, although others lived in communities in the villages and towns of Palestine. The Essenes at Qumran lived in a separate community with its own detailed regulations, and almost totally self-sufficient.

The scribes

The power of the scribes arose out of their study and interpretation of the law. In the first century they formed an emerging upper class, many of them holding important posts in the judicial system, in civil administration and in education. The more influential of the scribes tended to be Pharisees.

The cultural symbol of Judaism, until its destruction in **AD 70**, was the magnificent Temple in Jerusalem. It was a centre for pilgrimage, and was still thought of as the hallowed dwelling-place of the God of the Jews. Temple worship centred on the ritual sacrifice of animals which it was believed would bring forgiveness. The sacrifice was accompanied by ceremonial prayers and psalms, a blessing and the burning of incense. Festival days would be marked by sacrifical offerings on a grander scale. On these occasions it is thought that as many as 50,000 pilgrims would flock to the city; and at Passover the city more than doubled its population.

The high priest of the Temple, in theory a man-of-God appointed for life, the mediator between God and his people, was regarded with the utmost reverence. In practice the high priest was the victor of a bitter battle among rival wealthy families whose success owed much to corrupt means. The matter was complicated further by the recurrent interventions both of Herod and the Romans who for their own political ends would appoint and dismiss high priests. Nevertheless, despite these political elements, the high priest retained considerable authority both in the religious sphere and in his dealings with the Romans. He was assisted by numerous personnel including a temple police force, overseers responsible for the organisation of the Temple, and several treasurers to handle financial matters. In addition there were an estimated 20,000 or so priests and Levites, many who came to Jerusalem for short periods of duty, the priests being responsible for ritual matters, and the Levites serving as guards, singers and musicians, and servants.

The destruction of the temple in **AD 70** dealt a heavy blow to this symbol of Judaism. The first century, however, saw the continuing increase in the importance being given to the scriptures and to the need to undertake instruction in the doctrines and beliefs of Judaism. This development was of great significance in the unification of Judaism under rabbinic influences, particularly following the council in **AD 90** at Jamnia.

Mention should also be made of the Sanhedrin which was a Jewish council of 71 members. Its exact functions and history are uncertain, but it is likely that it concerned itself with both religious and political issues. Its powers and influence are difficult to determine from the limited information that is available, save to say that they tended to vary depending on the political circumstances and the attitude of the Roman authorities.

The original meaning of the word 'synagogue' is a meeting of people rather than a building, and originally these meetings, consisting of prayer and the study of scripture, took place in people's homes. By the time of Jesus' ministry these meetings are thought to have been held quite regularly, with some possibly taking place in buildings designed or adopted for that purpose. Whilst the archaelogical remains of only one such possible building have been found dating prior to the second century, in Acts there are numerous references to synagogues in Greece and the Middle East. The synagogue came to serve as a kind of community centre in which social and political gatherings would be held, and where children would receive instruction in the scriptures and basic education. There was no equivalent to the Christian priest, instead the synagogue was presided over by a council of elders assisted by an archisynagogos who was in charge of synagogue functions and services, and a hazzan who dealt with administrative matters. Services were centred around readings from the Scriptures.

Jewish religious thought in the first century

The Jews were generally well-educated in the Scriptures and accordingly the most popular teachings of the Old Testament played an important part in the moulding of the people's religious outlook. Their thinking was inevitably affected by current religious ideas, most notably those of the Pharisees, the Essenes and the Zealots. A central belief common to all Jews was that their nation enjoyed a favoured position in God's eyes, and in his plan for the world, for they were God's chosen people. They believed that God had given them his Law to enable them to show to the Gentiles the majesty of their god.

Throughout much of their history, however, the Jews had been subjected to the rule of foreigners. The Jews' subjugation to the Romans, their other misfortunes in history, and evil generally were explained by some as the result of evil impulses within men resulting in divine punishment, and by others as the work of Satan. The former belief was characteristic of the Pharisees, whereas the latter was held by those living at Qumran. Those believing the latter also believed that illness was a mark of the work of demons.

The political background

From **31 BC**, following Augustus' victory at the battle of Actium, the Romans had adopted a system of assigning provinces to one of two categories. Those provinces which had long been Roman and where their rule was secure, were governed by proconsuls selected by and answerable to the Senate. Other provinces were under the control of governors appointed by the Emperor. These were the provinces in which the Romans felt most vulnerable and in which all but one of the legions of the regular army were stationed. The provinces under imperial control were further divided. Some were governed by legates, men chosen because of their experience of both military and administrative matters. The legates commanded the armed forces in their province and were responsible for determining appeals from local magistrates in litigious disputes. The other imperial provinces, of which Judaea was one, were ruled by less experienced officials termed prefects, and later changed to procurators. Augustus created a new breed of official, the tax collector, thereby keeping control of revenue out of the hands of the governors and reducing any temptation to corruption. The primary source of tax revenue were the impositions on land and other property, the raising of which was greatly facilitated by the regular censuses that took place.

The political situation in the Middle East in the first century BC was one of turmoil, complicated by thirty years of internal strife and civil war in Rome. Herod had become ruler of Galilee by **49 BC**. He subsequently found that he was facing revolt, but was successful in **37 BC** in engaging the support of Mark Anthony with whose legions he entered Jerusalem. Six years later Mark Anthony was defeated by Octavian, but with characteristic political skill Herod won over Octavian who placed further territories under his control. He struck up close friendships both with Octavian (who henceforth assumed the name Augustus) and his chief minister Agrippa which were to prove the basis of Herod's policy, until his death nearly thirty years later.

On Herod's death his kingdom was divided among three of his sons. Archelaus succeeded to the throne of Judaea and neighbouring areas, Antipas was to rule Galilee and Transjordan as 'tetrarch' under Archelaus, and similarly Philip became the tetrarch of the remaining areas which had been under Herod's rule. Archelaus, however, could not boast the political dexterity of his father. He found himself embroiled in a number of problems which he handled poorly, and gained a reputation for cruelty. In **AD 6** he was denounced for marrying his dead brother's wife, contrary to Jewish law. He was exiled by the Emperor and Judaea was made a province. Philip and Antipas continued to rule as tetrarchs until their respective deaths in **AD 34** and **AD 39**. Antipas was tetrarch of Galilee and Transjordan, in which much of Jesus' ministry took place. He is referred to on several occasions in the Gospels and was responsible for the death of John the Baptist.

AD 37 had seen the death of the Emperor Tiberius. His successor, Caligula, installed his ally Herod Agrippa I as king of Philip's former tetrarchy, and two years later made him ruler of the lands which had been ruled by Antipas. Judaea and the other areas formerly ruled by Archelaus remained a Roman province. In Jesus' lifetime the stability of the province was frequently undermined by attacks from rebel nationalist zealots.

Pontius Pilate served as governor of Judaea from **AD 27** to **AD 36**. In addition to the reference to him in the Gospels he also features in the works of the historian Josephus and the Jewish author Philo. Both writers paint an unpleasant picture of him as an inflexible character willing to employ violent means to quell opposition. Indeed, according to Josephus, a massacre ordered by him of Samaritans connected to a messianic movement proved the final straw and Pilate was deprived of his governorship and returned to Rome.

Prior to his trial before Pilate, Jesus was first questioned before the Sanhedrin and only then taken to Pilate. Whilst most criminal charges were not heard by the governor but by the Jewish authorities themselves, the Roman administration generally insisted on determining cases in which the penalty was death. Pilate appears to have been somewhat reluctant to hear the case against Jesus and, noting that Jesus was from Galilee, sought to pass the Sanhedrin's case against Jesus to Antipas, although the latter refused to determine it and sent it back to Pilate. Pilate, afraid that the local Jewish leaders may send damaging reports about him back to Rome, felt compelled to submit to their demands.

Pilate continued as governor until his recall to Rome in **AD 37** after the massacre of Samaritans. In the brief period in which Judaea was without a governor, the Sanhedrin executed Stephen, the first of the Christian martyrs, having avoided referring the matter to the Roman authorities. In was during a similar interregnum that the Sanhedrin again took matters into its own hands when it ordered the execution of James, the Christian leader in Jerusalem.

In **AD 41** Emperor Caligula died and with the assistance of Herod Agrippa was succeeded by Claudius. Judaea was no longer to be a province under direct Roman control, but was instead added to Agrippa's kingdom. Agrippa proved a popular ruler, moving his official residence to Jerusalem, and remitting taxes. He was responsible for the execution of James, the son of Zebedee, and the arrest of Peter.

On Agrippa's death, Claudius determined that the whole kingdom should become a province under Roman rule. Under successive governors, relations between the Jews and their injudicious rulers deteriorated greatly. According to the historian Josephus, corruption was rife, which was no doubt one explanation for the increasing ferocity of the revolutionary nationalist party. The conduct of governor Florus provoked such bitter anger and resentment that the Jews rose up in arms in the Jewish War of **AD 66**. Florus had sought to levy a large amount of revenue from the temple treasury. Public protests followed and, unable to arrest those responsible, the governor's troops went on a rampage of looting in which many were killed. There followed a number of attacks against the Romans and within four weeks rebels had captured Jerusalem and much of Judaea. The uprising sparked rioting and rebellion throughout the Middle East, including the cities on the coast, and even as far away as Alexandria, with longstanding animosities between the Greek and Jewish communities resulting in many deaths. Local attempts to respond to the insurrections were largely unsuccessful and accordingly Nero assigned the task to the General Vespasian who recaptured Galilee in **AD 67**.

When Vespasian became Emperor, the campaign was taken over by his son Titus who in **AD 70** succeeded in recapturing Jerusalem. The geographical location of the city greatly facilitated its defence, and it was retaken only after a siege lasting nearly five months. The fall of the city led to the eventual defeat of the rebels and the dismantling of the Jewish state, including the abolition of the Sanhedrin and the position of high priest.

Jewish resistance continued into the second century with two further revolts in **AD 115** and **AD 132**, both of which were fiercely put down.

4.2　The Synoptic Gospels

The meaning of the term 'gospel' is good news, and in Christianity it refers to the life, teachings, death and resurrection of Jesus. The 'Gospel' was the spoken message of Christ and in the Gospel accounts we read of the Gospel being 'proclaimed'. This message was not at first recorded in writing. New Testament scholars offer several explanations for this: the early Christians were not particularly well educated, and would not have had the abilities, time or resources to put matters in writing; they expected that the end of the world was imminent and they saw no necessity for a comprehensive written account of stories which they found no difficulty in committing to memory.

Whilst scholars believe that there were a number of collections of stories about Jesus committed to writing in the early years after his death, these were never gathered together in one volume with the other purely oral teachings of the early church. The Synoptic Gospels have, at least up until now, proved impossible to date precisely, the present thinking being that they were all written between **AD 65** and **AD 100**. It is likely that the Gospel was committed to writing because, by this time, the first disciples were dying out or scattered and there was a growing appreciation of the need to preserve Jesus' teaching and message in a reliable form. These concerns must have been particularly heightened when, as seems likely, both Paul and Peter met their deaths in Rome in **AD 64** during Nero's persecution of Christians. A permanent written account was required to bear witness to the authenticity of the Christian Gospel when those who had seen and heard Jesus were no longer available to speak of what they themselves had witnessed. The need for authoritative accounts may have been seen as all the more pressing when in **AD 70** the Romans captured Jerusalem, putting down the revolt and destroying the Temple. The Jewish Christian community in Jerusalem fled to Pella and dwindled into obscurity, and Christianity's ties with its geo-graphical origins were severed.

It is likely that a written Gospel was also seen as having invaluable potential for contributing to Christian worship. Early Christian services often followed the practice of the synagogue of incorporating readings from the Old Testament – the addition of readings from Paul's letters or the teachings of Jesus would have been likely.

The authorship, sources and purpose of the Gospels remain uncertain. Neither Matthew nor Mark make any mention of their authors. In John, there is reference to the author as 'the beloved disciple', but his identity is not known, and in any event that reference is thought to be a later addition to the Gospel. In a preface to Luke and Acts, the author describes how others had written before him, that their accounts were based on information from those who witnessed the events in Jesus' life, and that he had recorded the details accurately. This information does not really assist in identifying the author or confirming authenticity – such a preface was standard requisite practice if an author was to speak with any authority.

Nor is there any reliable external evidence of the authorship of the Gospels. In the early fourth century Eusebius, credited as being the first church historian, refers to Papias, a bishop in Asia Minor in about **AD 130**, commenting that

Mark's Gospel was not written in an orderly manner. Papias attributed this to the fact that Mark was acting as an interpreter of St Peter, and Peter did not preach in an orderly fashion. Papias is also quoted as referring to Matthew drawing up a 'compilation of the Lord's utterances in the Hebrew language and everyone translated them as he was able'. It is universally accepted, however, that the Gospel of Matthew was originally written in Greek, and so Papias could not have been referring to the Gospel that we know as Matthew.

The lack of external evidence to assist biblical criticism forces the scholar to rely almost entirely upon a close examination of the Gospels themselves. The first task in such an enquiry is to attempt to ascertain which are the most reliable of the many New Testament manuscipts which have survived, and to acknowledge that even the texts selected in this way are unlikely to mirror precisely the words of their original authors.

A major advance in biblical criticism resulted from the work of Griesbach, in the late eighteenth century, who printed the three Gospels now known as the Synoptic Gospels side by side in columns. Scholars already appreciated that the Gospel of John was very different from the other three, but Griesbach's presentation of Matthew, Mark and Luke highlighted the striking similarities between these three books. They all recount a similar overall history, with events and stories in very similar sequence. The similarities are such that in many instances their wording is almost identical, as in the account of the healing of the paralytic (Matt 9: 2–8; Mark 2: 3–12; Luke 5: 18–26). Other examples include the feeding of the five thousand (Matt 14: 13–21; Mark 6: 30–40; Luke 9: 10–17) and Peter's denials (Matt 26: 69–75; Mark 14: 66–7; Luke 22: 56–62).

The agreement between these Gospels both in their order, but more particularly in their almost identical passages, has led biblical scholars to the inescapable conclusion that they shared some connection. The possibility put forward by some, that the Gospel stories had simply been passed on by word of mouth, and that the accounts had become stereotyped so that when they were repeated the speakers had come to use identical or almost identical language, has been rejected. The similarities are far too striking – either the Gospel writers copied from each other, or they shared the same written sources. The Gospels are not, of course, identical. There are important differences. Matthew and Luke each have many passages which are not duplicated in the other Gospels. In Mark, on the other hand, there is relatively little material which is not found in either or both of Matthew and Luke.

Augustine, writing in **AD 400**, advanced the theory that Matthew was the first Gospel to be written and that Mark, which is shorter, was an abbreviated version of Matthew. This theory has been generally rejected, although Roman Catholic scholarship until recently favoured this view. Whilst Mark is indeed shorter, the stories and accounts that are common to both books are almost invariably *more* detailed in Mark – Matthew is only longer because there is more raw material. Furthermore there are many important stories in Matthew, such as the account of the birth of Jesus which are not found in Mark, and which it is inconceivable would be omitted if the author of Mark had Matthew available to him as a source.

From the middle of the nineteenth century it has become almost universally accepted that Mark was the first of the Gospels. That hypothesis is based upon:

(i) The fact that nearly all the material in Mark is duplicated in Matthew and nearly two-thirds is duplicated in Luke. There is very little in Mark which is not found in Matthew and/or Luke.

(ii) The language used in Mark corresponds closely to that used in Matthew and/or Luke. There is very little correspondence between Luke and Matthew where they differ from Mark.

(iii) Mark is the shortest of the Gospels – it is far more likely that the later works enlarged upon the earlier text, and accordingly that Matthew and Luke were written later.

(iv) Both Matthew and Luke generally follow the same order as in Mark, and where each of them depart from Mark it is in different places but is always followed by a return to the order of Mark's Gospel, hence adding weight to the suggestion that they both shared Mark as source material.

(v) The language and style of Matthew and Luke are considered more refined than in Mark, making it unlikely that Mark copied from Matthew and/or Luke. There are a number of instances where Mark makes use of Aramaic words that Jesus would have spoken, but Matthew and Luke do not, preferring instead to keep to Greek.

(vi) Matthew and Luke alter descriptions in Mark which might have been disliked in the early church – thus Mark describes how Jesus was unable to perform 'mighty works' in Nazareth because of opposition to him there, whereas Matthew recounts how Jesus carried out 'many mighty works'. Mark refers to Jesus being angry, whereas Matthew and Luke refrain from attributing anger to him. Similarly instances in Mark in which the Apostles might appear in a poor light are edited in Luke and Matthew to omit such implication. This again suggests that it was Luke and Matthew who made use of Mark and that Mark was written first.

In addition to the material in Mark, however, Matthew and Luke have a considerable number of other verses in which they also agree. It is now almost universally accepted that Matthew and Luke shared a second common written but as yet unfound source, which biblical scholars have termed 'Q'. There is also still further material in Luke and Matthew which is unique to each book. The source for this material is generally considered to be the oral traditions of the early Christians.

Having reached the conclusion that both Matthew and Luke derived so much of their material from other written sources, at times making no or little alteration to it, it follows that it is most unlikely that either of them actually witnessed what they described – had they done so, one would have expected more individualised accounts.

The Gospel of Mark

How then did the first Gospel come to be written? To answer this question the only material available for consideration is the Gospel itself. It is made up of short paragraphs, each consisting of a self-contained story or narrative centred around something that Jesus has said or done. The obvious explanation for this literary structure is that Mark is not an original work in the sense that he embarked upon a new account of the life and message of Christ; rather he has simply drawn together separate stories from various sources, some written but many of them part of the oral traditions of the early church. Biblical scholars refer to these self-contained narratives by the Greek 'pericopes', meaning 'paragraphs'.

The pericopes are clearly sections of texts admirably suited for reading out aloud as part of worship or evangelising. Not only are they each easy to understand without reference to the rest of the Gospel, but they are each designed to concentrate on a specific point relevant to Christ's life or message with all superfluous detail being omitted.

There are a number of possible sources which may have been available to Mark, apart from oral material passed down by word of mouth:

- Eusebius, the first Church historian writing in about **AD 325**, records Papias, bishop of Hierapolis in about **AD 130**, quoting 'the Presbyter' as stating that Mark had written down what had been recounted to him by Peter. 'The Presbyter' was reputed to have said also that Mark himself had not seen the events of which he writes. The reliability of this account, at best third hand, is highly debatable. Many biblical scholars have nevertheless accepted that Peter was probably a source behind some of Mark's work, and in support of that view to the frequent references to Peter in Mark.
- It is thought likely that written sources are behind the parables in 4: 3–34, the collection of sayings at 9: 41–50 and much of chapter 13, and that these may have been used for teaching purposes.

As to the identity of the author, early Church tradition has it that the author was the John Mark referred to in Acts 12: 12; 25: 13; 5: 13; 15: 36–37; and also once in each of four of the Letters. The pointers as to the **authorship** are:

- The unrefined style of writing which leads to the conclusion that the author was not fully conversant with Greek. This is suggested too by the presence in this Gospel of Aramaisms which is a feature not found in the other Gospels. The character of John Mark as described in Acts – impulsive and not particularly reliable – has been said by some to point to him as the author.
- The confusing descriptions of the geography of northern Palestine, and Jesus' travels there. The writer almost certainly could not have been familiar with this region, whereas his account does suggest a familiarity with Galilee.
- The strong impression that the author did not witness the events himself.
- The concluding verses of Mark's Gospel (13: 9–20) were clearly written by a different author; the earliest texts finish at verse 8. The style is much more refined, and the content includes material contained in later books such as Luke and Acts.

Dating

If John Mark did indeed write this Gospel, then it must have been written not long after the events described in Acts. Biblical scholars are generally agreed that it was probably written between **AD 65** and 70, because:

- The deaths of Peter and Paul in **AD 64–65** would have provided an urgent need to record the events to which they could no longer bear witness.

- The Apostles and witnesses to Christ's life and teachings would have been dying out from about this time and earlier.
- When the reference at 13: 14 to 'the desolating sacrilege set up where it ought not to be ...' is repeated in Luke and Matthew, these authors alter the account in such a way as to remind the reader of the destruction of the Temple in Jerusalem by the Romans in **AD 70**. It is accordingly argued by many that if Mark had been writing after **AD 70**, or at least if he had known of the fate of Jerusalem, this verse would have contained some reference to it.
- The emphasis on persecution and suffering at various points in the Gospel. Some argue that the author was influenced by the persecution of the Church under Nero, and hence Mark must date from about that time.

The nature of Mark's account

Mark's Gospel is not a chronological account of the life of Jesus – almost certainly that was never the author's intention. The book is rather a series of pericopes fitted into a skeleton framework of the main events in Jesus' life. These major events are broadly in chronological order, whereas the pericopes are grouped together according to their subject matter. Thus, those concerned with Jesus' teaching in Galilee are contained in chapter 1; stories describing his conflicts with the Jewish hierarchy in chapters 2 and 3; parables of his teachings in chapter 4; acts of power in chapter 5; and the training of the disciples in chapter 6.

The development of Jesus' ministry is described primarily in stories of Jesus' power and of his conflicts with opponents, most particularly the Pharisees. The former show Jesus triumphing over different kinds of mental and physical ailments, multiplying food and overcoming spirits. The controversies with the authorities consist of Jesus explaining God's will and in so doing exposing the hypocrisy of his opponents. The Gospel presents Jesus as a figure of great power and authority.

The Gospel of Matthew

One feature of Matthew's Gospel is its clear structure. It does not start or finish abruptly as Mark does. It begins with a genealogy tracing Jesus' descent from Abraham, the father of the Jewish people, and ends with the command of the risen Jesus to the eleven to go and make disciples of all nations, and a promise that he would be with them always.

The material in Matthew follows much the same order as that in Mark. Chapters 3 and 4 mirror the order of Mark, as do chapters 8 to 12 and chapter 14 onwards. Matthew has added material from other sources, most notably sections of Jesus' teachings such as the Sermon on the Mount (chapters 5–7) and the parables in chapter 13. Even where the order follows Mark, Matthew has inserted matter from other sources, the Gospel being arranged in ordered collections of teachings on particular subjects and the form being akin to that of a manual of instruction for Christian life.

Much of the material which is unique to Matthew has a strong Jewish element. There are repeated allusions to, and quotations from, the Old Testament in an effort to demonstrate that Jesus was the fulfilment of Old Testament prophecies. Matthew presents Jesus' teachings as the consummation of Jewish law – hence in the Sermon on the Mount, Jesus quotes Judaic law only to explain a deeper underlying meaning. Matthew nevertheless portrays Jewish religious leaders in a highly critical light, more so than any other first-century Christian writer. Indeed many biblical scholars believe that Jesus was not as condemning as recounted by Matthew. In Matthew, Jesus confines his teachings to the Jews, telling his disciples 'I was sent only to the lost sheep of the house of Israel' (15: 24), and not until after his resurrection exhorting them to make disciples of all nations (28: 19).

Matthew is also notable for its emphasis on the miraculous. In 27: 51–3, the Gospel speaks of an earthquake with rocks being split, tombs being opened, and the bodies of saints who had fallen asleep rising. Elsewhere he embellishes stories taken from Mark, as with the account of the fig tree which in Mark withered the day after Jesus had spoken, whereas in Matthew the tree withers immediately after Jesus' words (11: 20). Matthew places great emphasis on apocalyptic themes, with several references to the 'weeping and gnashing of teeth' that will accompany the end.

One further characteristic of Matthew's Gospel is the reference to 'Church'. Matthew is the only Gospel writer to recount the story of Jesus telling Peter that he was the rock on which he would build his Church – indeed the word 'Church' does not appear in any of the other Gospels.

It is universally accepted that Matthew is not an account of an eyewitness, and further that even the sources used by the author were most unlikely to have been eyewitness accounts. The author of Matthew reproduces much of Mark, but with a less vivid style and with alterations suggestive of later influences. Scholars consider that the material unique to Matthew is the least reliable in the synoptics, with the account of Jesus' infancy conflicting with that of Luke and aspects of the events leading to his death, such as Pilate's dream, being of dubious authenticity.

The **author** of Matthew remains unknown, but is thought to have been a Jewish Christian seeking to explain how Jesus was the fulfilment of Old Testament prophecies and that by his teachings the old laws had been revoked. In the early church, the Gospel was attributed to the Apostle Matthew, probably as a result of the ascription of the Gospel to him by Papias. The overwhelming weight of academic authority today is against this and has concluded that Papias was:

(i) indeed referring to the Gospel that we know as Matthew, but was wrong in ascribing it to the Apostle, and in asserting that it was originally written in Greek; or

(ii) referring to another Aramaic Gospel which has been lost – such as the Gospel to the Hebrews or that to the Nazarenes which we know once existed; or

(iii) referring to a collection of sayings of Jesus, perhaps even Q.

Whilst it has not yet been possible to determine conclusively what Papias meant, the preponderance of opinion is that Papias did mean the Gospel of Matthew as we know it, but was simply incorrect in ascribing it to the Apostle and in believing that it was originally written in Aramaic.

As to the **date** of this Gospel, clearly it has to be later than Mark which is dated with some confidence to between **AD 65** and **70**. Commentators generally consider that Matthew post-dates the fall of Jerusalem in **AD 70**. Suggestions in the Gospel that hope of Christ's return was fading, together with the instruction to baptise in the name of the Trinity (28: 19) rather than in the name of Jesus (as in Acts), and the development of the more miraculous aspects of the narrative, must place it some years after Mark. Scholars have mostly settled on **AD 85** or later as being the likely time of composition.

The Gospel of Luke

Like Matthew, Luke follows the general framework of Mark, but instead of assimilating Markan and non-Markan material as Matthew has done, his Gospel consists instead of blocks of Markan and non-Markan script. It is therefore comparatively easy to see which source Luke is using as one reads his Gospel. Luke 4: 13 to 6: 11 is based on Mark 1: 21 to 3: 6; Luke 8: 5 to 9: 50 is taken from Mark 4–6 and 8–9; Luke 18: 15–35 is from Mark 10 and Luke 19: 29 to 22: 13 is from Mark 11–13. The rest of the Gospel consists of material from Q, other matter unique to Luke and a small amount of further script from Mark.

Biblical scholars have long debated whether Luke based his Gospel on Mark, as Matthew did, and added other material, or whether he wrote the Gospel from non-Markan material and added in the passages from Mark at a later stage. The proponents of the latter theory point to the following:

(i)   The beginning and the end of the Gospel are clearly non-Markan, suggesting that Mark was not the framework for this Gospel.
(ii) With the Markan passages deleted, the non-Markan material still reads as a coherent account, containing the essential events in Jesus' life. In contrast, the Markan passages taken alone do not make a readable story.
(iii) Luke contains passages of non-Markan material when compared with the same accounts in Mark. This suggests that either he had written the non-Markan material before the Markan material was added (perhaps because he had not seen it), or that he did his utmost to avoid using Markan material wherever possible. The latter explanation is unlikely in that, where he has used Markan material, it is often reproduced without amendment.
(iv) The fact that the Markan material is in blocks, rather than interwoven, again points to these passages being added after the book had been completed, at least in draft form.

If this hypothesis is correct, then the non-Markan 'draft' could be another early source, possibly written before Mark. The theory is not without its critics, who reject the notion that the non-Markan material forms a complete account, particularly given the absence of reference to the antagonism with the Jewish religious authorities.

Tradition has it that the **author** of Luke was a Gentile. The classical Greek style of his writing would support this. It is universally accepted that he also wrote Acts. The two volumes trace Christianity from its origins to its early growth in the Roman world and has been termed by some the first Christian apology, aimed as it appears to be at a wide readership in the non-Jewish world. In contrast to Matthew, Luke records Jesus as not restricting his teachings to the Jews. On no fewer than three occasions did Pilate attempt to release Jesus – the responsibility for Jesus' death is laid firmly at the door of the Jews.

Luke lays particular emphasis on Jesus' response to the poor and the outcast. Women play a far greater role in this Gospel than any other, featuring also in the parables. Throughout the Gospel, Luke presents the theme of the Spirit of God at work: in the conception of Jesus, at his baptism and temptations, and in his ability to heal. Similarly, prayer is given particular mention in Luke.

Undoubtedly Luke and Acts share the same **author** – their style and approach have much in common. The traditions of the early church held that these works were written by someone named Luke. An examination of Acts reveals three sections in which the writer refers to 'we', leading to the obvious inference that the author was present at those times, and was therefore one of Paul's companions. There are a number of phrases in Luke and Acts which some have taken to indicate that the author had some medical knowledge, but in reality they reveal no more specialist knowledge than any educated layman of his time might possess. However, among Paul's companions there is one named Luke, a doctor referred to in Colossians 4: 14. He is widely thought to have either written these two volumes, probably including extracts from his own diary in relation to events at which he was personally present, or to have kept a diary which formed part of the material used by the author, with the Gospel obtaining its title because of its connection with Luke's diary.

As to the **dating** of this Gospel, some have argued for a very early date on the basis that Acts ends with Paul's imprisonment in Rome, making no mention of Paul's execution, and that it must therefore have been completed prior to Paul's death in **AD 64–5**. This view has been generally rejected because of references in Luke suggesting that he knew of the siege of Jerusalem in **AD 69**. The preponderance of academic opinion is in favour of a date between **AD 75** and **85**, postdating the fall of Jerusalem and giving enough time for Mark to have become known to Luke, but at the same time completed before Paul's letters became widely read, as Acts suggests that they were not known to its author. Certainly the Gospel must have been written before **AD 96**, as it was known to Clement of Rome writing at that time.

4.3   The Gospel of John

Authorship

Nowhere in the Gospel does the writer state his name. In the Prologue with which the Gospel commences, he certainly infers that he had himself witnessed some of the events he describes and that he knew other eyewitnesses. Elsewhere at 21: 24 he states: 'This is the disciple who is bearing witness to these things, and who has written these things; and we know that his testimony is true'. It is not absolutely certain to whom 'this disciple' refers, but the most obvious candidate is the last disciple previously mentioned in verse 23 (described as the 'disciple who Jesus loved'), and someone who could have given a first-hand account.

The closing chapters of the Gospel contain other references to this 'beloved disciple', who was clearly someone known to Peter. That certainly raises the possibility that the author was John, son of Zebedee, one of the inner circle of disciples and mentioned as being with Peter in Luke and Acts, and in Galatians. The fact that John, son of Zebedee, is referred to in the Synoptic Gospels on no less than twenty occasions, but not once in John, would seem to support the theory that John is the 'beloved disciple' and author of this Gospel. Some commentators, however, have baulked at the idea that the author would have described himself thus. On the other hand, is it any more plausible that the author would have ascribed that title to another disciple, particularly when it is clearly not a reference to Peter? Other theologians have suggested that such an indirect reference to himself is an indication of the author's modesty in not wanting to mention his own name.

It is clear from the content of the Gospel that the author has a good knowledge of Jewish life, and understands aspects of Jewish ritual, since he refers to Jewish feast days and laws governing the Sabbath. Similarly he appears to have detailed information about the building of the Temple, is aware of the animosity between Jew and Samaritan, and knows of the high priests Annas and Caiaphas. He also appears familiar with landmarks in and around Jerusalem, which in the case of details he gives in the reference to the pool near the Sheep Gate, have been confirmed by archaelogical excavations. The evidence in the Gospel is fairly conclusive that either its author knew Palestine very well, or had access to someone who provided him with this detail. Similarly, on several occasions the writer puts names to people who in the Synoptic Gospels are only referred to anonymously.

A problem in relation to authorship arises because many scholars are of the opinion that the writer made use of both Mark and Luke. If that is correct, then one has to ask: is it plausible that one Apostle would have made use of texts written by men who had not themselves been Apostles and would not have had the detailed knowledge of Jesus that John, son of Zebeddee, would have possessed? Some biblical commentators dispute the theory that John had access to any of the Synoptic Gospels and point to the relatively small amount of overlap, which could be explained by oral tradition or other written sources; others see no difficulty in John using the second-hand accounts in Mark and Luke, given that he reproduces so little of their material in any case.

The historical accuracy of John has been the subject of repeated challenges. It is argued that if historically inaccurate, it is unlikely to have been penned by an Apostle. The charge is based in large part on the substantial differences between John and the Synoptic Gospels. It has been argued, not very convincingly, that John's Gospel is so different that it would only have been given credence in the early church if it was thought to have been the work of an Apostle.

The preponderance of academic opinion, however, is against John being written by an Apostle. The Gospel is strongly influence by Hellenistic concepts – the reference to 'the Logos' for example, that would be foreign to a Jewish fisherman from Galilee. This remains true, notwithstanding the discoveries of the Qumran literature which shared many of the abstract concepts characteristic of Greek thought. As to external evidence, the first writer who refers to the author of the Gospel is Irenaeus, who positively identifies John the disciple as the author and records him living at Ephesus. Eusebius recounts that Irenaeus received this information from Polycarp who in turn had been told by the Apostles. The early church fathers such as Tertullian and Origen all followed Irenaeus in attributing the Gospel to the Apostle John. This 'external' evidence, however, is viewed with considerable scepticism by most academic writers.

Dates for the composition of John from as early as before the fall of Jerusalem in **AD 70** to the last quarter of the second century have been put forward. Most scholars however date the Gospel between **AD 90** and **AD 110**, which if the Apostle John was indeed the writer, would make him a very old man when he wrote it.

The Synoptics and the accuracy of the Johannine account

A comparison with the Synoptic Gospels reveals the following differences:

(i)   There is a substantial amount of material in the Synoptic Gospels which is not referred to in John at all: the virgin birth, Jesus' baptism and temptation, the parables, the insitution of the Lord's supper, and the Ascension, to name but a few of many. The explanation generally put forward for the omission of so much important material is that John assumed that his readers were already familiar with the Synoptic Gospels, and saw no purpose in duplicating these accounts.

(ii) A large proportion of John's Gospel is composed of additional material which is not contained in the Synoptic Gospels. This includes Jesus' early ministry in Judaea, his meeting with the Samaritan woman, the healing of the blind man and the lame man in Jerusalem, and the washing of the disciples' feet, again to refer to just some of the additional narrative. The presence of this supplementary material is readily explained if John is seeking to supplement rather than improve upon the Synoptics, but it does call into question the authenticity of the matters which he alone recounts.

(iii) The dating of the cleansing of the Temple, the duration of Jesus' teaching and the dating of the last supper. The chronology of the Synoptics has been interpreted to give a period of one year only for Jesus' ministry, whereas the account in John is thought to indicate a period of almost three years. In relation to the last supper, the Synoptic Gospels record this as coinciding with the Jewish Passover, whereas John states that the last supper took place before Passover.

(iv) John's Gospel contains far more discourse and less narration than the Synoptics. Some biblical scholars have contrasted the two different presentations of Jesus and have questioned their compatibility. One explanation is that in John, Jesus invariably addresses his discourses to more educated audiences often in Jerusalem or in a synagogue, whereas in the Synoptics, Jesus is generally talking to crowds of people in the open air.

The contrasts between John and the Synoptics have not surprisingly led to much debate as to its accuracy. Many theologians have discounted John when constructing an historical portrait of Jesus, preferring the Synoptic account whenever discrepancies appear between the two. John is clearly a 'theological' work in which symbolism constitutes a continuing theme and accounts for the tendency to label this Gospel as unhistorical.

It is clear from an examination of the Gospel itself that its author certainly sought to portray his account as the 'historical truth' about Jesus, notwithstanding his theological and symbolic representation. John contains references to the timing of events, geographical description and details of Jewish traditions, all of which suggest that he was seeking to give his own factual account, not merely a theological interpretation of Jesus. On the other hand, however, how else could the writer give his message persuasive authority other than by setting it in a factual account that he presented as truthful and certain? The weight of academic opinion remains sceptical as to the historicity of John.

John portrays Jesus as the fulfilment of Old Testament prophecy, tracing Jesus' descent from Abraham and emphasising his Jewish derivation and authority, but at the same time representing the Jews as a hostile people who have rejected their own. A distinguishing feature of this Gospel is the spiritual character of Jesus' teaching, which is often understood on a superficial level only with the real message remaining unappreciated by his listeners. Jesus' life and passion are portrayed in the context of a developing relationship between the Father and the Son. Whilst the term 'Son of God' has its derivation in Judaism, John is clearly seeking to use the term in a deeper supernatural sense, more familiar to Greek thought. Jesus is a pre-existing divine being sent by the Father upon whom Jesus is dependent and whose commandments he will obey. John, more than any of the other Gospel writers, emphasises the role of the Spirit, with Jesus assuring the disciples that when he leaves them the Father will send another, the Spirit or Helper, who will remain with them forever.

Whilst Jesus' divine character receives special emphasis, as does his love for mankind, John nevertheless is at pains to portray Jesus' humanity, as in his tears at the grave of Lazarus, his washing of the disciples' feet, and his thirsting on the cross.

The author's purpose

A number of theories have been advanced as to the intentions behind this Gospel, the most notable of which are:

(i)   As an aid to evangelism. John 20: 31 proclaims that '... these have been written in order that you may believe that Jesus is the Messiah, the Son of God, and that through your faith in him you may have life'.

(ii) As a spiritual account of the life of Jesus that was distinct from, but designed to supplement the more factual accounts in the Synoptic Gospels. This was the view expressed by Clement of Alexandria. Clement states that he received this tradition from the 'early presbyters', and accordingly it is likely that this was a widely held view in the early church.

(iii) As a means of combating gnosticism. This theory is inevitably associated with a dating of John in the second century when the gnostic movements were flourishing. The proponents of this theory argue that the Gospel writer was motivated by a desire to counter Docetism, a brand of gnosticism which held that Christ only *seemed* to be human – he could not have really become flesh because this would have rendered him tainted with the world which was essentially evil. Hence, in John great emphasis is given to Jesus' humanity.

(iv) As a vehicle to present a Hellenised form of Christianity to the Greek non-Christian world. Accordingly, so it is claimed, the Christian message is packaged in 'religious' or theological language more suited to the Greek mind. This theory has been the subject of particular criticism, following the discoveries at Qumran which revealed that some of the terms to be found in John, and hitherto thought to have been of Greek derivation, were in fact in usuage in a Jewish context in the early years of the Church.

4.4 The Acts of the Apostles

The author's purpose

Acts is the one and only account of the earliest progress of Christianity. It tells of trials, persecutions, martyrs, escapes and travels set in locations throughout the ancient world, including Jerusalem, Antioch, Corinth, Athens and finally Rome. It was never intended as a comprehensive history of the work of all the Apostles, and indeed after chapter 13 is concerned primarily with Paul alone. Inevitably the author, Luke, was constrained in what he could include. Ancient writers wrote on a papyrus roll which provided at most thirty feet of manuscript and the text of Acts is sufficient to exhaust an entire roll. Furthermore, Luke was not engaged upon a detailed chronological history, rather he sought to tell a series of stories dramatising important events in the history of the early Christians.

The fact that Acts was written at all is in some ways remarkable. The early Church was waiting for the end of the world, and to early Christians a history of these years would have seemed an utter irrelevance. Christians were waiting for Christ's imminent second coming, but despite Paul's execution, the martyrdom of James and the fall of Jerusalem, the world had not ended and the second coming had not materialised.

Luke represents a rather different viewpoint, for he saw Jesus as not simply the end of history, but also as the beginning of a new history of the Church and of evangelism. Luke concluded that no one other than God Himself could know the timing of the second coming, and that until that time Christians should devote themselves to taking their mission throughout the world. Luke sees the history of the Church as the history of the continuing Gospel. The consequences of Luke's approach were that:

(i) He placed his account of early Christianity within the secular world, and tied in its advances to secular history.

(ii) He claimed a universality for Christianity, as for example in Acts 2: 9–11 in the Pentecost story, where visitors to Jerusalem from every country of the world heard the Gospel in their own tongue. The account in Acts is in large part the story of the Church's success in the Greek west.

(iii) The Church had to decide whether the Judaic laws that it had inherited from its Jewish roots were to be imposed on its Gentile converts. In summary, Luke's response was that Christianity was the true successor to Judaism, and that the taking of the message to the Gentiles was by God's command, a command which followed the refusal by his own people to listen to and accept Christ. The rejection by Christians of Jewish laws was not only in accordance with God's will but was also forced upon Christians by Jewish rejection of God.

(iv) Christianity ceased to be a permissible religion under Roman Law. In the Roman Empire only certain religions were authorised – the practice of others was forbidden and punishable with severe penalties, even death. The Jewish religion was tolerated, and at first the Roman authorities saw Christianity as a form of Judaism. The Jews, however, sought to persuade the Romans otherwise, and the practice of Christianity was forbidden. A chief motivation behind Acts is Luke's intention to portray Christianity as acceptable to the authorities and to commend it to them. Hence Luke repeatedly describes accounts of Roman officials demonstrating sympathy towards the early Christians, as for example in the attitudes of the tribune Claudius Lysias (Acts 23: 29) and Agrippa, Bernice and Festus (Acts 25: 25 and 26: 31) to Paul. Luke of course stresses that Paul was a Roman citizen.

A primary concern of Luke was to describe the incredible expansion of Christianity from its roots in the backwater of Palestine to its arrival in Rome, then the capital of the world. Luke is at pains, however, to demonstrate that this success was not as a result of human endeavours, but was brought about by the power of God through the Holy Spirit whose presence he repeatedly makes clear. Indeed Acts begins at Pentecost when the Apostles are filled with the Holy Spirit. Thereafter on the occasion of every decision the Church has to take, guidance is sought from the Spirit.

One of the greatly debated questions arising out of Acts is why it finishes where it does. From chapter 13 onwards, Luke is primarily concerned with the rapid and heroic progress of Paul and his dramatic voyage to Rome. The frustrating feature of the book is that Luke goes no further – Paul is left awaiting trial in Rome and the reader is not told the outcome. Several explanations for this have been advanced, most notably, that

(i) Acts was intended to be the second volume of a trilogy. However, the ending would still appear rather abrupt, and the theory has been rejected by many.

(ii) Paul was condemned and Luke did not wish to record this. Again this is not particularly satisfactory – Paul's condemnation would have been widely known, and there would have been no point in suppressing it.

(iii) Luke died before completing Acts. Christian tradition, however, has it that Luke lived well into old age.

(iv) Luke was unable to continue with the story because at the time of writing he did not know any more than he had recorded. This has led some to argue that Theophilus, to whom Acts is addressed, was the magistrate appointed to hear Paul's case, and that the book was written in support of Paul's defence.

(v) No explanation is necessary – Acts finishes where it does, because that is the end of the account which Luke sought to tell. In Acts 1: 8, the Apostles are directed to take the Gospel 'to the ends of the earth', and the arrival at Rome marks the completion of that story. Acts is therefore not the history of the Apostles' work, nor a biography of Paul, but the story of the trials and tribulations of its successful journey to the capital of the Roman Empire, at which point Luke's task is complete.

Dating

Various dates have been put forward, spanning nearly a hundred years from **AD 60** onwards. The four most conventional datings are:

(i) **About AD 60**: This is the date accepted by orthodox Roman Catholicism, and assumed by early Christian writers such as Eusebius and Jerome. The proponents of this view argue that it must have been written before Luke knew the outcome of Paul's trial – otherwise Luke would not have failed to recount details of the trial. They point out that if the book was written much later, after **AD 70**, one would have expected to find mention of the martyrdom of James in **AD 62**, the martyrdom of Peter and Paul, and of the destruction of Jerusalem and the Temple in **AD 70**. The historical setting of Acts, so it is argued, also suggests an early date. The Roman authorities, for example, are often sympathetic, occasionally protective towards Christians, and that is hardly likely to have continued after the persecution under Nero in **AD 64**, of which there is no mention in Acts. Similarly the fact that Jewish leaders are heading the prosecution of Paul in Rome, suggests that the Jewish nation has not yet experienced the devastation that befell them at the hands of the Romans in the fall of Jerusalem.

Two further features suggest an early date. Firstly the language of Acts – Christ is not yet used as a proper name for Jesus (Luke records Paul speaking of Jesus as 'the Christ'), Sunday is still the first day of the week and not yet 'the Lord's day', and Christians are still referred to as 'disciples', a word which does not appear in Paul's letters. Secondly there is no reference or hint of Paul's many letters, whereas it is thought that these had been collected and edited in about **AD 90** and should have been known to Luke some time before.

The arguments in favour of an early date appear very persuasive. The difficulty is that Luke's Gospel and Acts are undeniably two volumes of the same work, and academic opinion has concluded that Acts had to be written after Luke's Gospel. The latter, however, is thought by many to have been written after the fall of Jerusalem in **AD 70**. The basis of this thesis is that both Matthew and Mark appear to prophesy the destruction of Jerusalem as foretold in Daniel, but Luke appears to tell the same story as if it has already happened. Suggestions have been put forward that Luke uses different phraseology from Matthew and Mark because he was writing for Gentile readers who would not understand the reference to the prophecy of Daniel, and that it is reading too much into his account to conclude that he is writing of something that has already occurred.

(ii) **AD 75–90**: this is the dating which attracts the most widespread support. The proponents of this view claim that Luke's Gospel, both because its author uses Mark as a source, and because of the writer's apparent knowledge of the fall of Jerusalem, cannot be earlier than **AD 70**, and is likely to be some time later. As Acts is thought to have been written after Luke, Acts must have been written after about **AD 75**.

(iii) **AD 90–100**: arguments in support of this later date include the prevalence of the doctrine of the Holy Spirit in both Luke and Acts; the 'punishment miracles' which are not to be found in Matthew or Mark (in Luke, Zechariah is struck dumb; in Acts, Ananias, Sapphira, Elymas and Herod also are subject to punishments); the controversy over Jewish law is no longer a live issue in Luke and Acts; the Church appears to have developed a degree of organisation, with elders being appointed, deacons gaining status, the Church possessing its own funds, and baptism becoming a central part of Church membership. In Luke and Acts there are also references to speaking in foreign tongues (a later development than speaking in tongues), and to sects emerging within the Church teaching corrupt doctrines. In Acts, the author writes as if the missionary work in Greece had already been successful, and portrays Paul as a hero of legendary proportions, both of which suggest that the book was written later.

(iv) **After AD 100**: the proponents of this view claim that in several passages Acts relies upon extracts from Josephus's Jewish Antiquities. One passage is the speech of Gamaliel in the Sanhedrin in which he exhorts the Sanhedrin not to judge too hastily whether the Christian message was genuine and refers to Judas, who had earlier claimed to speak from God but whose movement had failed. The account in Luke is chronologically wholly wrong and, so it is claimed, based upon a misreading of Josephus, as Luke is invariably historically accurate. If Luke had indeed read Josephus's Jewish Antiquities, then a date after **AD 94** appears to follow, but whether he had remains an open question – the evidence is by no means conclusive.

Sources

Acts divides very clearly into two halves. The first fifteen chapters recount experiences of some of the Apostles, most notably Peter, in the days after Pentecost, whereas the second half is concerned almost entirely with Paul. When he came to write the first section, Luke would have had available to him Mark and Q, his own recollections of his travels with Paul in Palestine and oral traditions of the different Christian communities that he encountered. Some commentators have argued that there are a number of written sources behind Acts. Harnack, for example, claimed that Acts 5 and 6 contain a series of doublets, including two accounts of the coming of the Spirit, and two accounts of the arrest of the disciples, and claimed to identify four different sources.

The second half of Acts appears very different. In a number of passages, which have been called the 'we sections', the author writes in the first person. The significance of this has long been a hotly debated academic issue. One hypothesis is that these sections are taken from a travel diary and represent those parts of the Gospel in which Luke was himself a participant in the events that he is describing. Another theory is that the extracts are taken from someone else's diary, but is it likely that Luke would have retained the first person narrative? A third theory is that the first person was retained to make the text appear more of an eyewitness account. However, that suggestion faces one major objection – why do the 'we sections' form such a small proportion of the overall texts? Had the author been seeking to deceive, one would have expected that the first person would have been more prevalent. It is almost certainly the case that the 'we sections' are penned by the same author as the rest of Acts – the language alone points fairly conclusively to this: there are twenty one words and phrases found only in the 'we sections' and the rest of Acts, but nowhere else in the New Testament. It has been forcefully argued by some commentators that the use of 'we', far from being evidence of another source, is nothing more than the author indicating that he was present on these occasions.

Both Luke and Acts are each to be found in two different texts. That which is generally acknowledged to be the earlier text, the Alexandrian text as it is known, is the shortest. The later Western text includes a number of additions to the early version which essentially provide greater detail and more vivid and dramatic descriptions of the events recounted in Acts.

The historical accuracy of Acts

It is generally accepted that in the details he recounts, Luke is almost invariably correct. He employs the correct nomenclature for the various offical posts within the Roman Empire. Despite the fact that in some cases the offical titles varied from region to region, and even over time, he uses the correct terms for the time and the places about which he is writing. Luke has sufficient knowledge of current affairs to correctly set his work within the current political framework – for example, the information that he records about Herod Agrippa I and Herod Agrippa II, the Roman procurators Felix and Festus, and the priests of Zeus in Lystra, can all be authenticated by other sources.

It is clear, however, that the task which Luke set himself was not to compile a chronological history based on attention to fine detail, but a living account of the important events in the early history of the Church, the significance of which he explains and interprets.

Luke has undoubtedly omitted much that might have been included in Acts. Thus it is clear from Paul's letters, most notably II Corinthians, that much of the tribulations suffered by Paul do not feature in Acts at all. These omissions were no doubt in part forced upon Luke by the need to be selective about what he included, and of course he was not in any case seeking to write a biography of Paul, but rather to demonstrate the expansion of the Church.

A more important concern is not Luke's omissions but the alleged inconsistencies within Acts, and between accounts there and the accounts of apparently identical incidents in the Pauline letters. The most important are:

(i) **The story of Paul's conversion on the road to Damascas**. In fact there are three accounts of this in Acts alone which are all slightly different from each other. The most notable difference is the means by which Paul receives his mission – in one account it is passed to him by Ananias, in another in the form of a vision whilst praying in the Temple in Jerusalem, and in a third from Christ himself whilst on the road to Damascas.

(ii) **Events after Paul's conversion**. There are several discrepancies between Acts and the account in Galatians. For example, Acts records Paul staying in Damascus for 'many days', whereas in Galatians 1: 18 Paul is said to have stayed there three years. Elsewhere Acts portrays Paul as preaching in Jerusalem, but the writer of Galatians states that he was not known by sight in Jerusalem.

(iii) **The Council of Jerusalem**. An immense amount of academic debate continues over the connections between what many say are two different accounts in Galatians 2 and Acts 15 of the same event – the Council of Jerusalem called to determine the applicability of Jewish law to Gentile converts. Both accounts involve Paul and Barnabas, Peter and James, and journeys between Antioch and Jerusalem. Further, in both accounts there is a fierce debate, with former Pharisees demanding the submission of Gentiles to circumcision which results in the defeat of the Judaising party, so easing the lot of Gentiles accepting the Gospel.

It is easy to overemphasise the similarities between these two accounts. There is no doubt that the debate over the applicability of Jewish law to Gentiles raged for some time, and it would not be surprising if there had been more than one discussion or meeting on this subject before the matter was finally resolved. If that were the case, then it would have been more than possible that the discussions would have involved the same participants and the same issues. Indeed there are discrepancies between the two accounts which suggest that they do relate to different occasions. Thus Galatians 2 records that the debate took place in private, whereas Acts 15 refers to a large-scale public debate. Similarly the result of the meeting recorded in Galatians is far less detailed than the agreement which emerged from the debate recounted in Acts. Of significance also, is that after the meeting recorded in Galatians, Peter visits Antioch where he meets with Gentiles, but on the arrival of disciples sent by James is persuaded to reject fellowship with the Gentiles. This amounts to an incredible divergence from the account in Acts. In Acts, James is clearly in favour of relaxing the requirements on Christian Gentiles; and yet, in Galatians, apparently so soon after the conclusions reached in the Council, he has performed a complete about-turn, and persuades Peter and, indeed, Barnabas to reject the Council's deliberations.

The two accounts make much more sense, and fit more easily together, if they are understood as recounting two different occasions. Acts 11: 28 also describes a visit by Paul to Jerusalem with famine relief. It is perfectly possible – indeed likely – that the issue of Gentile obedience to Judaic law was discussed with the leaders of the Church in Jerusalem on that occasion, and more than possible that an informal solution was reached. Later the whole debate flared up again and it was resolved that a more formal and open discussion should take place in an attempt to reach a long-term solution. Hence it is only in Acts 15 that one finds the detailed regulations agreed upon. On this scenario, Acts must post-date the letter to the Galatians.

A number of biblical scholars argue that the picture presented by the author of Acts is so radically different from that contained in the Pauline letters that he could not have known Paul at all. These critics emphasise a number of features of Acts, including a different theological emphasis, but in particular:

(i)   That Luke states that the end of the Law is God's will, whereas Paul rejects the Law because he believes that it causes men to sin: in coming to rely on the Law, men learn to trust in their own righteousness and not in God.

(ii) In Acts, Paul performs miracles and is a brilliant orator. In the Pauline letters there is no mention of miracles and in II Corinthians 10: 10 it is alleged against Paul that he has no power of speaking.

Opponents of this viewpoint claim that its supporters are asking too much of the New Testament authors; they point to the fact that in his letters, Paul is writing with a limited purpose in mind and, further, that even within his own scripts Paul is guilty of inconsistency.

4.5　The thought of Paul

In his letters to the early Christian communities, Paul is not seeking to record his thoughts in any systematic manner; rather his writings are a response to situations which developed within the Church, and which he considered needed his urgent attention. In all there are thirteen letters which claim Paul as their author. In fact, however, it is unlikely that he wrote all thirteen. In Paul's era it was not uncommon for disciples to write in the name of their teacher in an effort to spread his teachings, or by way of homage to him. Whilst it is universally acknowledged that Paul was the author of the letters to the Romans, the Corinthians and the Galatians, and it is generally agreed that he probably wrote the letter to the Philippians and the first letter to the Thessalonians, the letters of Titus and Timothy are thought not to have been Paul's. Of the remainder, their authorship is not so clear.

Paul was a Jew, brought up and educated in the Jewish tradition, and inevitably that played an important role in the formation of his ideas. The Jewish faith, alone among the religions of the ancient world, was monotheistic. The central pillar of Judaism was the one and only God, a benign being who created the world and human kind, and who intervened in the world to bring about his own purposes.

The Jews, of course, claimed this God as their God, the God of Israel, with whom they had a special covenant – Israel was God's chosen people. It was to the Jewish people, in the person of Moses on Sinai, to whom this God had revealed his Law. This Law, whilst it contained rules of righteousness applicable to all people, was a Law known only to the nation of Israel. The Jews saw themselves as central to the unfolding of God's purposes for the world, and combined a high notion of morality with a sense of national assertiveness.

At the time of Paul, considerable efforts were being made to proselytise, to convert others into believing in monotheism, in a moral code and to make them part of God's chosen people. The missionaries did have some success and Gentiles were submitting themselves to Jewish Law. At the same time, however, many Jews, despite their knowledge of God's Law, chose to flout it. Offenders were chastised by the Rabbis, but the Jewish community was loathe to accept that any of their number could be rejected by their God. For Paul such a view lacked credibility, for not only was God the God of the Gentiles as well as the Jews, but he showed no favouritism between Jew and Gentile:

All who sin apart from the law will also perish, and all who sin under the law will be judged by the law. For it is not those who hear the law who will be declared righteous. Indeed, when Gentiles who do not have the law, do by nature things required of the law, they are a law for themselves, even though they do not have the law, since they show that the requirements of the law are written in their hearts.

Romans 2: 12–16

Whilst Paul acknowledges that there are both good Jews who obey God's law, and good Gentiles who act in accordance with its requirements, he warns that all men are subject to sin:

For I have the desire to do what is good, but I cannot carry it out. For what I do is not the good I want to do; no, the evil I do not want to do – this I keep on doing. Now if I do what I do not want to do, it is no longer I who do it, but it is sin living in me that does it.

Romans 7: 19–20

In Romans, Paul describes in detail the universal inner moral struggle which besets any righteous adherent to a higher moral code. The fact that Man is so subject to sinful and base desires is for Paul not only indicative of the gulf between Man and God, but only serves to emphasise Man's need for communion with the Almighty, his sole source of salvation. Given human weakness, reconciliation with God could only be achieved by a fresh intervention, a fresh initiative from God, namely the sending of Christ, an act which Paul describes as the 'Grace of God'. For Paul, Christ represents salvation for the world. What Paul meant by salvation, and how he saw Christ as God's gift to humanity contributed greatly to the development of Christian doctrine.

Paul speaks of Man being justified, redeemed and expiated in Christ. Justified because, Paul explained, before God all are sinners, all men are guilty, but God 'acquits' the guilty, who are thus relieved of their guilt; redeemed because Man is liberated from the slavery in which he is unable to do that which he wishes to do. Christ's life on earth, his suffering and death, are the price paid by God for the emancipation of Mankind: 'It is for freedom that Christ has set us free' (Galatians 5: 1). Lastly Christ represented a sacrifice. Sin brings with it not only guilt and impotence, but also a sense of shame and self-disgust. In ancient religions, sacrifice was perhaps the most favoured remedy of all to wipe away such defilement. The rituals of sacrifice to achieve expiation, practised in the religions of the Greeks, and by the Jews in the Temple at Jersualem, were familiar to Paul's contemporaries:

God presented himself as an atonement, through faith in his blood.

Whilst describing Christ as a sacrifice, Christ is clearly not a sacrifice to placate God's anger, for it is God also who suffers by this sacrifice. By Christ's self-sacrifice, God brings about a cleansing of the world.

Paul sees Christ's life on earth, his death and resurrection as a fulfilment of God's purpose and of the promises made to the Jewish people that he would send a Messiah. This is what the followers of Jesus were claiming, and after his conversion Paul embraced this claim with enthusiasm. The Messiah was not, however, the Messiah which dominated Jewish expectations – someone who would free the Jewish people by victory over the nations oppressing them. Rather the Messiah brings victory over the spiritual forces of evil, and the overcoming of the forces of sin which frustrate our good intentions.

Christ himself wrestled with these dark forces, but ultimately in his resurrection Christ was victorious, even over death, which Paul describes as the last enemy.

Paul's understanding of Jesus and his life originated from his encounters with the Christian communities which had grown up. At Paul's conversion it was Jesus who appeared to Paul, who chose him as his instrument to carry his name before the Gentiles, but it was in the early Church that Paul learned of the teaching of Jesus. This community of God's people Paul saw as the fulfilment of the promise made to Abraham that in time: 'All nations will be blessed through you' (Galatians 3: 8). In Galatians 3: 2, Paul writes: 'If you belong to Christ, then you are of Abraham's seed, and heirs according to the promise'. To Paul, the growing Christian Church was the true Israel or people of God, in whom all people would find salvation, and his missions to the Gentiles the consummation of God's purpose for the history of Mankind.

To belong to the new Israel required acceptance of Christ, no more, no less: 'There is neither Jew nor Gentile, slave nor free, male nor female, for you are all one in Christ Jesus' (Galatians 3: 28). Time and time again Paul refers to being 'in Christ', a doctrine which Paul develops and expands, but which was already present in the early Church practice of baptism and the breaking of bread. It was in baptism that the Christian community welcomed new believers, and for Paul the cleaning and renewal which this represented were a symbolic parallel to Christ's death and resurrection: 'We were buried with him through baptism into death in order that, just as Christ was raised from the dead, we too may live a new life' (Romans 6: 4).

Paul builds on and develops the ideas current in Jewish thought of Adam as representing all people, and of mankind being subjected to the same trials as Adam. Paul explains that just as mankind is in a sense incorporated in Adam, so the followers of Christ are incorporated in him. In contrast to Adam, however, Christ the Messiah brings life. To Paul, all men are saved by Christ's death but, in dying Christ intended men to live not for themselves, but in and for him. By following Christ, man choses to put aside his self in favour of a new different life:

> ... *count yourselves dead to sin but alive to God in Christ Jesus. Therefore do not let sin reign in your mortal body so that you obey its evil desires. Do not offer the parts of your body in sin ... but rather offer yourselves to God, as those who have been brought from death to life; and offer the parts of your body to him as instruments of righteousness. For sin shall not be your master, because you are not under law, but under grace.*
>
> Romans 6: 12–14

> *I have been crucified with Christ and I no longer live, but Christ lives in me.*
> Galatians 2: 20

To Paul, life in Christ was a deep personal experience.

As a result of Paul's efforts, the emerging Church grew rapidly in the early years, both in terms of numbers and geographically. Paul was welcomed with keen excitement as he took his mission to the many towns and cities of the Greek world. Greek society, however, was extremely individualistic. Rivalry and jealousies soon grew up, thereby threatening the unity of the infant Church. To Paul, the unity of the Church was essential. He feared that the Christian communities would follow in the steps of the ancient Greek city states which had been so beset by factionalism.

One major difficulty was the persistence by many in retaining rituals and ideas from their Jewish or pagan past, resulting in diversity and confusion. This problem was made all the worse by the fact that the Church had no doctrinal code of beliefs, thereby leaving the Church exposed to dangers from those who wished to misinterpret or distort Christ's message and teachings. It was in response to these threats that Paul developed his own doctrine, presenting the Church as a living body in which all the separate parts depend on and are subordinate to each other:

> *Now the body is not made up of one part but of many. If the foot should say, 'Because I am not a hand, I do not belong to the body,' it would not for that reason cease to be part of the body.*
>
> I Corinthians 12: 14

Paul presents the Church as the body of Christ in which Christ is working through each individual, using their talents and efforts for his purposes. For unity to be maintained, the members of the body must accept each other as manifestations of Christ working – individuals must avoid the temptation of claiming credit for their sucesses or qualities:

> *... those parts of the body that seem to be weaker are indispensable, and the parts which we think are less honourable we treat with special honour... God has combined the members of the body and has given greater honour to the parts that lacked it, so that there should be no division in the body but that its parts should have equal concern with it ...*
>
> I Corinthians 12

In developing his doctrine of the Spirit, Paul provided himself with a useful tool to counter the tendency towards individualism and factionalism. After the resurrection, Jesus' followers, believing that Christ had risen from the dead to a new life, were gripped by excitement and expectation and there were many instances of visions, hearing of voices, speaking in tongues etc. These occurrences were seen as manifestations of God speaking to men through his Spirit and a realisation of the Jewish messianic expectation that with the coming of the Messiah, God would pour out his Spirit.

This excitement and enthusiasm within the early Church was in one sense to be expected but, on the other hand, it presented dangers. Not all coinage is genuine, and counterfeit coinage can closely resemble the genuine. Paul exhorts in I

Thessalonians 4: 19: 'Do not put out the Spirit's fire; do not treat prophecies with contempt' but adds 'Test everything, hold on to what is good. Avoid any kind of evil'.

He used his doctrine of the Spirit to humble those who might take pride in the most ostentatious of the gifts of the Spirit. In Romans 11: 3 Paul states:

> *For by the grace given me I say to every one of you: Do not think of yourselves more highly than you ought, but think of yourselves with sober judgment in accordance with the measures of faith God has given you. Just as each of us has one body with many members, and these members do not all have the same functions, so in Christ we who are many form one body and each member belongs to all the others. We have different gifts according to the Grace given us. If a man's gift is prophesying, let him use it in proportion to his faith. If it is serving, let him serve; if it is teaching, let him teach; if it is encouraging, let him encourage; if it is contributing to the needs of others, let him give generously ...*

Paul points out that all qualities possessed by the individual members of the Christian community are gifts. That being the case, it was not appropriate for individuals to claim credit. Indeed a member's qualities were not his own at all, but belonged to the Church as the body of Christ, and any gifts received to help build up that body were gifts from Christ to his Church – they were manifestations of Christ working in his followers. The Spirit is not therefore some form of magic simply to impress non-believers, but the way in which Christ revealed himself to the Church and participated in it, in accordance with his purposes.

A crucial element of Paul's theology was that in Christ, men and women are set free from slavery to the law, because Christ had abolished the rules and regulations of the law. This was a message which proved to be readily misunderstood. Many Jewish Christians feared that this teaching left the converts from the Gentile world without any moral framework. Indeed, many early Christians took Paul to be speaking of an unrestricted freedom in which men were free to give in to their baser desires. Paul warned against such excesses: 'You, my brothers, were called to be free. But do not use your freedom to indulge the sinful nature; rather serve one another in love' (Galatians 5: 13).

In addressing the problem, Paul stood firm to his conviction that the law, the old covenant between the Jewish people and their God, in which detailed rules for life were laid down, had been superseded. The Christian life was not to be led from compliance with a written code, but by means of the Spirit acting within. In Romans 12: 2 Paul writes:

> *Do not conform any longer to the pattern of this world, but be transformed by the renewing of your mind.*

Christians were, not surprisingly, asking how they could recognise which feelings originated from the Holy Spirit and which from their own nature. Paul explains that the Christ who was living in them, was the same Jesus who had lived, and that Christians were able to test their feelings against what they knew of Christ from their knowledge of his teaching and Gospel. Christians should let their minds be reshaped by Christ, a process which continued throughout one's life. In Ephesians 4: 13 Paul speaks of the body of Christ being built up 'until we all reach unity in the faith and in the knowledge of the Son of God and become mature, attaining to the whole measure of the fullness of Christ'.

The law of the Old Testament is thus superseded by the law of Christ, that is his Spirit working in and through his Church. Knowledge of Christ is derived from his teachings, his example and his death and resurrection, and it permeates Paul's writing and ideas. Paul urges his readers to think of others, to accept others without passing judgement and to understand that because Christ died, they all belonged to the Lord.

In applying himself to ethical matters, Paul draws upon Christ's life, death and resurrection as his benchmark for describing what is 'Christlike'. He exhorts followers to mirror the gentleness of Christ, to learn from his willingness to forgive, to imitate his humility and obedience to God. For Paul, Christ's death was not only an ultimate sacrifice for others, but also the ultimate demonstration of his love for the world.

It is love, more than any other quality, that Paul identifies as fundamental to the Christian life, and which he so eloquently describes in that well-known passage in I Corinthians 13: Love is patient, kind, protecting, trusting, persevering, does not boast, keeps no record of wrongs – to mention only some of the aspects Paul speaks of. Without love, man is nothing.

'Love one another as Christ loved you' is the dominant theme in so much of Paul's writings, and it is love that is the means for the building up of the Church. What love requires is not described by Paul in any detailed code for life, but when real problems presented themselves to the Christian communities he was quick to provide guidance. Sexual immorality, impurity, obscenity and greed are decidedly not Christlike (Ephesians 5: 3). Similarly neither are drunkeness, hatred, jealousy, idolatry, witchcraft and factionalism (Galatians 5: 19). It is abundantly apparent from Paul's letters that these were very real problems for the early Church, and Paul is adamant that Christians should turn their backs on such behaviour, not by withdrawing from the world, but by being an example to the world.

As to marriage, Paul quotes Jesus himself as forbidding separation and divorce. Paul speaks of mutuality between husband and wife: 'The wife's body does not belong to her alone, but also to her husband. In the same way, the husband's body does not belong to him alone but also to his wife' (I Corinthians 7: 4). Marriage is a central feature of the Christian community, and in Ephesians 5: 25–33 Paul exhorts husbands to love their wives as Christ loved the Church. The sanctity of the bond of marriage is so strong that a pagan spouse belongs to God by reason of his or her marriage to a Christian partner.

As to slavery, Paul writes, in Colossians 3: 11 and elsewhere, that in Christ there is no slave, nor free man. Rather: 'For he who was a slave when he was called by the Lord is the Lord's freedman; similarly, he who was a free man when he was called is Christ's slave' (I Corinthians 7: 22). Whilst in Christ all are equal, Paul is not seeking to challenge existing obligations within society, but advocating a changing of individuals' conceptions. Thus, in his letter to the Colossians, Paul calls upon slaves to obey their masters as if obeying Christ, but at the same time urges masters to be just and fair with their slaves in the knowledge that they too have a master in heaven.

At the beginning of his missionary activities Paul, like his fellow believers, lived with the expectation that Christ would return within his own lifetime (e.g. I Thessalonians 4: 15). In his later letters, Paul is somewhat less concerned with Christ's second coming, and instead concentrates far more on Christ's participation in his expanding Church. Whenever the second coming might materialise, God in the meantime was making his wisdom known through his Church (see Ephesians 3: 10).

The Church, which transcended barriers of language, race, nationality, social status and tradition, was unifying humanity. The unity of Jew and Gentile within the growing Church was a microcosm of the unity which God intended for the world, and which he was going to realise through his Church. The Church was to be God's instrument, not only for reconciliation between peoples, but also between them and their Creator.

4.6   The book of Revelation

Revelation is probably the most difficult to read of the New Testament books, consisting of descriptions of successive visions in language with which modern-day Christians are unfamiliar. In contrast, the evidence suggests that Revelation had a wide circulation in the early Church, and in particular was well known to the early Church Fathers.

Authorship

The author calls himself John, and early tradition has it that he was John the Apostle. Such second and third century writers as Justin, Irenaeus, Clement, Origen and Tertullian all attributed Revelation to the Apostle John. None of these authors, however, explains how they came to accept or conclude this, and the later of them may merely be repeating the possibly erroneous views of their predecessors. One early writer, Dionysius, was the forerunner of many modern critics, disputing apostolic authorship on the basis of the glaring differences in the style and language between Revelation and the Gospel of John. In the Gospel there is no mention of the author's name, there are frequent discussions of such concepts as love, light and truth which do not feature in Revelation, and the Gospel is written in grammatical Greek whereas the Greek in Revelation is repeatedly inaccurate. On the latter point, however, many commentators maintain that the inaccuracies in the Greek are not the result of the author's lack of knowledge, but were quite deliberate. This conclusion is said to follow from the fact that Revelation contains a mixture of both incorrect and correct grammatical form, indicating that the author was fully conversant in Greek.

Aspects of the book itself do suggest that Revelation may have been penned by John the Apostle. The text starts with seven letters addressed to seven of the

Asiatic Churches. That the author writes to these Churches with such apparent authority, and in the name of John, would indicate that they at least probably understood these letters to have come from the Apostle John. The fact that John prophesies in his own name, when the practice was to attribute such prophecies to an ancient name in order to endow them with authority, also points to the author being someone of stature in the early Church. The whole tenor of the book is of the writer being inspired by God and bearing witness to a divine revelation.

The picture which one forms of the author of Revelation, in particular from the dramatic language he employs, is certainly consistent with the descriptions of John the Apostle in the Synoptic Gospels, in which John and James are described as 'the sons of thunder' and painted as prone to expressions of righteous anger. On the other hand, however, this representation of John is not readily discernible in the Gospel of John.

Most theologians nevertheless acknowledge considerable links between Revelation and the Gospel and also the three Johannine letters, with many concluding that they share a common authorship without necessarily accepting that that author was John the Apostle. These five texts share similar ideas. Thus, for example, both the Gospel and Revelation speak of Jesus as the 'Logos', and depict him as the Shepherd, and both describe Christ as the 'lamb'. These two books share also the frequent contrasting of opposites, in particular light and dark, truth and falsehood, the power of God and the power of men. One further characteristic common to the Johannine texts, and not found elsewhere in the New Testament, is the repeated symbolic reference to the number seven – as in the Gospel's seven signs and the seven-day account of the passion story, to mention but two examples.

A considerable number of biblical scholars remain unconvinced and decline to accept the traditional view as to the authorship of Revelation. A major obstacle for many is the irregularity of much of the Greek employed with broken sentences, incorrect genders, wrongly used participles, and odd grammatical constructions all at complete variance with the Gospel. A number of theories have been advanced to explain this discrepancy. One solution advanced is that the author's fluency in Greek had improved in the interval between writing the two books, a theory obviously rejected by those who consider that the inaccuracies in the Greek of Revelation are not accidental. Another suggestion was that Revelation was written in a form of entranced state and the author was accordingly unwilling to refine what he had produced. A third hypothesis is that when writing the Gospel, the author had the assistance of someone better versed in Greek but that Revelation was his own work.

Revelation itself is not without arguable pointers against apostolic authorship. The author himself lays no claim to this, but equally this is not surprising if he expected his readers to understand that the John he refers to is indeed John the Apostle. There are no references in this book to the incidents involving John in the Gospel, or any suggestion that the author had known Christ prior to his death. On the other hand, Revelation is about prophecy and the future, and this omission must surely carry little weight, if any, in this debate.

Contrast is also made by some between the emphasis on God's creatorship and power in Revelation and the emphasis on love in the Gospel and First Epistle. It is, however, somewhat of a large step to conclude from these differences that Revelation was written by a different author. Revelation is clearly intended to be a different type of work, and the divine anger portrayed is one that is in conflict with the forces of evil. A similar contrast can be seen between the victorious Messiah who rules over nations and the gentleness of Christ portrayed in the Gospel. Again it is essential to grasp the different purpose of the two texts, and indeed to note that even in Revelation, Christ is described as the Lamb of God, and the description of Logos is found in both the Gospel and Revelation. The reference to seven spirits in Revelation 1: 4 is perhaps difficult to understand – the repeated tendency to the symbolic use of that number is not a very convincing explanation given the importance of the Holy Spirit in John's Gospel, above all others.

As is apparent, there is evidence for and against the apostolic authorship of Revelation, and it is impossible to reach a firm conclusion either way. What of alternative authors? Papias (about **AD 70–145**) refers to a John the Elder. This was traditionally interpreted to be a reference to John the Apostle. However that is by no means clear, and it is argued by some scholars that this is in fact a reference to another writer who was the real author of Revelation. Supporters of this hypothesis point to Dionysius' reference to a second John who lived at Ephesus, but the only authority that he quotes in favour of what is in any event a somewhat tentative suggestion is a report from a traveller. Moreover, if Revelation was indeed the work of a second John and if indeed they both lived at Ephesus, the author would have known that by referring to himself merely as 'John', confusion as to the true authorship was likely to abound. The possibility that Revelation could have been incorrectly attributed so soon after being written does appear rather unlikely. On the other hand, had there been only one John living at Ephesus and had he been the true author, it is perhaps easier to understand why the early Church assumed that the author was the Apostle John and concluded, again erroneously, that the Apostle lived at Ephesus. There are no other obvious candidates for the authorship of Revelation. A number of earlier scholars suggested that John might be a pseudonym, but it would have been difficult to have succeeded in such a design, both during the Apostle's life, and indeed after his death, given the absence of an explanation as to why the work remained unknown in his lifetime.

Sources

As to the author's sources, he has clearly drawn considerably on the Old Testament, most particularly the books of Daniel and Ezekiel, in relation to the apocalyptic revelations, as well as many other parts of the Old Testament. Indeed, whilst there are very few direct quotes, the author is so immersed in the concepts of the Old Testament that less than a third of the 404 verses in Revelation are without any reflection of this earlier scripture. It has been claimed by some that so seemingly unconscious is the author's use of the Old Testament that it is as if the work was compiled under the inspiration of the Holy Spirit.

A good number of academics have argued that the Jewish apocalypses are a more likely source than the Old Testament. Whilst they do bear certain similarities with Revelation, there are major differences. The author of Revelation writes in his own name, not that of a pseudonym; he does not seek to appear to predict events which are in fact past to bolster confidence in his predictions about the future; and his work has more in common with the Old Testament writers on issues of morality.

Dating

Academic opinion tends to favour the period **AD 90–95** during the reign of the Emperor Domitian for the dating of Revelation. The preference for this date is not based upon any particularly convincing piece of evidence, but rather on a number of vague indications which, it is argued, point in the approximate direction of this period. Revelation clearly portrays a picture of a struggle between the Church and secular rulers, with the secular powers, by which is meant the Roman Empire, portrayed in the form of a beast who demands universal worship. This is a reference to the cult of Emperor worship, which is said to have arisen as early as Julius Caesar, but which had its greatest growth in the era from Nero to Domitian. Even in these years, not all the Emperors were particularly enthusiastic to develop this cult but some, in particular Domitian, introduced stringent measures to enforce it.

It was inevitable that Emperor worship would encounter resistance from Christianity, but the difficulty is determining the point at which such conflict reached the level which prompted the author of Revelation to express himself in the way he did. The answer is impossible to deterine, save to say that the information detailed would have been available to the author as early as the reign of Nero, and accordingly the book could date from any time between **AD 64** and the reign of Domitian, a considerable time range. A second pointer is the era of persecution which had either just begun or is anticipated. A major difficulty here, however, is that persecutions of Christians broke out from time to time on a local basis even outside those periods which witnessed more widespread and organised persecution. Indeed, on examination, all the references to persecution seem more likely to relate to either local incidents or outbreaks. As to the various references to Rome being drunk with the blood of the saints, these occur in visions and so they too do not assist in the dating of this book.

Whilst most scholars remain persuaded that the persecution described and foretold in Revelation points to the reign of Domitian as the most likely period in which the book was penned, the evidence is far from overwhelming. Indeed there is very little detailed evidence about the Domitian persecutions at all, and no firm evidence that such persecution extended beyond Rome itself.

The details of the seven Asiatic Churches contained in 2: 1 – 3: 22 are said to point to a Domitianic date. Some of the Churches (Ephesus, Sardis, Laodicea) are suffering from decline and this it is argued indicates a considerable interval between Revelation and the founding of these Churches. Again this argument contains little or no merit. Churches can flourish for decades before decay sets in, but equally they may decline much more quickly.

One further argument advanced in favour of the period **AD 80–85** is the many parallels that are said to exist with the Gospels of Matthew and Luke. The merit of this point is again open to attack, given the uncertainty about the dating of Matthew and Luke, and the fact that the parallels are capable of being explained by oral tradition.

The arguments for an earlier date, however, are not surprisingly also inconclusive. One such date that has been advanced is during or after the reign of Nero. Revelation 17: 10 is said to contain a reference to the sixth reigning Roman Emperor. Assuming that one starts from Augustus, the first to be proclaimed Emperor, Nero would be the fifth Emperor, and Revelation, so it is argued, came to be written in the years immediately after his death. A second theory in support of a Neronian date is the significance of the number 666. Numerous attempts were made to decipher what was thought to be some form of symbol, but it was not until the nineteenth century that one scholar calculated it on the basis of the Hebrew enumeration of the Hebrew transcription of the name Nero Caesar. Such an interpretation is somewhat puzzling – Revelation was written in Greek (although some scholars have argued that it was translated from the Aramaic), and the author would hardly expect the members of the Asiatic churches to comprehend such Hebrew symbolism. A further pointer towards a date around the reign of Nero is the absence of any reference to the fall of Jerusalem in **AD 70**, which would be difficult to imagine in a book about prophecy and judgement whose author was himself from Jewish roots.

The author's purpose

The first three chapters containing the letters to the seven Asiatic churches are clearly designed with the specific needs of those particular Christian communities in mind. The writer expresses the Lord's approval or condemnation on the various ways in which the Churches have developed. There is criticism of spiritual decline, of the incidence of immorality and of willingness to listen to false prophets, but there is also a call to repent accompanied by words of encouragement.

From chapter 4 onwards, these themes are of more general application, and one cannot resist the conviction that the text is meant for a wider audience. Indeed it is clear from early Christian writings that Revelation had an extensive circulation. The book becomes dominated by the recurring theme of the struggle between the infant Church and the mighty Roman Empire. This theme is not expounded by means of a structured text but rather by series of collections of visions each describing similar kinds of occurrences but in different ways. One scholar, Moffat, has spoken of a 'kaleidoscope of visions'. The imagery is frequently terrifying and vivid, the author painting a horrendous picture of the fate of those who assist the forces of evil. It is not until near the end of the book that the evil forces of the state and of Satan are finally vanquished.

Revelation, in brief, is both a message of hope and of ultimate victory for the Church in the troubled times to come, and a warning both of the warfare ahead and of the Day of Judgement.

Bibliography

C.K. Barrett, *Essays on Paul*, SPCK, London (1982)
C.K. Barrett, *The New Testament Background: Selected Documents*, SPCK, London (1996)
Leonhard Goppelt, *Theology of the New Testament*, Eerdmans Publishing Company, Grand Rapids, MI (1981)

Donald Guthrie, *New Testament Introduction*, Inter-Varsity Press, Leicester (1975)

H.A. Guy, *The Synoptic Gospels*, Nelson, London (1960)

Howard Clark Lee, *Understanding the New Testament*, Prentice Hall, Hemel Hempsteod (1983)

John Marsh, *The Gospel of St John*, Pelican, London (1968)

John Metcalfe, *Saint Mark*, John Metcalfe Publishing Trust (1996)

Bruce M. Metzyer, *The Canon of the New Testament: Its Origin, Development and Significance*, Clarendon Press, Oxford (1987)

Jerome Murphy-O'Connor, *Paul – A Critical Life*, OUP, Oxford (1996)

D.E. Nineham, *Mark*, Pelican, London (1992)

H. Ridderbos, *Paul: An Outline of His Theology*, SPCK, London (1977)

Christopher Rowland, *Christian Origins*, SPCK, London (1985)

E.P. Sanders, *Paul, the Law and the Jewish People*, Fortress Press, Philadelphia (1983)

E.P. Sanders and Margaret Davies, *Studying the Synoptic Gospels*, SCM, London (1989)

R.L. Wilken, *Judaism and the Early Christian Mind*, Yale University Press, New Haven, CT (1971)

A.N. Wilson, *Paul – The Mind of the Apostle*, Sinclair Stevenson, London (1997)

▓ ⊻ 5 The history of the Church: the early Church to AD 500

The study of the history of the Church is essential not only for an understanding of how Christianity came to have such a profound influence on the development of the Western World, but also for the Church itself, as a means of learning from the mistakes and errors of the past. The history of the Church consists of its geographical growth through missionary activity, spreading far and wide; its growth into a mighty organisation; the development of doctrine through argument and debate, division and schism, and determinations by Church Councils; and lastly its effects on the lives of individuals and nations.

5.1 Early sources

Much of the first century is hidden in obscurity – the writers of the times hardly refer to the Christians, so unimportant were they. The main source of knowledge of the early Church is from the few Christian writings, notably the New Testament. Difficulties arise in establishing when and by whom these works were written. Some New Testament documents were originally anonymous, and others were probably not written by the people whose names they bear – this applies for example to the Pastoral Letters, the Johannine Letters, the Petrine Letters, and James and Jude. Often we can only guess at the true authorship of a document. As to dating, none of the books of the New Testament state their dates of composition, and one can only hazard an estimate from reading their contents.

The Acts of the Apostles is one of the most important sources. Traditionally it was thought that Luke and Acts were written by Luke the Physician, although this is now questioned. The account in Acts indicates that the author's knowledge of the first days of the Church was patchy. Acts is essentially the writer's own description with the author telling a story. Whilst he must have used some sources, it is far from easy to isolate them. Acts is selective, and does not attempt to give a history of all the Apostles, but concentrates on two, Peter initially, and later Paul. Acts leaves many questions unanswered: What happened to the twelve? How did James come to be leader of the Church? Either the author did not know the answer to these questions or he chose not to include them. If Luke was writing towards the end of the first century, he would probably have had very limited information available to him. Christians at that time had little interest in recording the history of their faith – apart from anything else, the world was not expected to last long.

Luke's picture consists of relatively few incidents supplemented with general comment. He refers to 'many wonders and signs' (Acts 2: 43), but gives only one example – Peter healing the lame man. The conversion of first 5000 (Acts 2: 41) and later 3000 (Acts 4: 4) appears to have been grossly exaggerated – the total population of Jersualem at that time was no more than 30,000 and other evidence points against such a high proportion of Christians in the city. Luke's main theme is the expansion of the Church leading to the arrival of the Gospel in Rome. The picture is of a united and harmonious Church, with Jerusalem as its focal point. There is no reference to the delay in the Second Coming, and no discussion of the acrimonious debate over circumcision of the Gentiles or of the role of Jewish Law in Christianity.

Other Christian sources include the *Didache* or Teaching of the Twelve Apostles, *I Clement* and *Barnabas* (all first century works), seven letters of Ignatius of Antioch, the *Shepherd of Hermas* and *II Clement*. There is also a growing amount of material being discovered from the Christian 'underworld' originating from groups which were later to be regarded as heretical. In addition, correspondence between the Emperor Trajan and one of his Governors, Pliny, provides invaluable detail as to the position of Christians in the first years of the second century.

5.2 The Jewish background and the first Christians

The Jewish people were a race apart. They had a distinct sense of their own separateness and of their unity with fellow Jews. The first Christians were Jewish and they saw in Christ a continuation of the history of God's chosen people, not a break with their Jewish past. The mission of the early Christians was to persuade fellow Jews to acknowledge Christ as the fulfilment of the Old Testament, a 'new covenant' between God and Israel.

The Jewish people were spread throughout the Roman world, with large numbers living in most major towns and cities. It is estimated that there were about 5 million Jews living within the confines of the Empire outside Palestine, making up about 7 per cent of the total population. Not only were the Jews numerous but they had succeeded in attracting many Gentiles. Whilst circumcision was repugnant to most Gentiles, monotheism and the Jewish codes of moral conduct had considerable appeal. In contrast to the strict approach taken in Jerusalem, many of the Jewish emigrant communities were willing to embrace Gentile converts without requiring circumcision. For the first evangelists this meant that, in almost all towns and cities in which they sought to proselytise, there were religious groups familiar with the concept of one God and with codes of ethical conduct, and it was among these Gentiles that they made their first non-Jewish converts.

In the early years Christians made considerable headway in attracting fellow Jews, despite hostility from the Jewish establishment and their lack of attraction for the nationalist zealots planning the expulsion of the Romans. The Christians (called Nazarenes by the Jews) grew in numbers both in Jerusalem and in surrounding Judaea. The Church spread also among the Jews of Galilee and Damascas, and in Antioch the capital of Syria and the third most important city of the Roman Empire. This expansion caused great concern to the Jewish Establishment, resulting in the persecution of the early Christians. A central figure in that persecution was Saul of Tarsus, a Pharisee and fierce opponent of the Christians. Following his conversion Paul proved no less zealous, and was fired with a conviction of God's mission for him to preach the Gospel to the Gentile world, to ensure that Gentile converts adhered to the true faith and to bring about their acceptance by the Church in Jerusalem.

The mission to the Gentiles potentially faced serious obstacles arising out of the Jewish background and tradition of the early Church. Many adherents of the early Church were Pharisees anxious to preserve their Jewish religion from liberal assimilation to the surrounding Gentile world, and for a time the call to the Gentiles was a disputed matter. As to the Gentiles of the ancient world, they could make little sense of the contempt in which the Jews held any pagan cult, or their strict rules as to diet or their insistence on circumcision. Many Gentiles were converted, and the questions of whether they should comply with such laws and procedures of the Jewish Church were passionately argued controversies. Paul rejected the notion that non-Jewish believers should keep the Mosaic Law. The problem was debated at the Council of Jerusalem in **AD 49**, in which a compromise was reached. Paul successfully persuaded the Church not to require Gentile converts to undergo circumcision, but they were to be prohibited from eating food that had been sacrificed to pagan gods, and to accept the far stricter Jewish prohibitions on extra-marital sexual relations.

The expansion of the Church owed much to Paul – not only his success in the Council of Jerusalem, but also his ability to translate the Gospel into language which was intelligible to the Greek world.

Paul's rejection of the applicability of Mosaic Law to non-Jewish believers led many Gentile converts, unfamiliar with the strong moral code of the Orthodox Jewish family, to contend that freedom of the Spirit so emancipated them that they were free to behave as they pleased, most notably in sexual relations. Opposing groups argued that the life of the Spirit demanded rejection of marriage and sexual relations. The issue of sexual licentiousness at one extreme, and the rejection of marriage at the other, are two of the issues Paul addresses in his letters to the early Church.

In **AD 57** Paul was arrested in the Temple in Jerusalem and taken to Caesarea where he was detained for two years before being transported to Rome to stand trial. It appears that he was freed after about two years, when he returned to the areas where he had evangelised so effectively several years earlier. Paul was again in Rome prior to his execution in **AD 64** during the persecution under Nero.

Jerusalem remained the centre of the Church for only a short period. Jewish Christians left the city shortly before its downfall in **AD 70** and settled at Pella. Thereafter Jewish Christianity continued but failed to convert the Jewish people. In **135** Hadrian excluded all Jews from Judaea, and Jerusalem became a Greek city, thereby further distancing Christianity from its Jewish roots. In comparison to the growing number of Gentile Christians, the Jewish church was of little significance. The Jewish Christians faced hostility from the Jews, and little support and encouragement from Gentile converts who were critical of their continued observance of Jewish traditions and laws. Many Christian Gentiles came to interpret the Old Testament as the history of the Jewish people's perpetual failure to heed the prophets, and their rejection of Christ as a further demonstration of this.

5.3 The spread of Christianity and the encounter with the Roman world

To the south of Jerusalem Christianity spread to Egypt, and by the second century the Church was strong in Alexandria. To the north-east was the boundary of the Roman Empire and a language barrier. These proved difficult obstacles, and accordingly the main movement of Christianity was to the north and west. There were sizeable churches in several towns in Asia Minor and Syria. From there the mission extended into Thrace, northern Greece and Bulgaria. The church in Rome quickly took on significance, becoming the most important Christian city. It was not long before settlements grew up in Italy, southern France and Spain.

The spread of Christianity in the early years was greatly facilitated by the political, historical and social context in which the young Church found itself. The political unity of the Roman Empire and the relative peace had resulted in thriving commerce, with businessmen travelling all over the Roman world, many of them spreading the Christian message. The conquests of Alexander between 334 and 326 BC had spread the Greek language, providing an excellent medium for expressing theological ideas. The cosmopolitan nature of the Empire, with so many races, competing sects and rival faiths, meant that people were searching for certainty, and questioning their own traditional beliefs. The Empire was suffering from moral decline and its peoples were searching for hope.

Whilst Christ had been crucified by the Roman authorities, his death was seen as an act of the Jewish establishment, and the Romans as part of the Gentile world to be converted. The Empire facilitated the spread of Christianity which co-existed with the many different cults and mystery religions of the East. The Roman authorities tolerated them all unless they were seen to encourage revolt or weaken morality.

Unlike the adherents to the various cults, however, Christians stood out as people who would not conform to many norms of the time. They refused to have anything to do with idolatry and spoke out against the public games in which gladiator killed gladiator or where innocent captives were thrown to the lions to entertain the populace. They declined public office, and refused to carry out certain public duties such as the pouring of libations because this resembled pagan rites. The Christians came to be regarded as a sullen people, disliked by many.

Initially the Church benefited from the same tolerance extended towards others, until the great fire in Rome of 64. The unpopular emperor Nero was suspected of starting the fire himself and turned on the Christians as a scapegoat. His accusations fell on fertile ground, such was the universal hatred which they had by then engendered. Large numbers of Christians were slaughtered on the basis of their faith alone. Death was often but the final moment of a lengthy torture. Some of the early martyrs, fired by a conviction that a martyr's death guaranteed their place in the new kingdom, courted martyrdom by acts of provocation, such as destroying pagan images or showing contempt for the authorities under cross-examination.

It is likely that after this period the persecution continued intermittently but to a lesser degree. Under Domitian (81–96) it probably flared up again, in particular because the Christians were unable to demonstrate the exuberance required by the Emperor for the offering of divine honours to him. Trajan (**98–117**) did not favour such tests of loyalty and the position eased. Correspondence between Trajan and Pliny provides some detail of the early second century. When he became governor of Bithynia (south of the Black Sea) in **111**, Pliny found that the growing Christian communities had emptied the Temples and were making it difficult to sell the meat of sacrificial animals. Under pressure from local interests Christians were arrested. They were cross-examined, often under torture, to establish the nature of the enormities that it was thought they must practise; but although some Christians were executed and those who were Roman citizens incarcerated pending a trial in Rome, the authorities could find nothing to report. Pliny, unclear as to the nature of their crimes, wrote to Trajan seeking guidance. It is apparent from Trajan's reply that the Emperor did not regard the Christians as a threat. He advised the Governor that whilst Christians need not be sought out, those who were accused of Christianity could be tried and punished, but if found guilty they might be pardoned if they recanted.

Christianity remained a capital offence throughout the Empire, but the persecution was far from continuous or systematic. Whilst some governors actively pursued Christians, others protected the Church. The early persecutions, being both sporadic and local, did not slow down the growth of the Church. Indeed, if anything, they gave the Church notoriety and the time to grow and debate its own burning internal issues.

The second half of the second century saw renewed persecution under Emperor Marcus Aurelius (**161–180**). The Emperor had been instilled with prejudice against the Christians by his tutor Fronto. The walls of the Empire were being battered by barbarians in the East and at the Danube, he had a faithless wife and a profligate son. The Christians were a natural scapegoat for the source of public and private ills. There were outbreaks of terrible persecution in **177** at Lyon and Vienna. It started with the exclusion of Christians from places of public resort. Then the mob rioted and obtained a public examination of certain Christians. The Emperor ordered that those who recanted should be released. Of those who refused, the Romans were to be beheaded and the non-Romans thrown to the beasts. A notable heroine was Blandia, a female slave. Tortured for a whole day, her tormentors failed to extract a recantation. She was bound to the stake and exposed to the beasts, who refused to harm her. Eventually she was fastened in a net and gored to death by a bull.

Aurelius was succeeded by his son Commodus in **180**, and under his slack administration the persecutions slowly dwindled.

5.4   The life and organisation of the early Church

In I Corinthians 12, Paul lists in order of precedence the gifts of the early Christians: 'And in the Church God has appointed first of all apostles, second prophets, third teachers, then workers of miracles, also those having the gifts of administration and those speaking in different tongues'. The apostles, prophets and teachers were those engaged in missionary activity. However, the Churches established by these missionaries soon developed a number of offices of local clergy.

The office of elder is referred to in the New Testament by several other names, such as bishop, pastor, teacher, steward, preacher and minister. The term deacon had a distinct meaning – deacons were appointed to help in the administration and business of the Church to enable the elders to devote themselves to more spiritual and pastoral matters. Whilst the travelling missionaries co-existed with the local clergy for thirty years or so, within a generation or two there had been an almost complete transition from apostles and prophets to bishops, presbyters and deacons.

Christian life, including the organisation of the Church, was essentially simple. Formalism and pomp were absent, rather the worship was free and spontaneous.

An important text, which probably dates from the end of the first century, is the *Didache* or Teaching of the Twelve Apostles. This is almost a manual for communicants and clergy. It includes a description of examples of moral conduct which result in death or life. The work stresses the need to confess in church and exhorts its readers not to come to prayer 'in an evil conscience'. The book gives directions for the Eucharist and for baptism, permitting threefold aspersion where there is not enough water for immersion. The Eucharist is reserved for those who have been baptised. Detailed regulations govern the hospitality to be given to apostles and prophets: 'Let every apostle that cometh unto you be received as the Lord. And he shall stay one day, and if need be the next also, but if he stays three he is a false prophet. And when the apostle goes forth, let him take nothing save bread . . . but if he asks for money, he is a false prophet'. On the other hand, the author called upon ordinary Christians not to criticise what the prophets said 'in the Spirit' because the prophets were the people's high priests.

By the early second century, Christian communities had permanent pastors – chosen from among the presbyters or elders to preside over them. As to attire, they did not wear any special clothing, but by the third century some were wearing either black or white. One Christian writer of this period, Ignatius Bishop of Antioch, advocated obedience to the authority of the bishop, arguing that this was the best means of maintaining unity. He wrote to the Trallians: 'Respect the bishop as a type of God, and the presbyters as the council of God . . . '.

The bishop and his clergy represented a visible manifestation of the Christian community, and succession to these positions was a matter treated with some care. Whilst the people chose their bishop, the appointment needed the consent and the laying on of hands of the bishops from the neighbouring communities – three bishops were sufficient, although it was thought preferable for all the bishops of a province to attend. A bishop represented his church in the ordination of other bishops, usually carried out the baptisms, and gave out the bread and wine.

Christians aspired to a moral code unfamiliar to the peoples of the rough Roman Empire, and they were frequently misunderstood and denounced. Some of them defended their faith in writings known as 'Apologies'. Trained philosophers and rhetoricians, they sought to demonstrate that Christianity was the most intelligent and intelligible of all religions. The most significant of the early Apologists was Justin Martyr, a philosopher who converted to Christianity and who died a martyr in Rome in **163**. In his First Apology, addressed to the Emperor Antonius Pius, the Senate and the Roman people, Justin protests that the State had no right to punish except for proved crimes. He writes: 'You do not examine enough, but driven by unreasoning passion and scourge of evil demons you punish without investigation or consideration'. Justin answers the standard accusations levelled at the Christians – those of atheism, disloyalty, cannibalism, licentiousness and secret meetings. Justin attacks his enemies by asserting that Christians are simply putting a stop to the immoralities introduced into the world by the pagan gods.

Justin's works provide valuable insights into the life and worship of the early Christians, and the early development of doctrine. He explains how on a Sunday the brethren met together in one place, and would hear readings from the Gospels or from writings of the prophets; after which the president – simply one of the brethren chosen to preside – would give verbal instruction based on the readings. This was followed by prayer, the giving of thanks, and the sharing of bread, wine and water.

5.5   Internal crises: schism and heresies

In the course of the second century there developed many heretical sects, the most notably being:

(i) **The Nazarenes**: this sect grew out of the Jewish Christians who fled from Jerusalem shortly before its fall in **AD 70** to Pella. Unlike Jewish Christians elsewhere they held on to Jewish customs, observing the laws relating to circumcision and the detailed regulations for the observance of the Sabbath. This sect never had substantial influence but nevertheless continued to the early fifth century.

(ii) **The Ebonites**: this sect was determined to impose Jewish Law on all Christians, denounced the teachings of Paul, and accepted only the Gospel of Matthew which they rewrote to exclude any reference to the miraculous conception. They believed that Jesus was not divine – rather he became divine after his baptism when he received the Spirit which left him before his death, leaving a mere man to suffer on the Cross.

(iii) **The gnostics**: the influence of the gnostics was considerable. Gnosticism is a collective term used to describe various doctrines put forward by a dozen or so rival sects which split off from the Church between **AD 80** and **150**. By the early third century, gnosticism had invaded most communities throughout the Roman Empire to a greater or lesser extent. What is known of the gnostics, however, is primarily what is recorded in the attacks upon them by the orthodox Christian Fathers, rather than from their own writings. The gnostics believed that matter was inherently and permanently evil, and that salvation was achieved by overcoming and destroying matter. This could only be done by those who had knowledge or 'gnosis'. These were special people who were members of a 'spiritual class' and beneath whom were the 'psychic', consisting of prophets and other good Jews who were unable to reach beyond faith. There was then a third class, the 'hylic' consisting of the majority of mankind who were beyond help and irretrievably bonded to Satan and subject to their own lusts.

Gnostics resisted matter by rejecting even the most harmless of enjoyment lest they become contaminated. They practised a strict code of morals demanding an ascetic lifestyle with some even forbidding marriage, or prohibiting husband and wife from having sexual relations. This unnatural denial of human beings' deepest emotions proved too much for some, and some sects descended into sexual immorality, claiming to justify their conduct by pointing to Paul's teachings that in Christ a believer is set free from the law.

Gnostics taught that the Supreme Being is remote and unknowable, beyond time and change and without qualities. To explain how such an ineffable Being could create evil matter, they imagined a series of emanations from the Being. When one of these emanations was far away from the light around the centre of the Being, the Being created the world, but did so badly.

(iv) **Montanism**: this heresy developed in a period in which the Church was suffering considerable turmoil. Gnosticism was strong and attacking the very foundations of the Christian Faith. The Church had lost its spontaneity and rigidity had set it. Montanism arose as a reaction to these developments. The sect was started by Montanus whose utterances appeared to come from a spirit possessing him. According to Montanus, this represented something quite different, and was evidence of a new age in which Christ was to be superseded by the Spirit. Montanus claimed that he had received the Holy Spirit in a special revelation. He announced the establishment of a new Jerusalem near a small village in the far west of Phyrigia. Large numbers joined him until some of the towns of Asia had lost most of their Christian populations. The Montanists were condemned by several bishops and ultimately excommunicated, resulting in schism. His followers adopted strict discipline, with second marriages being forbidden and celibacy advocated as superior to the state of marriage. They categorised sins into those that could be forgiven and those that could not. They espoused a concept of an exalted priesthood – the clergy were seen as special people apart who were doing God's work. The Montanists were known for impassioned preaching and as a result preaching declined in the Church. One consequence of this was that the priest's role became more secretive and separate, and it was now supposed that the people needed them as their intermediaries in order to communicate with God.

5.6 The early Catholic Fathers (180–250)

By the last quarter of the second century the Church had undergone attack from the gnostics on the one hand, and the Montanists on the other. The Church was spiritually weak. At about this time a group of men – Irenaeus, Tertullian, Cyprian, Clement of Alexandria, and Origen (who were later given the collective title of the Catholic Fathers) – started tackling the difficulties which faced the Church, notably the New Testament Canon, the creed and Apostolic succession.

Irenaeus was the first of the great fathers. Two of his works survive complete: a short Presentation of the Apostolic Teaching (a manual of fundamental doctrines) and a series entitled *Refutation and overthrow of the knowledge so falsely called*, generally known as *Against Heresies*. Irenaeus deduced that the gnostics could only be overcome by drawing together the various scriptures into one authoritative canon. The difficulty was: which writings should be admitted? The gnostics had their own Gospels and Epistles which they were advocating should be included. Irenaeus argued that the real test should be whether the books were by the Apostles, or failing which whether they were penned by someone who had been closely connected with the Apostles. Irenaeus opposed originality which he saw as courting heresy. In contrast to the ever-changing fads of the competing sects, Irenaeus emphasised the enduring orthodoxy of scripture and traditions based upon the teachings of the Apostles, and of the apostolic succession. Innovation and speculation, he argued, were inimical to the true faith.

Similarly, as a further shield against heresy he advocated that those who sought baptism should be required to accept a rule of faith or creed, which developed into what we now know as the Apostles' Creed. Not surprisingly, Irenaeus was a keen exponent of the authority of those who had succeeded the Apostles in the role of presbyter or elder, which was at this time evolving and becoming more akin to what we now term bishop.

Three of the Fathers came from the Church in Carthage. **Tertullian** was a lawyer and the most important theologian in the West at the end of the second century. To Tertullian the divinity of Christ was apparent from the incredible nature of the claim made. 'I believe it because it is so outrageous' he says of the Crucifixion of the Son of God. Through his writings and eloquence he overwhelmed the opposition including, after his attraction to Montanism, the orthodox bishops. He was the first to use the term 'Trinity'. In *De Idolatria*, Tertullian raises issues such as what a Christian should do when invited by a non-Christian to a wedding or other event where a pagan rite might be performed. He advised that a Christian could not perform certain public duties, such as enter the army or hold public office, as he would inevitably be required to partake in pagan rites. Tertullian advocated ascetism. He condemned attendance at theatre and other public amusements, second marriages and military service.

Tertullian provides interesting insights into the daily life of Christians in the Roman Empire. The life of the Christian was very different from that of his pagan neighbours. In all his public and private life a Christian was surrounded by tokens of pagan worship, and he was faced daily with moral dilemmas. Certain trades were forbidden to him, such as idol-making, acting, fighting in the arena and those associated with immorality. Various allied professions were also closed to Christians, for example the polisher of sacrificial knives, or the cutter of bone tickets for the arena. The holding of civil office was not without problems in that ceremonies associated with public office often involved the recognition of heathen gods. Tertullian explained some of the difficulties that might arise between a Christian wife and a pagan husband: ' ... if fasts are to be kept her husband will be giving a feast on the same day; if she has to go out, never will family business be more hindering. For who would allow his wife to go round to other people's houses, and especially to all the poorer cottages for the sake of visiting the brethren? Who would willingly let her be taken from his side for meetings at night, if it should be her duty? Who, in short, would put up with her absence all night at the Easter solemnities without misgivings? Who would let her creep into a prison to kiss a martyr's chains? Or indeed meet anyone of the brethren for a kiss?'

Tertullian insisted that the Churches of the apostolic succession had the true doctrines. Like Irenaeus before him, Tertullian reasoned that the body of essential truth must have been known to the Apostles and communicated by them to the churches they established. The body of essential truth was thereafter guaranteed by episcopal succession. In contrast, heresy post-dated the Church and could claim no such authoritative lineage. Hence, he argued, the heretics should not be admitted to any discussions on the Scriptures. Attracted by its intense puritan morality, Tertullian embraced the Montanist prophecy and accused the Catholic Church of being unspiritual and institutionalised.

Alexandria, a city of perhaps two and a half million inhabitants by the second century, and the intellectual centre of the world, also boasted a sizeable church. Its Catechetical School became well-respected for its theology and also for its philosophy and science. **Clement** became head of the school in about **190**. He argued that pagan religions had aspects from which the Church could draw, and that the advent of Christianity was prepared by Greek philosophers as much as by Judaism. He helped rescue learning from the disrepute that had resulted from its association with gnosticism, arguing that it may be sufficient for the common people to believe and obey, but the intelligent needed to understand by reason. Clement was concerned to demonstrate that one could be educated and intelligent whilst accepting the principles of faith.

In *Stromateis*, Clement argued that philosophy, far from giving support to gnosticism, afforded an invaluable tool for its destruction. He stressed the need for the study of philosophy and interpreted biblical themes in language capable of being understood by the educated Greek world, arguing that Greek philosophy was a gift given to interpret the Gospel and to assist in the conversion of the Greek world. He sought to persuade his Christian readers that whilst his mode of expression was by no means biblical, the substance of his teachings corresponded with the message of the New Testament.

Clement believed that God had sewn his seeds of truth in all men, and that all truth and righteousness originated from him. Hence Clement's confidence that understanding and knowledge of God were to be found in the writings of the Greek philosophers. Clement's views were in complete contrast to gnosticism. He refuted the suggestion that sexual relations were inconsistent with leading a spiritual life, and disparaged the idea that marriage was evidence of, or resulted in, a lesser spiritual being. Clement saw the Christian life as a journey of progress in which the Christian strived to become Christlike. As the believer progressed he would err and would require correction and need to ask repentance. The Christian life was a school whose pupils were of differing abilities and at different stages in their Christian development.

Origen (184–254), considered to have been one of the best teachers and writers in the early Church, was a pupil of Clement and, unusually for one of the early Church writers, of Christian parents. In the same year that his father died a martyr's death, Clement became the head of the Catechetical School at the age of 18. He was a prodigious writer and is believed to have written thousands of works including letters and articles. He emphasised the deity of Christ and the doctrine of the Trinity.

Whilst the early Church had not dwelt on the exact nature of Christ's divinity, or the interrelation between his divinity and humanity, from the end of the second century new theories emerged, most notably Monarchianism which put forward two views to explain the nature of Christ. Dynamistic Monarchianists believed that a divine power came down onto the man Jesus, and this empowered Jesus to do the works of God. Modalistic Monarchianists believed that all the fullness of God dwelt in Christ, and he was a means of God's manifestation. God thus manifested himself sometimes as the Father, sometimes as the Son and at other times as the Holy Spirit. Each manifestation was of the same Divine Being, although differently revealed.

Monarchianist theories were bitterly criticised because they implied that the Father had suffered on the Cross. The Church's teaching was that Christ was truly God and that at the same time he had a personality distinct from the Father and the Holy Spirit, but yet was one with them. Origen put up a strong defence of this article of faith, and his thinking, in particular on the doctrine of the Son's eternal generation, set the seeds for the decision in 325 of the Council of Nicaea as to Christ's deity.

In his efforts to defend Christian orthodoxy against gnosticism, Origen sought to present comprehensive doctrines which answered the main questions raised by the gnostics. He drew on various strands of Greek philosophy to supplement the scriptures, which he argued should not be interpreted literally but symbolically, as a spiritual mystery. The influence of Greek thought is apparent in Origen's explanation of the Fall. According to Origen, God initially created a kingdom of spiritual beings but over time every human soul fell into the material world, which thus came into being because of the Fall. In the material world human souls were trapped in their bodies, waiting to be set free. The soul of Christ, however, did not fall but remained faithful to the Logos. When the Logos took on flesh, Christ's soul came with it, and entered the body of Mary. On the issue of the Trinity, Origen argued that the Son and the Spirit were subordinate to the Father, his teaching forming the basis of Arianism – a heresy which was to play such an important part in the development of the Church in the fourth century.

Cyprian of Carthage was converted to Christianity in 246 at the age of 46. A wealthy lawyer, he sold his valuable pleasure gardens and gave the proceeds to the poor. Two years after his baptism he was elected Bishop of Carthage by popular demand, something which aroused deep resentment among other presbyters, and resulted in schism and rivalry in his own see. Out of his particular position two issues arose: the method of election of a bishop and the bishop's authority within the Church. In contrast to his own election, Cyprian argued that to be elected a bishop it is first necessary to be chosen by the other bishops, secondly to be accepted by the laity and thirdly to be supported by the Judgment of God, by which he probably meant an uneventful election and consecration free of any inauspicious natural phenomena.

Cyprian insisted on the primacy of the bishop, whom he described as the glue which bound the Church together. In an impassioned tract *On the Unity of the Church*, Cyprian demanded unity within the Church, claiming that the bishops had absolute supremacy and that they received their authority directly from God. Failure to obey the bishop was a sin. That said, Cyprian was a strong believer in the autonomy of each bishop within his own church: whilst the whole body of bishops should where necessary decide issues together, the majority had no jurisdiction over any individual bishop within his own see. As to Rome, the bishop there was the symbol of Church unity, but was not vested with any power to impose his authority on any individual bishop.

Cyprian introduced the idea of the clergy as sacrificing priests – he considered that the offering up on the altar was of the body and blood of Christ. Whereas once Christians were distinct from pagan religions in having neither altar nor sacrifice, Cyprian set the seeds for the doctrine of transubstantiation.

5.7   The third century: growth, expansion and the great persecution

The late second century witnessed a partial persecution under the Emperor Septimus Severus (193–211). Whilst Septimus may not have been antagonistic towards Christians, his wife Julia Doma was the daughter of the High Priest of the temple of El Galal, the sun God of Emesa. It was probably in large part due to her influence that the Emperor passed an edict requiring official persecution, and prohibiting all proselytising by Jew and Christian. It appears that the edict was only enforced with any vigour along the Mediterranean, in particular the two main Christian centres. The Catechetical School in Alexandria was dispersed and Clement was forced to abandon the city in 203. Carthage was also attacked in the same year.

Thereafter for the first half of the third century the Church enjoyed comparative calm and was generally treated in a neutral or even a friendly way by the secular authorities. As a result it grew rapidly in numbers and prestige, even to the extent of freely penetrating the upper echelons of Roman society. The Emperor Alexander Severus (212–235) openly condoned Christianity, as he did all other faiths. Philip the Arabian, Emperor in 244–249, was thought to be a secret follower.

A key factor in the growth of the early Church was the opposition that the Christians provoked. This was no doubt one of the reasons why they maintained such a strong degree of cohesion despite the schismatic groups that prospered in what was by now a far flung church. The persecutions, the martyrdoms and the allegations of secret meetings at which unspeakable immoralities were practised were certainly sufficient to arouse curiosity. On the other hand, the proponents of the Gospel appeared to have much to offer. On a spiritual level they spoke of forgiveness of sins, the overcoming of evil, of immortality and belonging. On a more concrete level many Gentiles were impressed by the charity practised by the Church which cared for the poor, for the bereaved and orphaned, offered hospitality to strangers, responded to the needs that arose at times of war or natural disaster, and even extended such help and assistance to non-believers.

As Christianity grew, so too did the financial resources of the Church and by the year 251 the Church in Rome was able to support 46 presbyters, 7 deacons, 7 subdeacons, 42 acolytes, 52 exorcists, readers and doorkeepers, as well as provide assistance to more than 1500 widows and others in need. On a social level Christianity was radical. It emphasised the concept of the individual's moral

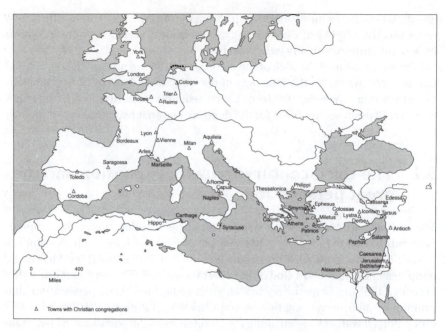

Map 3 The spread of Christianity

responsibility for his own decisions, it paid less heed to social divisions than did other beliefs, and preached the equality of men and women.

Christianity spread with particular speed into Syria and Asia Minor and Greece. To the north, however, was the frontier of the Empire and a language barrier. The most extensive missionary activity was to the West and within a few years there was a considerable Christian community in Rome. By **250** there were approximately 100 episcopal sees in Italy. In France there was an expanding Church based at Lyon, and by the end of the third century there were bishops at Arles, Rouen, Paris, Bordeaux and Reims, to name but some. As for Britain, it is likely that there was no significant Church presence until the middle of the third century. By the end of the fourth century Britain had been largely brought within the Church, until that is the Saxon invasions began when the local Britons retreated into Cornwall, Wales and Ireland. The conversion of the Saxons did not start in earnest for another two centuries.

In Egypt, missionaries had progressed some considerable way up the Nile by the second century, and on the north coast of Africa the Church established itself at a very early stage. By the time of Tertullian in about **200**, the Church in Carthage had a substantial following.

In contrast to the first half of the third century, much of the period from **250** to **260** was one of terrible persecution. The Roman Empire was in turmoil with barbarians threatening many of its borders and repeated rebellions and mutinies. Decius (**249–251**) believed that security meant reverting to ancient customs and determined that this meant that Christianity had to be obliterated. He appointed Valerius to oversee a campaign against the Eastern religions which he saw as undermining the strength of the Empire. Valerius' efforts had much popular support. There was a growing public resentment and hostility towards the Church, which in Alexandria in **249** had found expression in mob riots against the Christians.

The persecution under Decius was unique: it was official rather than mob-led, it was universal and it was systematic. It was aimed at the destruction of the Church and sought to force Christians to denounce their faith. The campaign was particularly directed against the bishops. They were forced to choose between staying with their Church and refusing to denounce their faith, in which case they faced imprisonment, torture and in some cases execution, or fleeing and guiding their congregations from afar. Some chose flight in the belief that they were needed to ensure the continuation of the Church. Others, such as Origen, suffered greatly in prison and were subjected to repeated torture. Some – such as Fabian, the Bishop of Rome – were eventually executed.

Whilst the bishops were selected for special treatment, all were subject to the campaign. On fixed days, citizens were required to appear before the local magistate and a special commissioner and give sacrifice or at least throw incense upon the altar. If they complied they were given a certificate (libellus) to confirm their observance. In the inital stages there were many who were prepared to renounce their faith, and others who thought their consciences would be clear by obtaining a libellus by corrupt means rather than by offering sacrifice. After a while, however, the oppression encountered much stiffer resistance.

The persecution was eventually interrupted by the death of Decius whilst fighting the Goths. His death resulted in two years of anarchy, exacerbated by the afflictions of the plague. The chaos was brought to an end by the succession of Valerius as emperor in **253**. Valerius renewed his campaign of oppression, supplementing the methods of his earlier reign of terror by confiscating the property of wealthy Christians. Valerius also suffered in his efforts to protect the Empire – he was captured by the Persians and later died in captivity. Gallienus (**260–268**) ended the persecution and returned the property that had been seized from the Church.

In the remainder of the century, the Church enjoyed a prolonged period free from oppression and went from strength to strength. The turn of the century, however, brought in a new tide of persecution under Diocletian caused by fear of Christianity and of Christian penetration in the army. Diocletian was an experienced military leader chosen by the generals to carry through a comprehensive reorganisation of the state apparatus and of the army. The massive Empire was being attacked on many frontiers, and with a border of six thousand miles to protect, the military budget was a considerable burden. Within the ranks of the army itself there was dissension.

Diocletian considered that extensive change was required to ensure the survival of the Empire and carried out major reforms of the army, currency, taxation and prices. Appreciating that it was the army, and not the Senate, which was governing the Empire he moved his court from Rome to Nicomedia, which was nearer the frontiers. He sought to incorporate his likely rivals and accordingly he divided the Empire into two, appointing Maximian to rule the Empire to the west of the

Adriatic as a second but subordinate Augustus. Each of them had a second-in-command – a Caesar, with Constantine controlling the West and Galerius the East. This reorganisation proved successful for a number of years.

The Church continued to expand and extend its influence. The Emperor's own wife, Prisca, had converted to Christianity and the increasing prominence of the Church provoked fierce anti-Christian sentiments, including from the Emperor's son-in-law, the Caesar Galerius, who purged the army of all who failed to comply with his requirements for the offering of sacrifices. Galerius pressed the Emperor to take more far reaching steps. Eventually the Emperor gave in and in **303** commanded that all churches be destroyed, that all biblical scripts be burnt, and prohibited all meetings for worship. Within a few weeks there were two fires in the palace, both of which were blamed on the Christians. A second edict followed, commanding the arrest of the clergy. The prisons simply could not hold all the clerics incarcerated and a further edict was issued granting liberty in return for offering sacrifice. Those who refused were tortured. A fourth edict in **304** extended the persecution – all citizens were to be required to sacrifice, and those who refused were to face death.

Notwithstanding the extreme requirements of the edicts, the persecution was enforced with differing degrees of severity in East and West. No executions were carried out under Constantius in Britain, Gaul or Spain. On the death of Constantius in **306**, his son Constantine was declared Emperor by his troops and sought to impose his rule in the West. A civil war ensued, with several claimants announcing their right to rule as Augustus in the West. Whilst not himself a Christian, Constantine had been exposed to Christian influences. His control of the western provinces of Britain, Gaul and Spain and subsequently over other provinces meant that these areas escaped the ravages of the persecution.

In the East, however, after Diocletian retired in **304**, Galerius was free to unleash his unrestrained brand of oppression and in some parts the persecution was especially brutal. Eventually, as he lay on his death bed, Galerius issued an edict acknowledging that the persecution had failed to bring Christians back to the religions of their forefathers, granting religious toleration and exhorting Christians to pray for him and for the defence of the Empire. Galerius' death was followed by civil war in the East too, where Maximian and Licinius engaged in battle to succeed him.

Out of this turmoil emerged two victors. In the West, in **312**, Constantine overpowered his last remaining challenger, Maxentius, in a battle which he won against the odds. Prior to engaging in combat, Constantine had called on the assistance of the Christians' God and is thought to have seen a flaming cross of light in the sky with the inscription in Greek: *In this sign you shall conquer.* The result of this experience was the conversion of Constantine to Christianity. His victory was a momentous event in the history of Christianity, for it was to result in the first Christian Emperor of the Roman Empire. The same year saw Licinius gain overall control in the East and in **313** the two rulers met and concurred on a policy of toleration for all religions, and agreed that all property seized from Christians should be returned. From this point onwards, whilst there were episodes of sporadic persecution under Licinius in the East, persecution in the West was largely unheard of.

5.8 Constantine, toleration and the Council of Nicaea (325)

A decade after the accord between the two rulers, Licinius embarked on a fresh campaign of oppression in the East. At the same time he was also experiencing immense difficulties in upholding the Empire's frontiers, and in 323 the barbarians crossed the Danube. Constantine rushed to his aid, but after repelling the invaders he turned on Licinius and in alliance with the Armenian Christians who were being harassed by him, Constantine overpowered Licinius at the battle of Chrysopolis in 324.

Thereafter Constantine ruled alone, supported by a huge army. He decided to construct an impressive capital. Rather than move to Rome he chose Byzantium. Situated between East and West it was an ideal location for communications between the two halves of the Empire, and from which to counter the threats coming from the East. Having taken control of the whole Empire, Constantine's priorities were to strengthen his hold and to cement the unity of East and West. His years as Emperor witnessed momentous advances by the Church. Whilst Constantine did not make Christianity the official religion of the Empire, his initial policy being one of equality between the various religions, as his reign progressed his policy increasingly became one of favouritism. When Constantine became Emperor in 323, about 10 per cent of his subjects were Christians, but under Constantine they grew in numbers and influence throughout the Empire.

Constantine restored property confiscated during the persecution, paid for the production of copies of the Bible, constructed many church buildings, endowed the bishops of Rome with a splendid episcopal residence, and allocated a substantial slice of provincial revenues to the Church's charitable purposes. The Church was permitted to accept legacies, Sunday was made a day of rest and given the same status accorded to pagan holy days, and official sacrificing was abolished, facilitating the acceptance by Christians of the office of magistrate. Christian ethics also found expression in some of Constantine's social legislation. Criminals were no longer to be branded on the face, the crucifixion of slaves was forbidden, families of slaves were to be kept together when they were sold, married men were forbidden from keeping mistresses, measures were introduced for the protection of children, and severe penalties were imposed for failing to obey the moral laws.

Emperor Constantine kept close friendship with the bishops, and attempted to settle the different disagreements and maintain peace and unity. At Alexandria an esoteric controversy arose between a presbyter Arius and his bishop Alexander. Arius put forward an explanation of Christ's divinity at variance with the accepted teachings of the Church. He taught that Christ had 'come into being out of non-existence' and that he was 'created not made'. On this account, the Son was the first of all created beings but was obviously inferior to the Father, and was neither eternal nor divine. Arius was successful in enlisting influential support from bishop Eusebius of Caesarea, and the bishop of Nicomedia, also named Eusebius. The Greek churches were divided, and at a synod in 321 attended by bishops from Egypt and Libya, Arius's teachings were rejected and he was excommunicated. In 323 Constantine decided to intercede, and wrote to Arius and Alexander requesting that they resolve their differences which Constantine saw as a matter of mere semantics.

Constantine sent his friend and adviser Hosius, bishop of Cordova, to attempt to resolve the disputes, but to no avail. Finally Constantine decided to call a huge synod of bishops to settle the matter. Initially this was to be held at Ancyra but Constantine ordered that it should meet at Nicaea, not far from the imperial residence at Nicomedia. This ensured his personal supervision over the proceedings, but it also made it more of an ecumenical gathering rather than being limited to the East.

The Council of Nicaea opened on the 20th May 325 and lasted over three months. It was attended by about 220 bishops, almost all were Greek, and only a handful were from the West. Of the bishops present, about twenty were supporters of Arius. The opening day was held in a large hall in the imperial palace. Times had changed indeed – many of those present were maimed or scarred as a result of persecutions perpetrated on the Church by the Emperor's predecessors. Constantine exhorted those assembled to reach agreement, and as a demonstration of his reaction to their disunity he publicly set fire to correspondence he had received from the bishops disparaging one another.

The discussions at this first Council centred around whether Christ was of the *same* essence as God, or merely of a *similar* essence. The orthodox party carried the day, and at the close of its deliberations the Council adopted a creed which amounted to a complete repudiation of Arianism. The Nicene Creed consisted of a series of formulations about God, Christ and the Holy Spirit. Christ was declared to be 'the Son of God, only begotten of the Father . . . very God of very God'. To emphasise the rejection of Arianism, however, several further clauses were added denouncing Arian beliefs, in particular the claim that Christ was metaphysically or morally subordinate to God. To the relief of the Emperor, and in spite of the fierce controversy that the issue had aroused, all but two of the bishops endorsed the creed. The apparent unanimity was only achieved because the different signatories interpreted the creed in different ways. The creed declared that the Father and the Son were the same. To some this meant that the Father and the Son shared the same identity, to others this merely meant that they were of the same kind. Nevertheless, despite this ambiguity, the solution reached and the apparent unity achieved were seen as a success for the Emperor.

In addition to this doctrinal feud, the Council also addressed other issues concerning discipline and the structure of Church organisation. Canons were issued providing that a bishop should preferably be consecrated by all the bishops and granting a power of veto to the bishop of the provincial metropolis over the appointment of bishops. These measures strengthened the move towards an hierarchical system of church government, although it is interesting to note that there was no mention of any universal rights vested in the Bishop of Rome. In the East there was no single dominant see to which the others were subordinate. The reality was that issues of Church policy were under the control of the Emperor himself, and those who were able to determine policy often did so by virtue of their being in favour with the Emperor.

5.9 Church, state and society after Constantine

The success of Christianity brought its own problems. From now on, Christianity became a means of social advancement, of prestige, and many were motivated by their thirst for status, power or wealth in their conversion to the Christian faith. At the time of Constantine's death, Christianity was still the religion of only a minority, but within the next hundred years or so most educated Roman townspeople had come to embrace Christianity, as had the majority of the ruling elite. As to the people, they had embraced the Church even earlier, and in the late fourth century many cities in various parts of the Empire had been faced with riots by fanatical Christians destroying temples and other pagan symbols. This was so especially in the East where Christianity was strongest. By the **450s** there were few pagans still to be found in Roman towns. In rural districts, however, the population remained faithful to their pagan roots and traditions for far longer, and in the West the Church was to be engaged in eliminating pagan influences for several centuries to come.

Christians had turned the tables. Initially the mobs and later officialdom imposed their own persecution on the pagans. In the years after **390** legal penalties were imposed against pagans, but were also directed against heretics, schismatics and Jews, all of whose loyalty to the state was seen under the Christian Emperors to be open to doubt.

There were healthier factors at work, such as the influence of Christian spouses on their pagan families. Others were converted by the accounts of miracles, especially the claims made for healing powers, or attracted by the fellowship associated with belonging to a Christian community.

Christians were part of a broader society and to a large extent they shared a common culture with their pagan neighbours. At all levels of society, religion now in fact made little outward difference to life. Christians still took part in Roman festivities, even consulting magicians, or using charms in an attempt to cure their ills, or getting drunk at celebrations, just as non-Christians did. It became difficult to distinguish outward obedience from genuine commitment, and this prompted some to resort to asceticism to differentiate themselves. From the later years of the fourth century, monasticism provided one means of living such a life, dedicated to sexual abstinence and other forms of self-denial and poverty.

Publicly Christians allied themselves with the social framework of the Roman Empire. Many, such as Eusebius, came to think of Christianity and the Empire as being part of God's plan – a universal Christian society, with the Emperor the representative of divine authority in the world. In the minds of some there was a tendency to merge Church and Empire. The Emperor, a divine representative, was responsible for the well-being of the Church. Heresy was seen as a form of revolt and missionary activity as a means of imposing law and order. Beyond the confines of the Roman Empire was barbarity and disorder. The Empire represented civilisation and Christianity.

The institutions of the Church also underwent development. Christian communities were strongest in the urban centres, and there grew up a network of bishoprics formed into provinces headed by a metropolitan bishop, generally based in the provincial capital. In large part the geographical structure of the Church mirrored that of the State. The third and fourth century saw increasing imperial intervention, including in the appointment of bishops to the most important sees. In the early years the congregations had had a free hand in choosing their bishops, but gradually this was eroded, and neighbouring bishops came to impose considerable control in the selection of their brethren. By the last quarter of the fourth century the metropolitan sees had gained pre-eminence in what was becoming an increasingly hierarchical organisation, with the Emperor exerting substantial and often decisive influence, both within the Church and by means of legislation. Laws were introduced imposing restrictions and penalties on heretics, and bishops unseated by the various councils were invariably sentenced to exile with the intention of disarming them.

In the fourth century there developed a passion for commemorating the sufferings of the martyrs, with the Christian calendar filling up with celebrations of the anniversaries of their deaths. The commemorations were more than simply celebrations in which the Christian community would meet together – they provided a bridge which enabled Christians to make the move from the experience of years of persecution to the era when the Church was privileged and powerful, and an appearance of continuity between the suffering Church and the new, privileged position it now enjoyed. In Rome, under Pope Damasus, martyrs' shrines were ostentatiously embellished, giving the impression that Rome's acclaim was of Christian rather than pagan origin.

By the end of the fourth century the corpses of the martyrs were being moved from their graves into the urban churches and placed in ornate buildings. In cities throughout the Christian world the martyrs' cults shifted from the cemeteries outside the towns to the new churches, and the commemorations were incorporated into the communion services of the urban Christian community. Prior to the fourth century, buildings and sites did not acquire any special holiness, but the presence of the martyrs in the urban churches changed this. Churches ceased to be simply gathering places of Christians, and became sacred places. Similarly, the locations of the New Testament miracles became sites for pilgrimage.

By the beginning of the fifth century the Empire had been devastated. The whole of the West was under the hand of the barbarians and had split up into smaller states. It was an age of uncertainty for the Christian communities, living together with both Arians and pagan conquerors. Over time, the pagans slowly converted to Catholicism. As to the Bishop of Rome, the fall of the Empire, accompanied by the flight of great patrician families from Rome, left him the major influence in the city.

5.10 The Arian controversy under Constantine and his sons

From the Council of Nicaea (325) until Constantine died twelve years later, the Nicene Creed prevailed. The Christian faith had officially drawn upon the language and concepts of Greek philosophy, and was now expressed in terms that had much in common with earlier religions. Whilst Constantine had imposed a settlement upon the Council, Nicaea was only an early event in what was to be a prolonged period of doctrinal definition. In 327 Constantine granted an amnesty leading to the return of the Arian exiles driven out after the Council of Nicaea, and the remaining years of his reign saw the supporters of Arianism re-establish themselves. Their chief proponent, Eusebius of Nicomedia, was one of the most eminent scholars of his day. Nicomedia was but a short distance from Constantinople and the Emperor's residence, and he was able to exercise considerable influence. Whilst he had been a signatory to the Nicene Creed, it was no secret that his interpretation of the ambiguous formula was far different from the meaning ascribed by the orthodox bishops. In the following decade Eusebius succeeded in discrediting and ousting three of the most influential critics of Arianism by cunning designs, rather than in theological debate.

The first victim was Eustace, Bishop of Antioch, who was charged with disparaging the Emperor's mother, Helena. He was deposed at a synod and then sent into exile by Constantine. The second casualty was Athanasius, Bishop of Alexandria, one of the most vociferous critics of Arianism. When Athanasius was accused by a dissident group in Egypt of brutality, Eusebius sought to use this to his advantage. His supporters brought about Athanasius' excommunication and deposition after he was condemned by a synod of conduct unbefitting a Christian Bishop. Athanasius appealed to the Emperor, but Eusebius had obtained evidence that Athanasius had threatened to interrupt the supply of corn from Alexandria to Constantinople should his appeal not succeed. This guaranteed the success of Eusebius, and in 336 Athanasius was sentenced to exile. At this time Constantine was celebrating the thirtieth year of his rule, and called a meeting of reconciliation for all the Arians who had returned to acknowledge the authority of the Council of Nicaea. Marcellus, another strong proponent of orthodoxy, refused to attend and was subsequently exiled.

The following year Constantine died, and the Empire was divided up between his three sons. Constantine controlled the western provinces, Constantius the East, and Constans ruled Italy and North Africa. By 353, however, Constantius had gained overall control of the whole Empire. His brothers had quarrelled and in the resulting warfare between the two Constantine had been killed. A decade later Constans was himself assassinated by the rebel Magnentius who was ultimately defeated by Constantius. This political turmoil, and the eventual victory of Constantius, a staunch opponent of the Nicene position, were of immense significance in the Arian controversy.

At a Council in Antioch in 341, on the occasion of the dedication of the new cathedral, ninety seven Greek bishops drafted an additional creed to supplement that agreed at Nicaea, most of which was designed to counter the teachings of

Marcellus. The following year, however, saw the death of Eusebius, and the resulting division over his successor left his supporters without a leader.

The two Emperors, Constans and Constantius, initiated a council of bishops from both East and West which met at Serdica in **343**. The result was disunity. The western bishops were resolutely committed to Nicaea, the eastern bishops were equally passionate in their opposition to it. The two factions split and held separate councils each broadly reaffirming their positions. One development which was to have considerable future significance was that the western bishops issued a canon providing that any bishop rebuked by his provincial superior had the right to appeal to the Bishop of Rome. The stalemate was to some extent reversed by a further Council held in Antioch the following year when compromise was more or less imposed by the Emperors. Athanasius was to be allowed to return from exile to the East, and the western bishops agreed to end their support for Marcellus.

The cessation of hostilities was short-lived. During his years of exile, Athanasius had succeeded in winning considerable backing from the western bishops, making genuine reconciliation between East and West even more remote. The success of Arianism was assured by the reunification of the Empire under Constantius in **353**. The Emperor was keen to force the Church to accept a new Arian creed. He was conscious too that, whilst Athanasius had a strong body of support in the West, there were still many bishops in the West who appeared to have little understanding of the dispute, and might be more amenable. At Councils in Arles in **353**, and in Milan in **355**, the Emperor pressured the bishops into repudiating the Nicene Creed and adopting the formula that the Son was unlike the Father, and denouncing Athanasius. Such was the role of the Emperor in these proceedings that when the Bishop of Rome, Liberius, declined to agree to the new creed, he was condemned to exile.

The difficulty with the position taken at these two synods was that it appeared to deny that Christ was divine in any way at all. This stance, which soon gained the title Dissimilarian, was contrary not only to the Nicene Creed but also to the position taken up by the majority of the Greek bishops, that Christ and God were of like essence. The latter represented an obvious possible compromise in that it asserted unqualified similarity but fell short of 'identity of essence' which merged Father and Son into one being. The Greek bishops, led by Basil, Bishop of Ancrya, succeeded in convincing Constantius that their position was the only means of uniting the Church in a compromise solution. This was counter to the extreme Arian stance that Constantine had previously taken under the influence of his adviser, Valens the Bishop of Mursa. The two bishops vied with each other, Valens calling for a description limited to the likeness of Father and Son, and Basil urging that a statement of faith should refer to essential likeness.

At a synod in **358**, the description that Christ was '*of like essence*' to God was adopted. This version incited stiff opposition from the extreme Arians who had previously prevailed. Constantius decided to call a council of East and West which met in **359**. This resulted in a major victory for the Arians. The Emperor, who wished to settle the matter finally and end the disunity, was persuaded by Valens of the political expediency of the vague formula of likeness. This ensured success for the Arians, the Council submitted to the Emperor's wishes, and Christ was declared to be simply '*like*' the Father.

5.11 The Arian controversy to the Council of Constantinople (381)

The following year Constantius faced a rebellion. Rebel forces declared their leader Julian as Emperor, and the two men prepared for war. Before they could engage in combat, however, Constantius died. Julian became Emperor without a battle, and the growing permeation of Christianity into Roman society received an abrupt but short-lived reversal. Julian was a passionate convert to paganism, and promoted pagans, especially former Christians who had renounced their faith, to influential positions in the state administration. He adopted the policies and practices that had so well served Christianity. An hierarchy of priests was developed, and priests were to receive stipends and dispense charity to those in need. Pagan temples and property which had been confiscated were returned. Christian reaction was varied, in some areas extending to attacks on pagan temples and idols. Several Christians were martyred as a consequence of the resulting repression. After only two years in power, Julian was killed during his military campaign against the Persians in **363**.

Under Julian there was no imperial interference in the Church's theological debates. His successors generally continued the previous goal of a broad united church that incorporated Arianism. Despite imperial policies, however, opinion was moving in favour of those committed to Nicaea.

In the early years of the second half of the fourth century, theological debate was dominated by new controversies concerning the Trinity and the person of Christ. The first concerned the divinity and nature of the Holy Spirit. The second arose out of the difficulty in expressing the separateness of God and Christ, and caused such acrimony that in Antioch in **362** there were bishops advocating different positions and vying with each other for control of the see. The third new issue to vex the Church was the assertion by Apollinaris, an old ally of Athanasius, that what made Christ different from other men was that his human mind had been replaced with the divine word or Logos. His teaching represented a denial that Christ had been fully human.

The most prominent of the orthodox bishops during these controversies was Basil, Bishop of Caesarea, who together with two other theological thinkers became known as the Cappadocian Fathers. After becoming Bishop of Caesarea in **370**, Basil sought to develop a firm basis of support for the Nicene position and endeavoured to ensure that posts were filled by sympathisers. The Cappadocian Fathers taught that the divine substance of Father, Son and Spirit had existed always, and was of the same essence. The Trinity, they asserted, should be described as being '*God in three persons*'.

In **381**, Theodosius I called the council of Constantinople. The council, although supposedly ecumenical and attended by 186 bishops, was not attended by any representatives from Rome. The Council asserted the deity of the Holy Spirit, and acknowledged the position taken at Nicaea that the Father and Son had an identity of substance. The Council's pronouncements on doctrine heralded the end of Arian ambitions in the Church of the Roman Empire, although outside the Empire Arianism continued to flourish among the Goths converted by Arian missionaries. Before dispersing, the Council issued a canon confirming Rome's position as the primary see of Christendom and announcing that Constantinople was the New Rome and should rank as the second see after Rome.

5.12   Asceticism and the growth of monasticism

As the Church gained power and status in Roman society from Constantine onwards, increasing numbers began to question whether the Church was losing some of its moral authority, and becoming too detached from the discipline and austerity of the early Christians. Many reacted by cutting themselves off, seeking isolation and practising self-denial, believing that celibacy and deprivation would lead to true knowledge, a unity with Christ in his sufferings and elevation to a higher standard of Christianity.

The monastic communities were preceded by the Christian hermits who lived alone in caves in the Egyptian deserts, and in Syria and Mesopotamia. In Egypt their self-denial was generally limited to depriving themselves of food and sleep, but elsewhere there were those whose zeal to surpass others in the excesses of self-sacrifice was such that they ate only grass, or lived in trees or in the open air with no protection from the sun. Other ascetics lived in close proximity, but met together only for worship, with no common life. One of the originators of the more organised monastic communities was Pachomius (**290–345**). He had served in the Roman army, and started a community by the Nile. The ascetics there practised chastity and poverty but also lived together, submitting to a strict code of discipline and undertaking hard manual labour. Even within these communities, individuals were permitted to compete with each other on the degrees of deprivation they would impose upon themselves.

The monastic life was given greater structure by the interventions of Basil, the Bishop of Caesarea, in the second half of the fourth century. He established a series of rules for the monastic life, requiring an organised time-table for common worship and meals, the movement of the monastic communities to nearer the cities, the insistence on obedience and hard labour, the pursuit of learning and the prohibition of individual excess in self-sacrifice.

Monasticism spread quickly but its success brought with it a thorny problem for the Church leaders. The monasteries were almost entirely communities of lay people outside the authority of the local churches and bishops. The bishops became determined to bring the monasteries under their control. When he founded the communities in the fourth century, Basil of Caesarea had insisted on submission to the local bishop. The issue remained a vexing one, and in **451** the Great Council of Chalcedon formally directed that all communities were subject to the authority of the bishops.

5.13   Division between East and West

In the fifth century, differences of opinion between East and West took on far greater significance. This is apparent from the fierce disagreements which arose over the teachings of Origen, who had hitherto been respected as an able Christian scholar. From the late fourth century, Origen's teachings came under a series of attacks, primarily on the grounds that his theories involved theological speculation which was not only unnecessary given the teachings handed down by the Apostles, but amounted to an infiltration of paganism. In **399** Theophilus, Bishop of the important metropolitan see of Alexandria, denounced the Origenists and outlawed them from Egypt. The exiles travelled to Constantinople where they enlisted the support of the new Bishop, John Chrysostom.

Constantinople had for many years been growing in importance, both as the capital of the eastern Emperors, and as the dominant Christian centre in the East. At the Council of Constantinople in **381**, the see had been designated as second only to Rome, a decision that had caused deep resentment at Alexandria. When the anti-Origenist monks expelled by Theophilus turned to the Bishop of Constantinople this was to bring the two sees into collision, and Theophilus resolved to oust the new Bishop. Circumstances were on his side. On being appointed Bishop, John, an ardent ascetic, had initiated many reforms to strengthen discipline in the Church, had offended many by failing to provide the now usual luxurious hospitality to guests to the bishop's house, had alienated the wealthy by his sermons denouncing riches and, most importantly of all, had greatly upset Eudoxia, the wife of the eastern Emperor. In short, by the time Theophilus sailed to Bosphorus in **403**, John had many enemies. Theophilus called together a Council at Chalcedon and succeeded in having his rival, who had refused to attend, deposed. The Emperor obliged, confirmed the decision and ordered John's exile.

This dispute bears witness to the growing rift between East and West. In **404** Pope Innocent I, with the support of the western Emperor, had called for a new council, but the request was rejected. In retaliation, Innocent excommunicated Chrysostom's accusers. At Constantinople many refused to acknowledge his successor, and with Roman approval met for worship outside the city. Even after John's death in **407** the dispute lingered on, when the eastern metropolitan bishops continued with their refusal to exonerate Chrysostom.

The ultimate split between East and West was greatly facilitated by the administration of the Empire. In periods under the rule of a sole Emperor, the location of the Emperor's residence in Constantinople had meant increased influence and status for the papal see in Rome far in excess of that enjoyed by the Bishop of Constantinople, who faced rivalry from the two competing sees of Antioch and Alexandria, and was subject to the authority and interventions of the Emperor. In the East it was the Emperor who was in ultimate control. As a consequence, the Christian peoples on the borders of the Empire, who were increasingly seeking their own national identity, became reluctant to acknowledge the authority of a Church so compliant to imperial wishes. After the death of Theodosius in **395** the administration of the Empire was again divided into half, but within only a few years the barbarian invasions were threatening Rome itself, and the western church was largely left to itself to settle its disagreements. In **410** the Goths entered Rome. In the ensuing turmoil it was the Church, not the civil administration, that remained effective, and it accordingly gained in stature. The difference between East and West was pronounced – in the West the Church dominated, whilst in the East it was largely subordinate to the Emperor.

5.14 Augustine, the Donatist controversy and the emergence of Latin theology

It was not until late into the fourth century that western Christianity began to participate fully in theological debate. Hitherto theological questions and controversies arose from the ideas and writings of theologians in the Greek East, and the uninformed Latin churches had shown little interest. By the middle of the fourth century, however, Rome was beginning to increase its influence. Rome's sense of importance had been greatly strengthened under Pope Damasus (**366–384**), in particular by the veneration he promoted of saints and martyrs and the growing emphasis given to the roles of St Peter and St Paul in the city's foundation as a Christian centre. The western church was growing in self-confidence and was ready to develop its own thoughts and doctrines. Of the theologians to emerge from the West, Augustine more than any other was to leave his mark on the future progress of Latin thought.

Augustine's conversion to Christianity came in **386** at the age of 32. He established a monastic community in his hometown of Thagaste, in North Africa, but in **391** was eventually prevailed upon to become ordained, being appointed four years later as assistant bishop of Hippo. The city of Hippo, in common with the rest of the Christian world in North Africa, was still bitterly divided over the Donatist controversy that had now been continuing for nearly a century. Both communities held to the same creeds, and the same Latin Bible. The focal point of the controversy between them was the memory of Bishop Caecilian of Carthage. The Donatist's rejection of the Catholics arose from their belief that those who had consecrated Caecilian as bishop had turned traitor during the persecution by giving up copies of the scriptures. The Donatists claimed that theirs was the only pure and true Church and that the Catholic ordinations lacked validity. The African Catholics venerated Caecilian as a saint.

The two camps differed in their concepts of the Church and the administration of the sacraments. For the Donatists, the Church was reserved for the pious and pure. The Catholics, however, rejected the notion of such a select community. For the Donatists, the sacrament was only valid if received within the Church. Those who had consecrated Caecilian were tainted, and accordingly were not part of the true Church of the martyrs which had stood firm during the years of persecution. The Catholics, however, held that the validity of the sacraments was not determined by the orthodoxy of the priest: the sacraments were administered by Christ, and merely through the priest.

Augustine attempted to enter into dialogue with the Donatists, and pressed the Catholic bishops to reach agreement on aspects of church discipline in order to strengthen Catholic unity in the debate. These moves came at a time when imperial prohibitions and restrictions against pagans and heretics were severe, and those with imperial influence were pressing for a strengthening of the persecution. Initially Augustine had rejected a policy of threats and intimidation, reasoning that the resulting conversions would lack sincerity, and generate bitter resentment. Eventually, however, he was persuaded to change his mind. In **411** a Great Council was held at Carthage, instigated by the imperial government and watched over by an imperial commissioner. The conference was attended by 279 Donatists and 286 Catholics. The imperial will again prevailed, and the Emperor Honorius ordered Donatist clergy into exile, seized property belonging to Donatists and imposed penalties for those expounding their beliefs.

It was in this controversy that Augustine formed his doctrine of the Church. His theory of ministry was of priests invested with an authority which transcends their moral characters. It matters not that the minister administering the sacraments is a heretic, for it is Christ who is in truth administering the sacraments. Accordingly those baptised by the Donatist Church did not require to be rebaptised. On the other hand, those receiving baptism in schismatic communities could not receive grace until they were reconciled with the Catholic Church. As to man, Augustine saw him as utterly depraved, lost without God. God, however, gave his Grace to those who he had predestined to accept Christ and to receive the sacraments.

In *On the Trinity*, Augustine advanced a doctrine of God which rejected all talk of subordination within the Trinity. He asserted that all three Persons of the Trinity were equal, and that the Spirit proceeded not just from the Father, but from the Son also. This doctrine gradually came to be incorporated into the creeds of the western churches, and by the seventh century was becoming a matter of controversy between East and West which was going to have consequences of immense importance.

The height of the Donatist controversy coincided with the success of the barbarian attacks in the most western provinces, and the entry into Rome of the Goths in **410**. Many wondered how God could have foresaken the city of St Peter and St Paul. In his book *City of God*, Augustine seeks to counter the suggestion that the misfortunes of the Empire stemmed from the rejection of the pagan Gods. Augustine argued that the Church endured for the Kingdom of God, and was not to be seen as tied to the interests of the Roman Empire. The interests of the Church were above those of the particular temporary secular administrations – the invading barbarians should be seen not as enemies but as potential converts to the city of God.

5.15   The debate concerning the nature of Christ

In the course of the fourth century, a controversy had been growing over the relationship between the divine and human natures in Christ. There were two competing schools of thought, based at the two Christian centres of learning at

Alexandria and Antioch. The Alexandrians stressed the divinity of Christ, whereas the Antiochian school wished to preserve the fact of Christ's humanity. The theological debates between these two schools became extremely heated, the controversy fanned by the ecclesiastical rivalry between the two sees. Apollinarius, a proponent of the Alexandrian School, maintained that in Christ the human soul had been replaced by the Logos, from which it followed that Christ had not been truly human. This extreme form of Alexandrian thought was condemned at the Council of Constantinople in 381. In opposition to Apollinarius were Diodore who preached that Christ was a temple in which the Logos dwelt, in much the same way as God had dwelt in the prophets. Christ was to be distinguished from the prophets, because in him the Logos dwelt completely and for eternity, whereas his dwelling in the prophets had been but limited and temporary.

The teachings of Diodore, and his pupil Theodore, were in conflict not only with Apollinarius but with the very fundamentals of the Alexandrian school, and provoked vigorous opposition. The struggle for supremacy came to a head after Nestorius, a well-known Antiochian preacher, was appointed bishop of Constantinople in 428. Nestorius taught that Christ was a perfect man, a human-being who was worthy of being united with God, and that Mary could not be called the Mother of God, but merely the Mother of Christ. Such teaching caused great offence at Alexandria where the Bishop Cyril maintained that the Logos had assumed human form in the womb, and Mary was accordingly rightly termed the Mother of God. Cyril succeeded in arming himself with the support of Pope Celestine I who wrote a formal demand to Nestorius, sent via Cyril, demanding his acknowledgement of Christ's divinity on threat of excommunication. When forwarding the Pope's command, Cyril also wrote to Nestorius demanding that he renounce a further amplified set of Antiochian teachings. However, by the time these arrived the two Emperors Theodosius II and Valentian II had already called a general Council to meet at Ephesus.

At the opening of the Council, the bishops overwhelmingly condemned Nestorius and his supporters, the arrival of the forty or so Nestorian bishops having been delayed. When the bishops arrived from Antioch, they formed a Council of their own and denounced the demands that Cyril had added to the Pope's command, the 'Twelve Anathemas'. Emperor Theodosius felt compelled to intervene. He had the two leaders arrested and in vain attempted to achieve some reconciliation before finally dissolving the Council. The Emperor bowed to the will of the majority and eventually Cyril was allowed to return to Alexandria. Nestorius was exiled to Egypt where he died not long before the Council of Chalcedon in 451.

The majority Council at Ephesus also directed its attention to the heresy of Pelagianism. Pelagius was an Irish monk who had arrived in Rome at the turn of the century and was appalled at the extent to which life in the affluent capital diverged from the teachings of the Gospel. He reacted fiercely to an extract from Augustine's *Confessions*: 'Thou commandest continence; grant what thou commandest and command what thou wilt'. Pelagius saw in this a rejection of Man's free-will and individual moral responsibility. Whilst acknowledging that men are sinful, he claimed that this was a result not of original sin, a concept he eschewed, but of a path men chose to take which with faith and effort they could reject. Pelagius had succeeded in enlisting considerable support among the Nestorians, but was condemned by Pope Innocent I and, albeit under some pressure from Emperor Honorius, by Pope Celeste I. The Council of Ephesus finally closed the chapter.

Support for Nestorianism was, however, far from dead. Whilst the Antiocheans were obliged to accept the exile of Nestorius, Cyril was subsequently persuaded to agree to a compromise under imperial pressure, in which Christ was described as 'perfect God and perfect man consisting of rational soul and body, of one substance with the Father in his Godhead, of one substance with us in his Manhood, so that there is a union of two natures'.

The theological truce lasted just over a decade. Cyril died in 444 and the new bishop Dioscorus took a more robust anti-Nestorian stance. The Emperor Theodosius II was by now strongly under the sway of his courtier Chrysaphius whose godfather Eutyches, an abbot, was an ardent opponent of Nestorianism. Eutyches claimed that Christ had two natures before the Incarnation, but that at the Incarnation the two natures were merged into one. Dioscorus and Eutyches enlisted the assistance of Chyrsaphius in an attempt to put an end to the theological truce and to assert the dominance of Alexandria. In the bitter controversy, both camps sought support from Rome. Pope Leo responded by way of a tome in which he denounced Eutyches' teachings, and insisted upon the distinction of Christ's divine and human natures after Incarnation. However, Dioscorus and Chrysaphius persuaded the Emperor to call a Council, which met at Ephesus in 449 attended by about 150 bishops. Pope Leo did not attend but sent papal legatees who brought with them Pope Leo's tome. The Council was presided over by Dioscorus. Pope Leo's tome went unread, the Council condemning Flavian who was immediately exiled. Such was Dioscoros' success that he was able to ensure that the vacant see at Constantinople was filled by his own presbyter.

Within two years Dioscorus' fortunes underwent a complete reversal. Pope Leo remained hostile to the victors of the Council of Ephesus and by 450 not only had Emperor Theodosius died, resulting in the ousting of Chrysaphius, but Dioscoros' protege, Anatolius, for whom he had secured Constantinople and Alexandria, constructed the *Henoticon*, a statement of doctrine designed to appease monophysites in Egypt and Syria. It asserted that Christ is one and not two, and avoided any mention of 'nature'. The *Henoticon* succeeded in uniting the Greek churches in the East, but infuriated the Pope who in 484 excommunicated its chief author Acacius, Bishop of Constantinople. The *Henoticon* regulated the faith in the East until 518 when under the Emperor Julian the doctrines of Chalcedon again prevailed at court and were imposed as the standard of orthodoxy throughout the Empire.

5.16   The Papacy

From the very early days, the Church in Rome enjoyed an eminent position, conscious that it was the guardian of the Apostolic tradition, founded by St Peter, the rock on which Christ was to build his Church (Matthew 16: 18) and chosen by Paul as a jewel in his missionary ventures. The Bishop of Rome traced his apostolic succession to Peter, and could claim that he was the guardian of the faith, transmitted by the Apostles through apostolic succession. In the West, the development of Rome's authority was greatly facilitated by the absence of any rival. In the East, however, at first Alexandria and Antioch struggled for supremacy, and were later joined by Constantinople and Jerusalem.

By the fourth century, Rome was already enjoying considerable authority in juridical and disciplinary questions. In **330** Constantine moved his capital from Rome to Constantinople, shifting the political centre of the Empire to the East. One result was a substantial increase in the status of the bishop of Constantinople, who at the Council of Constantinople in **381** was given precedence over the other eastern bishops and granted appellate jurisdiction over the eastern church. Constantinople was henceforth to become a rival of Rome. A second result was that the Bishop of Rome gained a degree of independence in Church affairs completely at variance with the persistent imperial interference in the eastern churches.

From Pope Damasus (**366–384**) onwards, the Bishops of Rome began to widen their claims for authority. Damasus concluded from the divisions arising from the growth of Arianism that the Church required greater regulation and a stronger hierarchical structure. The Council of Nicaea marked an important step on this path, endowing the metropolitan bishops with authority over local bishops. Damasus wished to build on the success of Nicaea, but importantly he asserted that the authority of the Council derived from the ratification of its canons by Pope Sylvester. Damasus availed himself of Christ's description of Peter as a rock, in developing a biblical basis for the claims for Rome's jurisdiction.

In the West, the many Church Councils of the fourth and fifth centuries were seen as far less significant than in the East, and accordingly western bishops seldom attended and never in significant numbers. It was to Rome that the western bishops directed their requests for guidance and it was from Rome that they accepted authority. This is exemplified in the acceptance of the decisions of Nicea, which had papal approval and which remained unquestioned in many parts of the West, despite the subsequent controversies that raged in the East. In a determination to strengthen discipline and to impose greater control, Damasus issued regulations governing Church life covering celibacy, conditions for admission into the priesthood, and marriage between Christians of common descent.

The status of the Bishop of Rome understandably varied according to the personality and strengths of the occupant of papal office. Innocent I (**402–417**) gained particular prestige by his handling of Church affairs and his insistence on primacy. However, the most distinguished of all the fifth century ecclesiastical leaders was Pope Leo I (**440–461**). Leo built on the theological and biblical basis for supremacy advanced by Damasus half a century earlier. He claimed that he was not merely the historical successor of Peter but that Peter spoke through him, giving papal utterances a unique authority. Leo had believed that in the monophysite controversy his tome should have been accepted without question. The Greek bishops at the Council of Chalcedon begged to differ, and approved the tome only after thorough debate. In response, Leo asserted that the statement of faith produced at the Council derived its authority from the fact of its papal ratification. The reality was, or course, that the Council had been called against the wishes of the Pope, who had seen no necessity for such an assembly, and had reached its decisions under the watchful eye of the imperial commissioners.

5.17   The barbarians and the Church's response

The defeat of the Emperor Decius by the Goths in **251** represented the previously unspeakable and left a period of anarchy in its wake. Whilst the Empire recovered under Valerian (**253–260**), the memory of this terrifying event weighed heavily on Roman minds. Over the following hundred years the Roman army largely maintained the frontiers, but with the increasing assistance of the Goths who came to play an important role in the army. In about **370** a dispute between two of the Gothic leaders resulted in one of them, Fritigern, agreeing peace terms with the Emperor and converting to Christianity, whilst his Gothic rival set about persecuting the Christians in his own territories. From about **375**, the movement of Goths into the Empire became a flood. The Huns advanced from the south of modern-day Russia, and decimated the Ostrogoths, who settled within the Empire in Thrace. In **386**, 40,000 Goths were added to the soldiers under imperial command. In the winter of **406**, the Danube, part of the northern boundary of the empire in the West, froze over and the Vandals, Alans and Suevi crossed into Gaul. The invaders continued into Spain and in **429** the Vandals breached the Straits of Gibraltar, a decade later reaching Carthage. The success of the barbarian hordes resulted in anarchy, as Roman government and authority crumbled, leaving the Church to rally the people. In the early years the threat from the barbarians had been seen as short-lived, but as the enemy increased in strength so did the desire of the Church to convert them to the Christian faith.

Earlier missionary work had been undertaken among the Goths by the orthodox Church, but the most significant success was that of the Arian Ulfilas who had been made bishop of the Goths in **341** at the Council of Antioch. Ulfilas initiated the formation of an alphabet for this language which hitherto had little literature to speak of, and translated the Bible into Gothic. When he was expelled in **348** he continued his mission among the vast numbers of barbarians now living within the Empire. That there were also orthodox Christian barbarians within the Empire is evidenced by a direction from the Council of Constantinople that the Churches of the barbarians should be governed according to the customs of the Church. Outside the Empire, missionaries reached the Caucasus and the Huns.

The Arian Goths, in turn, took the Christian Gospel to the other Germanic races. Increasingly these barbarian races came to live within the Roman Empire, and their arrival was generally followed by their conversion to Christianity. However, the vast majority were not orthodox but Arian, leaving them both racially and religiously distinct. The barbarian tribesmen came to rule over large parts of the Empire, and whilst in some provinces the Catholic communities were subjected to occasional periods of persecution, in general a policy of collaboration was successful, if only because both faced a common pagan enemy in the form of the

Hunnish tribes. The same policy was pursued in Italy where, until the last quarter of the fifth century, the office of Emperor survived if only nominally. In **476**, however, the barbarian commander Odoacer appointed himself King of Italy, so formalising the collapse of the Empire in the West which in reality had already been completed with Alaric's march into Rome in **410**. In the East there remained a powerful Emperor firmly in control and still claiming sovereignty over the West. The western Church, however, as will become apparent, came to concentrate its attentions on the barbarian rulers, rather than look to the old links with the Emperor in the East, thereby further widening the divergencies between the Greek and Latin churches.

Bibliography

H. Chadwick, *Early Christian Thought and the Classical Tradition*, OUP, Oxford (1984)

H. Chadwick, *The Early Church*, Penguin, London (1993)

D.J. Chitty, *The Desert a City*, [on the origins of monks and nuns], Continuum International Publishing Group, US (1977)

J.G. Davies, *The Early Christian Church*, Weidenfeld & Nicholson, London (1965)

W.H.C. Frend, *Martyrdom and Prosecution in the Early Church*, OUP, Oxford (1965)

W.H.C. Frend, *The Rise of Christianity*, Fortress Press, Philadelphia (1984)

A.H.M. Jones, *Constantine and the Conversion of Europe*, Penguin, London (1972)

J. Stevenson, *Creeds, Councils and Controversies*, Seabury, New York (1989)

R. Williams, *Arius: Heresy and Tradition*, Wm B Publishing Co, US (2001)

■ ⊻ 6 The history of the Church: the thousand years from AD 500 to 1500

6.1 An overview

By the sixth century the Roman Empire, which had ruled the Mediterranean world for so long, was disintegrating. Christianity now found that the state and administration under which it had grown were collapsing around it. In the following thousand years Christianity was to lose as much territory and as many followers as it was to gain. The inhabitants of Northern Europe were to embrace the faith, but most of the north coast of Africa, much of the Nile Valley, part of south-east Europe, most of Asia Minor, Syria and Palestine and the position it had held in Arabia, Persia and Central Asia were lost. It is highly unlikely that there were any more Christians in **1500** than there had been in **500**. A major factor was Islam, which was making alarming headway, even capturing areas where Christianity had flourished since the first years of the early Church. Throughout nearly the whole of these thousand years, Western Christendom lived in fear of Islam invasions.

On the other hand, by **1500** Christianity was to become securely and permanently established in north-western Europe, and had regained nearly all the areas in south-western Europe which it had only temporarily lost to Islam. Furthermore, the populace of Western Europe was to fashion a new set of ideas and mores which were far more influenced by the Christian faith than hitherto.

Eastern Europe in this period witnessed the conversion of the Russians, who took their faith with them as they expanded into Asia, the Pacific and North America, preparing the way for a rapid expansion of Christianity in the four centuries after **1500**. This period was to coincide, of course, with the conquering voyages of the north-west European explorers to the New World.

These years witnessed immense movements of populations, with hordes of barbarian and semi-civilised peoples frequently attacking and disrupting the centres of Christian civilisation. This was in marked contrast to the earlier relative stability enjoyed by the Church under the Empire. It was these population movements that in large part accounted for the advances and set-backs for the Christian Church in this period. A brief historical summary is illuminating:

410	Rome is sacked by Alaric and the Goths
5th century	The Visigoths are in Spain, the Vandals in North Africa, the Burgundians, Alamanni and Franks in Gaul, and

	the Anglo-Saxons settle in Britain. The West is invaded by Attila and the Huns
6th century	The Lombards conquer northern Italy and establish a kingdom which was to last for 200 years. The Avars dominate much of central Europe, and pose a recurrent threat to the Teutonic states of Western Europe, and in the 7th century even attack Constantinople
7th century	The Slavs overrun north-eastern Germany and penetrate into the Balkans and Greece, even menacing Eastern Europe. The new invaders, the Arabs, establish their faith in much of the Orient, North Africa and most of Spain, dominate Sicily, threaten Italy and even reach into Central Asia
8th century	Viking raids commence, with Ireland, Britain, the coast of France, Spain and parts of Morocco being subjected to pillaging in the following century, with Britain and Normandy coming under Viking rule
11th century	A massive eastern movement of people associated with the Crusades, leaving colonies on the islands and coastlines of the Mediterranean with merchants and missionaries penetrating far inland
13th century	The Mongols, who were to become opponents of Islam, conquer Persia, Mesopotamia, China and much of Russia, for a time threatening Western Europe
15th and 16th centuries	The Ottoman Turks dominate the eastern Mediterranean, and threaten central Europe. The extensive migration of north and western Europeans begins, carrying Christianity around the world

These massive migrations brought with them ruthlessness and destruction, in stark contrast to the spirit and teachings of Christianity, of which the half-civilised pagan conquerors were scornful. The invaders were nevertheless to some extent in awe of the civilisation that they were subjugating, and in time sought to take on the cultures and customs of their subjects. The primitive polytheism of their own religious beliefs were no match for the attractions of Christianity, and they assumed both the faith and the civilised mantle of the Mediterranean world – Christianity's only rival being Islam which successfully converted many Christians away from the Western faith.

Christianity itself underwent significant change, influenced in turn by the migrants into the Christian world. This period saw the development of the magic power surrounding the sign of the cross, the increasing sophistication of Church rites and the belief in powers to cure disease and ward off calamities. Though subject to change, the Church, its clergy and bishops stood out as bulwarks in the West. Whilst the administration of the Roman Empire crumbled around it, the Church took on its mantle of prestige, assuming much of the functions hitherto performed by the Roman State.

By **500** the Church had already grouped itself into a few main communions, the largest being the Catholic Church. In theory it preserved unity within its jurisdiction, but there were many divisions between the Western churches allied to the Bishop of Rome, and communicating in Latin, and the Eastern churches which were predominantly Greek speaking and looked more to the Patriarch of Constantinople than to Rome.

It was the Western Catholic Church which generated the greatest efforts to spread the Christian faith, with a continuous stream of energetic missionaries establishing many new churches that were to become of major significance in the future growth of the faith. The only other major communion, the Arian Church, was to disappear, and the other small groupings either died out or remained as declining isolated movements. There were also groups such as the monophysite Church in Egypt, who expanded up the Nile to Sudan and Ethiopia, and the Nestorians who penetrated into India, Central Asia and China, but they were the exceptions.

The Western Catholic Church enjoyed the prestige of representing the faith practised by the large majority of the peoples of the Graeco-Roman world, and benefited from the endorsement and support of the state – in contrast to Arianism which went into decline after losing official backing in the East. The Byzantine Church, unlike the Church in the West, was very much under the domination of the Emperor. Moreover, throughout most of these thousand years the East was harassed by the expansionism of an aggressive Islam, whereas the West had to deal mainly with segmented primitive religions which could not ultimately resist being overwhelmed by Christianity.

There were no new denominations or schismatic movements of any significance during these years. The Catholic Church in the West developed far more extensively than the Church in the East, Nestorianism waned, and the smaller communions contracted. Within the Catholic Church there had developed new monastic orders, fresh formulations of theology, modifications of ritual, and new forms of art and architecture. Generally, however, both the creed and the organisation of the Christian communities had changed little in a thousand years, and it was not until the Protestant Reformation in the sixteenth century that new forms of faith were to emerge. What is notable, is the increasing importance of the miraculous, the elaboration of liturgy, the growing tendency to veneration of relics and signs, and the development of popular movements such as the Franciscans, Waldenses and Lollards, and of schools of mysticism.

As to the conversion of non-Christians, many individuals were won over by merchants, captives or monks. They tended to live in small isolated communities, often persecuted but with little impact on their own people. Most of the converts, however, were drawn into the Church not by their own conviction but by the decision of their leaders, over which they had no choice. This political weapon of conversion en masse brought huge numbers under the umbrella of Christendom. Not surprisingly, mass conversion was often under duress, with baptism enforced as a mark of allegiance or submission. The clergy rarely protested at the means by which converts were brought to embrace the Church. These years witnessed the infliction of cruelty and conduct at complete variance with the Gospel against those to be converted, with the perpetrators often claiming to espouse Christian spiritual and moral ideas and even practising these when it came to their own people.

The work of proselytising abroad, and of teaching the coerced converts, was taken up by missionaries, for the most part monks, who played a vital role in the expansion of Christianity. The secular clergy generally only took on importance once Christianity had become more established and organised. The increasingly important monastic communities were set apart, their members seeking individual salvation, rather than the saving of the souls of others. They generally chose to live away from the towns and cities, often in remote parts, and accordingly they frequently inhabited areas where the populace was not Christian. Some monastic communities attracted visitors and converts impressed by their rigorous and devoted way of life. Whilst the monks remained apart, they nevertheless often took a role in religious teaching and in education.

The Christianity of the new converts, in particular those coerced into accept-ance, was not surprisingly somewhat superficial. The religious education was learned primarily from the monks whose exacting regime was held up as a model of Christian perfection. It took several hundred years before a concept of lay Christianity became established, offering a different set of Christian ideals.

The papacy was also directly engaged in the task of furthering the spread of Christianity, at least in the West. Gregory the Great, for example, instigated several missions, as did a number of other Popes, although many were less enthusiastic. More importantly, the Pope represented a focal point of unity. The papacy was a source of authority, settling disputes, conferring prestige on the secular clergy, bestowing blessings on the missionary clerics, and bolstering the determination of local Church leaders to maintain their independence from secular leaders. The papacy was a vital contributor to the spread of the faith, in a world in which the Christian cause depended so much on the protection and goodwill of the secular authorities. The civil leaders repeatedly sought to control ecclesiastical appoint-ments and the papacy was the only balwark against these intrusions, although it was far from always successful in its resistance. The determination of the papacy depended in large part on the incumbent who, in many cases, was unable or unwilling to exercise papal authority. Nevertheless, notwithstanding the frequent reality of weakness, the papacy remained a symbol of the moral authority of the Christian Church and its autonomy from the state. Indeed the position of the papacy compared favourably with that of the Church in Eastern Europe which was far less able to assert itself, less united, and dominated by the secular rulers in Constantinople.

The manner in which Christianity spread inevitably meant that it took some time before the populations supposedly under the umbrella of Christendom could truly be said to have embraced the faith. Indeed it was several hundreds of years before the tribesmen of northern Europe were converted, and even then their faith could hardly be said to be profound or comprehensive. It was not until the eighth century that the Germans of the Rhine valley could be said to be even superficially Christian, and it was not until the end of the twelfth century that the Scandinavians could be said to have thoroughly adopted Christianity. The speed of conversion was much less rapid than in the first five hundred years, or indeed compared to the expansion from the sixteenth century onwards. Whilst the growth of Christianity was slowing down, nevertheless it did continue. There were important exceptions, most notably where it encountered Islam. In these areas, Christianity experienced catastrophic setbacks. In the seventh century most of the Iberian peninsula was overrun, later to be recaptured. In the fifteenth century much of south-east Asia was lost. Further afield, the impact of Islam was even more marked with major setbacks in North Africa and Western Asia in the seventh century. Elsewhere there were advances. Nestorianism flourished in Central Asia, India and the Far East between the seventh and the fourteenth centuries, but thereafter faded rapidly.

In a work of this nature it is impossible to present a detailed and comprehensive account of the history of these thousand years, still less to present the various strands that make up this history in strict chronological order. Accordingly, in the sections that follow we have identified the crucial issues that dominated this period, in an attempt to enable the reader to gain an overall picture.

6.2   The growth of the papacy

The five hundred years to AD 1000

It was the latter half of the second millennium that was to witness the permeation of papal power and influence throughout Western Europe and into every feature of the lives of its peoples. The earlier years were very different. Certainly the Pope had authority. He was seen unquestionably as the successor of St Peter whose tomb was enshrined in Rome. Christendom had not yet, however, adopted any sophisticated doctrines of papal supremacy. Instead St Peter was seen as continuing Christ's work on earth through the Pope, a directing force, and an invaluable unifying foundation.

In these years, the papacy sought to exercise relatively little control. Monasteries were established, and ecclesiastical appointments made by local civilian rulers without protest from Rome. The bishops exercised a considerable degree of independence within their own sees, and councils were held, and rules decided, without papal involvement. Whilst Rome remained throughout a symbol of unity, this was centred on Christendom's conviction of the presence there of St Peter. There was no huge papal entourage or network of papal legates, instead the only points of contact between Rome and the local churches were the archbishops, who for many years exercised considerable independence. From the seventh century onwards, however, an archbishop was not permitted to assume office without first receiving the special vestment, known as a pallium, from the Pope. This could only be obtained after first making a written statement of his faith, the orthodoxy of which then had to meet with papal approval. This form of authority was also insisted upon by many archbishops in relation to their suffragan bishops, hence laying the foundations for an hierarchy of obedience and conformity.

One incumbent of the papacy in this period stands out for his efforts to revive the Church and to extend papal influence. Pope Gregory the Great (590–604) stressed the need for an hierarchical structure. He promulgated the claim of the papacy to universal jurisdiction over Christendom, and sought to develop the

Church in the West, both by cultivating links with pagan rulers and the leaders of the Germanic tribes, and by initiating and actively supporting missionary activity. Gregory, himself a monk, did much to advocate asceticism and the cause of monasticism, and gave considerable encouragement to the growing practice of venerating saints and relics.

AD 1000–1300: the move to Avignon and the era of expansion

The foundations of what was an era of great papal initiative and a rapidly expanding papal machine are to be attributed, in large part, to Leo IX who occupied the papacy for but a relatively short period from **1049** to **1054**. It was in these years that the practice of appointing papal legates directly responsible to the Pope became a more comprehensive tool of papal power and influence, that the volume of papal correspondence increased markedly and that the political alliance with the Normans was formed. Leo astutely advanced officials keen to forward his vision of a papal monarchy. A notable successor to such ideals was the former monk Hildebrand who became Pope Gregory VII in **1073**. Gregory laid claim to complete sovereignty in all matters, asserting the infallibility of the Roman Church, sole authority to make new laws and to establish new bishoprics, the right to absolve subjects from their allegiance to secular authorities, the precedence of papal legates over all bishops, and the predominance of an appeal to the papal courts over all other tribunals. Within a short period these grand pronouncements were far from mere pretensions but became accepted as part of the order of the day, and are indicative of the pervasive influence of the papacy throughout Western Europe.

By the twelfth century St Peter's role was in decline, and the incumbents of the papal see began adopting the more authoritative title of 'Vicar of Christ' in place of Vicar of St Peter, thereby giving form to their claim for universal sovereignty. In the two hundred and fifty years to **1300** a sophisticated, elaborate and efficient papal administrative machine took form which became a central force in Europe.

The growth of papal government is well illustrated by the increasing use of the main papal tools of influence, the Councils, the papal legates and papal correspondence. In the four hundred and fifty years to **1100** there were but three Councils, all held in the East, and with little input from the Church in the West. In contrast, in the following two hundred or so years to **1312** there were a total of seven General Councils, all summoned by the Pope, all held in the West, all conducted primarily in Latin and all were presided over by the Pope. The same period witnessed a major growth in the number and influence of papal legates, and a rapid increase in papal business, with the average number of surviving papal letters rising from very few in the first 500 years of this millennium to 35 a year under Leo IX, rising again under Innocent II by the middle of the twelfth century to 72. This figure was to increase to 280 by the end of the century, to 730 by the middle of the thirteenth century and to 3646 (and this is still per year) under John XXII (**1316–24**).

Whilst it is true that life in Europe was becoming more organised and complex across the board, and the organs of state administration were experiencing growth generally, nevertheless the papal machinery was expanding like no other administration. The driving force was not so much the pretensions of the holders of papal office as the demands on the papacy by the faithful, who petitioned the Pope for every imaginable form of remedy. Medieval government prospered and maintained its authority by granting benefits and dispensing justice, and the papacy was the supplier *par excellence* of these highly sought-after commodities. The gifts of the Pope were eternal, and were not subject to an appeal to a higher court.

A substantial proportion of papal correspondence originated from monastic communities seeking approval of their land rights and customs and independence from the bishops. The single most important cause of the expansion, however, was the incessant demand from litigants for the determination of a vast range of different disputes, arising out of every conceivable aspect of ecclesiastical administration throughout virtually the entire continent of Europe. In addition to disputes arising out of appointments to all levels of clerical office, the papal court was petitioned to inquire into heresies, to confirm the privileges of religious orders, to have debts to moneylenders reduced, to reverse excommunications and other religious sentences, to determine the sincerity of religious vows, to allow those born outside wedlock to enter Holy Orders despite their illegitimacy, to approve the conditions of loans, and even to approve the terms of a queen's dowry.

This flow of litigation resulted in a complex and comprehensive system of laws governing every feature of Christian life from baptism to burial, from confession to penance, from alms to usury, from marriage to regulations for monastic life.

One striking aspect of litigation before the papal court is the extraordinary resilience and determination of the claimants who frequently incurred costs which appear quite disproportionate to any benefit or remedy they could conceivably have received. Many were even prepared to burden themselves or their monastic communities with loans under the conviction that, if successful, the benefits they would procure for their family or community would endure for all time.

The administration of papal justice brought in valuable revenue by way of fees charged to litigants, and was an indispensable and highly practical means of furthering papal political objectives. Papal gifts and papal justice served to win allies and punish enemies.

By the later years of the twelfth century the papal legal administration had become an effective and efficient machine, probably employing over a hundred scholars with legal expertise, and heading a legal system processing the various forms of proceedings, recording judgements, making copies of important documentation and drafting the documentation required to implement the decisions of the papal court. The Popes themselves were inexorably caught up in overseeing the legal machine. Indeed it is a telling feature that every Pope of any note from **1159** to **1303** had trained in law!

The power and influence of the papacy was nevertheless limited by the political reality of being an administration without the physical means to impose its will on its secular adversaries. At the end of the day, papal rulings and excommunication were ineffective or in some cases counterproductive. In ecclesiastical matters, papal power and influence were understandably less vulnerable, in large part because the papacy could bestow far more valuable benefits on the secular clergy and the monastic communities than it could offer its political adversaries.

The fourteenth and fifteenth centuries

In the early years of the Middle Ages, the Pope's authority was firmly rooted in his role as successor to St Peter, whose remains were enshrined at Rome where his bodily presence was thought to remain and from where he directed the Church through his Vicar. The strength of papal authority by the beginning of the fourteenth century is well illustrated by the ability of the papacy to continue and develop its administration after moving to Avignon in 1309, where the papal government remained for a period of seventy years. The move to Avignon, far from undermining the Pope's authority, made the papal court more accessible to the faithful in that geographically it came within far easier reach for most of the inhabitants of Western Christendom.

The years following the move witnessed the continued growth of the papal machinery of government. Inevitably, like all organisations, as the administration grew it generated increasing numbers of officials and gave birth to increasingly complex procedures. Its efficiency began to diminish, thereby limiting its own effectiveness. By the fourteenth century, the still increasing level of business handled by papal government was no longer serving to further enhance papal power and influence, and accordingly the papacy sought other means to effect this. These means were to prove effective only in the short-term, as each effort to enhance papal power seemed to generate a counterbalance. The net effect was to further suffocate papal power.

A major feature of the fourteenth and fifteenth centuries is the granting of papal indulgences. This originated in 1095 when Urban II proclaimed that those joining the Crusade would be ensured of a place in Heaven. The granting of indulgences was rare, for the most part limited to those participating in the subsequent Crusades. A hundred years later, eligibility was broadened to include those who assisted the Crusaders with finance or advice. A hundred years further on, by the beginning of the fourteenth century, they had become a tool to be used to advance the Pope's goals. By the middle of the century, indulgences had become a source of revenue, as individuals were permitted to purchase an absolute indulgence for the time of their death.

These centuries also saw the granting of indulgences to those making a timely pilgrimage to Rome. In 1300 Pope Boniface VIII bestowed absolute indulgences on all those who visited the shrines of Rome in that year and every hundredth year thereafter. The interval was subsequently reduced by successive Popes, eventually to every twenty five years by 1470. These pilgrimages resulted in substantial, although diminishing financial benefits to the papal purse. The first 'Jubilee', according to some accounts, attracted well over a million visitors to the city in 1300. Thereafter the volume of tourists decreased, but nevertheless had a significant beneficial impact on the prosperity of the city and the papacy.

The papal entourage proved innovative in its exploitation of indulgences by framing different and separate circumstances in which they were granted, thereby creating an individual's demand for a variety of indulgences to ensure salvation whatever the cause of his demise. The system became extremely complex. The consequence of such widespread granting of indulgences was inevitable. As they increased in circulation they declined in value, the downward process exacerbated by growth in the manufacture of forged copies of documents evidencing indulgences.

In international politics too, the papacy underwent changes in the manner in which it sought to further its influence. In theory, the Pope was the supreme secular authority in the same way as in ecclesiastical matters. The reality was somewhat different. The Pope's secular power could only be exercised through the secular rulers to whom, so the claim ran, he delegated power. This theory was nowhere more concretely demonstrated than in the case of the Emperor himself. Uniquely, succession to the imperial throne was not hereditary but required coronation by the Pope. The Emperor, more than any other ruler to whom power was in theory delegated by the Vicar of Christ, should defer to papal wishes. Successive popes found the situation was more complex. Henry V, for example, whom the Pope crowned as Emperor, proved far more dangerous than Henry IV whom he had refused to crown. The reality was that the Pope could only be effective against his secular adversaries by the destructive means of forming alliances, instigating wars and thereby destroying his enemy. The result was always chaos. Whilst the Pope could bring down his adversaries, what he was not able to do was to rebuild out of the mayhem that ensued.

This frustration in secular affairs resulted in the papacy taking a growing role in international diplomacy. There were many opportunities: in the Middle Ages, wars, once started, tended to be long lasting. The papacy, keen to enhance its status and prestige, stepped in as an arbitrator to negotiate first a truce and, if successful, a settlement of the dispute. Equipped with a papal office staffed by lawyers well versed in the art of negotiation and determining disputes, together with the wide range of benefits he could himself bestow to ease the path to settlement, the Pope was an ideal arbitrator. In performing this role, however, the Pope was not exercising any compulsion, or asserting his temporal sovereignty over the parties – far from it. The reality was that the powers of those appointed by the Pope to conduct the negotiations were restricted to those agreed by the warring parties. The claim to secular supremacy had been relinquished, under the pressures of political reality.

It was political reality too that determined who eventually controlled appointments to ecclesiastical office. The protagonists in this struggle claimed to be adhering to the same guiding principle that had governed the early Church, namely that appointees should be the representatives of, and chosen by, those to whom they minister. Election to ecclesiastical office accordingly should require the consent of the laity, the clergy and the bishops. How the will of these different constituents was supposedly ascertained and aggregated was not determined.

As to the papacy itself, up until the eleventh century the Emperor laid claim to represent the clergy and peoples of Western Christendom in any papal election. Himself crowned by the incumbent of the papal see, he affirmed his authority to express the will of the Church. By the latter half of the eleventh century, however, the Emperor had come to play a much reduced role. It was instead those with influence in Rome itself, that is the cardinals and the local nobility, who wielded the power in selecting a new Pope. In 1059 Pope Nicholas II decreed that the cardinals alone were to elect his successor, but this did not prevent the Emperor and the local nobility from exercising more indirect influence through cardinals whom they could win over. The situation was even more confused by the fact that some cardinals were entitled to vote, but others merely to be consulted. There was no effective mechanism for resolving disagreements, and in the one hundred and twenty years after the decree there were repeated disputes over papal succession. At the Lateran Council of 1179 a clear procedure was at last adopted in which all cardinals had equal votes, and a valid election required a two-thirds majority. In the following two hundred years, there was only a brief period in which the succession was in dispute.

As to appointments to the episcopacy, from the eighth to the eleventh centuries the principle of selection by local clergy and people gave way to the reality of nomination by local secular rulers. In time, the local clergy came to reassert their own claims to select their bishops, and by the latter half of the twelfth century the canons of a cathedral church were acknowledged as entitled to elect their own choice as bishop. The result of ousting the control of the secular rulers was that frequently there were disputes as to the outcome of elections, leading to lengthy and costly appeals to the papal court. Ultimately, in the fourteenth century, the papacy declared its exclusive power to appoint successors to the episcopacy. Ironically, however, the net result was that the power of electing bishops was taken from the local clergy and returned to the secular leader, for the papacy was unable to impose its own choice in the face of opposition from the local secular leader who found it easier to impose his own wishes than he had done when dealing with the local clergy.

As to other appointments, these followed a similar pattern. At the beginning of the second millennium the right of appointing clergy had been assumed by local secular leaders. In the twelfth and thirteenth centuries the papacy increasingly laid claim to the power to appoint its own candidates. By the fourteenth century the Pope had assumed the habit of making large numbers of grants of minor ecclesiastical office to aspirants from all over Europe, in many cases promising the same office to a number of applicants, who on the position becoming vacant would then assert their competing and inconsistent claims. The net result, as with episcopal appointments, was that the candidate who could count on the support of the local secular leader generally won the day.

Whilst the power of the papacy in these thousand years peaked in the thirteenth century only to decline thereafter, the papacy remained very much part of European life, representing, despite its obvious faults, a symbol of permanency and continuity, of moral authority and the path to salvation.

6.3   The encounter with Islam

In the first six hundred years Christianity had continually grown in strength and numbers, overcoming persecution, establishing itself as the religion of the Roman Empire, dominating Western Europe even as the Empire collapsed and was overrun by semi-civilised invaders, and penetrating northward far beyond the boundaries of the former Empire.

Islam was to present an entirely different threat. In the following nine hundred years, Islam succeeded in winning over many peoples who had formerly professed

Christianity. The setbacks were to totally outstrip any reverses sustained before or since, including even those suffered by the later Church in the advance of totalitarian communism. Whilst Christianity had overcome the less advanced religious tribal beliefs of semi-civilised peoples, Islam acknowledged Jesus as a prophet, but vigorously asserted its claim to supersede Christianity.

The initial progress of Islam was startling, the speed of its advance far exceeding the earlier rate of growth of Christianity. Mohammed began his teaching in about **610**, and by his death in **632** the whole of Arabia was committed to his teachings. Within a century Islam had spread as far as Morocco in the west, and Pakistan in the east. The Muslims were led by 'caliphs' or 'successors', fired with religious fervour and combining both secular and religious office. They created a religious Empire consisting of a series of 'caliphates' based largely upon Mecca, Baghdad, Damascas and Cairo together with a series of separate states, their military commanders generally assuming governorship of occupied territories. Whilst the caliphates were not part of a single state or administration, they nevertheless shared a common Arab culture and a single language, in addition to the unifying zeal of the new, and growing faith. No translations of the Koran were permitted and accordingly the Arabic language dominated both in religious matters and in the laws and teachings which Islam generated.

The advances of Islam at the expense of Christendom were in two separate phases. In the seventh and eighth centuries Islamic leaders took control of Arabia, Syria, Mesopotamia, Persia, Palestine, Egypt, North Africa and the Iberian Peninsula. There followed a period of five centuries when the progress of Islam into Christian territories came to a standstill. In these years Christianity succeeded in further expansion into northern Europe and had a few ephemeral victories against Islam in the Middle East. At the same time, Franciscan and Dominican missionaries made considerable but piecemeal progress in some areas, even penetrating into Central Asia and the Far East. In the thirteenth and fourteenth centuries, however, Islam again made significant advances in the form of conquests by Turkish and Mongol converts. In the conflict, many pagans adopted Islam, as did a number of peoples in Central Asia who had professed Christianity. In the latter years, the Ottoman Turks imposed Islamic rule in Constantinople and the Balkans, resulting in many conversions away from Christianity, and a good deal of outward migration. In the sixteenth century Christianity again made successful progress in Asia, as indeed did Islam. After **1500** the advances made by both religions were not generally to the detriment of the other.

The expansion of Islam at the expense of Christianity was almost entirely a consequence of military and political victory, followed by conversions within the newly conquered territories. The commonly held belief that there was wholesale forced conversion is simply incorrect. Whilst coercion was applied, this was the exception. The numerous conversions which followed the military conquests resulted rather from the damage to the prestige of the Christian faith and the belief of many that God had deserted the Church, and from economic and social discrimination, with Christians being subject to special taxation. Outside the areas under Muslim control there was practically no apostacy from Christianity to Islam.

Coercion was employed by Muslim armies, but against pagan faiths, not against Jews and Christians whose religious beliefs were seen as preceding their own and accorded a considerable degree of toleration. The present-day belief in the violent aggression of Islam is accurate in so far as it concerns other religious beliefs, but it is questionable whether the Muslims were any more guilty than Christians in the use of the sword to impose their faith on pagans. On the other hand, it was only Christianity which sought to evangelise by systematic missionary activity.

Christianity, and indeed Judaism, had a marked influence upon the Islamic faith. It had already made substantial progress in Arabia even before Mohammed began his teaching. How familiar Mohammed was with Christian thinking is not clear. Whilst there are sections of the Koran discussing Jesus and Christianity, they do not point to a thorough understanding of Christian doctrine or of a knowledge of the New Testament. What is unquestionable is that in the course of his life Mohammed did come to know something of Jesus, whom he considered to have been a prophet. After Mohammed's death, Christianity was to have a more marked influence as the infant Islam began to develop a more comprehensive set of beliefs. The new Christian converts to Islam brought with them their own culture, practices and thought processes, and inevitably had a considerable impact on their new rulers, who were impressed by their subjects' culture and training in such areas as philosophy, physics and medicine.

The ease with which Islam spread so rapidly is to be attributed not merely to the religious enthusiasm of its adherents, but also to the historical context into which Islam was born. For years, the Persian and Byzantine Empires had been locked in an exhausting struggle, the Arabs had been threatening the borders of both empires, and several of the peoples within the Byzantine Empire were becoming defiant.

Islam advanced with extraordinary speed. Within four years of Mohammed's death, Syria and Palestine were practically under Islamic rule. Jerusalem was conquered two years later in 638, and Muslim troops had entered Alexandria by 642 and entered Mesopotamia and Persia in the same decade, later to reach the Punjab and well into Central Asia. In the early years of the eigth century Islam advanced from Carthage (captured in 697), overrunning the entire coastal area of North Africa and most of Spain. In the ninth century, Italy itself was subjected to conquest in the south, and for two hundred years the Muslims held Sicily.

The new rulers were quick to impose restrictions on their Christian subjects, who were compelled to make public their faith by wearing a special mark or clothes, and obliged to pay a special tax. Restrictions were imposed on the building of new churches and public worship. Enforcement of these measures was varied, but there was no widespread attempt at coerced conversion – indeed the authorities feared the loss of revenue from the discriminatory taxes that would result, and even took steps to penalise those who converted to Islam.

Notwithstanding the absence of forced conversion, however, the Church inevitably declined faced with migration of Islamic peoples, the more numerous progeny of polygamous Muslim men whose children from Christian wives were of course born into Islam, and apostasy sometimes motivated by social and economic reasons, sometimes stemming from conviction at one extreme or persecution at the other. Seldom did anyone return to the fold, or the Church attract converts from Islam – the punishment for such was death.

The prestige and confidence of the Church took a severe battering. Appointments to clerical office, including the episcopate, were frequently the prerogative of local Muslim rulers who even called Councils and placed Jews and fellow Muslims in them. The martyrdom of the early Church was seldom repeated, the majority of laity and clergy alike keeping a low profile.

By the mid-ninth century Islam had become firmly rooted throughout the southern half of the Mediterranean basin, Christianity was in retreat, Rome was under threat, the great former Christian centres of Alexandria and Carthage were under Muslim rule, the Muslims were creating their own culture, and northern Europe was fearful of incursions by Scandinavian tribesmen. The future for Christianity looked dim.

In the following six hundred years Christianity made a substantial recovery from the brink of disaster. Christendom was fortunate in that the ability of its opponents to continue their advances became severely inhibited by internal quarrels and personal and family dissent, and a loss of enthusiasm by many Muslims for the trials and tribulations of further conquests. On the other hand, Christianity experienced a revival of its fortunes, with the Byzantine Church in the ninth and tenth centuries prevailing over the pagan beliefs of the various tribes that had previously breached its borders. The invaders were now embracing Christianity and the Byzantine Empire was confidently pushing its borders northwards, and retaking areas that had been captured by the Muslims in Syria and Cilicia and converting their inhabitants. For about a century these areas were to remain under Byzantine rule. The Western Church, likewise, was successful in bringing the northern tribesmen, including the previously marauding Scandinavians, at least nominally within its ambit.

It was Western Europe, however, that produced the effective challenge to Islam, first by force of arms in the Iberian Peninsula, Sicily and in the Crusades, and later by an unparalleled surge in missionary activity.

Spain and Portugal

In contrast to the speed of the Muslim conquest, the recapture of the Iberian Peninsula took an eternity with the last Islamic state of Granada not falling until 1492, the struggle having lasted in all some eight hundred years. The first defeats for the Arabs came at Asturias in 718 and at Tours in 732, and within about thirty years they were driven back to the Pyrenees, with Barcelona falling to the Emperor Charlemagne as early as 801. Thereafter progress was slower, with the Christian advance hampered by dissension and warfare between the various Christian rulers and a revival of Muslim fortunes under Almanzor, the minister and general of the Caliph of Cordova. From 1034 the Muslims suffered severely from the loss of the leadership of the Caliphate of Cordova. Not only were the Muslims divided, but they faced opposition from the many Christians in the territories under their own control who were anxious to assist in their overthrow. Dissension in Christian ranks continued to hamper progress, but by about 1250 only Granada remained in Muslim hands.

The campaigns to recapture the Iberian Peninsula witnessed the use not merely of civilian force of arms, but also of the Crusading orders, like the Order of

Christ, enforced baptism and exile, and attempts at conversion by missionary activity in the areas recaptured. In contrast to the Crusades and despite an order of the Pope, the Spaniards and Portuguese fought with little assistance from the rest of Christendom.

As to the Muslims who fell under Christian rule they were generally granted religious tolerance, but required to pay special taxes. They were treated in much the same way as Christians had been treated under Islamic rule. Many Muslims left for North Africa, and others embraced the Christian faith, perhaps persuaded by the efforts or the enthusiasm of the missionaries who followed in the wake of military advances, especially in what were the early days of the Franciscans and Dominicans in the first years of the thirteenth century.

Whilst religious toleration was the rule, there were exceptions, particularly from the late fifteenth century with the Inquisition being set up in Spain, charged with the task of hunting down those claiming to be Christian but who were clandestinely Jews or Muslims.

Asia Minor and the Crusades

In **1071** at the battle of Manzikert, the fierce Seljuk Turks defeated the armies of the Byzantine Empire and invaded Asia Minor, seizing more than half the Empire. Eastern appeals for help were eventually acted upon by Pope Urban II who in **1095** spoke passionately of Turkish atrocities being inflicted upon the churches and holy shrines of the Middle East, of the rape of Christian women, and of murder and torture. The Pope sent legates throughout Europe to join a Holy Crusade against the Turks, his initial motivation being not to forward the Gospel but the rescuing of holy shrines, and the defence of Christians in the East against Muslim aggression. In the following two hundred years the Crusades were to become an important feature of European history.

There can be little doubt that religious zeal constituted an important force behind the Crusades. However, there were other factors at play. The Crusades represented both a continuation of the migrations of the Teutonic peoples that had featured in the collapse of the Roman Empire, and the beginnings of the expansion of Western Europe which was later to result in the voyages of discovery and the emigration of Europeans throughout the globe.

In all there are said to have been seven crusades, but it is more accurate to see the Crusades as a continuing military campaign involving not just larger expeditions but also many smaller expeditionary forces. Indeed by **1150** there was a regular flow of soldiers, pilgrims and merchants from Europe to Syria. The First Crusade, however, was by the far the most successful, in large part because of Muslim disunity. Jerusalem was captured in **1099**, and four crusader states were established. Elsewhere the advance of the Seljuk Turks was halted, temporarily putting off the collapse of the Byzantine Empire. The success of the Crusaders, however, could not continue when unity began to return to Muslim ranks, and in **1187** Jerusalem was recaptured. In the thirteenth century the Crusaders were limited to a coastal strip with Acre as their capital, and although Jerusalem was reoccupied it fell again into Muslim hands in **1244**. In the late thirteenth century the Sultans of Egypt gradually whittled away at the Crusader States, and Acre was finally captured in 1291, ending Christian rule in Syria.

The Crusades were accompanied by the growth of trading posts and colonies along the Eastern Mediterranean, from which missionaries set out into the hinterland. However, few converts were made among the Muslims, rather Christians from the several Eastern Churches were brought under the umbrella of Rome.

Missionary activity and dialogue

Force of arms and trade were not the only points of contact between Christians and Muslims, for intellectuals engaged in debate, each side seeking to demonstrate the truth of their faith through dialogue. By the middle of the thirteenth century, when it was clear that military victory over Islam was elusive, Christian thinkers, such as Raymond Lull, one of the most noteworthy missionaries of the thirteenth and fourteenth century, began to move away from the idea of permanent war with Islam, in favour of persuasion. Others were growing tired of the constant warfare, and support grew for peaceful missions. Thus, in the fourteenth century, several university chairs were created for Oriental languages to train prospective missionaries, as advocated by Raymond Lull and others.

The missionary task was taken up by the Franciscans and Dominicans who adopted a completely different outlook from earlier religious orders, who were primarily preoccupied with asceticism and the salvation of their own souls. With papal support, the two orders went out to nearly all parts of the Muslim world in which, whilst they won over relatively few converts, they administered to Christian merchants and captives.

In the fourteenth and fifteenth centuries, Christianity again sustained considerable reverses as a result of a fresh phase of Muslim invasions. In the eleventh century the Seljuk Turks had converted to Islam, and continued to press south and west, advancing into the Byzantine Empire. Here, as in the Iberian Peninsula, the Muslims practised religious toleration, though Christianity steadily declined because of the extent of Turkish migration into Asia Minor and the inevitable acceptance by many Christians of Islam. The Mongols who followed the Turks were rather more ruthless. Initially they attacked Christian and Muslim alike, but on adopting Islam they concentrated their efforts on Christianity. In the thirteenth and fourteenth centuries new Muslim invaders, the Ottoman Turks, were threatening Western Christendom. They made advances in Asia Minor, in 1453 capturing Constantinople and defeating the Byzantine Empire, and thereafter continuing into Greece and the Balkans. The defeat of the Byzantine Empire, and the expansion of the Ottoman Turks into Eastern Europe, proved devastating for the Church, since the state religion was now under the shadow of a Muslim sultan. Many thousands were converted. The churches rapidly declined, becoming identified with the remaining Eastern minority nationalities under Ottoman rule. In the late fourteenth and fifteenth century Christendom was subjected to further attacks in Central Asia, Persia and the Caucasus, and suffered setbacks in Egypt, the Sudan and Ethiopia.

By 1500 Christianity was virtually confined to Europe. Islam, on the other hand, controlled much of the Mediterranean and, apart from losses in the Iberian

Peninsula, was still making advances in many parts of the globe. The fortunes of Christendom, however, were set to take a new turn.

6.4 Dissent, persecution and inquisition

In the early Middle Ages, heresy was mainly confined to individual academics or eccentric preachers, and the Church did not feel the necessity to take any systematic measures to counter it. However, in the twelfth century, dissident movements began to make considerable advances, in particular the Waldensians and the Cathars, against whom the Church took rigorous steps.

The **Cathars** prospered in Western Europe in the twelfth and thirteenth centuries, especially in southern France and northern Italy. So successful were they, that by the turn of the twelfth century it was feared that they might completely replace the Catholic Church in southern France. The Cathars believed in two gods: a benign god who created the spiritual world, and an evil god who created the material world. Humanity and the earth were dominated by the evil god of the Old Testament, and Christ, a spirit, had been sent by the good god to lead men to salvation. They believed in a spiritual baptism by the laying on of hands, which cleansed the recipients of orginal sin, permitting them to join the kingdom of the good god after their death. Those who had received this baptism were known as the Perfect, led a life of asceticism and were revered by the Believers, who chose to delay receiving baptism until death approached out of a reluctance to submit to the rigours accepted by the Perfect.

The lifestyles of the Cathars represented a marked contrast to the corruption within the established Church, and their success caused such concern that in **1208** Pope Innocent III instigated a crusade against the Cathars of southern France.

The **Waldensians** sought to imitate Christ by a life of poverty and preaching in the vernacular, and gained great popular support. The Waldensians refused to accept the authority of the hierarchy of the established Church, and Church customs which were not derived from the New Testament. They rejected the observance of feast days, the doctrine of purgatory, prayers to images of saints, liturgy, indulgences and so on. Like the Cathars, they formed themselves into two levels, with the higher believers acting as evangelising missionaries, living austere lives, and dependent for support on their lesser brethren. Their unworldliness, like the holiness of the Cathars, highlighted the faults in the Catholic Church. In **1184** they were excommunicated by Pope Lucius III who instigated a campaign of inquisition against them and other dissident movements. Notwithstanding this opposition the Waldensians gained strength, particularly in Provence and Lombardy, and by the beginning of the fourteenth century had spread throughout most of continental Europe, later becoming particularly strong in central and eastern Europe. Their ideas were to influence the Protestant movement in the following century.

The persecution of dissident movements that began in the twelfth century was initially conducted by local secular and ecclesiastical leaders. However, by the end of the century the papacy was taking a more active role. In **1184** Lucius III issued an edict requiring bishops to organise inquisitions to counter the main heresies and to transfer convicted heretics to the secular authorities for punishment. Innocent III (1198–1216), irritated at the failure of the local episcopacy to root out the Cathars, sent out members of the Cistercian order into parts of France, followed by the Dominicans who were to come to play such a central role in the Inquisition. In 1224 further ferocity was added when Emperor Frederick II decreed that heretics should be burnt, a policy adopted and approved by Pope Gregory IX in 1231. The machinery of the Inquisition was by now firmly established with the Dominicans serving as the Pope's agents and with the infliction of torture offically sanctioned by Pope Innocent IV in 1252.

The method of the inquisitors was to descend upon a town without warning, together with a team of examiners, advisers, prison officers and notaries to record evidence. The local population would then be addressed and all those who suspected heresy in themselves were called to confession and absolution. Suspected heretics who had not come forward were then arrested and detained until they could be tried. The evidence against suspects was frequently tenuous and difficult to challenge, all the more so when supported by a confession extracted under torture. The trial was held in camera with the inquisitor acting as prosecutor, judge and jury with power to convict on the testimony of two witnesses. No one was prepared to risk their own safety by representing those accused.

More lenient sentences included attendance at masses, pilgrimages, or fines. Other penalties were the wearing of special signs to publicise the offender's crime, the confiscation of property, disqualification from holding office or from entering into contracts, and imprisonment. For the insubordinate, impenitent and relapsed the sentence was frequently death at the stake, for which punishment the Church handed the offender over to the civil authorities.

The intensity of the Inquisition varied according to the approach taken by the local secular rulers, the enthusiasm of the local church leaders, and by the occasional steps taken by the papacy to curtail its most extreme zealots. In Spain the Inquisition was pursued with great vigour, after 1480 becoming part of the monarchy's machinery of government and remaining a real force in the country for a further four hundred years. In France and parts of Italy the Inquisition was very active until the fifteenth century, although the Waldensians in the Alps were fortunate to outlive its rigours. England for the most part avoided the terrors of the Inquisition. Germany experienced intermittent episodes, but the power of the papal inquisitors was somewhat limited. In the late fifteenth century the Inquisition declined, only to be rejuvenated in the middle of the sixteenth century when a new reign of terror was inaugurated to deter the spread of Protestantism.

6.5   The Eastern Church

The Byzantine Church and the West to 1054

In the seventh and eighth centuries the East suffered major setbacks as much of the Empire was invaded and occupied by Slavs in Greece, the Mongol Avars in Eastern Europe and the Bulgars in the Danube valley who laid waste to monasteries and centres of learning. As ever, the fortunes of Christianity were closely related to those of the secular rulers. It was not until the second half of the ninth century that Latin and Greek missionaries eventually succeeded in the conversion of these barbarian tribesmen. The hundred years from **650** saw the Church sustain further major reverses, this time at the hands of Islam, again with the East suffering the greatest impact including the loss of Asia Minor and Egypt, and the historically and intellectually important eastern patriarchal centres of Alexandria, Jerusalem and Antioch. After these Islam advances, the West was largely ignorant of Christianity in the eastern cities and their surrounding provinces for centuries. Rome and Constantinople, however, were still parts of the same Christian Empire, with the Byzantine Emperor ruling much of Italy including Rome. The links between the two cities were strong. The Greek language and culture were very evident in Rome, with many Greek and other foreign monks having fled there from the Islamic advance, and there were regions in Italy where the Greek churches predominated. The papacy in the century between **650** and **750** was dominated by Popes with a Greek background, these outnumbering the Latins by two to one.

The presence of such a strong Greek influence at Rome appeared to bode well for the future unity of Christendom. This appearance was further strengthened by the visit in **663** of the Greek Emperor to Rome, and by the reception given in **710** to the Pope on his visit to Constantinople.

The appearance was illusory. The Greek Emperor's visit to Rome was not repeated for seven hundred years, nor were subsequent Popes welcomed in Constantinople. By the end of the eighth century there was not even a pretence of political unity between these two halves of Christendom, and by the twelfth century they had come to see themselves as very separate indeed. The causes of this separation, and the recurrent attempts at reunion were, in part, political: while the Byzantine Emperors held dominion in southern Italy, the Popes generally sought imperial approval of their election but, when the Lombards shrugged off imperial rule, the papacy became more independent, and the bonds with the East less important. The success of the Lombards, however, did leave the papacy vulnerable, and accordingly in the mid eighth century the Pope forged an alliance with the Carolingian king Pepin. This was to remain an important feature of the political scene for most of the Middle Ages, with the Carolingians taking over dominion of Byzantine territories in Italy. This marked a turning point, with the Pope choosing to defy the Byzantine Emperor and to forge closer links with political allies in the West, a change of direction which was given dramatic form in the coronation of Charlemagne in **800**, reviving the Empire in the West.

A further factor was rivalry between the Pope in Rome and the Patriarch in Constantinople. As Rome shrank in political importance and Constantinople grew to become the greatest political and cultural city in Europe, the Patriarch became less and less inclined to acknowledge papal supremacy. The Emperors too were not keen to accept jurisdiction over their subjects by an ecclesiastical power outside their control. The various attempts at reunion always had some political imperial motive, as was abundantly apparent when imperial forces were failing to keep back the Ottoman Turks and military help was needed from the West.

Even by the seventh century there were many divergences in customs between the two halves of Christendom, to add to their different languages. The Greeks excommunicated those who missed communion for three successive Sundays, the Romans did not; the Greek monks refused to have slaves, the Roman monks thought this acceptable; the Greeks admitted widows as nuns, the Romans did not. Whilst these differences were relatively trivial compared to the areas of agreement, they were seen by many as a problem for the imposition of discipline and unity.

The divergence which gave rise to the greatest controversy was the Nicene Creed. This statement of belief had been accepted by the whole Church and declared that the Holy Spirit comes 'from the Father'. At some stage, an unknown individual or Christian community in the West had added the words 'and the Son'. This usage was given wide practice after its adoption at the chapel of Charlemagne, and by the eleventh century was in use throughout nearly the entire Western Church, ironically with the exception of Rome which only adopted it fully by about 1030.

An essential difference was that in the East there was no single Church ruler. The most important Christian centre was Constantinople, the great imperial and cultural capital of the East. From the reign of Constantine, the Emperors of the East had taken a major role in the governing of the Church. From the first ecumenical council of Nicaea in 325 until the seventh council in 787, also at Nicaea, the Emperor presided over proceedings, often in person. The Emperor was seen by many as head of the Church. This concept of his ecclesiastical role became embedded, and no doubt accounts for the assumption of that role by Russian Emperors following the collapse of Byzantine imperial rule. Whilst the Imperial will generally prevailed, often motivated by the desire to achieve and enforce unity, it was not without opposition, and controversies which have the appearance of being doctrinal often were in large part an expression of attempts by the Greek Church and the Patriarch of Constantinople to assert independence.

Success in controlling ecclesiastical leaders did not stifle deep-seated doctrinal controversies. One explanation for this was the relative independence of the episcopacy. Whilst the lack of authority over local bishops of the Patriarch of Constantinople weakened his position *vis-à-vis* the Emperor, it also made it more difficult for the Emperor to enforce uniformity.

Whilst the Western Church was far freer from the political interference that plagued the Eastern Churches, Western Christianity nevertheless remained indebted to the more cultured and educated East. The East had been the cradle of Christianity, and boasted the main centres of learning including Antioch and Alexandria. The upper echelons of Eastern civilisation were well educated, whereas illiteracy still prevailed among their Western counterparts. In the task of civilising and educating the barbarian invaders, the West benefited greatly from Eastern influence as is apparent, for example, in the churches and mosaics to be found on the Adriatic coast and along the shores of North Africa and Gaul, and in the growth of the veneration of the cross.

Doctrinal controversies originating in the East had on occasion an important impact in the West. The Iconoclastic controversy lasted from 726 through to 842. The struggle originated out of efforts in the East to counter the growing reverence given to icons. By the seventh century many of the cities had one or more local saints whose icons were said to have special powers. The bitter dispute culminated in the restoration of icons, but served to heighten even further the domination of the secular rulers over the Eastern Church, and damaged further the ties with the Church in the West. In **726** Emperor Leo II issued an edict declaring his opposition to icons, and a few years later called for the destruction of all religious icons in churches and in all public places. The Pope condemned the Emperor's actions, and in response the Emperor transferred Sicily, southern Italy, and the whole of the western part of the Balkans and Greece away from the papal see to the Patriarch of Constantinople. This served to increase the forces pushing the papacy into alliance with the Franks.

The motives behind the imperial policy of iconoclasm were mixed. Whilst Leo no doubt shared the abhorrence of the educated classes for superstition, it also served to reduce the influence of the monks, who were proving more effective than the episcopacy in asserting their freedom to decide ecclesiastical issues for themselves. Not only were monks exempt from military service, they were immune from taxation and their monasteries derived considerable income from visiting pilgrims. The iconoclast policy continued under Emperor Constantine V (**741–75**). It is estimated that 50,000 monks and other holy men fled from Constantinople and its surrounds to avoid the persecution. It was not until the Council of Nicaea in **787** that veneration of icons was again made lawful and relations with Rome were eased. The dispute flared up again in **815** when a new Emperor again espoused iconoclasm. Whilst he removed the Patriarch at Constantinople, he did not pursue the policy with the same vigour as his predecessors and there was none of the severe persecutions of the earlier years. The policy faded after the decision of the Council of Nicaea was reaffirmed in **842**.

The history of divisions and reconciliations between East and West between the fifth and the eleventh centuries was finally brought to a head in **1054** by an angry rift between the papal legate, Cardinal Humbert, and the Patriarch of Constantinople, Michael Cerularius. Additional foundations for this particular dispute had been laid thirty years earlier, when the Greek Emperor had sent an envoy to Pope John XIX requesting his consent for the Patriarch of Constantinople to be termed universal within his sphere, as Rome was within the whole Church. The Pope rejected this request, thereby alienating many in the East who considered that Rome held only a primacy of honour. The rivalry between the two Christian centres was fuelled by developments in southern Italy where Greek churches in Bari vied for supremacy with the Latin churches in Apulia. The politics of the region were further complicated by the occupation of large parts of Italy by the Normans. Cerularius feared an alliance between the Pope and the Emperor to drive out the Normans, which might result in the transfer of jurisdiction over the Churches in Bari to the papacy, and a weakening of his authority as Patriarch.

Cerularius set out to undermine any such alliance. He encouraged criticism of Latin practices, and in **1053** ordered the closing of all churches of Latin rite in Constantinople. In response a papal legation at Constantinople, led by Cardinal Humbert, excommunicated the Patriarch. The papacy itself had not been directly involved, the Pope having died before the excommunication. Cerularius, however, determined on establishing his own ascendancy, denounced the Cardinal. The Patriarchate of Constantinople emerged victorious, but the victory ultimately proved pyrrhic. Thereafter reconciliation proved impossible, rendering far less effective the Crusades of the following two and a half centuries, and facilitating the fall of Constantinople to the Turks in **1453**.

The rift did indeed prove irreversible. Over nine hundred years later, by a joint declaration on the 7th December **1965**, Pope Paul VI and Patriarch Athenagoras expressed their ' . . . regret for the offensive words, the unfounded accusations and the despicable acts which, from one side or another, marked or accompanied the sad events of this period'.

Attempts at reunion

In the years between **1054** and the fall of Constantinople in **1453**, several policies were contemplated to effect a reunion, ranging from military conquest, through to a settlement based on negotiation and discussion to counter religious divergence. The primary choice of the papacy was diplomacy aimed at persuading the Byzantine Emperor of the wisdom of religious unity with Rome, with papal support in return for the obedience of the Eastern churches. To the Emperor, faced with the advancing forces of Islam this was an attractive proposition. However the monastic communities, the intellectuals and, indeed, the Christian populace in the East were not amenable to imperial authority on such important ecclesiastical issues.

The Paulicians and the Bogomils

The **Paulicians** were a sect which gained some prominence in the Byzantine Empire after **650** and which survived for many years in central Europe. They repudiated the formalism of the Orthodox Church and professed to base their teachings on the New Testament, rejecting the use of images, crosses, relics, incense and candles. They believed that Jesus was a mere man until he was baptised, when he became the Messiah. The Paulicians were persecuted by the Orthodox emperors, but tolerated by the Iconoclastic Emperors. In the ninth century, tens of thousands of Paulicians were massacred on the orders of Empress Theodora, and many organised themselves for armed resistance and were crushed in **874**. Others were transported from their home in Armenia to the Balkans, where they faced attacks from the Bulgars and the Slavs, whom they had substantial success in converting.

The **Bogomils** were another sect that prospered in the Balkans and proved similarly persistent. The movement is thought to have been founded by a tenth century priest, Bogomil, in reaction against the Orthodox Byzantine Church and what was seen as the poor morals of the orthodox clergy. Bogomilism saw matter as evil and favoured asceticism. Despite persecution by both Roman Catholic and Orthodox Churches it prospered for some time in Serbia, Bosnia, Croatia, Dalmatia, Hungary and Slovenia. After the Turkish invasions of the fifteenth century many adopted Islam, although it is thought that the sect continued into the seventeenth century.

6.6 The Orthodox Church in Eastern Europe and Russia

In the latter half of the ninth century, in response to a request from Ratislav, the Prince of Moravia, the Patriarch of Constantinople sent two Greek brothers as missionaries to the Slavic tribes who had spread throughout Eastern Europe. Cyril and Methodius were both familiar with the Slavic tongue and set about constructing an alphabet for this previously unwritten language. They proved to be two of the most effective Christian missionaries, spreading not only their faith but with it the Byzantine culture which was to have such an important role in the future development of these peoples. Whilst initial success in Moravia was reversed by the invading Magyars, their teachings lived on in the Bulgarians to the south, and in 927 the chief bishop of the Church in Bulgaria was granted recognition as a patriarch. From Bulgaria, Byzantine Christianity spread to Serbia and Roumania, with a patriarch appointed for Serbia in 1219.

In the late tenth century the pagan prince of Kiev, Vladimir, adopted Byzantine Christianity and ordered the mass baptism of Russians, thereby laying the foundations that led to Orthodoxy becoming the state religion of the Russian people, a position it was to retain until the overthrow of the Czar nine hundred years later. Under the rule of Vladimir's successor Yaroslav, the Patriarch of Constantinople appointed a bishop to hold office in Kiev thereby inaugurating a period of nearly four hundred years in which Constantinople had primacy over the Church in Russia, with the head of the Russian Church invariably a Greek appointed by the Patriarch. In the split with Western Christendom after 1054, the Russian church sided firmly with the East.

In the thirteenth century the Russians came under pressure from both the Mongol hordes led by Genghis Khan, and from a Catholic crusade led by German knights. Alexander Nevsky led the Russians to victory over the Western invaders in 1242, but surrendered to the rule of the Mongol leader. For the next two hundred years the Russian Church lived under Mongol rule, with appointments to the Metropolitan of Kiev being subject to approval of the Khan. In the fourteenth century the Byzantine Empire was suffering setbacks, and the Ottoman Turks occupied Bulgaria and Serbia, in 1453 taking Constantinople and killing the Emperor. Within a short time the Russians, under the leadership of Ivan III of Moscow, had overthrown Mongol rule. Russia was now a powerful nation state and many Russians proclaimed Moscow as the Third Rome, the new head of the Eastern Church.

6.7 Monasticism, the religious orders and the growth of learning

The religious orders constituted an extremely important feature of medieval Christendom. In England and Wales alone there were some 800 monastic communities, at a time when these countries were but sparsely populated. In the first half of the Middle Ages the different monastic communities had much in common, with the Benedictines being pre-eminent. The late eleventh century, however, saw the beginning of a proliferation of different religious organisations each seeking, at least in their formative years, to establish their credentials as legitimate successors to Christian ideals. These religious organisations were, nevertheless, inevitably affected and moulded by the medieval society in which they existed and with which they had regular encounters. These points of contact embraced their property rights, the sources of their income (being most notably endowments) and recruitment, as well as the backgrounds and perspectives of those who held sway in the orders. The religious orders, like many Christian institutions throughout the ages, provided a route for social advancement the like of which was not available elsewhere in the Middle Ages.

The Benedictines

In the early Middle Ages the Benedictines coexisted with other forms of monastic communities, the most notable being the Celtic monks of Ireland renowned for their missionary work in Britain and Europe. Celtic monasticism with its demands of asceticism and cultural achievements had considerable impact in continental Europe, with its missionary Columbanus founding the Abbeys of Luxeuil (**590**) and Bobbio (**612**) in northern Italy.

After **600**, Benedictine monasticism increasingly dominated the scene, retaining its primacy for five hundred years after which it continued to influence ecclesiastical affairs. The Benedictine Rule appealed to many secular leaders as a means of bringing order and regularity into an important sphere of medieval life. It was for this reason that the order received the backing of the Carolingian rulers and others, who enforced the Benedictine Rule in their domains.

The central feature of the Rule, a document of 12,000 words, was obedience centred around a life of rigorous demands – obedience not only to the teachings derived from the Gospel and to the Rule, but also to the abbot, who was portrayed as Christ's representative within the monastic community. The theme of the Rule was obedience through self-denial, leading to communion with God.

Monastic life was not immune from the pervasive influence of secular society, in which it played important functions. As Western Europe was expanding there were insufficient life opportunities for the children of the nobility. The rule of primogeniture, and the social and economic reasons which prevented its demise, produced a pressing need for positions for other children of noble families. Increasingly they channelled their sons and daughters into the monastic communities. One consequence was an enrichment of the monasteries from endowments by the nobility. Europe was still but sparsely populated, with vast tracts of land unexploited and of dubious value to owners, who bestowed large gifts of land on monasteries within their domains.

Another result was a reduction in the manual work performed by monks who came to devote themselves more to liturgy, learning and art, making the monasteries the cultural and educational centres of Europe, most notably those at Reichenau, St Gallen and Corbie. The monasteries came to boast extensive libraries with monks making ornate copies of theological manuscripts, and of ancient works of literature and learning.

The monastic orders performed two other valuable functions in a world where the concept of the supernatural was very pressing. Secular rulers and their subjects looked upon the monks as pursuing a holy existence, but not just for their own individual salvation. Monks were seen as carrying out a religious role on behalf of all, defending the secular rulers and their kingdoms against invisible supernatural enemies. This was an age too in which fear of eternal damnation was ever present. The Church imposed penances which for many offences were severe, but the system of penitential punishments usually provided for commutation of a penance on payment of a sum of money. In the Middle Ages a penance was seen more as a debt to the supernatural, rather than an individual responsibility, and accordingly what mattered was that the debt should be paid, and whether it was paid by the offender was immaterial. The monasteries played a central role in this system – founders and benefactors of monastic communities could ensure that their penitential debts were paid. Who better to fulfil this role than those who were so strongly motivated in their desire to gain eternal life, and whose communities were destined to continue indefinitely? Praying on behalf of all mankind and undertaking penance and intercession for others, the monks were seen as the spiritual equivalent of the feudal knights.

From the ninth century onwards there were repeated attempts at reform, primarily to introduce greater asceticism with less study in favour of more manual labour, and fewer contacts with the outside world. An important reform movement originated from the abbey at Cluny in central France in the tenth century. Cluniac reforms emphasised worship; in Cluny itself, almost the entire daily life of the monks was engaged in prayer and Church services. The abbots of Cluny created a large centralised organisation, a network of dependent houses with priors appointed by the abbot of Cluny, and owing a duty of obedience to the abbot. This was a marked change, as earlier monasteries had been largely independent from each other.

The twelfth century saw a marked downturn in the fortunes of the Benedictines and the development of new rival alternatives critical of the wealth of Benedictine monastic communities and seeking to pursue a more austere regime. The two orders that rose to prominence were those of the Augustinian canons and the Cistercian monks.

The Augustinian canons

The Augustinian canons looked back to one of the foremost theologians of the past, Augustine, and to biblical teaching. They adopted a Rule far simpler and more general than the Benedictine: to share all property, to pray together at appointed times, to wear the same form of dress and to obey a superior. Two schools developed among the Augustinians – those who practised abstinence, silence and manual labour, and those who considered that the only necessary requirement was that all property should be owned in common. In the late eleventh and early twelfth centuries initially small, and later more sizeable communities appeared throughout Western Europe, living together under strict rules, but going out to work among the populace. By the thirteenth century there were many communities living under the Rule of St Augustine.

In contrast to the Benedictine monasteries, Augustinian communities were created at little cost and with little formality. The Augustinian canons were not rich, nor could they boast leading intellectuals, nor did they give great emphasis to prayer and Church services, but they played an important role in the towns and castles where they were generally at work, and attracted modest donations from many less wealthy benefactors. Usually living in small branch communities, they organised schools, ran hospitals, provided care for the sick, the poor and the aged, and renovated churches that had fallen into disrepair.

The Cistercians

Whilst the Cistercians prospered in the same years as the Augustinians, they could not have been more different in their outlook. Augustinian canons worked in small groups in the heart of the secular world, encountering and tackling the problems of society. The Cistercians established monasteries on the frontiers of Western civilisation where they sought a return to the virtues of the Rule of St Benedictine, free of the traditions and customs of the Benedictine order and asserting the principles of self-denial, poverty, purity, withdrawal from society and submersion in the spiritual life. They eschewed the contacts with society which brought revenue to other orders.

The constitution of the order was drawn up in **1119**, and undoubtedly contributed to the success of the organisation of the order, which was essentially hierarchical. The abbot of the founding monastery at Citeaux visited each house

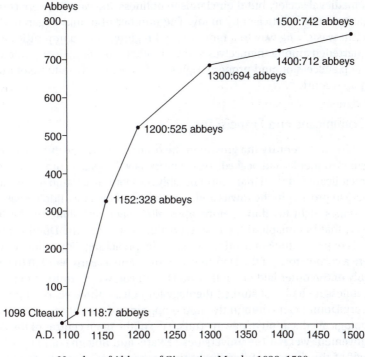

Number of Abbeys of Cistercian Monks, 1098–1500

annually, and the abbots of all the houses would attend each year at a legislative assembly at Citeaux at which rules and regulations governing the order would be promulgated. By 1300 there were over six hundred monasteries and nunneries.

Originally committed to poverty, the Cistercians became an extremely wealthy order based on exploitation of their extensive agricultural estates, and of the labouring conversi ('lay brothers'). The Cistercians were not the first religious order to turn to outside labour, but their exploitation of such labour represented a new development. The conversi were generally illiterate and admitted into only partial membership of the order. They lived on the monastic estate but in separate buildings away from the monks, with their own chapter house for Sunday worship. They were required to give an oath of life-long obedience and celibacy, and were subjected to a severe regime, mostly of manual labour. They were prohibited from entering the full Cistercian order. They were not permitted, let alone encouraged to learn to read and write.

This subservient disciplined workforce, often two or three times more numerous than the monks themselves, brought great wealth to the Cistercians. As to the secular authorities, they welcomed the stability brought by the Cistercians and the supervision they exercised over the frontier territories. That so many conversi were prepared to accept such a terrible existence, deprived of family, freedom and any chance of betterment, says much about the conditions on the borders of Christian civilisation. By the end of the twelfth century, this previously docile workforce became increasingly rebellious, and by the end of the next century the conversi had largely ceased to exist as a source of labour.

By the late Middle Ages the monastic communities were an established integral part of medieval society but their claims to holiness and sanctity were coming to be regarded with scepticism by many. The number of monks began to decline, asceticism was giving way to a more relaxed regime, and communities increasingly quarrelled among themselves and with others, resulting in arguments over leadership succession and property rights and an extensive volume of litigation at the papal court.

The Dominicans and Franciscans

By the thirteenth century the growth in the order of the Augustinian canons and the Cistercian monks had peaked. This century saw the establishment and growth of the mendicant orders of friars, most notably the Dominicans and the Franciscans who were to prosper in the towns and universities of the late Middle Ages.

The friars sought to adopt a more 'apostolic' way of life along similar lines to the ideals that had inspired the first Augustinian canons. The Dominican order had as its objective the eradication of heresy by preaching. Education and learning were a cornerstone of the Dominican efforts, and as early as 1228 the general assembly of the order laid down that no Dominican was permitted to preach in public unless he had first studied theology for at least three years, and required that every Dominican community should appoint a friar with responsibility for the theological education of new recruits. Two of the main centres of the Dominican movement were at the universities of Paris and Bologna, and by 1234 well over half of the doctors of divinity at the Sorbonne are thought to have been

Dominicans. The study of languages, including Eastern languages, was encouraged by the orders to enable their missionaries to communicate with Muslims and pagans. Many scholars joined the Dominican order, and later others became Franciscans to the mutual benefit of all concerned. The friars gained masters trained in theology to educate their preachers and missionaries, and the academics were provided with the means of pursuing their studies without financial worry and the necessity of a concurrent career in secular or ecclesiastical administration.

The Dominican and Franciscan orders, especially the former, facilitated the rejuvenation of theological study and debate aimed at the conversion of heretics, the rejection of Islam and the enlightenment of the errant Byzantine church. Dominicans, in particular, produced some of the leading theologians of the Middle Ages such as Thomas Aquinas.

Both orders eschewed the wealth associated with the earlier religious communities, and instead espoused a simple apostolic way of life. Francis, in particular, advocated imitation of Christ and literal obedience to biblical commands by selling all possessions and giving to the poor. The Franciscans, more than any others, elected to suffer the deprivations of the most poverty stricken, with poverty representing a goal in itself, indicative of communion with Christ.

The efforts of both orders were concentrated in the towns in which they found their audiences, their first recruits and the modest charitable donations on which they survived. In marked contrast to the earlier orders, the friars, prohibited by their orders from owning more land than they needed to house themselves, never became substantial property owners or owners of great wealth. Their modest income came primarily from small donations, often in kind, or from legacies or fees for burials and masses for the dead. The orders were not dependent upon the wealthy, their benefactors being from a wide range of donors.

Recruitment to these orders differed from their predecessors. It was acceptable for a child of the nobility to enter a prestigious and wealthy Benedictine or Cistercian monastery, but it was quite another matter for those children to be enlisted into the impoverished mendicant orders. In contrast, the Dominicans and Franciscans, particularly in the early years, often attracted those already obliged to beg for a living, in addition to those of the nobility, and more particularly the scholars who were attracted to their ranks.

The thirteenth century saw the rapid expansion of both orders. Though far less organised and regulated than the Dominicans, the movement initiated by Francis already had large numbers of followers throughout most of Western Europe by 1218. The Dominicans were never as numerous, but by the early fourteenth century they had about six hundred houses, with the Franciscans having about fourteen hundred. Estimates of the number of friars vary greatly but it is likely that there were well over twenty thousand Franciscans and over ten thousand Dominicans, concentrated in the Mediterannean basin, but undertaking a world-wide missionary task.

The growth of learning

Education in the first half of the Middle Ages was almost entirely the province of the monasteries, with novice monks and young men from the local nobility being taught by a scholar appointed from the monastery. The eleventh century saw the establishment of cathedral schools which in the following century gradually eclipsed the monasteries. There students received tuition from the chancellor in theology and the seven liberal arts: grammar, logic, rhetoric, arithmetic, geometry, astronomy and music. The cathedral schools, in particular those at Laon, Paris, Chartres and Cologne, fostered theological debate, one of the controversies culminating in the acceptance in the late eleventh century of the doctrine of transubstantiation. Another debate centred around the meaning of the Crucifixion, and laid the foundations of modern day orthodox thinking. Hitherto the dominant thinking had been that through sin, mankind had subjected itself to the devil, and that a ransom had to be paid in the form of someone free from sin to cancel out the devil's claim to mankind. Anselm (**1033–1109**), an Archbishop of Canterbury, argued that by sin, men alienate themselves from God, and that a sacrifice was required by God for the forgiveness of men's sins. That sacrifice was Christ, sent by God's mercy to die on the Cross for the redemption of mankind. Anselm was the first to put forward the ontological argument for the existence of God, an attempt to demonstrate God's existence from reason alone.

One of the later scholars to emerge from the cathedral schools was Abelard who helped develop the systematic method of reasoning in which belief is questioned and doubted in an effort to discover fundamental truths. Valiant attempts were made by Abelard and other scholastics to reconcile Christian faith with the reasoning of the philosophy of Aristotle.

By the thirteenth century the universities of the Sorbonne, Paris (the first university, founded in **1256**) and Bologna were the leading centres of learning in Europe, with universities also being founded at Salerno, Oxford, Cambridge, Montpellier, Padua, Salamanca and Toulouse. Undergraduates were taught Latin and the liberal arts, especially logic and philosophy, with graduates receiving tuition in medicine, law and theology. Students would pay a fee to each professor after a class, in which they would be read an extract from a text and listen to the tutor's comments on it. Books were still few in number, and as parchment was expensive, students frequently had to listen and remember, in order to learn.

6.8 Women and the religious life

The early Middle Ages saw great numbers of monastic foundations whose purpose was to provide a safe haven for the unmarried daughters and widows of aristocratic families. These nunneries often boasted women of high social status and considerable education, with Hilda at Whitby and Etheldreda in Ely gaining particular renown. These nunneries were ruled by an abbess, who in the early years exercised authority over the communities of monks who were often attached to the nunneries (double monasteries) to minister the sacraments.

The growth of monasticism in the two hundred years from the early tenth century coincided with a reversal in the status of women within the monastic way of life. As the liturgical and intercessional role of monks increased, so did their relative importance. Double monasteries suffered a decline and then virtually disappeared. The nunneries played but a minor part in the development of monasticism in this period. This is aptly illustrated by the fact that of all the numerous monastic communities established by the abbots of Cluny, only one was for women – and that was founded for the express purpose of providing a safe refuge for the wives of married men who had been persuaded to join the Cluny order. It was strictly supervised by the abbot of Cluny.

In the tenth and eleventh centuries there were insufficient nunneries to cater for the number of women seeking to avoid or forget matrimony in favour of the religious life. The demand is evident in the development of new religious orders from the beginning of the twelfth century. The leader of one of the earliest was Robert of Arbrissel who travelled throughout the Loire valley preaching. He attracted a considerable following of women from all social levels, and established a monastic community for them at Fontavrault. This monastery was soon showered with gifts and endowments, with many of the benefactors seeking to introduce their daughters to the community. Initially accepting women from a variety of social backgrounds, within a few years the community became the sole province of aristocratic families.

In northern France, St Norbert, the founder of the Premonstratensian canons, also encountered a keen demand from women to participate in a monastic way of life. Large numbers of women joined the order, which renewed the practice of setting up double monasteries. The presence of so many women roused opposition from many within the orders and among the general populace. Repeatedly in the mid twelfth century the papacy issued edicts demanding that the women's rights be preserved, but the Premonstratensian order began forbidding double monasteries and by the end of the century had determined to admit no more women to the order.

The pressure, particularly from the aristocracy, for the continuation of monastic communities for women remained so strong that even the Cistercian order was unable to exclude them. As the order expanded, nunneries appeared throughout Europe endowed by the great aristocratic families seeking the protection of the order. These communities, though often established in the proximity of settlements of Cistercian monks and often with the assistance of their abbots, retained a large degree of independence over their own affairs.

In the early thirteenth century the General Chapter of the order imposed increasing restrictions, limiting the foundation of new settlements and the number of new entrants to existing communities and seeking to regulate aspects of their daily life. These attempts were completely unsuccessful. By this time there were nearly as many nunneries as there were male monastic communities – about 650 as against 750 – and in some areas such as Germany and the low countries the nuns were more numerous than their male counterparts. The attempts at control met with fierce resistance from 1242 to 1244 when these attempts were at their height. In large measure the efforts to control the nuns were abandonned.

A completely different religious phenomenon was that of the beguines. They were essentially a movement of women, free from male control. They based their lives on no definite rule, they had no formal structure or disciplinary code, they were not cloistered in any monastic community, they did not seek endowments or wealth but instead engaged in the secular world though living in small convent communities. The movement originated in the early thirteenth century around

Liège in the west of Germany, and with considerable rapidity spread as far south as the Alps, to the shores of the Baltic and to Bohemia in the East. At first the beguines, charged with heresy, faced persecution and even death, but their simplicity and the absence of any challenge to Orthodox Christian beliefs attracted much sympathy and support from a number of leading churchmen, and the allegations of heresy died out.

Whilst the beguines often receive little mention or no mention in works on Church history, they were in fact a major feature of many European towns and cities for a period of over four hundred years from the beginning of the thirteenth century. In Cologne, for example, by **1400** when the movement was probably near its peak, and when the population of the city was probably in the region of 25,000 to 30,000, there were over one hundred and fifty beguine convents in which there lived about 1500 beguines – well over one-tenth of the adult female population! Even in the late eighteenth century there were still beguines living and working in Cologne.

The beguines committed themselves to chastity and to the service of God. They were to be found working in hospitals, administering to the poor and needy, embroidering ecclesiastical vestments, as well as in prayer and contemplation. They faced opposition from a number of quarters, for many such as the priests whose congregations were depleted, parents who did not approve of a daughter's choice, or disappointed aspiring husbands did not approve. However, the secular and ecclesiastical authorities were generally sympathetic in the early years and continued so until the latter half of the thirteenth century.

The repression began to take official form in **1274** following the Council of Lyon which condemned religious orders that had not received formal papal approval, and continued through the fourteenth century. The process of bringing the beguines and other unauthorised religious communities under central control, drawn together in established monastic communities, was well under way by the early fifteenth century when papal orders were issued requiring the episcopacy to search out and dismantle any such remaining informal communities.

Bibliography

G. Baraclough, *The Medieval Papacy*, WW Norton & Co, New York (1968)

R. and C. Brooke, *Popular Religion in the Middle Ages*, Thames & Hudson, London (1984)

J.M. Hussey, *The Orthodox Church in the Byzantine Empire*, Clarendon Press, Oxford (1990)

M.D. Lambert, *Medieval Heresy: Popular Movements from Bogomil to Huss*, Blackwell Publishers (1992)

C.H. Lawrence, *Medieval Monasticism*, Longman (2000)

C. Mango, *Byzantium: The Empire of the New Rome*, Orion, London (1980)

Hans Eberhard Mayer, *The Crusades* – translated by J. Gillingham, Oxford University Press (1988)

C. Morris, *The Papal Monarchy: The Western Church 1050–1250*, Clarendon Press (1991)

J. Riley-Smith, *The Crusades*, Tale University Press, New Haven, CT (1987)

R.W. Southern, *History of Christianity: Western Society and the Church in the Middle Ages 2*, Penguin, London (1990)

W. Ullman, *A Short History of Papacy in the Middle Ages*, Barnes & Noble (1974)

W. Ullman, *The Growth of Papal Government in the Middle Ages*, London (1979)

◼ ▾ 7 The history of the Church: the Reformation

7.1 The condition of Western Europe

As the Middle Ages drew to a close, many in Europe still lived in fear of the two great menaces of the era – the plague and the Turk. In **1347** The Black Death had claimed about one-third of all the inhabitants of Western Europe, and the centuries that followed witnessed further outbreaks of the plague which represented an ever present threat. As to the Turks, by **1453** they had captured Constantinople from where they pressed north and west, their advance not being checked until after they had reached Vienna in **1529**. In **1480** Turkish forces had even come ashore in southern Italy, an unnerving reminder to all who lived near the Mediterranean of their vulnerability. For some, the condition of Western Christendom was a punishment for the errors of the Church. By the late Middle Ages the Church was riddled with corruption, with clergy often poorly educated, disinterested, indulging in absenteeism and sexual immorality, and with the papacy itself incriminated by its own promotion and protection of abuses. Increasingly, Popes became embroiled in Italian affairs, which only increased the growing resistance in England and elsewhere to papal demands, particularly for ecclesiastical levies for Rome. The papal court too had fallen into disrepute, not only because of corruption but also because it had become overburdened with bureaucratic procedures, rendering it largely ineffective in meeting the needs of its clients.

Socially and politically, Western Europe had undergone significant changes. The later Middle Ages had seen the rise of a merchant 'middle' class unwilling to accept feudal traditions and an authoritarian Church. This new merchant class was educated and had access to the reading material produced by the new printing presses which played such an important role in the development of Protestantism. It was from the merchant classes that the majority of Protestant leaders emerged. On the political front, a sense of nationalism was developing as the unifying appearance provided by the last effective Emperor, Charles V, and the Pope crumbled. Indeed, the Reformation can be seen on one level as a rebellion of the Teutonic peoples who had been outside the confines of the old Roman Empire against domination from Rome – for it was primarily in those areas that Protestantism established itself, in contrast to those countries where the culture of the Roman Empire had long dominated and in which the language spoken was still of Latin derivation, as in Italy, Portugal and France.

The last effective Emperor, Charles V, faced a host of problems as European nations emerged with a sense of their own autonomy and independence, and an ability to exercise greater control within their own borders. In France, the destruction of the power of the feudal nobility in the Hundred Years War with England enabled Louis XI to extend and enhance his control and authority. In England, the end of the War of the Roses in 1485 saw the rise of an effective Tudor monarchy. In Spain, the monarchy was also emerging as a substantial force following the expulsion of the Muslims in the late fifteenth century, and the conquests of the New World flowing from the voyages of Bartholomew Diaz, Vasco da Gama and others.

The Middle Ages were followed by and the Reformation preceded by the Renaissance, which saw the revival of classical Greek and Roman culture in the arts, politics and public debate. The Renaissance originated in Italy following the arrival of many Greek scholars seeking refuge from the Turks after the fall of Constantinople in 1453. They brought with them Greek manuscripts and culture, and revived the Greek language which had fallen into disuse. The humanists, i.e. the scholars who read the classical Greek and Latin writers and endeavoured to adopt their wisdom to their own lives, rejoiced in the beauty of the world and the human body, and paid tribute to the literature of pagan predecessors to Christianity. The Renaissance saw a revival of the arts, and a conviction in the power of human reason. Christianity was not denied or attacked by the humanists, rather many sought to harmonise Christianity with ancient classical thought. Other humanists were more sceptical, with some rejecting Christian concepts of morality. In Germany, in particular, the Renaissance saw a revival in religious learning with the publication of not just the classical writers but also of the Church Fathers, and the foundation of nine universities between 1456 and 1506 where both Greek and Hebrew were taught to facilitate biblical studies. In England, the leading figures were Colet, More and Erasmus who advocated ecclesiastical reform from within, acknowledging papal authority but desiring a return to the teachings of the New Testament. Erasmus worked on a new edition of the Greek New Testament with an accompanying Latin translation which was published in 1516, a turning point in the history of biblical criticism. Erasmus' contribution ensured that the Renaissance was not entirely secular and pagan.

A crucial factor in the spread of the Reformation was the development of printing which opened up a new dimension in the circulation of knowledge and thought. Hitherto texts, including the Bible, had been invariably in Latin. In 1456 Gutenberg produced the first book – the Bible – published in the Western world, and within a few years printers were producing texts in vernacular languages throughout Europe, facilitating the rapid dissemination of the thoughts and teachings of the first leaders of the Reformation.

7.2   Reformation and the rise of Protestantism

The desire for change was not new for there had been previous attempts to carry out reformation within the Church. Indeed the reformers saw themselves in this context. They called for a revival of the Church, the removal of abuses and a return to the purity of the past. They were not concerned to establish a new break-away Church or even to introduce fresh innovations. The underlying convictions of the reform movement were a belief in the absolute authority of the Scriptures, a rejection of the traditions of the Church save where they were justified in the Scriptures, and a belief in salvation by Faith alone. Their conception of the Church was of a priesthood of all believers in which Christians were not dependent or inferior to the ordained clergy, but were equal before God, and had the right and indeed the duty to read the Scriptures and participate in the governing and decision-making of both Church and society.

7.3 Luther

The catalyst for the start of the Reformation came from a professor of biblical studies at the newly founded University of Wittenberg in Germany, **Martin Luther**. On All Saints Day, 31st October 1517, Luther nailed his ninety five theses to the door of the castle church in Wittenberg calling churchmen to debate the sale of indulgences. His theses were academic and moderate in tone – the doctrine of indulgences *per se* was not attacked, only its abuses but, within two weeks, news of them had spread throughout Western Europe, generating much popular support and sparking a bitter controversy.

Luther's condemnation of the abuse of indulgences coincided with the need of Pope Leo X for money to finalise the construction of St Peter's in Rome, which the papal office was seeking to satisfy by declaring indulgences for all who contributed. Trenchant replies to Luther's theses followed, the most notable being those of Eck, the Professor of Theology at Ingoldstadt, and from Prierias, the Master of the Papal Palace, who declared indulgences to be in accordance with papal authority and condemned any challenge to the practice as heretical. Luther, a member of the Augustine order, was called before the Chapter at Heidelberg but when he refused to back down he was summoned to Rome. The Elector of Saxony interceded and the matter was heard before a papal legate in Augsburg in October 1518. Compromise proved impossible and when the legate demanded that Luther retract, Luther appealed to the Pope and to a General Council.

The Pope, however, was keen on mediation and reconciliation, and anxious not to endanger his relations with the Elector of Saxony as the Imperial elections were imminent. The controversy was bitterly debated at the Leipzig Disputation of 1519, by which time Luther was increasingly doubting the whole basis of papal authority. Enticed by Eck, Luther denied the infallibility of the Pope, and indeed of General Councils. This, in contrast to his earlier criticism of the abuses of indulgences, was indeed a challenge to the Church authorities, and in the face of such heresy the Pope had little choice but to excommunicate Luther, which he did in June of 1520. The Elector declined to enforce the Bull of Excommunication, which Luther publicly burnt in the university at Wittenberg.

Luther had already written and published three further tracts known collectively as his *Primary Works*. In *The Appeal to the Christian Nobility of the German Nation* he challenged papal authority, arguing that all Christians are priests, and that where the Pope fails to take action, the secular authorities were entitled to intervene. In *The Babylonish Captivity* Luther attacked the doctrine of transubstantiation, and the withholding of the Sacrament from the laity, which he saw as an attempt by the clergy to subjugate the faithful. In *The Freedom of the Christian Man* Luther argued that salvation came from faith alone, not from the performance of good works.

The controversy raged against a background of a political struggle in which the German Electoral Princes sought to maintain and entrench their influence over the Church in their domains. At the same time, in **1519** the succession as Emperor fell to Charles V whose preoccupation with his struggle with Francis I of France for territorial gains in Italy, and his debt to the Elector of Saxony for help in securing his election, provided time for the Reformation movement to make further advances. In **1521** the Pope issued a further Bull against Luther and called upon the Emperor to enforce it. Instead, Charles called a Diet at Worms. Luther was called upon to recant, but adamantly refused. The Emperor felt compelled to act, and declared his resolve to combat the growing heresies by cementing an alliance with the Pope. Luther, however, received the protection of the German princes who saw in Luther's opinions a means of enhancing their own authority against that of the papacy. Luther spent the next ten months in the safety of the Elector's castle at Warburg where he translated the New Testament into German. Luther had the support of many of the German people, in particular among his fellow Augustinians, and the growing merchant classes. The latter welcomed Luther's emphasis on a Christian laity, which contrasted with the monastic life which hitherto had been held out as the Christian ideal.

Developments continued at Wittenberg where Luther's colleague, Colstadt, was encouraging some of the secular clergy to marry, and calling for changes to the liturgy, the abolition of vestments and the presence of images in church. These radical opinions were not shared by Luther who returned to Wittenberg to channel the reformation movement in a more orderly direction. In the same year the Diet of Nurnberg was held, to which the new pope, Adrian VI, sent his nuncio with assurances that reforms would be introduced, provided heresy was repressed. The Diet decided that Luther should suspend his attacks provided a council was held in Germany within the near future, and called for a papal response to the demands of the Germans which had become known as the 'Hundred Grievances'. A Council, had it met, would in all probability have served to unify the German reformers. However, it was not to be. Pope Adrian died, and was succeeded by the politically more astute Pope Clement VII whose legate succeeded in drawing together support for the papacy among the more pliant princes of the south of Germany.

The progress of reform was slowed to some extent by the Peasants' Revolt which broke out in **1524**. Failing in his attempts at negotiation and mediation, Luther gave his support to the nobles in their brutal quashing of the rebellion in which 100,000 peasants are thought to have died. The following year saw Charles V victorious in battle against Francis, resulting in the Treaty of Madrid in **1526**, and the possibility that the Emperor might at last deal with the reform movement head on. Attention was, however, again diverted away by the advance of the Turks on Hungary. At a Diet in Speier which was still in session as the Turks advanced, agreement was reached whereby each state was to be left to itself to determine the religion to be practised within its own borders.

In the following three years Luther set about the reconstruction of the Church in Saxony with the assistance of John the new Elector, a keen supporter of the reformation. John ordered that a series of Instructions, drafted by the great academic theologian and reformer Melanchthon, be implemented thoughout his dominions, with secular government taking on responsibility for providing pastors. The mass was to be in German and preserved as a Sunday morning service only, rather than daily, with an afternoon service having a sermon based on readings from the Old Testament.

On the political front the Emperor Charles V was gaining in strength, in 1527 entering Rome and taking Pope Clement captive. When Charles agreed peace terms with both the Pope and the King of France, his brother Ferdinand saw an opportune moment to call a further Diet, again held in Speier, in 1529. This time the Catholics had the upper hand, and the Diet reversed the earlier decision that had allowed each ruler to determine the religion practised by his subjects. The Elector of Saxony, the Landgrave of Hesse and the fourteen imperial cities of upper Germany joined with other reform leaders and appealed to the Emperor in protest, hence giving rise to the term Protestantism.

7.4 Zwingli

Whilst the catalyst for reform in Germany had been sparked by Luther, a similar but very distinct movement for reform was developing in Switzerland, a movement destined to give birth to the great Reformed Churches. The foremost leaders were Zwingli and Calvin, both of them far more radical than the rather conservative Luther. Whilst both branches of the Protestant Reformation held to the same underlying principle of salvation by faith alone, there was a great deal of disagreement between them. The characters of these movements differed considerably, largely because of the contrasting political environments in which they developed. In Switzerland, the Reformed Churches took on the traits of the democratic republics of the Swiss confederation, whereas secular government in Germany was autocratic.

Zwingli had served as a chaplain to papal troops, and had been granted a papal pension in return for his loyal service. No doubt Pope Adrian was reluctant to be too severe with someone so valuable to the papal cause. Nevertheless, Zwingli expressed his conviction that the claims made for papal authority were not born out by the Scriptures, and vociferously condemned the sale of indulgences. In 1519 Zwingli was elected as the People's High Priest in Zurich, where he began preaching the message of reformation with the blessing of the secular authorities. Zwingli condemned all customs not based on biblical precedent or authority and attacked the taking of monastic vows, the practice of celibacy, the doctrine of purgatory, the belief in salvation by good works and the concept of the mass as a sacrifice. He called for sermons in the vernacular and for images and relics to be removed from the churches. The demands for reform soon extended to other cities in Switzerland, provoking bitter opposition in some cantons where the Catholic cause remained strong and resulting in armed conflict in which Zwingli was to die in 1531.

Both sides sought to strengthen their positions, with Zurich and other towns and cities favouring reform joining together in the Christian Civic League, prompting Austria and other Catholic states to form a 'Christian Union'. Zwingli contemplated a united Protestant front, but this proved impossible given the disagreement among the reformers, in particular concerning Scripture and the sacraments. On the former, Luther's stance was that anything was capable of acceptance provided it was not contrary to the Scriptures, whereas for Zwingli nothing was permitted unless justified by the Scriptures. As to the Eucharist, Zwingli saw the bread as symbolic only of Christ's body, whereas Luther believed in the theory of consubstantiation. A conference of the reformers in Marburg in **1529** to settle differences failed to overcome the latter point.

In **1530** Charles V called a Diet at Augsburg in an attempt to divide the reformers. Melanchthon, fearing war, sought to highlight the differences between his own Lutheran position and the opinions of the more extreme reformers such as Zwingli, and to emphasise the areas of common ground with the Catholics. Luther refused to be party to any compromise, and war proved inevitable. The years **1530–31** could well have seen the subjugation by the Emperor of the Protestant camp, were it not for further invasions by the Turks prompting a suspension of hostilities pending a new Diet. When the Turks were repulsed, however, Charles became preoccupied with other matters.

7.5 Calvin

Luther and Zwingli represented strands of Protestant thinking which were poles apart. A new school of thought, adopting a position between these two, emerged from the reform movement in France, and was promulgated most notably in French-speaking areas of Switzerland by **Calvin**. Calvin had trained both in law and for the priesthood and had been influenced by the writings of Luther and Erasmus. From **1541** until his death in **1564** he worked in Geneva. He held no high ranking position, serving only as a parish minister, but his power and influence were considerable. Calvin advocated a theocratic state in which there was a strong alliance of Church and State, with the State empowered to enforce ecclesiastical doctrines, discipline and morality by civil remedies of punishments and penalties. It was along these lines that, under Calvin's influence, the small autonomous state of Geneva came to be governed. The authority of the Church was exercised by a consistory of pastors and elected laymen, supported by a machinery of government vested with the power to investigate the private lives of the faithful and which had much in common with the Inquisition. Adultery was punishable by death, a child who hit its parents was beheaded, as was the offender who affixed a placard to the pulpit in Calvin's church.

Calvin's work *The Institutes of the Christian Religion*, primarily concerned with the teachings of the Scriptures, is one of the major texts of the Reformation. Calvinist theology was centred around the concept of the absolute sovereignty of an omnipotent God against whom man, tainted with original sin, has rebelled. Men are powerless and utterly dependent on God's grace. Law was provided to preserve man's hope of salvation, a salvation only made possible by Christ who was both God and Man, and whose death exculpated man's sin. Redemption is only possible by faith, a gift of the Holy Spirit. As to the Eucharist, Calvin rejected the beliefs of both Luther and Zwingli, claiming that although the communicant did receive Christ's body, this was not to be accounted for by the doctrine of transubstantiation but came about because of the faith of the believer.

7.6 The Anabaptists

The most radical of the attempts at reform came from various groupings which their opponents came to term 'anabaptists'. They believed that baptism of infants was inappropriate and should be postponed until adulthood and a proclamation of faith. They gained notoriety in Zurich in 1525 when the city council refused to allow radicals to meet together or to promulgate their opinions. The Anabaptists failed to comply, seeing themselves as missionaries charged with bringing those who considered themselves Christians to a true and deeper understanding of faith. The Anabaptist movement spread throughout German-speaking Europe as its adherents sought to evangelise in small groups of two or three missionaries. The central common strands were a belief in a discipleship which followed the example of Christ, and strict obedience to the Word of God as set out in the Scriptures. They practised pacifism and the redistribution of wealth within their communities, in which all took part in decision-making. They insisted upon the separation of Church and State and condemned the involvement of secular authorities in religious matters.

The secular and religious authorities, both Catholic and Protestant, saw the revolutionary views of the Anabaptists as a serious threat to social stability, as well as to their respective religious positions, and they united to stamp it out by whatever means necessary. In the twenty five years from 1527 thousands of anabaptists were killed, with many others repudiating their beliefs. The persecution came to a head in 1540 when the Anabaptists came to power in the city of Munster. The city was besieged by an army led by the bishop of the city and the defending Anabaptists were killed or driven out. The Anabaptists were not, however, exterminated and they experienced a period of revival in the sixteenth century. Thereafter only three groupings survived: the brethren in Switzerland and south Germany; the Mennonites in the Netherlands and northern Germany; and the Hutterites in Moravia. Their numbers expanded again in the late nineteenth century, and again in the 1970s when there were an estimated 750,000 adherents world-wide.

7.7 The advance of Protestantism

Calvin's ideas gained ground in much of Germany where they encountered Lutheranism, and also in the Netherlands where the growth of the reform movement became intertwined with political opposition to the rule of the foreign Catholic Emperor Charles V, and his son and successor King Philip II of Spain. It has been claimed that 100,000 Protestants were killed in the six years from 1567 to 1573. Eventually in 1618 the Dutch provinces were successful in breaking free of the Spanish Crown and the Roman Church. The Dutch Reformed Church, dominated by the ideas of Calvin both in terms of its faith and its presbyterian form of organisation, thereafter underwent a bitter theological struggle concerning the nature of predestination. In Scotland, too, the Protestants had great success, facilitated by Scotland's links with France and the influence of the French reform movement. The Scottish reform leader, John Knox, spent some time in Geneva and was much attracted by Calvinist ideas which he took to Scotland where they were to a large extent taken on board by the Scottish reform movement.

In England, Henry VIII proclaimed himself Head of the Church of England, but although the power of the papacy and monasticism were both destroyed, the King and hence the nation remained Catholic in doctrine and practice. Under his son, Edward VI (1547–53), the Reformation made considerable headway, only to be persecuted under Queen Mary (1553–58) who attempted to restore papal authority. Two hundred bishops and scholars were burnt at the stake with many Protestants fleeing to continental Europe. In the forty-five years of the reign of Elizabeth I, Protestantism was restored and permanently established. Catholic leaders were replaced with Protestant, but the episcopacy and liturgy were retained.

In France, the reform movement suffered considerable persecution. The policy of Francis I had been to encourage the reformers in the hope of causing difficulties for Charles V. However, in 1545, after that quarrel had subsided, Francis proclaimed his allegiance to the Catholic Faith and ordered the extermination of the Waldensians, a Europe-wide movement of dissenters who practised a life of poverty based on biblical teachings and which had aroused papal condemnation. This heralded a period of vicious persecution. Despite this opposition the Protestants increased in number and spread throughout most of France. They were greatly influenced by Calvinist thought with many of their pastors receiving their training in Geneva, the focal point of French Protestantism. From 1562 to 1598 the country was ravaged by a series of eight religious civil wars in which many Protestants died. By the Peace of Ambroise, in 1563, the Huguenots were allowed to practise their own worship in a number of cities, and they developed a form of separate existence with national structures within Catholic France and a capital at La Rochelle. This pattern of 'refuge cities' proved to be the basis of subsequent peace agreements in these troubled years. The Protestant cause suffered major reverses following the terrible massacre on St Bartholomew's Day in 1572. Eight thousand Huguenots were slaughtered in Paris, with many more killed in the violence that broke out in the provinces. By the Peace of Monsieur, in 1576, the Huguenots were granted permission to worship throughout France save in the vicinity of Paris. This only provoked renewed efforts to defeat the Protestant minority and further warfare. The Catholics were victorious, and although the persecution was to some extent reversed by the Edict of Nantes, in 1598, the toleration was but limited. Towards the end of the following century the persecution was renewed with increased fervour, causing Huguenots to leave the country in fear of their lives.

In Germany, Emperor Charles V came to realise that he must ally his forces with the Church and defeat the Protestants by force of arms. By now both Francis I, King of France, and Henry VIII had died, removing previous limits to Charles' ambitions. The Protestant princes were in disunity, with the Elector of Saxony facing a rival in his cousin Maurice. At the battle of Muhlberg in 1547 the Elector was taken captive by Charles, who thereby secured a major victory against the

Protestants which could have brought the whole of northern Europe under Catholic domination again. However, following a deterioration in his relations with the Pope, Charles called a further Diet at Augsburg, at which in return for allowing the laity to take communion and the clergy to marry, the Emperor demanded acceptance of the seven sacraments and the doctrine of transubstantiation. The compromise was accepted by most of the German princes, but it was welcomed neither by the Pope, nor the reformist Churchmen. Within a short time, an alliance between King Henry II of France and the German Protestants completely changed the political picture. Following the battle of Augsberg, in which the French captured the city, Charles agreed to call another Diet. By the Peace of Augsberg, in 1555, religious unity was finally abandoned. Henceforth all disagreements were to be settled in the Imperial Chamber. Each secular leader was free to impose Catholicism or Lutheranism within his own territories, but there was no toleration of Catholicism within Lutheran states, or of Lutheranism within Catholic states. Calvinism remained unrecognised.

7.8   The Roman Catholic Reformation

These were turbulent times. The year in which Luther was excommunicated, 1521, saw the death of the last of the Renaissance Popes, Leo X; the Turks pressing further on Europe's borders; and the annexation by Spain of the New World. It was against this background that there were not one, but two reformations, the second within the Catholic Church itself. Whilst the Church was slow to respond to the need for reform, change was inevitable, if only to counter and reverse the advances of the reformers and to correct the glaring abuses within the Church. In the process, the divisions between the Roman Church and the Protestants deepened as central doctrinal issues became more precisely defined, making compromise impossible. Central to a comprehension of the Roman Catholic Reformation is the influence of St Ignatius de Loyola and the Council of Trent.

7.9   Ignatius Loyola, the Jesuits and other religious movements

Ignatius Loyala is credited with playing a greater role than anyone in countering the progress of the Protestant reformers. In 1521, at the age of thirty, Loyola underwent a conversion experience which led him to a life of poverty and asceticism, and to a conviction in the primacy of the papacy to which he preached unbending loyalty and obedience. Loyola's *Spiritual Exercises* were a guide to meditation and prayer aimed at bringing the believer into complete obedience to God and to the Church. The Exercises became, and indeed still are, a central element of the training for the Jesuit priesthood. The tenor of the work, and of Loyola's life, is well illustrated by the Thirteenth Exercise entitled '*Rule for Thinking with the Church*' in which Loyola exhorts:

To arrive at the truth in all things, we ought always to be ready to believe that what seems to us white is black, if the hierarchical Church so defines it.

In **1534** Loyola and five others formed the Society of Jesus, pledging themselves to poverty, chastity and the unquestioning service of the Pope. They eventually earned papal recognition and approval in **1540**, becoming a disciplined mendicant order of highly educated men bound to the Pope. In the sixteen years to Loyola's death, the influence of the society spread throughout Europe and the Spanish and Portuguese colonies. It became one of the most effective missionary groups in the history of Christianity, leading the Church of Rome into a new period of rapid expansion from **1550** to **1650** when Mexico, Central and South America, and much of the Philippines came within the Catholic domain, not to mention the smaller communities in Africa, Asia and elsewhere. The Jesuits were at the forefront of the campaign of counter-reformation, and in France, modern-day Belgium, southern Germany and above all in Eastern Europe they recaptured large areas for the Roman Catholic Church. Wherever they went the Jesuits established schools to educate the faithful in the true ways of the Church, providing a high standard of education for both laity and clergy.

The Jesuits were instrumental in the establishing in Rome of the Inquisition which had become such an effective tool of government in Loyola's native Spain. In the Middle Ages the Inquisition had primarily been under local control, and towards the end of the Middle Ages had waned, until it was introduced in Spain in **1477** under the auspices of the Spanish monarchy. However, in **1542** Pope Paul III established a papal office in Rome, the Supreme Sacred Congregation of the Holy Office, to oversee a universal Inquisition under papal control, and governed by six cardinals. Attempts at conciliation were replaced by propoganda, censorship, coercion and persecution. Books could not be published without the authority of the Inquisition which kept the Index of prohibited material. In 1564, for example, the Inquisition effectively censored well over half the books then being printed in Europe. No one was exempt from inquiry by the papal inquisitors – into their actions and their minds. The Inquisition was far more cruel and pervasive than that under local control many years earlier. For the good of the victim and the Church, heretics were sought out. If they could not be brought back into the fold, by whatever means, they were to be eradicated before they contaminated others.

Not surprisingly, the Jesuits attracted hatred from those who lived in fear of them, envy from those within the Church who resented their influence, and distrust from secular authorities doubtful of the loyalty of those so greatly committed to the service of the Pope. In the eighteenth century they were exiled by the civil authorities in France and Spain, and in **1773** the Society was suppressed by the Pope only to be revived again in **1814** and regain a permanent influence within the Catholic Church.

The Catholic Reformation saw the establishment of new monastic orders, many as a result of the influence of a group of clerics and laymen known as the Oratory of the Divine Love, which had been founded in **1527**. They included Caraffa (who subsequently became Pope as Paul IV) who founded the order of the Theatines which sought to reform the secular clergy by requiring them to take the monastic vows. Other orders include the Capuchins, the reformed Franciscans, who advocated a return to the ideals of the early Church, the Barnabites and the Ursulines, a teaching order of nuns.

In Spain, the counter-reformation was characterised by the growth of mysticism, a development not particularly welcomed by the Church authorities, in that it emphasised a personal relationship with God outside the auspices of the priest. One of the greatest mystics, and one of the most formidable women in the history of Spain, was St Theresa who became the prioress of the new order of Carmelites, founding sixteen separate houses of nuns and a further fourteen for friars. In 1562 she published her autobiography in which she described her visions and her form of prayer in which the will is silenced but memory and understanding remain alert. With the assistance of her follower, John of the Cross, she rejuvenated much of the spiritual life of the faithful in Spain.

7.10   The Council of Trent

The Council of Trent, called at the instigation of Emperor Charles V, was held at intervals between 1545 and 1563 to debate the organisation and doctrines of the Church, and was the most important Council between Nicaea in 325 and Vatican II in 1962–65. The Emperor hoped that the Council would be a vehicle for reconciliation, but the Jesuits and the leader of the papal party, Cardinal Caraffa, had other ideas, and in the field of doctrine the Council only served to heighten the differences with Protestantism, which it declared heretical. The Vulgate was ruled to be the only authorised version of the Scriptures, and Church traditions and teachings were declared to be of equal importance to the Bible on doctrinal questions. The Council reasserted the traditional view that there were seven sacraments, and reaffirmed the doctrine of transubstantiation, the existence of purgatory, indulgences and the celibacy of the clergy. Luther's claim to salvation 'by Faith alone' was rejected – whilst God's grace is essential, justification also required obedience and good works. Significant reforms were aimed at strengthening the Catholic Church for battle against the reformers by reasserting the primacy of the Pope, reorganising and preserving the heirarchical administration of the Church, providing better training for the secular clergy, tackling corruption, and addressing the question of pluralities and absenteeism.

The years before the completion of the Council's deliberations saw advances in battle for the Catholic cause by the Emperor's armies. At the height of these successes, when it appeared that the Protestants would be routed, the Pope's jealous rivalry caused him to move the Council to Bologna in 1547. The Emperor reacted by compelling Pope Paul III to accept the terms of the Interim of Augsberg in which some measure of conciliation was accorded to the defeated Protestants, including an invitation to the Council to a number of Protestant leaders in Germany when the Council sat again in 1550 to 1552. The attempts at discussion and compromise were however fruitless: there were divisions among the Protestant representatives who were discontented at the pace and direction of the reforms, and warfare had in any event resumed.

There followed a ten-year interval before the Council reconvened. That decade saw an alliance between King Henry II of France and the Protestant princes, resulting in their victory against Charles V, and his abdication in 1556, with his son Philip succeeding to Spain and the Netherlands, and his brother Ferdinand becoming Emperor. In 1559 the new Pope Pius IV summoned the Council to meet again, inviting representatives of the Eastern Churches, and some of the Protestant churches. The invitations were declined. In the remaining years of its deliberations, the Council codified Catholic doctrine in the Profession of Tridentine Faith which was to be recited by all those to be appointed to episcopal sees or other offices, and consisted of affirmations of acceptance of the Nicene Creed, a precis of the doctrinal issues decided by the Council and of the rulings of previous Councils.

7.11   The end of the wars of religion

The Catholic Reformation was accompanied by the wars of religion that broke out all over Europe after the failure to reach agreement, and which were complicated by the struggle of the German princes with Imperial authority. The Peace of

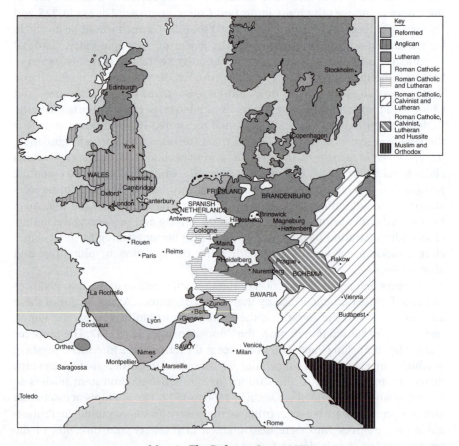

Map 4   The Reformation at 1570

Augsberg in **1555** represented a compromise between the Lutheran and Catholic causes in Germany under which each secular leader was to determine the religious affiliations of his subjects. In many parts of Europe, including France and the Netherlands, religious wars continued to rage intermittently, invariably with political undertones. The last of these wars, which we will return to in Chapter 8, was the Thirty Years War which in large part resulted from the success of the Catholic Reformation after the Peace of Augsberg and was eventually resolved in **1648** by the Peace of Westphalia. As in the Diet of Spier, a hundred and twenty years earlier, this settlement provided for religious affinities to be determined by the secular leaders. The religious map of Europe had hardly altered at all, nor has it done in the three and a half centuries since.

The net result of the Catholic Reformation and the events of **1517** to **1648** was to create a rejuvenated, belligerent, expansionist Roman Catholic Church with a much greater emphasis on piety, discipline and a more precise definition of orthodoxy. The growth of Protestantism in Europe was halted, and in many places its advances reversed, and Roman Catholicism came to be embraced by people throughout the globe.

Bibliography

J. Bossy, *Christianity in the West 1400–1700*, Oxford Paperbacks (1985)
Owen Chadwick, *The History of the Church 3: The Reformation*, Penguin, London (1990)
A.G. Dickens, *The Counter Reformation*, Thames & Hudson, London (1977)
A.G. Dickens, *The English Reformation*, Fontana, London (1986)
R.B. Scribner, *The German Reformation*, Palgrave (1986)
G.H. Williams, *The Radical Reformation*, Truman State University Press (1999)
A.D. Wright, *The Counter Revolution*, St Martin's Press – now Palgrave, New York (1982)

■ ⊻ 8 The history of the Church: 1500 to date

The seventeenth and eighteenth centuries

The seventeenth century witnessed the Thirty Years War from which the papacy emerged with its power and influence in Europe much reduced, and with Protestants having made substantial advances. It saw too the great revival in France, and in Britain the rise, decline and resurrection of Anglicanism. Whilst Protestantism became a permanent phenomenon, religious toleration remained absent. The religious affiliations of subjects were still determined by their rulers, and it was not until the eighteenth century that ideas of religious freedom began to gain ground, initially in Germany, Austria and England.

8.1   The Thirty Years War, 1618 to 1648

The events which sparked the Thirty Years War were centred around Bohemia with its long history of racial tensions between Slav and Teuton, and the more recent animosity between Catholic and Protestant. In 1606 when a Catholic procession in the mainly Protestant town of Donauworth was set upon, the Duke of Bavaria forced the town to accept a Catholic dominated Council. When the Catholics denounced the Peace of Augsburg, claiming that this had been negated by the decrees of Trent, Protestants – both Lutheran and Calvinist – combined together into an Evangelical Union, prompting Catholics to organise themselves into a Catholic League. Religious tensions increased over the following decade. When in 1618 Protestant politicians threw three Catholics out of a window, this provided the catalyst for three decades of conflict.

The first period of the war ended in 1629 with the German Protestants utterly defeated. When Emperor Matthias died, the Protestants of Bohemia offered the crown of Bohemia to the Protestant Frederick, the Elector of the Palatinate, which it was hoped would lead to Frederick's election as Emperor. Frederick accepted but in 1620 he was defeated by the forces of the Catholic League under Emperor Ferdinand. The Protestants were in disarray and, but for the intervention of Christian IV of Denmark, they might have been forced to capitulate earlier. By the Peace of Lubeck in 1629, Christian gave up claims to the bishoprics bordering upon his own dominions, the Catholics had taken control of the Palatinate and the Protestant cause appeared defeated.

The following five years saw Gustavus Adolphus, King of Sweden, come to the aid of the Protestant side, motivated in large part by his own political ambitions to control the Baltic. He rallied Germanic forces to counter the Emperor and the advance of the counter-reformation. In **1631** he won a great victory in the battle of Breitenfeld, and went on to seize control of the episcopal states on the Rhine. It was now the Catholics who were facing calamitous defeat, but in a further battle of Lutzen in **1632** Gustavus was killed. The Peace of Prague of **1635**, reached after the Swedes lost the battle of Nordlingen, saw the two sides back to the position of **1627**.

The war continued for a further thirteen years, culminating in the Peace of Westphalia which recognised the independence of the German states, the Swiss cantons and the United Netherlands. After a generation of warfare in which Germany was drained, with its population falling from 16 million to 6 million, Protestantism was now permanently established and dominant in large parts of Europe, and the papacy was set to experience a long period of decline in its power.

8.2   Religious revival and decline in France

The civil wars of the second half of the sixteenth century, in which religion had been such a key feature, were brought to an end by the Edict of Nantes in **1598** when Henry IV granted religious freedom to the Huguenots and gave them political control of parts of the country, most notably La Rochelle. Whilst Roman Catholicism remained the religion practised by the overwhelming majority of the French, Henry IV refused to abide by the Decrees of Trent. Under Louis XIII (**1610–43**) Richelieu sought to enforce and strengthen Catholicism. The Huguenots resisted by force of arms, but were defeated in **1625**. Two years later, La Rochelle itself was besieged. The surrender of the city brought an end to thirty years of Huguenot political autonomy. Their religious freedoms were protected, but henceforth they came under the increasingly centralised French administration. Richelieu approached the papacy with a similar assertiveness. He sought to mould the Church into a national institution, with bishops being required to recognise allegiance to the State, and the King deciding appointments to ecclesiastical office.

The seventeenth century was marked by an increasing nationalism within French Catholicism, and by a revival of learning and piety. Francis de Salle (**1567–1622**) succeeded in converting many 'heretics' back to Catholicism. Saint Vincent de Paul (**1576–1660**) was notable for his founding of charitable institutions for the sick, the orphaned and the poor, and for establishing the Congregation of Missions at Chartres, to train priests in the skills of evangelising, and also the Sisters of Charity. M. Olier and Père Eudes were responsible for missions in the Auvergne and Brittany and were leading figures in the successful efforts to train and educate the priesthood, a task which had been neglected for decades. Several seminaries were established, notably that at St Sulpice.

The development of the Catholic Church into a national institution continued under the reign of Louis XIV (**1643–1715**) and his minister, Mazarin, is characterised by the dispute over the regale – the practice whereby in some areas of the realm the King appointed bishops and laid claim to the income from the sees pending the appointment of a new incumbent. By **1675** Louis had extended this practice throughout most of France. In retaliation the Pope refused to recognise bishops appointed by the King. In **1682** the Four Articles of Gallican Freedom in Affairs Ecclesiastical were issued, denying papal authority over kings other than in spiritual affairs. By this time there were as many as thirty five bishops without papal approval. So matters remained until **1689** when, in a different political environment, Louis XIV recanted in return for papal approval of the bishops he had already appointed.

The King's desire to establish and strengthen a national ('Gallican') church under the watchful eye of the monarchy no doubt partly explains his introduction of stringent repressive measures against non-Catholics, and the revocation in **1685** of the Edict of Nantes. Many Protestants reconverted to Catholicism, and thousands fled to Geneva, Germany, England and America. This senseless persecution of a group which had become politically integrated into the French nation, and which was dominated by professional people and skilled craftsmen, is thought to have had a significant impact on the French economy. Under Louis XIV, similar persecution and atrocities were inflicted upon the Waldensians in Savoy, and Protestants in the Cevennes.

The two issues that caused the most acrimonious controversy within Catholicism in seventeenth century France were those of **Jansenism** and **Quietism**. The former took its name from Cornelius Jansen who in his work *Augustinius* adopted Augustinian thought, asserting a doctrine of predestination in which obedience to God's commands was impossible without special grace, and resistance to God's grace was likewise impossible. Thus men's conduct and response are determined either by their nature or by God's grace. The Jansenists provoked bitter opposition from the Jesuits, and their teachings received papal condemnation in **1658**. In **1713** they were forced to flee to the Netherlands following the anti-Jansenist bull Unigenitus. Under the Archbishop of Utrecht they became the old Catholic Church, and after **1870** were joined by the opponents of papal infallibility. Quietists held that men should approach God by surrendering themselves in prayer without caring for their own salvation. Proponents held that any wrongs they committed did not count as sins at all, because they did not result from their own wills. Quietism was also condemned by the Pope in **1697**.

The development of Gallicanism provided a precedent for similar movements of Febronianism in Germany and Josephism in Austria. Nicholas van Hontheim, co-adjutor to the Archbishop of Trier, penned the book *De statu Ecclesiae* under the pseudonym Febronius to avoid papal wrath. He concluded that St Peter was the first bishop among equals, with bishops deriving their authority directly from the Church. He exhorted secular leaders to reform their own national churches in accordance with the advice of their bishops. In Austria, Maria Theresa, and in particular her son, Josephus, implemented such policies, thereby coining the term Josephism – the Inquisition was forbidden, the minimum age of admission to monasteries was reduced to twenty five, the Jesuits were expelled, the clergy's exemptions from taxation were abolished, and discriminatory measures against Protestants and Orthodox were lifted.

The condition of the Church in France in the latter half of the eighteenth century left much to be desired. The expulsion of the Jesuits in 1764 did not result in any improvement. The hierarchy were closely identified in the minds of the people with the monarchy – they were generally of aristocratic origin, wealthy and disinterested in the spiritual and pastoral role of the Church. As a result, the Church and the clergy suffered greatly at the hands of the revolutionaries. In 1789 the Assembly seized all Church lands, and within a few months had abolished religious orders, and nearly half the bishoprics in France. A further measure provided for bishops and parish clergy to be elected by the populace. Most of the bishops refused to swear allegiance to this new constitution, and a schism ensued. Those who refused to co-operate were forced to flee, and a total of 40,000 went into exile. The following year the State announced that religion was abolished, and the Reign of Terror commenced in which thousands were killed. In 1795 the worship of reason had clearly failed and religious toleration was introduced. A national council of clergy met in 1797, partly in the hope of healing the schism. The council acknowledged the supremacy of the Pope, but reaffirmed its commitment to the Gallican Articles of a hundred years previously.

The eighteenth century, and later the nineteenth century, saw drastic changes for the Roman Catholic Church, culminating in the loss of nearly the entire geographical territory over which the Pontiff had presided as temporal ruler, the loss of political influence, but an enormous increase in his spiritual claims and influence. The history of the papacy in these years is characterised by the increasing assertiveness of secular rulers, even in Catholic countries, as they attempted to control the Church and its hierarchy within their own borders. In Spain, where the Reformation had had the least impact, the monarchy was anxious to curb the power of the Church and inaugurate a national church along Gallican lines. On more than one occasion the monarchy abandoned its plans in the face of fierce opposition led by the Inquisition. In Portugal, too, the government was concerned to undermine the power of the Jesuits. Ironically, support came from Pope Benedict XIV himself who objected to Jesuit willingness to incorporate local and tribal customs in the Christianity practised by Indians in the New World. The Jesuits were expelled from Portugal in 1759, and following their apparent implication in a plot to kill the Portuguese King, distrust of them grew. In 1764 they were expelled from France and three years later from Spain too. Many of those in the Catholic hierarchy had likewise mistrusted the Jesuits, and been jealous and fearful of their influence. As opposition to them increased, there were calls for the society to be abolished, which it was in 1769 when Pope Clement XIV ordered its total suppression.

8.3 England and Britain in the sixteenth and seventeenth centuries

On her succession following the death of Mary, Elizabeth was declared Supreme Governor of the Church in England She sought uniformity in Church and State (the Elizabethan settlement), which she enforced vigorously. Opposition came from those who rejected what was in reality but partial reformation, with reformers both within and outside the established Church advocating a return to the practices of the early Church. In response to dissent, Elizabeth, with the assistance of Whitgift (Archbishop of Canterbury, 1583–1603), sought to strengthen her efforts to impose uniformity. A Commission for Causes Ecclesiastical was established which was to remain an effective instrument of control throughout much of the seventeenth century. A further Act of Uniformity introduced in 1593 established a scale of penalties for failure to attend parish church, and for attending unlawful assemblies. Some refused to conform and were imprisoned or hanged. Many fled to the Netherlands to form a movement which was to play such an important role in seventeenth century England. Repressive measures were also introduced against Catholics. It became a crime to say or hear Mass.

The history of the Church in the seventeenth century is characterised by the rise, fall and then the revival of the Anglican Church, its close association with the State, its acceptance of the divine right of kings to rule, and the growth of the Separatist movement, the forerunner of the modern Free Churches.

The accession of James VI of Scotland in 1603 raised the hopes of many persecuted reformers. On his way to London, the new king was presented with the Millenary Petition requesting the abolition of various abuses in public worship. James, however, had a hatred of Presbyterianism. At the Hampton Court conference, held to hear the Petitioners' requests, a new Bible was promised (resulting in the publication in 1611 of the Authorised Version) and changes to the Prayer Book were planned, but the Puritans otherwise gained nothing of substance. Indeed, the following year, acceptance of the sovereign's supremacy, the Prayer Book and the Articles were imposed and many Protestant clergy who refused to comply were forced out of their livings.

In 1605 the Gunpowder Plot, instigated by Catholics disillusioned with the new monarch, justified the introduction of further repression, including the prohibition against any Catholic practising as a barrister or doctor or being appointed guardian or trustee.

James' reign saw the continual growth of Puritanism and antipathy towards the Anglican clergy as they became inextricably linked with the royalist claims of the Stuart monarchy. Charles I, who succeeded to the throne in 1625, proved to be an even more ardent believer in the divine right of kings. He appointed Laud as his Archbishop of Canterbury. By means of the Star Chamber and the High Commission, further repressive anti-Puritan measures were introduced. This resulted in the emigration to the New World of even greater numbers of Puritans, the hardening of opposition within England, the rise of Puritan influence within Parliament, and thereafter the impeachment of Laud and the Earl of Strafford in 1640, the commencement of the civil war two years later and ultimately in the execution of the King in 1649.

The end of the civil war witnessed the transfer of power not to parliament, where the majority favoured establishing a new church along Presbyterian lines, but to Oliver Cromwell who ruled as Lord Protector, employing many of the rights and powers formerly exercised by the deceased king. Cromwell, like the majority of his victorious army, was an Independent and rejected the replacement of priest by presbyter. Under Cromwell a number of extreme separatist groups, such as the Levellers and the Diggers, were allowed freedoms hitherto denied them. Anglicans were effectively barred from ecclesiastical office. A Commission of Triers was established to interrogate those seeking appointment, and later the Commission extended its remit to examining clergy appointed before its creation. In 1655 the dispossessed clearly were prohibited from taking positions as teachers or chaplains, or administering the sacraments, or even reading from the Prayer Book. The decade of the Commonwealth provided non-conformity with a prolonged period in which it was able to permanently entrench itself in England.

On Cromwell's death in 1659, there followed a period of anarchy. In 1660 Charles II accepted the invitation to the throne. Any hopes that Presbyterians might have had of compromise and religious toleration were soon dashed. Charles and the reinstated Archbishop Laud, encouraged by popular support for measures against Catholicism, set about restoring the status quo. The dispossessed Anglican clergy – an estimated 1000 – were returned to their parishes with Parliament ensuring that all lands taken were to be returned. About 2000 Puritan ministers were compelled to leave their parishes. The Presbyterians were forced to ally themselves with the Separatists and together they were to lay the foundations of the English Free Churches.

The Clarendon Code consisted of three Acts designed to suppress non-conformity. The Corporation Act of 1661 required all officers of a corporation to receive Holy Communion in the Church of England; the Conventicle Act prohibited assemblies of more than five worshippers; and the Five Mile Act made it illegal for dispossessed preachers to approach within five miles of their last living. The Act of Uniformity in 1662 imposed conformity in episcopal ordination and the acceptance of the Common Book of Prayer. Parliament, fearful that the King might attempt to bring about the return of Roman Catholicism – indeed a secret treaty had been agreed in 1670 with Louis XIV aimed at securing that goal – introduced repressive measures. These culminated in 1673 with the introduction of the Oath of Supremacy which required all holders of civil and military office to denounce transubstantiation as well as receive Holy Communion within the Church of England. Popular opinion was frequently whipped up into expressions of anti-Catholic fury – not least of all by the revelation in 1678 by Titus Oates of an attempt to reinstate the papacy. That such fears were not totally without foundation was born out by the King's deathbed profession of Catholicism.

James II succeeded his brother to the throne and sought to relax the restrictions on the liberties of Catholics. This prompted a fierce reaction fuelled by events in France where the Edict of Nantes was revoked in 1685, and the Huguenots were being subjected to horrific persecution. Opposition within the established Church was led by the Archbishop of Canterbury, Sancroft. There was widespread support for the invitation to William of Orange to succeed to the throne.

The accession of William, a calvinist from the home of many an exiled English Puritan, was especially welcomed by the non-conformists. The Toleration Act granted freedom to worship to all save Roman Catholics and Unitarians on condition they take the oath of allegiance and reject transubstantiation. The Act reasserted the position of the Anglican Church which, however, was split when Sancroft and other bishops refused to swear allegiance to William and Mary, believing themselves bound by their conviction in the Divine Right of Kings and their previous oath of allegiance to James. The group was expelled from the Church but remained in existence as a separate episcopal church for nearly a century.

Two non-conformist movements which attracted most opposition were the **Quakers** and the **Unitarians**. They were overlooked in the Toleration Act of 1689 and had to wait to 1813 until they were granted freedom to worship. George Fox rejected formal religion, believing that the Church in England was too willing to subject itself to State control, seeking State protection at the expense of spirituality. Fox preached in the open air to thousands, especially in the North West of England, proclaiming the power of Christ to liberate from sin, rejecting creeds and liturgies, and calling upon men to seek God in their hearts. Fox drew together a band of men and women who set about the task of evangelising both in England and abroad. They earned the nickname 'Quaker' because at their meetings they sometimes shook with emotion, but they termed themselves the 'Children of the Light' and later the Society of Friends. By the end of the seventeenth century there were over 100,000 Quakers from all social classes. They spread to New England and other parts of the New World, having particular success among the aboriginal peoples. The Unitarians rejected the doctrine of the Trinity in favour of a belief in one God. They did not emerge in England until the mid seventeenth century during the upheaval of the civil war, and by the second half of the eighteenth century had had a major impact on the English Presbyterian and General Baptist Churches. The year 1773 saw the opening of the first Unitarian Church, after which the movement expanded with some momentum, organising itself into a denomination in 1825.

The reign of Queen Anne (1702–14) saw the growth of two parties, Whigs and Tories, which were to dominate British politics for many years. The Tories represented the views of the squires and country clerics; the Whigs had much support in the towns among the merchant classes and non-conformists. The practice developed of dissenters who wished to gain public office practising 'occasional conformity', i.e. the taking of Holy Communion in the parish church prior to their election to office. With royal approval, the Tories secured the passing of the Occasional Conformity Act outlawing this practice. In 1714 Anne died and was succeeded by George I of Hanover who was greeted by non-Conformists with enthusiasm. The following century saw the growing participation by non-Conformists in the social, political and economic life of the nation.

8.4 Pietism and the Evangelical Revival

In the late seventeenth century the German Lutheran Church had lost its reforming zeal and had developed a scholastic rigidity. It was in need of spiritual revival. The **Pietists** breathed new life into the Church, emphasising the importance of personal faith and the role of emotion. Pietism derived its origins from earlier English works such as Bunyan's *The Pilgrim's Progress*, and the Dutch Reformed Church of the early seventeenth century. German Pietism began with the attempt of Philip Spener to raise spiritual awareness. He gained particular influence after one of his supporters, Augustus Herman Francke, was appointed to a professorship at the new university of Halle in **1691**, from when Halle became the centre of Pietism. Francke initiated a number of important educational and welfare projects, but in particular was central in the development for the first time among the German Lutherans of a desire for missionary work. After his death in **1727** German Pietism declined.

One of Francke's pupils, and a godson of Spener, was the nobleman Nicolaus von Zinzendorf who determined to make his own contribution to the spiritual enhancement. German-speaking Moravians had fled to Saxony in the Thirty Years War and Zinzendorf invited them to settle on his lands. They lived in a monastic type community with children brought up together but separately from their parents, who were thus free to engage in missionary work in obedience to Christ's commandments to spread his Gospel. The Moravians led the way for Protestant missionary work and were active world-wide, most notably in America. Zinzendorf lived much of his later life in England and through him pietism had a substantial impact on the developing **Evangelical** or **Methodist Revival**.

The Church in England had become stale, dry and lifeless. Both John and Charles Wesley were prominent members of a group at Oxford University in about **1730** which met together to read the New Testament in Greek and visited the local sick and those in prison. They were nicknamed '**Methodists**' by fellow students because of their '**methodical**' compliance with the practices of their High Church religion. In **1736** they both sailed to Georgia as missionaries and in the course of their travels John Wesley came into contact with Moravian missionaries and pietism. On his return home John Wesley met Peter Bohler, a Moravian who had carried out missionary work in Britain, and from whom he came to understand the possibility of spontaneous emotional conversion of a kind he himself later underwent in **1738**. This conversion produced in Wesley an ardent desire to evangelise, and he travelled the length and breadth of the country preaching the Gospel. His work coincided with the early years of the mass movement of people from the country to towns and cities before the Church had organised itself to cater for their needs, and when it was largely indifferent to the command to spread the Gospel.

People flocked in thousands to hear Wesley, generally in the open air, as he preached of his experience of a new birth following a conscious and emotional experience of conversion, and of the possibility of Christian perfection. Wesley did not advocate the creation of a new Church outside the Church of England in which he and his brother had been tutored. However, his message of a 'new Gospel' could not help but suggest something lacking in the teachings of the clergy and he was not welcomed in the parishes. Moreover, as the movement gained momentum, some form of organisation was clearly called for, and lay preachers were appointed to assist. These developments pushed the Methodists in the direction of Dissent. In **1760** lay preachers celebrated Holy Communion, and in **1784** Wesley himself ordained Dr Coke and two other men for missionary work in America. In **1787** Methodist chapels were formally licensed under the Toleration Act, and although on his death in **1791** he still considered himself an Anglican, he had established a new denomination which today has some thirty million worshippers.

A second branch of Methodism owed its development to George Whitfield who had been a member of the same 'Holy Club' at Oxford. Unlike Wesley, who believed in Free Grace for all, Whitfield was a calvinist. He gained a powerful patroness in the Countess of Huntingdon. She built chapels throughout England and Wales and established training colleges, some of whose entrants remained within the Church of England.

The Methodist revival brought feeling and emotion into worship, expressing itself in the hymns of Charles Wesley which so effectively brought home the Christian message to ordinary people, who had hitherto been largely overlooked. Methodism, forced to become a separate denomination by the rejection of the Established Church, nevertheless left its mark upon it. Students in the colleges of the Countess of Huntingdon laid the seeds, especially at Cambridge, of an evangelical wing within the Church of England which was to play a pivotal role in creating the various missionary societies in the late eighteenth century. Methodism had its impact too on the social and humanitarian movements that developed in the following 100 years, including those for the emancipation of slaves, the reform of prisons and the combating of the evils of the Industrial Revolution.

8.5 Deism and the Enlightenment

The seventeenth and eighteenth centuries saw a number of challenges from thinkers who renounced dependence upon the supernatural and maintained that everything could be judged by human reasoning. One of the first to propound such rationalist views was Descartes (**1596–1650**) who resolved to doubt everything, claiming that doubt was the first and essential tool for human enquiry and constituted proof of his own existence – 'I think, therefore I am'. From this initial argument Descartes constructed the ontological argument, demonstrating the existence of God.

Christian thinkers sought to justify their theological beliefs through an appeal to the existence of the Universe, its detail, order and symmetry. This all pointed to the existence of a God and his plan for mankind – a God whose power and goodness gave him the ability and the desire to reveal himself to men, a revelation recorded in the Bible. One school that drew on Descartes' thinking was that of the **Deists**, who subjected Scripture to human reason and who tended to discount or minimise the importance of revelation. Rather, Christianity was merely a restatement of basic principles of 'natural religion' which could be understood entirely from 'the light of nature'. Thus belief in God, worshipping him, leading a virtuous life, seeking forgiveness of sins and expecting punishment or reward in the afterlife do not require or depend upon acceptance of the Bible.

One of the most influential of the Deist writers was John Toland (**1670–1727**) who sought to demonstrate in his work *Christianity not Mysterious* that everything is capable of being understood by man's intellect and only that which is clearly demonstrable is true. Deism encountered opposition in England, in particular from Bishop Butler who argued that God's very essence is mysterious.

The **Enlightenment** is the term used to describe the period in the history of Western Europe, in particular Britain, Germany, France and also the New World, when man matured and came to understand that he was not bound by the authority of dogma or ancient customs, but was free to reach his own conclusions. The Enlightenment distinguishes mankind's development from its primitive condition in the Middle Ages, or indeed in the Reformation. In England it is evident in the ideas of the Deists which spread to Germany. **Rationalism** was the dominant force in continental Europe and achieved particular influence as a result of the efforts of Lessing (**1728–81**) who rejected the concept of revelation and of miracles, and believed that humanity was outgrowing its dependence on Christianity, which had developed in a period of ignorance. Enlightened philosophers tended to believe that nature and scientific enquiry held the answer to every question and looked with suspicion at what they saw as the attempts by Church and State to stifle progress and enquiry. One of the greatest philosophers of the eighteenth century, Immanuel Kant, maintained that God's existence could not be proved by reason, but was indicated by the sense of moral feelings that men have within themselves. As we shall see later in this chapter, Kant's writings were influential through much of the nineteenth century.

8.6 England in the nineteenth century

It was in Britain that the Industrial Revolution first emerged, heralding the movement of vast numbers of people from the countryside to urban areas. In the early nineteenth century the Church of England was in decline. Hampered by its inability to create a new parish without an Act of Parliament, it failed to adapt to the rise of the industrial populations, among whom the non-conformists were to make great advances. In the middle of the eighteenth century it is estimated that little more than one in twenty working men attended church or chapel, with religious attendance in urban areas even lower. In the course of the century, however, the condition of the Church of England improved greatly through the rise of the Oxford Movement and the revival of Evangelical elements.

The year **1828** saw the repeal of the Test and Corporation Acts which had restricted the rights of dissenters, evidencing the growing influence of non-conformists both inside and outside Parliament. The following year, measures were passed providing for Catholic Emancipation, and in **1833** a bill was introduced to bring about substantial changes in the administration of the Church of Ireland. This latter measure, and the growing possibility of the disestablishment of the Church of England, aroused much opposition from within the Church, led by a group of men centred on Oriel College, Oxford. The **Oxford Movement** is said to have begun in July **1833** with Keble's sermon at St Mary's Church in Oxford in which he protested against the infringement of the Church's prerogatives in Ireland, and accused the state of interfering in apostolic rights and denying the sovereignty of God.

The leaders of the movement, also known as the Tractarians – John Henry Newman, John Keble, Edward Pusey and Hurrell Froude – emphasised the authority of the Church's traditions, claiming that the Church of England was closer to the early Church than the corrupt Roman Catholic Church, and distinct from the non-conformist churches who could not lay claim to the apostolic succession, the guarantee of the authority of the Church of England. From St Mary's Church, Oxford, where he presided from 1828 to 1843, Newman exercised considerable influence. In the latter half of the nineteenth century the Oxford Movement increasingly became 'Anglo-Catholic', placing great emphasis on the authority of the priest and adopting much ritual from the Roman Catholic Church. Whilst their main contribution was in liturgy, they revived pilgrimages, retreats, regular communion for laity, confession and religious communities. Successors to the Oxford Movement exercised considerable influence in the Church of England during the first half of the twentieth century, and remain one of the three strands of thought competing for influence today.

The movement provoked considerable opposition. The traditional hostility to Roman Catholics was still very much alive in Victorian England. In 1780 London had witnessed the Gordon Riots when the mob had rampaged through the city demanding the reversal of measures intended to relieve Catholics of some of the worst injustices against them. Anti-Catholic riots continued intermittently throughout the nineteenth century. Popular literature was characterised by much anti-Catholic sentiment with such books as 'The Female Jesuit or the Spy in the Family' and 'Geralda the Demon Nun' being on sale well into the twentieth century.

The publication in 1841 of Newman's Tract 90, in which he argued that the Thirty Nine Articles were essentially Catholic in origin, prompted protests in the House of Commons, and caused the Bishop of Oxford to reprimand him. Newman was forced to leave Oxford, and within a short time converted to Roman Catholicism. On Newman's departure, leadership of the Oxford Movement was assumed by Pusey, who together with the majority of the prominent Tractarians remained loyal to the Church of England. The movement continued to prosper, exercising a key role in raising the standards of worship, and of pastoral care in the industrial areas and in the East End of London.

This period also saw the revival of the Roman Catholic Church after the removal in 1829 of the remaining restrictions on participation by Catholics in the life of the nation. A number of influential clergy defected from the Church of England, but numerically by far the greatest impact was from the stream of Irish immigrants – by 1851 an estimated 400,000 were living in Britain. One of the Anglican defectors, Manning, was appointed a cardinal in 1875, and took the initiative in establishing educational facilities, mainly elementary schools to provide a Catholic education.

The eighteenth century Evangelical Revival had seen the Methodists, the Calvinists and the Anglican Evangelicals establish themselves. An influential group of evangelicals which drew from all three was the Clapham Sect whose members founded the Church Missionary Society, the British and Foreign Bible Society, and the Religious Tract Society. One such evangelical was William Wilberforce who spearheaded the campaign against the slave trade. An Abolition Committee, established in 1787, oversaw a prolonged propaganda campaign, seeking to win over both public opinion and the minds of Members of Parliament. Slavery was at last abolished in 1807, but it was a further twenty six years before slaves in the British Empire were finally emancipated. Wilberforce also penned the extremely influential book entitled *A Practical View of the Prevailing Religious System of Professed Christians in the Higher and Middle Classes in this Country contrasted with Real Christianity*. He emphasised what he saw as the duties of the rich to the poor, and the need for the prosperous to transform their nominal Christianity to a faith of genuine personal commitment. The book proved extremely popular and helped bring about a change in social habits in the first twenty years of the nineteenth century. Hitherto Christians, especially the Established Church, had shown little concern for the victims of the Industrial Revolution. Indeed those most prominent in evangelising were so preoccupied with the message of personal salvation that they appeared blind to the practical problems of humanity, such as poverty and slum housing.

Participation in Methodist chapels gave many working men experience of decision-making, public-speaking and leadership, and it was from this background that many social reformers and the leaders of the trade union movement and Labour Party were to evolve. A body of Christian thought emerged which argued that redemption was not limited to the spiritual but should be total; just as man needed spiritual salvation, so too he needed to be saved from physical deprivation. Christian influences, again for the most part outside the Established Church, are also to be found in the various legislative measures introduced in the nineteenth century to limit the abuse of the industrial workforce. It was not until the twentieth century that Christian Socialism emerged as an important influence in the Church of England, being at its most significant in 1942 to 1944 when William Temple was Archbishop of Canterbury.

The late eighteenth century had seen the creation of numerous organisations for overseas missionary work, and for evangelising at home. These societies engaged in the mass distribution of Christian literature, arranged public meetings to evangelise, and organised Sunday schools for children in the towns and cities. From the 1840s the various churches developed their own inner city missions ministering to the social as well as the spiritual needs of the people, and providing soup kitchens, clothing clubs and savings 'banks'.

The evangelisation of the working classes posed a difficulty. There was much truth in the jibe that the Church of England represented the Tory Party at prayer. As to the Wesleyans and Congregationalists, their followers were dominated by the middle classes. The problem was exacerbated by the fact that the children of working class churchgoers often moved up into the echelons of the middle classes. Even the Methodists had less impact on the further increasing population of the industrialised areas. Baptists and the Primitive Methodists, however, did succeed in attracting large working class congregations. In 1865 William and Catherine Booth abandoned mainstream Methodism and opened a mission in a tent in Whitechapel in London to take the message of salvation to the working classes. To the annoyance of many in the Established Church, this venture proved a success and led to the birth of the Salvation Army, with its emphasis on uniforms, corps and citadels. For some time 'General' Booth, as he styled himself, was primarily concerned with spreading the evangelist message of spiritual salvation, but came to appreciate a link between evangelism and social liberation.

The Salvation Army grew into a movement which became world-wide. Today there are an estimated 55,000 'soldiers' in the United Kingdom, with as many as one and a half million world-wide.

8.7   The fortunes of Roman Catholicism in France and Germany

By the Peace of Tolentino in **1797**, the Pope had been forced by the victorious French army's arrival in Rome to abandon claims to a substantial portion of papal territory, and was taken captive to France. In **1799** Napoleon was declared First Consul, and believing in the stability associated with a national Catholicism, he reached new terms with the Pope in the Concordat of **1801**. The First Consul acknowledged that the majority of Frenchmen were Roman Catholic and returned the papal states to the new Pope. In exchange, Pius VII annulled all the sees in France and cancelled the appointments of all incumbent bishops. New bishoprics were created. The incumbents were to be appointed by the Pope but the First Consul was to have the power of veto. Likewise the State was permitted to veto the appointments by bishops of lower clergy. France thus had a new church hierarchy. Some 'old' bishops refused to abandon their sees and were excommunicated by the Pope. A schism resulted, with the bishops and recalcitrant laity forming La Petite Eglise which was to continue for nearly a century. The French Catholic Church remained a 'national' church with the Pope prohibited from publishing any Bull without the consent of the government.

In **1806**, on the crowning of Napoleon as Emperor, the Pope participated in the ceremony in Paris by annointing the Emperor, though the latter insisted on placing the crown upon his own head. From **1808** to **1814** this Pope too was taken prisoner by the French. Following Napoleon's defeat, Pius VII began reasserting the authority of the papacy, assisted by the Jesuits who were reinstated after having been outlawed since **1773**.

The following sixty years saw a revival of Romanism – whilst the Pope's temporal power and authority had largely disappeared, his spiritual authority was to rise with the growth of **Ultramontanism**. The adherents of this new movement were fiercely loyal to the Pope as the ultimate authority on issues of faith and practice. They were first prominent in France, where the history of the church in the nineteenth century was characterised by the Ultramontanes' struggle with Gallican nationalists. After Napoleon's defeat, Ultramontanism rose to pre-eminence throughout Catholic Europe. This same period saw a series of religious revivals in Protestant Europe and a continual struggle between Catholicism and political liberalism and republicanism. Italy still consisted of a patchwork of small rival states, but a democratic movement began to develop, known as the Carbonari, pressing for the unification of Italy. The year **1848** witnessed revolutions in France and Germany. In Italy, an army led by Garibaldi marched on Rome and forced Pius IX into exile from which he was returned by the French two years later. Unification came in **1861** when Victor Emmanuel was proclaimed King of Italy.

Under Pius IX who occupied the papal throne from **1846** to **1878**, the doctrinal supremacy of the papacy was greatly enhanced. In **1850** he re-established the Catholic hierarchy in England, and three years later did so in the Netherlands. In **1854** he proclaimed the doctrine of the Immaculate Conception, laying a solid foundation for the devotion to Mary and reinforcing his spiritual authority. In **1864** the papal office issued the Syllabus of Errors, a list of heresies following the earlier encyclical *Quanta Cura*, condemning separation of Church and State, political liberalism, democracy, rationalism in theology, anti-clericalism, religious toleration and even the Bible societies (for distributing the Scriptures without the comments of the Church fathers).

In **1870**, the year that Rome was seized by the victorious King Victor Emmanuel, the Vatican Council concluded its deliberations, resulting in a triumph for Ultramontanism and the defeat of Gallicanism, Febronism and liberal Catholicism. The Council almost unanimously approved the doctrine of papal infallibility, whereby the Pope when speaking *ex cathedra*, i.e. in the discharge of his papal office, is beyond error. There had been considerable opposition within the Roman Catholic Church to this development, but when the vote was finally taken, only two votes were cast against – in particular that of the academic Dollinger, who had substantial support in Germany. As a result of his opposition Dollinger was excommunicated. Many, inspired by his views, formed a separate church, known as the Old Catholics, which still survives in Germany and Switzerland and is based upon episcopal succession.

The Declaration of Infallibilty provoked opposition from Bismark, following the proclamation of King William of Prussia as Emperor in **1871** after the end of the Franco–Prussian War. Bismark initiated the Kulturkampf against the Roman Catholic Church, giving concrete expression to the tensions which had been growing between the Prussian rulers and the papacy for several decades. He expelled the Jesuits from Germany and passed the anti-Catholic Falk Laws in **1873**. He also brought education totally under State control, limited bishops' powers of discipline and established a supreme church court under the auspices of the Emperor. The Falk laws were subsequently repealed following Bismark's conviction that Roman Catholicism represented an effective balwark against socialism.

In France, there developed a prolonged antipathy between Church and State lasting well into the twentieth century. In **1901** religious orders were prohibited from participating in education, and in **1904** fourteen thousand schools were closed down by the government in response to the refusal of the Jesuits and others to comply. By La Loi de la Séparature of **1905**, ecclesiastical property was deemed to belong to the State and religious bodies desiring to make use of it were obliged to form associations. All privileges hitherto enjoyed by the Church, such as subsidies, were withdrawn. Pius X called in vain on Catholics to disobey the Separation Law.

8.8   Science, philosophy and biblical criticism

The nineteenth century was the age of doubt in which Christianity was confronted with scientific, philosophical and historical challenges. Darwin's theory of evolution, philosophical questioning of the traditional concepts of a Christian God, and historical inquiry of biblical texts all served to question the authenticity of the Christian Faith. The debate over evolution came to prominence in England, the ideas of Darwin being taken up in particular by the scientist Huxley. To many, their theorising seemed in complete contradiction to the biblical account in Genesis 1. Over time, however, in part because of developments in biblical criticism generally, the Genesis story came to be seen by most believers as purely symbolic.

In Germany, the century saw the growing influence of Immanuel Kant (1724–1804) who had successfully challenged previous philosophical thinking that God's existence was susceptible to proof by reason. Kant argued that our understanding is limited by our concepts of time and space, and any attempts to go beyond that only result in confusion and uncertainty. In *Critique of Pure Reason* (1781) Kant claimed that although the existence of God cannot be demonstrated through reason, his existence is indicated by the feelings men have within themselves of moral values. God's existence is necessary if man is to face consequences for his actions in the form of rewards or punishments in an after-life. In the nineteenth century, philosophers sought to respond to Kant's position. Schleiermacher (1768–1834), who has been termed the father of modern theology, acknowledged the force of Kant's criticism of rational attempts to demonstrate God's existence, and argued that belief in God was justified by religious experience, and that religion is not susceptible to rational analysis in the way that it is applied to behaviour or science.

Hegel (1770–1831) again took a different position, claiming that God is a spirit which is manifested and present *in* the world (as distinct from the orthodox position that God is over and above the world). The world is itself a manifestation of God. For Kant and liberal Protestant theologians, Jesus became a teacher of moral religion; whereas, for Schleiermacher and Hegel, he was a form of the divine presentation sent to unite God and humanity. Hegel's view of the world as a manifestation of the Absolute Spirit was transformed by his pupil Feuerbach (1804–72) who thought that the Spirit of which Hegel spoke was no more than nature itself, and our conception of God no more than our vision of our own purified nature.

German scholars were also engaged in scrutinising the historical bases of the claims of Christianity and subjected the Bible to sceptical analysis. Some, such as F.C. Baur, sought to highlight the substantial divergence between the Church of St Peter and the teachings of Paul. Others promulgated the argument that, whilst Jesus of Nazareth existed, the Christ depicted in the New Testament is essentially a myth. In addition to such criticism challenging traditional views, the nineteenth century also saw the reconstructing of the Bible with the assistance of newly discovered texts. In 1881 a Revised New Testament in English was published – a more accurate translation than the Authorised Version.

8.9   The New World and the expansion of Christendom

The years 1500 to 1750 saw the emergence of Christianity as a world-wide religion, no longer primarily confined to Europe. In contrast to the limited success of the missionary activity of the Middle Ages, these years saw the opening up of new worlds in which Christianity became permanently established. It was the Roman Catholic Church which took the lead and which was almost the sole beneficiary of this rapid expansion, in large part because the two foremost colonial nations, Spain and Portugal, were Roman Catholic. The Iberian governments took responsibility both for secular matters, and for the advancing of the Christian faith in the lands under their dominion. These were still the early years of Protestantism and the Protestant states of northern Europe, with England and the Netherlands yet to develop into the great trading nations that they became.

The participation and interference of government in missionary work in the early years declined as the secular authorities came to realise that it was not necessary for, and indeed often hampered, their political and colonial policies. Government interest was superseded by new initiatives originating from early in the seventeenth century, and which became the main vehicles for the spreading of the faith from the eighteenth century. Voluntary associations were founded, beginning with the creation in **1622** of the Congregatio de Propaganda Fide under Pope Gregory XV, which still oversees the missionary work of the Church, and the subsequent foundation of its seminary for training missionaries in **1627**. In France, this development was later mirrored by the Société des Missions Etrangères formed in **1658**, one of whose founders was instrumental in the launch of the French East India Company which gave free passage to missionaries.

In England, the first missionary association, the New England Company, was founded in **1649**, with the influential Society for Promoting Christian Knowledge (SPCK) being formed in **1698**, and the Society for the Propagation of the Gospel in Foreign Parts following in **1701**. The latter was created to minister to the English settlers and the natives they encountered in North America and the West Indies, but later took on a world-wide mission as Britain extended its influence and power.

The Protestant missionary effort was slow in building up momentum. As late as **1784** there were still only six missionary societies, and two hundred Protestant missionaries, at least half of whom were Moravians. The Roman Catholics had had marked successes, but even by the end of the eighteenth century less than 20 per cent of the world's population was Christian, and this was still almost entirely European.

The Protestant missionary zeal of the later eighteenth and nineteenth centuries arose out of the Evangelical Revival in England and the growth of Pietism in Germany, representing a desire to move Protestantism away from preoccupation with rigidity and doctrine, in the direction of devotion and holy life. Moravians, closely associated with the rise of Pietism, took the lead and between **1732** and **1752** established a number of missions, prompting the foundation of societies in England in the last decade of the eighteenth century, and the early years of the nineteenth, most notably the interdenominational London Missionary Society in **1799**. These developments prompted similar Roman Catholic foundations, such as the Society for the Propagation of the Faith in **1844**.

It was only in the **1820s** and **1830s** that overseas missions began to be an important aspect of church life in Britain. The latter half of the nineteenth century opened up vast opportunities for missionary work throughout the world. The year **1858** saw the Treaties of Tientsin with China, and Yedo with Japan facilitating the growth of European and Christian influence; the disbanding of the East India Company which had opposed missionary work; and the pioneering explorations of Livingstone in Africa.

South and Central America

In the late fifteenth century, Pope Alexander VI divided the new lands of the Americas between Spain and Portugal, whose kings were given power to preside over the new churches in these lands, and the duty of bringing the natives to the Christian faith. Their conquistadors, prepared to convert by force, inflicted many brutalities on the native populations and indeed on each other in their thirst for wealth. The Europeans treated all native American Indians as savages, making no distinction between the advanced cultures of the Aztecs and the Incas on the one hand, and the savage cannabalistic tribes on the other.

The missionaries, however, often stood out as champions of the natives in the face of the cruelty of the Spanish conquistadors and the authorities. Las Casas gave up his Indian slaves, became a Dominican and sought to obtain legal protection for the Indians. He was instrumental in the passing of a new law in **1542** restricting slavery, but which was almost universally ignored in the colonies. His convictions led him to write a book entitled *On the Only Way to Call People to God*, but no one was prepared to print it. The opinions of Las Casas did prepare the way for the later efforts of the Jesuits, who established reservations for the Indians in various parts of the Spanish and Portuguese Empires, including Guatemala and southern Brazil, but most notably in Paraguay. These Jesuit 'reductions' consisted of large stretches of land reserved for the Indians and governed by the Jesuit order. The Indians were thus protected from the violence and exploitation of the colonists and were educated and taught the Christian faith in semi-communistic monastic communities in which no one could own property, but everyone was free to leave. In the early years, many of these unarmed reductions were destroyed by white bandits, but in **1648** were given permission by the King of Spain to carry arms. The reductions in Paraguay covered an area the size of Great Britain in which there were thirty three Indian cities. These colonies aroused resentment among the Spanish and Portuguese and in **1750** they determined to expel the Jesuits, who six years later were recalled, resulting in the collapse of the reservations.

Whilst there were American Indians who became ordained or who taught Christianity as lay preachers, the demands placed on them of a knowledge of Latin, theological doctrine and the acceptance of celibacy meant that in the sixteenth and seventeenth centuries at least there were relatively few Indians in the ranks of the clergy.

North America

In North America, Christianity was introduced by the French with Champlain founding Quebec in **1608**. Both the Franciscans and the Jesuits were at the forefront of missionary work, with earlier efforts being concentrated on the Huron tribe. The Ursuline order of nuns played a major role in educating the women and children of many natives, in particular the Illinois. Further south, the Pilgrim Fathers had landed at New Plymouth in 1620. Massachusetts became a Congregationalist centre. One of their ministers, John Elliott, translated the Bible for the local Indians, becoming known as the Apostle to the Indians. The first Anglican priest celebrated communion at Jamestown in 1607, where nearly a century later the first Anglican College was established.

The largest groups in the English colonies were the Congregationalists and Presbyterians. The first Presbyterians originated from the Dutch Reformed Church, but what was to become mainstream Presbyterianism came from Britain, with many Scottish and Irish Presbyterians seeking refuge from the Stuarts, and many more emigrating following the economic sanctions imposed on Ireland. There were smaller communities of English and Welsh Baptists, and a Quaker settlement in Pennsylvania.

By 1690 the settlers numbered some 250,000. They were all British save for small numbers of Huguenots, Dutch Calvinists and Mennonites. The early eighteenth century saw the arrival of large numbers of German Protestants, primarily Lutheran. By 1750 there were no fewer than 200,000 German immigrants, with as many as 70,000 in Pennsylvania alone.

The evangelical enthusiasm of the Protestant churches among the British settlers had waned considerably by the eighteenth century, and as the century progressed there were various calls for a revival. 'The Great Awakening' took place in Northampton in Massachusetts under Jonathan Edwards in 1734 and influenced religious developments both in the colonies and in Britain. The revival began in response to a series of sermons on justification by faith alone, to which people flocked, and continued for several years, reaching a peak in 1740. A key figure in the revival was George Whitfield, a pioneer in the English Revival, who arrived in New England in 1740 and undertook a six-week tour of the colonies. He preached to large open-air audiences, his last sermon being to a crowd estimated at 20,000.

The Awakening spread to New York, New Jersey, Pennsylvania, Maryland and Virginia, with several Churches, including the Baptists led by evangelists such as Daniel Marshall, making many converts. One consequence of the revitalisation was the revival of attempts to evangelise among the Indian tribes.

The nineteenth century saw great geographical and political expansion, the excesses of individualism, and a devastating civil war that split the nation in half. At the beginning of the century there were signs of a second Awakening which was to last for over half a century. It was characterised by large meetings in which families encamped for several days in the open air and joined together in common worship and prayer, usually becoming worked up to a high emotional pitch resulting in hysterical conversions. The Methodists and Baptists co-operated in what was to become an Evangelical United Front to win over the masses to Christianity. By the middle of the nineteenth century there were over a million and a half in the Methodist Church and over a million Baptists.

The Protestant Churches generally took a positive role in social matters such as women's rights to vote, public education, penal reform and the campaign for the abolition of slavery. They were similarly vociferous in their opposition to alcohol, prostitution, immigration, offending against the Sabbath, Roman Catholicism and slavery. In the civil war (**1861–65**) the Churches split over the issue of slavery. Reconciliation did not follow the victories of the northern armies, with the northern Churches convinced that their southern brethren were in need of evangelising. As to the emancipated slaves, they invariably chose to join the Baptists or Methodists.

In the years after the civil war, missionary efforts were aimed primarily at the growing urban populations and abroad, rather than at the frontiers. This period also saw mass immigration, including that of many Roman Catholics who today form the largest Christian body in the United States. Whilst the Protestant population is more numerous, it has been contintually prone to rifts, there being well over a hundred different sects.

India

In India, the Portuguese advanced the interests of their traders and the Church by force of arms, with little regard for the local population. The main Portuguese settlement was in Goa where both Dominicans and Franciscans were active from the early sixteenth century. Whilst there were a number of campaigns which resulted in mass conversions, in particular as a result of the efforts of Francis Xavier, a founder of the Society of Jesus who arrived there in **1541**, Christianity failed to become established apart from in Goa and its surrounds. There was, however, considerable success among the lowest castes, whose descendants remain Roman Catholic. In the south of India, the Jesuits carried out their missionary work without the assistance of a secular power. In **1606** Robert de Nobili adopted native customs, and lived as a brahmin, in an effort to win over the highest caste, and several missionaries with this object in mind refused to seek the conversion of the lowest castes. The movement initiated by de Nobili had considerable success, at its highpoint boasting over 200,000 Christians. In 1744 the policy of 'Indianisation' of the faith was condemned by the Pope and the Jesuit mission was not long afterwards recalled.

Protestant missionary work in India began with the Lutheran Christian Schwartz, who was active in missionary work from **1750** until he died in **1798**. In 1792 the English Baptist Society sent William Carey to Serampore. Carey translated the New Testament into Bengali. In **1806**, in Calcutta, the Anglican Henry Martyn began translating the New Testament and the Book of Common Prayer into Hindustani, although his missionary work bore no fruit. A college was founded in the same city by Bishop Middleton for the preparation of Indians for missionary work. In the early decades of the century the Anglican Church created bishoprics to administer the churches. In **1830** the Scottish missionary Alexander Duff also went to Calcutta where he was responsible for establishing the first of the numerous schools in which members of the higher castes were educated. The remaining years of the nineteenth century, and the twentieth, saw the creation of many educational institutions by the missionaries, ranging from primary schools to establishments for higher education and training for the ministry.

The churches had to grapple with the thorny issue of the caste system, with the Roman Catholic and Lutheran Churches permitting its retention among their brethren. The Anglican Church took a more principled stance, and as a result was abandoned by many Christians in favour of Roman Catholicism. In southern India, the Anglican Church made significant advances among the outcastes however, where in the Diocese of Dornakal the number of Anglican Christians rose to 85,000.

Japan

The Jesuits had their greatest success in Japan where Xavier arrived in 1549 and spent two years evangelising. In large part due to the efforts of his companion Juan Fernandez, a lay missionary who successfully grappled with the local language, and the work of Dominicans and Franciscans, it is estimated that nearly a million were converted in the following fifty years. This remarkable progress was brought to an end by a prolonged period of persecution carried out by the secular authorities, suspicious that the missionary activities were but a first step in the plans of the Spanish and Portuguese to conquer the country. In 1638 alone, over 17,000 Christians are said to have been slaughtered. Europeans were effectively excluded from entering the country and churches disappeared. Europeans were not allowed into Japan until the mid nineteenth century, when they discovered a number of congregations still alive, having practised their faith in secret for two centuries. Anglican missionaries sent out from America and England were active, and in 1887 they united their organisations into the Holy Catholic Church of Japan which subsequently established its own theological college.

China

In China, attempts in the seventh and thirteenth centuries to establish churches had little success. Matthew Ricci in the late sixteenth century succeeded in immersing himself in Chinese culture, language and learning, and gained the approval of the Emperor to undertake missionary activity. There were about 2500 Chinese Christians by the time of Ricci's death in 1610, the number growing to about 300,000 by the end of the seventeenth century. In his efforts to win converts, Ricci permitted incorporation of ancestor worship, resulting in later opposition from the Dominicans who referred the matter to the Inquisition. The issue was not properly resolved and acrimony over the 'naturalising' of the faith continued to split the different missionary groups, and only served to hamper progress. In the mid eighteenth century, forces within China sought to oppose the continuing spread of the faith, and in 1746 the Emperor ordered that missionaries be deported, thereby beginning a long period of proscription.

Protestant missionaries started their work in China in the early nineteenth century, which they were permitted to do under treaties between the Chinese authorities and Western governments, some of which were extracted by force. The London Missionary Society sent Robert Morrison to Macao in 1807, who translated most of the Bible into Chinese. Other missionaries followed, most notably American, British and Canadian. Within a century there were about one and half million Protestants in China, the number of Catholics having grown to about five million. The Boxer Rising of 1900 saw several missionaries murdered, and progress was halted for a time. In 1912 the various English-speaking Anglican missionary groups joined together to form the Holy Catholic Church of China. In the context of such a largely populated country the numbers were relatively small, but among the Chinese Protestants, in particular, there were many who were well educated and contributed much to Chinese society.

Initially the Communist Party under Mao expelled Western missionaries who were seen as agents of imperial capitalism, but Chinese Christians were left alone. Following the Cultural Revolution in 1966 the churches disappeared underground, reappearing after the revolutionary zeal had calmed down. The churches remained subject to restrictions in their activities, especially concerning contact with foreign churches.

Africa

In Africa, Christianity made little progress in the sixteenth and seventeenth centuries. On the Mediterranean coast, Christianity had been destroyed by the Islamic advance, save in Ethiopia, and to a certain extent in Egypt. Elsewhere the Portuguese were active on parts of the coast, but the dominating motive was the trade in African slaves, and the spreading of the Christian faith came a poor second. It was not until the nineteenth century, following the explorations and trading activities of primarily the British and French that Christianity, and in particular the Protestant faith, came to dominate much of the continent.

The nineteenth century Christian missions in Africa were initially centred on the communities of freed slaves brought together on the coast of West Africa, as many as 50,000 living in Sierra Leone by 1846. These colonies had been founded to provide a haven for freed slaves, and a base for further missionary work in Africa. In the second half of the century the small population of Sierra Leone produced many ministers and missionaries who ventured into the rest of Africa, including Samuel Crowther who in 1864 became the first African Anglican Bishop.

Even though the British Parliament had made the slave trade illegal in 1807 and had ordered the emancipation of slaves in 1833, there were more slaves than ever being shipped across the Atlantic, and West Africa was becoming depopulated. The evangelical Sir Thomas Fowell Buxton maintained that West Africa could be saved by the three C's – Christianity, Commerce and Civilisation. He argued that the slave trade could be most effectively countered by developing more lucrative commercial activities to take away its attractions. Following the failure of the Niger Expedition – which it had been intended would bring about anti-slavery treaties with inland tribes, set up model farms and report on the prospect of commercial development – this theory was dismissed by many until the later successes of David Livingstone in East Africa designed to counter the Arab slave trade.

By the mid eighteenth century some Christian missions themselves engaged in commercial activities, such as the Church Missionary Society which developed cotton growing in parts of Nigeria. From the outset the Christian missions laid great stress on education and literacy, with the establishment in many places of grammar schools along British lines, and the creation of further education establishments, in some cases affiliated to a British University. It was not until the end of the nineteenth century that the Roman Catholic missions took a significant role in education, but when they did they established many primary schools which they used as a tool of evangelisation.

In the scramble for Africa from **1870**, the British missionaries generally welcomed the extensions of British Imperial rule, sometimes out of fear that their missions might come under Portuguese misrule, or that they might be displaced by Roman Catholic missions under the rule of a Catholic power. That said, the missionaries were often the greatest critics of colonial administrations, and the colonial governments were often apprehensive about their activities. One effect of the advent of Imperial rule was the ousting or effective demotion of native educated leaders who had been trained to participate in the leadership of their countries, and in the teachings of the Christian faith. These leaders often took an active part in the nationalist and independence movements.

8.10 The Eastern Church

The Orthodox Church never had the unity and centralised hierarchical structure that was characteristic of the Roman Catholic Church. Instead it was made up of independent churches, which whilst acknowledging the Patriarch of Constantinople as the head of the Orthodox Church, were closely identified with their respective secular governments. After the fall of Constantinople in **1453**, the Orthodox Church became divided as so many Orthodox Christians came under Turkish rule.

In Constantinople the Turkish rulers tolerated the Christians. They sought to exploit the Orthodox Church to assist them in governing and taxing their new subjects. The Patriarch, as the head of the Orthodox hierarchy, became an intermediary between the Christians and their Turkish rulers. The Sultan, conscious that the papacy was a unifying force against Islam, was all the more willing to support the Patriarch. In internal Church affairs, in contrast to the days when the Eastern Emperors had so frequently intervened, the Patriarch was pre-eminent in most matters. The Sultan, however, made the Patriarch responsible for the payment of taxes on Christians. The Patriarch recovered these sums from the bishops by selling appointments. The bishops looked to recoup their losses from the clergy, and they in turn from the people.

The sixteenth century onwards also saw the increasing influence of the Phanariots. They were Greeks who originated from a wealthy district of Constantinople, and by their ability to purchase ecclesiastical office they came to dominate the upper echelons of the ecclesiastical hierarchy not only in Greek-speaking areas but also in Serbia, Bulgaria, Roumania and even Antioch. In the following centuries they embarked upon a process of Helenisation that caused great animosity among the peoples of the Balkans.

The Eastern Orthodox Church was not untouched by the Reformation, but the reformers achieved little headway until the seventeenth century when Cyril Lucar, the Patriarch of Constantinople, came under the influence of the teachings of Calvin. Lucar's opinions prompted much opposition, leading to a Counsel of Jerusalem in **1672** at which Calvinism was denounced and the doctrine of transubstantiation approved.

The story of the Church in the Balkans is dominated by the tumultuous history of its relations with the ecclesiastical authorities in Constantinople, and the

Turkish secular leaders. Bulgaria had its own independent Archbishop, but this position was permanently occupied by the Phanariot Greeks who ruled over the Bulgarians in Church affairs, just as the Turks did in secular matters. The process of Helenisation became even more systematic when in 1767 the position of archbishop was abolished and direct control from Constantinople was enforced. In 1860 the Bulgarian Church repudiated rule by the Patriarch and, after a period of struggle, gained and maintained its independence from Constantinople. A similar pattern was witnessed in Roumania where the Turks sold ecclesiastical offices to the Greeks. In 1864 the Church declared itself independent from other orthodox churches, but remained subservient to the State which seized its monasteries and placed them under firm State control.

The late fifteenth century had seen the King of Russia, Ivan III, unite the Russian princes. Encouraged by his wife Zoe, the daughter of the last of the Eastern Roman Emperors, he assumed the mantle of successor to the Eastern Emperors and guardian of the Orthodox Church, whose ecclesiastical leader was under Turkish domination in Constantinople. The Orthodox Church started its own missionary activities by setting up monasteries in the northern regions in an effort to evangelise the primitive tribes living there. As in Western Europe, monastic communities – both the Urban who established themselves in the towns and cities, and the Desert who lived in the more remote areas – came to possess huge areas of land amounting by the middle of the sixteenth century to about a third of all productive land in Russia.

The son and successor of Ivan III, Ivan IV the Terrible, was formally crowned as successor to the Russian Emperors, and sought to establish Moscow as the ecclesiastical capital of the Orthodox Church. In 1589 the Patriarch of Constantinople was prevailed upon to establish a separate Patriarchate at Moscow on a par with those of Antioch, Jerusalem and Alexandria. The authority of the Patriarch of Moscow, and the unity of Church and State were assured when the first Czar of the Romanov dynasty, Michael, was elected to the throne in 1613. Michael was only 16 and was dominated by his father Filaret, who remained Patriarch for the next twenty years until his death in 1633.

In the middle of the seventeenth century the Russian church was rent in two by bitter controversy over minute liturgical differences. 'The Old Believers' attached great significance to the external forms of worship and considered that any change amounted to a betrayal of Moscow as the capital of Orthodoxy. The controversy culminated in the 'Old Believers' breaking away. In the course of this debate, the Patriarch Nikon sought to claim that in ecclesiastical matters the Patriarch was the supreme authority and that the Czar had no right to the title of head of the Church. This debate, in which Nikon was defeated, and the schism over liturgy greatly weakened the power of the Church, which remained even more firmly under State control. The 'Old Believers' were persecuted by the authorities, but continued to survive, numbering four million at the outbreak of the First World War.

The power of the State over the Orthodox Church was further strengthened in 1721 when Peter the Great abolished the office of Patriarch, replacing it with the appointment of a Holy Synod. This resembled a committee presided over by a Procurator appointed by the Czar which governed church affairs. The Russian Orthodox Church henceforth became virtually a department of State and an instrument of government and was to remain so for two hundred years. The Czar seized monastic and other ecclesiastical revenues, and introduced measures to require priests to inform the State police of any information detrimental to the State which came to their notice in the confessional or otherwise. Under Catherine II the Church underwent a further attack when almost all monastic property was confiscated by the State.

The Russian Orthodox Church nevertheless remained the dominant faith of the Russian people, boasting some ninety million adherents and sixty thousand non-monastic clergy in the nineteenth century. The clergy, however, were split between the upper or 'black' clergy, bishops and monks, and the lower 'white' parish clergy. The former were generally prosperous and received the support of the secular authorities, but the latter were invariably poverty stricken.

Under Nicholas I, who succeeded to the throne in 1826, a secret police force was established to enforce political and religious loyalty and to punish heretics. When Nicholas crushed the Polish republicans in 1831, he waged a ferocious war against heretics there and against the Uniate Church whose adherents sought reconciliation with the Orthodox Church to escape persecution. In 1853 his efforts to support the Orthodox Christians under Turkish rule brought him into conflict with England and France, who saw his religious zeal as a mere mask to justify territorial ambitions. Under Nicholas' successor, Alexander II, Philaret the Metropolitan Bishop of Moscow succeeded in drafting the edict of 1861 which emancipated nearly twenty three million serfs. The effect, unfortunately, was to render those freed more destitute and poverty stricken than they had been as slaves. Alexander sought to introduce other reforms such as establishing secondary schools and arranging for the foundation of elementary schools, but the clergy failed to engage themselves in these developments. In 1877 the Russians success-fully went to war against the Turks, appalled at the accounts of massacres of Christians in Bulgaria. These social and military advances, however, came to an end with the murder of Alexander II in 1881 and the beginning of a period of reaction under Alexander III.

In the early twentieth century, several clergy began calling for political and ecclesiastical reforms and for a while liberal voices were heard in the Synod. The Procurator of the Synod, however, was still carrying out the instructions of his political masters, and maintained a policy of intolerance and persecution of those daring to dissent. In the period of uncertainty following the abdication of the Czar in 1917, many churchmen felt free to speak out, with a number being critical of the Bolsheviks. A National Assembly of church leaders (the Sobor) met in 1917 and reinstated the position of Patriarch. Three candidates were chosen by ballot, and the new incumbent, Tikhon, was chosen from among the three by lot.

By this time the Bolsheviks were embarked upon confiscating Church lands, taking schools out of Church control and introducing civil marriage. Subsequently they withdrew all State subsidies to the Church and engaged in a campaign of persecution in which twenty eight bishops, over 1200 priests and up to 5000 monks lost their lives. The State purged the universities of Christian influence and imposed a stranglehold on libraries and the press, making the publication and distribution of Christian material almost impossible. Within only a few years the Bolsheviks embarked upon a propaganda campaign to ridicule religion and to advocate atheism. Patriarch Tikhon spoke out in protest but was imprisoned, and whilst detained was persuaded to agree to a group of more progressive priests taking decisions in the administration of the Church. When Tikhon objected to the sale of all Church valuables to support the relief effort for the famine in 1922, a number of the progressive priests broke away and formed what they termed the 'Living Church', which initially received considerable State support. In 1923 the Sobor accepted the reforms of the Living Church, acknowledged the separateness of Church and State, and pledged loyalty to the government. The State introduced rigorous controls over the Church and religious bodies, requiring every congregation to be registered, and all religious conferences to be authorised by the State apparatus in advance.

In the 1930s Stalin implemented a policy of centralised economic control with the object of transforming the country into a modern industrialised nation. Those who resisted were killed or sent to work in labour camps. Persecution was accompanied by massive propaganda campaigns and the creation of youth organisations to capture the minds of the young. The Soviet State was irreconcilably hostile to Christian beliefs. The Church was seen as a reactionary force standing in the way of progress towards a classless society and Communist ideals. At a very tangible level, God, and especially the Church, represented an alternative, indeed a higher authority than the State itself. Christianity could not be tolerated and the Church underwent a period of severe persecution. Thousands of clergy were imprisonned, with others being constantly harassed by the police. The atheist propaganda, the persecution and the controls decimated the Lutheran Church and the various non-conformist denominations, and almost caused the institutional collapse of the Orthodox Church.

Stalin's policy towards the Churches saw a marked alteration following the outbreak of the Second World War. He came to see the Orthodox Church as a means of promoting Soviet interests abroad, and bolstering morale at home. He permitted a revival of the patriarchal Church, and toned down the restrictions on Church activities. The Church began to flourish again, although it remained under close State supervision. In 1943 a Council for the Affairs of the Russian Orthodox Church was created, with a second Council for other religious groups following in 1944. These served as intermediaries between the government and the Churches, and enacted regulations for the administration of religious affairs.

In the Cold War, leading figures in the Russian Orthodox Church sought to bring Churches in other countries under their control, and in their travels abroad advocated Soviet foreign policies and spoke highly of conditions in the Soviet Union. After Stalin's death in 1953 the Orthodox Church participated in the Soviet-led peace campaigns, and in 1961 joined the World Council of Churches, despite intensified persecution from 1959. It was not until the 1980s that control over the Churches was significantly relaxed. The policies of *perestroika* and *glasnost* saw the influx of Bibles, the opening of churches, the growth of religious education, and the free participation of the Orthodox Church in international Christian organisations and gatherings.

In the Communist states of Eastern Europe the Churches were also subject to stringent controls, especially in Albania where religion was prohibited completely, and in Bulgaria and Roumania. In Poland, the Roman Catholic Church had comparatively considerable freedom, and played a major role in the Solidarity movement, resulting in the formation of the first non-Communist government in the Eastern bloc in **1989**. Other Eastern European countries followed the same path, with the Church and Christians forming a focus for the forces opposed to Communism. Church leaders often acted as intermediaries between the reform movements and Communist officials, and by their calls for moderation helped bring about political transformation without bloodshed.

8.11 The twentieth century: totalitarianism, oppression and the Cold War

The twentieth century has been the age of capitalist imperialism, xenophobic nationalism, class struggle and Communism. It has been the age of systematic mass persecutions and total warfare in which millions have died. The early years of the century saw several peace initiatives, the establishment of peace societies, the holding of international conferences, and the formation of the Permanent Court of International Justice at the Hague. Imperialist ambitions, however, proved overpowering, the assassination of the Crown Prince of Austria–Hungary at Sarajevo in **1914** being merely the catalyst that started a conflict that was inevitable. The peoples who waved their soldiers off in high jingoistic fashion had no conception of the impending carnage or the length of the war ahead. The State assumed total control of all economic and political activity, and citizens were subjected to manipulative propaganda campaigns to further the war effort. To a large extent, Church leaders in all the warring nations became part of their respective government's machines, providing moral support and justification. The presentation of moral arguments by European Christian leaders in the United States played a crucial role in bringing that nation to the assistance of the Allies.

At the end of the war, many Church leaders argued for the creation of supranational organisations to resolve future international disputes. The League of Nations was established in the hope that it would perform this role. The organisation was probably doomed from the start – the exclusion of Germany and the Soviet Union undermining its authority as a world institution.

The inter-war years saw significant changes. The United States and Japan emerged as world powers, Britain was obliged to grant autonomy to its white dominions, and both Britain and France faced resistance in their various colonies. Europe and the United States, in particular, experienced the evils of unemployment and depression, with increasing demands from a workforce whose representatives were for the first time beginning to participate in the political process. These years saw the appearance of totalitarian regimes, most notably in Spain, Italy, Germany and the Soviet Union. The all-powerful State regulated nearly every feature of the lives of its citizens, and countenanced no challenge to its authority which it enforced with utter ruthlessness, employing a network of police and intelligence services.

Mussolini was the first Fascist to seize power in 1922, gaining support from elements fearful of the threat of Communism. The Roman Catholic Church shared these fears, none less so than Pope Pius XI elected in 1922 who had witnessed the recent Bolshevik attacks on Poland. In the Lateran Agreements in 1929, the Pope allowed the abuses perpetrated by the regime to pass without criticism, in return for the recognition of the Vatican as an independent state, compensation for its abandoned territorial claims in Italy, recognition as the established church, and permission to instruct secondary school pupils in Roman Catholicism.

Mussolini's sole aim in his dealings with the Church, whose influence he resented, was to gain political mileage. He was outwardly critical of the Church, and attempted to impose stringent restrictions on the activities of Catholic Action, a lay organisation charged with meeting social and educational needs. The Pope responded by denouncing the attempts to stifle Catholic Action and, although restrictions remained, Mussolini allowed it to continue its functions. In principle, however, the Roman Catholic Church was generally supportive of Fascist regimes. It supported Franco in the Spanish Civil War, Antonio Salazar in Portugal and Ferenc-Szalasi in Hungary, and was sympathetic to Mussolini's attempt to conquer Ethiopia.

Hitler became chancellor of Germany in 1933, and within a short time the Nazi party had brought about the political and economic transformation of Germany, imposing highly regulated structures of control throughout industry and in every sphere of daily life. The underlying feature of Nazi ideology was the unity and exclusivity of the German people – the chosen race. Foreign influences were seen as undermining and perverting German purity, and the Jew its most pernicious enemy. There is no need in a work of this kind to detail the atrocities committed by the Nazis against the Jewish race, and indeed against the peoples of Eastern Europe, save to remind the reader that the persecution continued for a decade, began with the public humiliation of Jews and the denial of their rights to property and participation in political, economic and social life, and from 1940 onwards involved a highly organised campaign of punishment and extermination culminating in the deaths of six million Jews alone. The theoretical basis of these policies was set out for all to read in the text of *Mein Kampf*, the discrimination against the Jews was carried out in public with public support and participation, and the policy of liquidating the Jews was labour intensive and required thousands of German citizens to take an active part in the whole outrageous enterprise.

German Christians, Catholic and Protestant, participated and acquiesced in the horror of the holocaust, whilst at the same time taking part in the activities of their various Churches. That is not to deny that Christians themselves were at risk of persecution, but the vast majority either made no protest or carried out their allotted tasks with enthusiasm. German Christians were attracted by the ideology of national pride and to Hitler's anti-Communist rhetoric, and influenced by the apparent importance given to family life, the rearing of children, and the opposition to pornography and to homosexuality. Many persuaded themselves that once Germany had achieved greatness and established itself on the world stage, policies exploiting racial hatred would lose their appeal and be abandoned.

Christian support for the regime took concrete form with the Catholic Centre Party supporting Hitler's move to rule by decree and the Catholic trade unions effectively abdicating their role to represent the workforce. The Vatican entered into a formal agreement. The German State promised religious freedom, public subsidies, and the right to maintain Catholic schools and to minister to soldiers, the sick and those in prison. The Vatican continued its diplomatic relations with the Nazi regime, and assured its leaders that its priests and hierarchy would not engage in political activity. The Vatican's dialogue with the Nazi regime gave the latter respectability both within Germany and internationally. In reality, however, this attempt to guarantee the protection of the Church's activities was futile, for as the Nazi regime gained in strength it saw no necessity for complying with its promises. The many Catholic organisations were forced to disperse, the Catholic press was stifled and the Catholic schools closely controlled.

It was not until **1937** that the papacy at last responded. The encyclical 'With deep regret' was secretly distributed to each Catholic Church and read out on Palm Sunday. In it the Pope did not condemn the Nazi regime *per se*, but denounced the persecution of the Church and called upon the faithful to remain loyal to Christian principles of morality and to submit to the authority of Rome. Hitler responded by increasing the restrictions on Church activities.

As information about the atrocities increased, Pope Pius II was placed in a dilemma. To have vociferously condemned Hitler and to have attempted to rally German Catholics to resist could have resulted in the desertion of German Catholics from the Roman Catholic faith, and further persecution of the Church and its leaders. The Pope declined to mount an attack on Hitler, preferring instead to hope that this omission might save the institutional Church from destruction. What difference a more principled approach would have made will remain an unsolved question.

As to the Protestant Churches, in **1933** they underwent a consolidation into one organisation, adopted an hierarchical structure, electing a Nazi Ludwig Muller to lead them, and forbad the employment of anyone of Jewish extraction in the administration of the Church. Within two years Hitler had brought the Protestant Church under complete State control with the formation of the Ministry of Church affairs.

The growth of Nazi philosophy within the Christian communions was not without resistance. In **1933** a Pastors' Emergency League was established to counter the ideas of the Christian Nazis, and a second Protestant Church administration, '**The Confessing Church**', was established under the influence of Karl Barth and professing a faith based on true and orthodox Christian teachings. The teachings of the Confessing Church were seen by the Nazi State as a challenge to its authority, though they were not intended as such. Even the Confessing Church, with some notable exceptions such as Dietrich Bonhoeffer, failed to publicly criticise or chastise the Nazi regime. A small number of Christians, both Roman Catholic and Protestant, did voice opposition. Two leading opponents, Dietrich Bonhoeffer and the Jesuit Alfred Delp, were sentenced to death.

In the United States, Christians in the **1930s** were divided in their response to the dictatorships in Europe. A number enthusiastically supported the Fascist regimes as representing an effective bulwark to the spread of Communism. Liberal Christian leaders welcomed Roosevelt's 'New Deal' at home but on matters of foreign policy many remained staunchly isolationist. In the post-war period, the conservative Protestant Churches were vociferously anti-Communist, at least until the era of *détente* in the 1960s.

Through much of the early post-war period, racism was endemic in many churches in America, resulting in the formation of separate black Churches. The latter, supported by some groups within white Christian society, were at the forefront of the Civil Rights movement. Christian groups in the United States, particularly since the 1960s, have exercised considerable influence in the political process, claiming Christianity as inextricably linked to the American way of life and seeking to exert pressure on matters such as abortion. Presidential candidates as a matter of routine seek to establish their Christian credentials.

In China, Mao eventually defeated the nationalists in 1949 and pursued a policy of persecuting the Church with the expulsion of foreign missionaries. After Mao's death, and the warming of relations with the United States in the 1960s, churches reopened and the number of Christians grew, rapidly reaching an estimated three million Catholics and two million Protestants, until a further period of persecution followed the massacre of Tienanmen Square in 1989.

The rest of Asia saw modest growth in the Christian communities – by 1980 there were over one and a half million Christians in Japan and by the late 1980s there were an estimated fourteen million Christians in South Korea, representing nearly one-third of the population. Similar growth has taken place in Indonesia where many have been converted from Islam; in India, with an estimated Christian population of over thirty million in 1990; and also in Burma, Cambodia, Hong Kong and Taiwan.

The post-war period also saw the racial bitterness flowing from the introduction of apartheid in South Africa, where white Christian leaders largely lent their support to the apartheid regime. Some Christians were outspoken in their opposition, such as Bishop Desmond Tutu, Allan Boesak and Alan Paton, to name but three. In the 1980s they increasingly gained widespread support among Christians, and their voices came to dominate the South African Council of Churches and later the mainstream Churches.

By the beginning of the twentieth century, Christian missionaries had carried the Gospel throughout the globe and now Churches and Christian organisations, such as the Student Volunteer Movement, sought to strengthen the world-wide Church through further evangelisation. In Africa, thousands of missionary schools were established in the British colonies, and elsewhere the Roman Catholic Church set up educational establishments from primary schools to universities. Among the Protestant churches in the post-war period it was those in the United States that led the way, providing the majority of missionaries and most of the finance. Today most of Africa south of the Sahara is Christian. In Catholic Latin America, the Protestant Churches, especially the Pentecostals, have experienced a remarkable growth from very small beginnings.

In many countries, 'indigenous' Christianity is flourishing outside the mainstream Roman Catholic and Protestant Churches. These Churches incorporate varying degrees of the pre-Christian culture of the local populace, sometimes retaining elements such as witchcraft which find no place in authentic Christianity. Africa, Asia and Latin America have given birth to numerous different sects, many led by individuals who seem dominated by a desire to further their own interests or ideas.

Inevitably the missionaries took with them Western economic, political and social values. The result was the creation of a demand for Western style economic and political development, social upheaval and a demand for liberation which went far beyond spiritual liberation. At a political level this resulted in the independence movements in the various colonies ruled by Britain, France, the Netherlands etc. In Latin America the effect was ultimately to unite many Christians with those committed to using violence to bring down repressive regimes. This theology of liberation is examined elsewhere, but it certainly shares the same underlying idea adopted by the evangelical social reformers of the nineteenth century – that liberation through Christ has to incorporate material and not simply spiritual liberation. It was the means of effecting material liberation that distinguished liberation theology from earlier Christian ideas on this subject.

8.12   The ecumenical movement

The history of the Christian Church has been characterised by debate, controversy and at times division from its very earliest days. This has taken very concrete and long-lasting form in the great schism between the Roman Catholic and Orthodox Churches in **1054**, the Protestant Reformation, and the religious wars of the sixteenth and seventeenth centuries. Within Protestantism itself there have arisen many divisions, particularly within England and the United States, and more recently evidenced by the growing number of separate Pentecostal Churches world-wide. Division and separatism have not been without opposing forces. The medieval Church sought to impose uniformity through the Inquisition, and the Anglican Church of the sixteenth and seventeenth centuries was assisted by the passing of Acts of Uniformity, not to mention more repressive measures against Dissenters and Catholics.

The nineteenth and more particularly the twentieth century have witnessed rather different attempts at unity. The nineteenth century saw the increasing activities of the interdenominational missionary societies, and the early years of the twentieth century saw the creation of the ecumenical Student Voluntary Movement, the forerunner of the Student Christian Movement. A major milestone in unifying missionary activities among the Protestant Churches was the World Missionary Conference in Edinburgh in **1910**, attended by over 1000 delegates from many denominations, at which great emphasis was placed on the relationship between the Church's mission and its unity. The International Mission Council was formed in **1921**, and at an international conference in Oxford in **1932** proposals were drawn up for a world council of churches. In Amsterdam in **1948** the plans became reality when representatives of 142 churches, including nearly all major Protestant Churches in Europe, and most of those in America and Australasia, several Orthodox Churches and the Old Catholic Church, united in a joint declaration heralding the establishment of the World Council of Churches.

As to the Roman Catholic Church, little sign of any official desire for unity or reconciliation was apparent until Pope John XXIII (**1958–63**) called the Vatican

Council, which initiated a willingness to engage in genuine ecumenical dialogue, most notably with the Anglicans, Lutherans, Methodists and the Reformed Churches. Ecumenical debate, however, with the notable exception of the fusion of the Presbyterians and the Congregationalists into the United Reformed Church, has not resulted in any degree of unification of the main churches, nor is any such union likely to be achieved in the foreseeable future. Indeed, the most lively and enthusiastic evangelical Churches are outside the mainstream structures and are suspicious of ecumenical efforts. Uniformity appears as elusive as in the days of the early Church, notwithstanding the creation of structures designed to give it form.

Bibliography

Owen Chadwick, *The Christian Church in the Cold War*, Penguin, London (1993)

Owen Chadwick, *The Secularisation of the European Mind in the Nineteenth Century*, Cambridge University Press, Cambridge (1975)

Peter B. Clarke, *West Africa and Christianity*, Edward Arnold, Leeds (1986)

J.S. Conway, *The Nazi Persecution of the Churches*, Regent College Publishing (1997)

G.R. Cragg, *The Church and the Age of Reason 1648–1789*, Penguin, London (1960)

Jane Ellis, *The Russian Orthodox Church: a contemporary history*, Palgrave (1996)

S. Haliczer, *Inquisition and Society in Early Modern Europe*, Routledge (1987)

Adrian Hastings, *The Church in Africa 1450–1950*, Clarendon Press (1996)

Hugh McLeod, *Religion and the Peoples of Western Europe 1789–1989*, Opus (1997)

J.L. Mecham, *Church and State in Latin America*, University of North Carolina Press

E.R. Norman, *Church and Society in England 1770–1970*, OUP, Oxford (1976)

J.H. Parry, *Trade and Dominion: The European Overseas Empires in the Eighteenth Century*, Weidenfeld (1999)

D. Pospielovsky, *The Russian Church under the Soviet Regime 1917–1982*, St Vladimir's Seminary Press, New York (1984)

R. Rouse and S.C. Neill, *A History of the Ecumenical Movement 1517–1968*, CCBI Publications (1993)

G. Rupp, *Religion in England 1688–1791*, Clarendon Press (1986)

▮ ▾ 9 Modern theology – the main theologians

In an introductory work of this nature it is impossible to provide a comprehensive account of the development of modern theological thought. Instead, having put the subject in its historical context, we set out brief synopses of the thoughts of the chief contributors to modern theology, and some of the more recent concerns.

The development of theology in the nineteenth and twentieth centuries has to a large extent been determined by the Church's need to respond to the Enlightenment, which saw the emergence of a new man, determined to reject rules and dogma based on tradition in favour of exercising his own 'scientific' reasoned judgement. The Enlightenment was a declaration of independence, as the human person discovered his own powers and abilities and his freedom to reject limitations imposed by custom. Man saw himself as free to form his own judgements and hence free to renounce Christian doctrines and beliefs. A concomitant to man's realisation of his intellectual powers was the adoption of a critical approach to all that had appeared to be true and had hitherto been so accepted. Simply because something appeared to be so was no longer sufficient proof that it really was so.

9.1 Schleiermacher

The theological response to the Enlightenment arose out of the thoughts of **Frederick Schleiermacher (1768–1837)**, often described as the father of the nineteenth century. In his book *On Religion: Speeches to its Cultural Despisers*, Schleiermacher argued that if a person wishes truly to fulfil his potential as a human being – to experience a unity within himself – he must encourage and nurture his religious awareness, for it is only with a religious element that all other aspects of human life can be brought together in unity. We can only be truly fulfilled by our search for something beyond ourselves, and Christianity, claimed Schleiermacher, best fulfils the need in man for a religious life. 'Romanticism' was essentially a reaction against some of the teachings of the Enlightenment. Romantics such as Schleiermacher denied that reality can be known only by human reason and appealed to the human imagination and stressed the limitations on human comprehension. The Romantics maintained that reason restricts the human mind, whereas imagination liberates the human spirit. Human religious feelings thus become important. Human subjectivity and inward feelings were seen as mirroring the infinite, as the path to the mystery of the ultimate. Rationalism, argued the Romantics, was incapable of answering real human needs.

Schleiermacher argued that religion was a question of feeling or 'self-consciousness'. Theological thought in the late nineteenth century was dominated by liberal theology which concluded from the analysis of Kant that religion was what accounted for man's concept of morality and argued that Christian belief in the historical person of Christ could be grounded on study of the evidence, as with any other figure in history.

9.2 Barth

Schleiermacher's basic concept of religion as bringing sense and unity to our lives was adopted by **Karl Barth** (**1886–1968**), but he rejected 'liberal' theology as a betrayal of Christianity, in as much as it was a human-centred concept of religion. He rejected the idea that the only events of importance are those which can be subjected to historical research and analysis. The history of God's relationship with mankind is not susceptible to such an examination. Many in the early twentieth century, appalled at the carnage of the First World War, reacted against the teachings of the Enlightenment in which men were supposedly liberated from traditional (and religious) beliefs and customs. A human-centred approach was discredited. Barth stressed the 'otherness' of God.

The *Epistle to the Romans* (1919) was a work of dialectical theology (a theology of crisis) in which Barth describes what he sees as the contradiction between God and humanity rather than continuity, and stressed the cross of Christ as both God's 'No' and 'Yes' to the world – his word of both grace and judgement.

In the years after the *Epistle to the Romans*, Barth sought to reverse modernity's approach of seeking to rationalise faith. Why, he asked, should discussion about the Kingdom seek to justify faith's convictions by reference to the world? Barth argued that this approach was misconceived and that the analysis must start with Christ and man's response to him. We should not ask about Jesus' place in the history of mankind but our place in his. The attempt by religion to get closer to God is unnecessary – God is already with us and need not be sought after. The task of theology is to demonstrate faith's own internal coherence and to keep the proclamation of the Church faithful to its foundation in Christ in accordance with what has already been revealed to mankind in Scripture. Theology is not about responding to mankind's concerns and predicament, it is about responding to the Word of God.

Barth firmly rejected the doctrine of natural orders of creation promulgated by Nazi ideologists to justify the racial policies of National Socialism. He argued that Nazism entailed a rejection of the Church's foundations in Christ – the Jew through whom God had united Jew and Gentile. Barth was instrumental in drafting the Barmen Declaration which helped result in his expulsion from Germany in 1934 and his return to his native Switzerland where he became Professor of Theology at Basle.

Barth maintained that God created the world in order that there would be Jesus Christ, for him to be one with sinful man. The world is the external basis of his covenant, as the place in which the history of the covenant unfolds. In order for God to make a covenant apart from within his own triune fellowship, there must be something other than God; and for that reason he undertook Creation. God created the world to be one with his creature through Jesus Christ. The Incarnation, Barth argued, happened in God before all time. God revealed himself to mankind through the Incarnation. The importance of revelation is simply that it did and therefore can occur. Revelation is the self-unveiling to mankind of the God who cannot be unveiled to us. The unveiling is made possible by God 'distinguishing himself from himself'. What is revealed is that revelation can occur, that is God is such a God as to reveal himself. In revelation, God's essence remains unknowable – we do not know what God is, but we do know that he is, and that as promised in Scripture, he is with us. It is through the Incarnation and the doctrine of the Trinity that Christianity identifies its God.

9.3   Bonhoeffer

Dietrich Bonhoeffer (1906–1945), a Lutheran theologian, lectured at the theological faculty at Berlin where he wrote his two works *The Communion of Saints* and *Act and Being* at the ages of 21 and 24. He was an outspoken opponent of Nazism, and within days of Hitler's rise to power delivered a radio address in which he warned of the dangers of Führer worship. As a leading member of the Confessing Church he resisted the attempts to control the Protestant churches. In **1936** he was prevented from teaching at Berlin university, and was later forbidden to publish or speak in public. He joined the underground resistance movement and assisted the military resistance in relaying messages to the Allies through his ecumenical church connections. In **1943** Bonhoeffer was arrested on suspicion of assisting Jews and later the Gestapo discovered documentation tying him to the attempt on Hitler's life in July **1944**. He was placed in a concentration camp and in April **1945** he was hanged following orders to execute all resisters.

In *The Communion of Saints*, Bonhoeffer set out a theology based on divine revelation but stressed the importance of social relations. He drew upon both the revelational emphasis of Barth and the social concerns of the liberal theological tradition in Berlin. Bonhoeffer argued that every human being is an image of God, and that the difficulty of knowing another human being mirrors the difficulty of knowing God: the other person must reveal himself through an act of self-revealing love. Humans are like God, not because of any shared attributes such as a soul, but because their relationships to each other mirror God's relationship to them. Bonhoeffer's view of the Christian community is one of love centred on a 'structural togetherness' in which its members act for one another out of love. Bonhoeffer defines the Church as 'Christ existing in the community' with the Holy Spirit calling believers to faith and to this Christian community, uniting them as the Body of Christ. The Church is both the Body of Christ and a religious human fellowship prone to sin and imperfection, which the Holy Spirit is constantly working to transform.

For Bonhoeffer, in so far as the Church lives a life of faithful obedience to God's will, the Church is a form of revelation, and is 'Christ existing as community'. In *Act and Being*, Bonhoeffer teaches that 'Being in Christ' means believing, praying and proclaiming, but also understanding the sin, guilt and loneliness of one's pre-Christian existence, and acknowledging and appreciating oneself as a part of the community of Christ. Bonhoeffer analyses conscience as a device used by a sinner to justify himself and with which we rule our lives by the past, whereas Being in Christ involves having one's present determined by the future.

In his lectures, Bonhoeffer interpreted the story of Adam and Eve as reflecting our own story – the temptation of the serpent is the questioning of the truth of God's word, which results in our losing access to the tree of life, and in alienation, shame, loneliness, bondage and death. Christ heralds a new tree of life.

In *The Cost of Discipleship*, written during the Church struggles of the 1930s, Bonhoeffer calls upon Christians to respond to Jesus' teachings in the Sermon on the Mount. He attacks what he calls 'cheap grace' in which we calculate the minimum cost of being Christian and argues that discipleship and the Way of the Cross are the only path to joy and peace. He insists that faith alone is meaningless – only those who obey God's will believe, and only those who believe obey – faith and action in obedience are inseparable.

In *The Cost of Discipleship*, Bonhoeffer, in a clear reference to events in Germany, emphasises that all human beings share the image of God in the Incarnation and that an attack on any human being is an attack on Christ. In his lecture, Bonhoeffer described the Church's relationship with the State as one of judging its actions from the standpoint of the Cross.

For Bonhoeffer, theology is inextricably linked to ethics. He rejected a 'religious' view of God and emphasised the worldliness of the Christian faith. He argued that in the Incarnation, the world and God have become united in Jesus Christ, and that there is no ethical division between the spiritual and the secular. The whole world and the forms in which we participate in the world – work, marriage, government and Church – are related to Christ. Christians must follow an ethics of responsibility in which they willingly act as deputies for others, obeying Christ's Gospel by total response to the world. It was this sense of responsibility which caused Bonhoeffer to enter into the conspiracy against Hitler. Bonhoeffer came to see the world as having undergone 'secularisation' – the rejection of a religion in which God exists over and above the world, and is called upon by men to assist them in their individualistic concerns. Bonhoeffer welcomed humanity's outgrowing of this concept of religion which does not correspond with the biblical picture of God as being with us in our everyday sufferings. Bonhoeffer called for non-religious explanations of the faith, a social interpretation. God is neither external to the world, nor within us, but in the midst of our lives.

The Christian life, argued Bonhoeffer, is one of proclaiming Christ's Gospel of praise and prayer, but also of right action – of assisting in the liberation of the oppressed. The concept of a suffering God and a Christian response to oppression has found voice also in liberation theology, black theology and feminist theology.

9.4 Bultmann

Rudolf Karl Bultmann (1884–1976), the son of a Lutheran pastor, was a student at a time when the radical historical criticism of the 'history of religion school' was at its height. The application of critical historical methods to the New Testament, along with the 'demythologising' of the Bible and the consequences of these for a knowledge of God, are central to Bultmann's work.

Liberal Protestantism rejected the traditional religious framework for biblical studies. Believing that all truth originates from God, they advocated a rationalist approach to the understanding of the Bible. They recognised that whilst rational research and study could not supply a knowledge of God, it could contribute to a knowledge of God within a basic theological framework which permitted discussion about God.

In *The Epistle to the Romans*, Barth had written about God's judgement and grace by interpreting Paul, and it was this approach of practising theology through the New Testament which found favour with Bultmann. Both theologians sought to emphasise revelation through faith and the proclamation of the Word.

Bultmann differed from Barth in that, in his view, Barth failed to appreciate the humanity of Paul whose fallibility had to be taken into account in endeavouring to understand and evaluate his expression of the saving act of God in Christ. For Bultmann, theological interpretation went hand in hand with theological criticism. An understanding of the New Testament Scriptures requires the theologian to analyse in the light of his understanding of the Word. It is this point which marked the divergence between Barth and Bultmann, the former insisting on complete loyalty to the biblical text, the latter rejecting an identity between the Word of God and the words of Scripture.

Bultmann's theology cannot be considered in isolation from his New Testament scholarship, for him the two formed an integrated whole. Bultmann's approach was based on a belief that the historical accounts in the Bible were not merely a means of reconstructing accounts of past events, but that they speak to us today to challenge and transform our understanding of ourselves. In this way historical study is essential to the work of the theologian, and historical research is crucial to theological understanding.

The History of the Synoptic Traditions, in which Bultmann highlights the importance of rabbinic and other influences, remains one of the classical form-critical analyses of the Synoptic Gospels. Bultmann and the history-of-religions school drew not only on the Jewish context of the New Testament, but also on Hellenistic and oriental material, as for example in their endeavour to find a pre-Christian gnostic redeemer myth which might account for the unusual language of St John's Gospel. Bultmann stressed the importance of the recently discovered Manichean and Mandaean sources for understanding the Gospels – arguing that the evangelist transformed his gnostic sources in a Christian direction, correcting them where he felt they failed to express the Gospel adequately.

In accordance with his Lutheran roots, Bultmann saw revelation as taking place as the Gospel or Word is preached and interpreted. In *The Theology of the New Testament* he explained his understanding of theological statements – they cannot be the object of faith, they can only be an interpretation or explanation of the understanding that is 'inherent in faith itself'. Bultmann saw the theological thoughts of the New Testament – primarily the writings of Paul and the Fourth Gospel – as the unfolding of faith as it develops out of that 'new understanding of God, the world and man which is conferred in and by faith'. Bultmann emphasises that in order for mankind to have the possibility of developing this self-understanding, theological statements must be explained in ways which clarify their understanding of human existence. For Bultmann, human existence is central to Christian theology – theologies must express and explain their faith in Christ through a theological understanding of human existence.

Bultmann identified John's Gospel and the writings of Paul, more than any other New Testament works, as seeking to explicate God. Bultmann maintained that John gives a theological interpretation of human existence. The various Johannine concepts are said to relate to human existence seen from the standpoint of God's eschatological self-revelation in Jesus. It is impossible, argued Bultmann, to attempt to understand and interpret the subject matter of a text without some prior understanding, and in the course of reading a text our prior understanding reacts with our attempts to interpret. In analysing the writings of Paul, Bultmann approaches his task with a prior understanding derived not only from his reading of Paul, but also from his understanding of the Gospel which is determined in part by Paul, and in large part by other sources. Bultmann claimed that using this prior understanding, he can refine and correct Paul where Paul fails to say what he means, or what he ought to mean. Bultmann thereby invests the interpreter with a right to criticise the biblical writers and introduces the difficult issue as to how the text is left with enough authority to confront the reader.

Bultmann is best known for the debate provoked by his lecture on *The New Testament and Mythology* and his system of 'demythologising' the New Testament. He argued that there is a distinction between what a text *says* and what it *means*, and that what a text means is to be ascertained by a critical analysis of the text from the position of our prior understanding. Bultmann was adamant that the Gospel is not a myth but that the understanding of its essential meaning requires the elimination of myth.

Bultmann attracted the hostility of many religious conservatives who saw him as attacking the historicity of the Gospel and undermining Christian doctrine. On the other hand, there were many liberal theologians who considered that Bultmann had given biblical texts far more weight than they could reasonably merit. For Bultmann, however, as for Barth, the revelation of God in Scripture is not something which can be demonstrated by human reason. Indeed, when understood from within faith, the Bible facilitates a revelation of God which is not capable of rational and historical examination. This highlights the major divide in modern theology between those who seek to rationalise theology and those who use theological statements to explain and interpret faith from a starting point of belief, but remain open to knowledge and recognise the critical role of reason.

9.5 Tillich

Paul Tillich (1886–1965) underwent a transformation in response to his experience of the wholesale slaughter of the First World War, and by **1918** had espoused religious socialism. An outspoken critic of Nazism, he was suspended from his post at Frankfurt in 1933 for his attack on Nazi ideology in his work *The Socialist Decision*. Tillich fled to the United States where he started a new academic career in a language with which he was largely unacquainted. He remained little known until the publication in 1948 of a collection of his sermons under the title *The Shaking of the Foundations*, which proved a best seller. This was followed by the publication of three successive volumes of his *Systematic Theology*, and his appointment to a professorship at Harvard University. At his death in 1965 Tillich was probably the best known academic theologian in the United States.

Tillich's main theological concern was to present Christianity in terms that were comprehensible and convincing to a sceptical twentieth century audience. His method was to seek to reconcile contemporary culture and historical Christianity. In *Systematic Theology*, Tillich endeavoured to demonstrate that 'religion' and 'culture' are inextricably intertwined in that 'the form of religion is culture and the substance of culture is religion'.

Tillich maintained that the fundamental questions arising from our humanity are expressed by our cultures in different ways through their art and religious traditions, providing answers expressed in terms of religious symbols. He identified five questions arising from our human existence, with five answers in the form of biblical religious symbols:

- How can we possess knowledge of which we are certain? *Symbolic answer*: Logos.
- How can we resist the destructive forces that threaten to disintegrate our lives? *Symbolic answer*: God as Creator.
- How can we remedy the loneliness and alienation we experience? *Symbolic answer*: Jesus Christ.
- How can our lives be genuine given the complete ambiguity of our morality, religious practices and cultural self-expressions? *Symbolic answer*: The Spirit.
- Is there any meaning in history? *Symbolic answer*: The Kingdom of God.

Tillich approached these correlations by considering our 'essential nature', the 'existential disruption' in which we exist, and the 'actuality of life'.

Essential nature

Tillich maintained that for something to exist it must constitute an integral whole; it must form part of a greater integral whole with whose members it interacts; and it must be vulnerable to disintegration and to becoming detached from the whole of which it forms part.

Tillich argued that 'being' is constantly threatened by 'non-being' – a threat which we experience in our moments of utmost meaninglessness but which we resist. In resisting, we experience the presence of the 'Power of being'. Where, Tillich asks, does this power to counter the threat of non-being come from? His answer is the Christian symbol of 'God as Creator'. God is creator and, as the power of being, is constantly and mysteriously actively supporting our being as it is attacked by the threat of non-being. Our vulnerability to the threat of non-being is apparent in all our dealings with the world. We have to reach a compromise between pursuing our individuality ('Individualisation') and participating in our common community ('Participation'). Psychological and social problems can be seen as resulting from an imbalance between these two opposites. Tension is also present between 'dynamics' and 'form'. Whilst we need rules (form) in order to preserve order and certainty, form without the dynamics of creativity and change is stultifying; we also experience tension between 'freedom' and 'destiny'. Our destiny is determined by the conditioning we have undergone to date, which facilitates and limits our future, but we nevertheless have a freedom in deciding our actions. Thus we are inherently vulnerable to interacting with the world in which we experience these tensions and imbalances.

Our knowledge is of course acquired through our interrelation with the world, but our attempts to come to terms with reality are constantly threatened with meaninglessness and uncertainty. The answer to this threat is in the Christian symbol Logos. Our attempts to understand and to influence reality are threatened because of the limits of our reasoning. Our reason is subject to tensions between yearning for certainty and yearning for change. Similarly we experience a tension between relying on our own autonomy and relying upon external authority such as tradition or an authority figure. Tillich maintains that the tension arises out of the opposition between the 'structure' and the 'depth' of reason. The structure of reason is that which enables us to understand and influence reality; but these processes inevitably involve our making value judgements, which we do on the basis of standards. Even though not conscious of doing so, we undertake natural transactions based on those standards – the depth of reason.

The presence of these ultimate standards to reason is the presence of the power of being to the mind. Not appreciating this presence, we switch between reliance upon ourselves and reliance upon an external authority. In the uncertainty of this tension we crave knowledge in which the standards are neither subjectively determined by ourselves, nor imposed upon us. The desire for such knowledge, maintains Tillich, is a desire for revelation, and understanding of the meaning in life. Revelation has two sides – the receiving side of people united in faith, completely seized by the revelatory event; and the giving side which Tillich calls miracle. Miracle is some concrete event or person acting as a religious symbol through which the ground of meaning in life makes itself present. Whilst the ground of reason may be permanently present to reason, we only recognise it in revelation. The ultimate revelation is Jesus who in the crucifixion emptied himself. Through Jesus we come to know the reality of mystery and that we are related to it. We become aware of the unity of the structures and depth of reason and overcome the tension between internal and external authority.

Existential disruption

In our existence we are alienated from our essence, from ourselves and from the power of being. The threat from non-being is continually present. Isolated from the power of being, we cannot hold the tensions between individualisation and participation, between dynamics and form and between destiny and freedom in balance as we react with the world. The result is chaos, guilt, isolation and emptiness, devoid of meaning. The Christian symbols for this are 'Fall', which expresses the destiny which we share with others, and 'Sin', which describes our personal responsibility. The power for new being is the symbol of the Messiah who reveals the power of being. Salvation and revelation describe the same reality. Salvation is brought by the healing of the existential isolation by a reconciliation with the power of being and with others. Receiving this revelation in faith is a momentary insight in which one experiences unity with the depth of reason. This revelatory event is but fleeting and ambiguous. Existential disruption continues but the memory of the insight and the yearning for repetition remain.

Traditional Christian doctrine depicts Jesus as having both divine and human natures. Tillich calls for a restatement of this christology but with a different formulation. Jesus was human, Tillich argues, because he shared men's essential nature and was vulnerable to disintegration and alienation. On the other hand, Jesus was divine in that through him the power of being is mediated to others. In Jesus' life the unity between God and man were fully actualised without existential disruption (that is, without sin). In our turn, we can find the power to cure our personal 'existential disruption' through relationship with Jesus, who can mediate to us the healing power of new being.

Actuality

Actuality means our concrete lives in which our essence and existence become united. The spiritual dimension of our actuality involves self-integration, self-creation and self-transcendence. *Self-integration* consists of integrating our experiences into ourselves. All our actions, even those considered as 'moral', involve the sacrifice not only of acts that would have better served our own self-integration, but also of acts that would have provided greater benefit to others. Our humanity leads us to seek our own self-integration and accordingly we have to ask whether we can succeed in this whilst being unambiguously moral. *Self-creation* consists in our creating ourselves by producing things that have meaning to us and which make up our culture, but our culture is ambiguous in that its different traits can be both enlivening and stultifying. *Self-transcendence* occurs when we engage in truly religious activity – the search for the ultimate. Self-transcendence interacts with self-integration and self-creation in that there is a religious element in all moral and cultural acts, and it is moral and culturally creative lives that experience self-transcendence. However, the religious quest finds its expression in tradition, myth and organisations and all these are inherently ambiguous.

Concerns about ambiguous morality, culture and religion find their answer in the Christian symbol of 'Spiritual Presence' and 'The Kingdom of God'. Spiritual presence is the experience of God which we yearn for and occasionally experience in our human existence. Such experience involves the coming together in unison of our essence and our existential being when God reveals himself. These experiences, Tillich stresses, are always social and spasmodic. Tillich describes the process of being taken into this transcendent unity as the state of 'love' and argues that this can only take place in community, transforming it into a spiritual community. He is not referring, however, to the Church, for he maintains that spiritual community can be found in secular groups, and is frequently absent within churches. Moments of spiritual community bring with them an unambiguity not only in our self-transcendence, but also in our cultural self-creativity and moral integration. Our cultural and moral lives are momentarily self-transcending and religious.

The Kingdom of God is the symbol which represents the answer to historical aspects rather than to social aspects of unambiguous life. The Kingdom of God is the definitive instance of Spiritual Presence in the history of a given community because it represents that moment when the community experienced self-integration, self-creativity and self-transcendence which was truly unambiguous. The Kingdom of God is also, of course, the answer to the question: Is there any meaning in history? – and describes the unambiguous and eternal sharing in the eternal life.

9.6 Rahner

Karl Rahner (1904–84) joined the Jesuits at 18, and was ordained as a priest ten years later. He was subsequently appointed to a professorship of theology at the university of Innsbruck. He was strongly influenced by his Jesuit education, and in particular by the mysticism of the *Spiritual Exercises* of St Ignatius Loyola, with their stress on spiritual contemplation, self-analysis and prayer. He studied at a time when there was a renewed interest in the classical writings on Christian doctrine and thought, in particular the works of St Aquinas and medieval scholasticism, and also in patristic sources including the works of the Early Church fathers.

Rahner's theology is set out primarily in numerous essays on a wide variety of theological subjects. His style is unsystematic, mystical, philosphical and ecclesial. His picture of God is of a holy Mystery, a personal divine presence which enfolds the world and transforms us through its divine Grace. For Rahner, this holy Mystery is a source of infinite and unbounded knowledge and love open to us through contemplation and communion. He argues that mankind, created by God, has an in-built and inherent predisposition to receive his grace.

Rahner endeavoured to find new approaches to bring vitality to the study and expression of Christian faith. His theological starting point was the early Church's claims about Jesus. He saw his theological purpose not in seeking to prove the ultimate truth of Christianity, but rather as one of using the tools of philosophical analysis to demonstrate the coherence and intelligibility of the Christian faith both in its simplicity and in its depths.

One of Rahner's concerns was the failure of theological curricula and textbooks to present a full, coherent and unified picture of the Christian faith with the appropriate emphasis on the fundamentals. There was a tendency for theology to be compartmentalised, partly owing to the breakdown of the discipline to facilitate academic study, and partly because of the inclination of academics to engage in narrow debates over particular theological subjects. Rahner saw the need to present and explicate a comprehensive picture of Christianity to the modern world which he sought to do by 'transcendental method'. The central approach of transcendental arguments is to explain beliefs by establishing that the pre-conditions for the beliefs to be true do in fact apply. What Rahner sought to demonstrate was that there are good reasons to believe in God, that the truths revealed to man by him form a coherent and comprehensible whole, and that Christ's doctrines are compatible with our human experience of the world.

Rahner applied his transcendental method to his doctrine of God. He argued that our human experience of the mystical divinity itself holds the foundations of our belief in him. He bases his analysis on the structure of knowledge, maintaining that humanity is inherently predisposed to affirm being and that such affirmation is necessary before we can have knowledge of any kind. Accordingly, knowledge of a thing presupposes a predisposition to affirm its existence and indicates that the human mind is geared towards a context of being, the horizon of which is limitless and is Absolute Being. Rahner claimed that knowledge is orientated to God or Absolute Mystery and it is our prior experience of God through knowledge that predisposes us to the standard arguments put forward to prove his existence.

In revelation, the Absolute Mystery has chosen to communicate with mankind. What is it, Rahner asks, about human knowledge that enables us to accept and understand revelation? The answer, Rahner claims, is that man is already predisposed to receive revelation. At the same time, however, Rahner emphasises that God is never completely understandable but is mysterious and infinite, surpassing our abilities to comprehend him.

In his writings about the relationship between the natural and supernatural, and between nature and grace, Rahner sought to regenerate the system advanced by Thomas Aquinas concerning the character of the supernatural. Twentieth century theology tended to follow earlier Augustinian ideas, holding, firstly, that everything supernatural was beyond the natural in the sense that it was impossible for nature in itself to acquire any of the qualities of the supernatural; and, secondly, that where the supernatural does chose to interact with nature then this is a gift which is unmerited. Accordingly the supernatural is both transcendent and gratuitous. Aquinas had previously gone beyond this model, maintaining that the essence of the supernatural was participating in the divine life and that transcendence and gratuity are elements of that participation. Rahner was laying out the main element of the doctrine of grace.

The emphasis on the Augustinian concept of defining the supernatural as transcendent had tended to produce a dualistic view of the natural and supernatural as separate and parallel worlds, but Rahner emphasised the participational character of the supernatural and its continuity with the natural. There is a unity, he argued, between the natural world created by God and the natural world which is being transformed by his grace.

Rahner held that a central feature of revelation was that it involved an invitation to respond by committing ourselves to God completely. His conception of grace and revelation, however, was universal. He saw revelation as unfolding and continuous with the history of humankind, which man has sought to describe through different symbols. The history of these expressions follows the history of mankind. Rahner emphatically does not claim that Christianity is merely one of a number of particular histories of revelation. Christianity is essentially different in that in Judaism and Christianity God reveals himself directly, engaging in a relationship with mankind. In Christianity there was a climax in revelation in that his revelation in Jesus Christ was definitive and the human response to it in Jesus Christ was perfect.

Rahner's concern for a unified vision of the Christian Faith is also evident in his concerns about the separatist practice of theologians of debating the doctrine of God, his existence and nature, before turning to consider the doctrine of the Trinity and the interrelationship of the divine persons. For Rahner, the result was that the Trinity had come to be seen not as mystical but as baffling – something tagged on to the doctrine of God. Rahner maintained that the essence of God was his internal trinitarian relationships. He emphasised biblical revelation about the Trinity and called for a return to the understanding of divine nature promulgated by the Church Fathers in which the term 'God' generally meant God the Father. Rahner's position attracted some controversy, with a number of scholars criticising an approach to the Trinity which starts from God the Father, arguing that this tended to produce a subordination within the Trinity, a feature of much of the Greek trinitarian theology of the Church fathers. Other theologians have argued that the Scriptures are consistent, perhaps more consistent, with a unitarian approach and that the trinitarian concept of God is a philosophical tool to enable us to contemplate the one transcendent divine being whom Christians know, address and worship as Father, Son and Holy Spirit.

Rahner insisted that Father, Son and Holy Spirit are not merely characterisations which God adopts in his process of revelation, or our cultural and subjective conceptions of him. The external trinitarian manifestation of Son and Holy Spirit are extensions of God's innate essence – the Trinity is of the essence of God, and although we can never fully understand him in our human condition, in his revelation of himself through the Trinity he is giving us the gift of insight into the knowledge of his being.

Rahner is perhaps best known not so much for his often controversial, and indeed successful, efforts to expose the richness and depth of particular doctrines, but for his foundational emphasis on God the Holy Mystery, and on the importance of prayer, meditation and contemplation in our efforts to begin to understand God and his divine revelation.

9.7 Schillebeeckx

Edward Schillebeeckx was born in Antwerp in 1914. Educated at a Jesuit school, he entered the Dominican Order at the age of 20, and was ordained a priest seven years later. He was appointed to teach dogmatic theology to seminarians. After the war he returned to academic studies and held a professorship at the University of Nijmegen in the Netherlands from 1957 until 1983. He was closely associated with the reform movement initiated by the Second Vatican Council, and on three occasions his orthodoxy came under investigation by the Vatican Congregation of the Doctrine of the Faith.

Schillebeeckx's work is characterised by two pressing concerns: how to express the Gospel and Christianity in terms that are understandable to modern-day believers; and how the salvation gift from God in Jesus Christ is experienced by Christians in their individual lives and communities. In one of his earlier works, *Christ the Sacrament of the Encounter with God*, he advanced a highly personal approach to the sacraments, arguing that they constituted a personal encounter with Christ.

In his work in the **1970s** and **1980s** he laid great emphasis on research into historical sources in developing his ideas for the doctrine of Christ and the concept of ministry. In *Jesus* (**1974**), he lays particular stress on the Jewishness of Jesus, Jesus' experiences of God as *abba* and what Jesus reveals about the Kingdom of God. In *Christ*, he enquires into how Christians experience salvation, discussing human experience and revelation. He develops his ideas of salvation in a social direction and seeks to review the foundations of social ethics.

Schillebeeckx speaks of Jesus as 'the parable of God and the paradigm of humanity'. Jesus and God cannot be understood in terms of statements about their natures. Rather, to know God we must proclaim the Gospel of Christ and live that Gospel in our own lives. In this way we come to see Jesus' life as a clear revelation of the Father, and the perfect example to be mirrored.

In his work on ministry, Schillebeeckx responded to the growing modern problem for the Roman Catholic Church – the shortage of priests. Schillebeeckx argued that the receiving of the Eucharist must be given priority, and if the entrance requirements to the priesthood were depriving Christians of receiving the Eucharist, then the requirements must be relaxed either temporarily, or if necessary permanently. He advanced his case with considerable authority relying, in part, on historical precedent, in particular in the first thousand years of Christianity, when the needs of the Christian community were given priority over the demands of the Church's established practices and traditions. The response of Schillebeeckx's critics, including the Vatican's Congregation, to his emphasis on experience, is exemplified in the reaction of some to his arguments on the priesthood: are there not some matters, such as the nature and the form of the priesthood, which must be held on to dogmatically and not subjected to evaluation by experience? Schillebeeckx's answer is that history and experience must be taken seriously – but this, of course, does not explain how history and dogma are to interact.

Schillebeeckx's concerns have centred around the relationship between the Church and the world – hence his emphasis on what salvation means today, the history and destiny of the world, the living of the story of Jesus' life in our own lives, and the social aspects of salvation. Schillebeeckx's thoughts are strongly influenced by his understanding of the role of experience in belief, the importance of suffering in history and the boundless love of God. Human experience, argues Schillebeeckx, is the conduit by which revelation is imparted to us. Revelation is communicated to us by means of the whole range of human experiences, including events. Whilst reason elucidates experience, experience cannot be limited to or broken down into concepts or rationality because our experiences have a quality of mystery – as exemplified in Schillebeeckx's description of our encounter with God in the sacraments.

Of all human experiences, Schillebeeckx maintained, our experiences of suffering are the most revelatory. In suffering, we question all our ideas about life. Out of suffering evolves a critical approach to the world and to our experiences that provides the energy for the struggle for justice, and the further revelation of what it is to be human. This suffering experience is seen at its most intense in the life and crucifixion of Jesus. Jesus' ministry and death demonstrate the extent of God's identification with man's suffering, and his limitless love. Through creation and history God reveals himself to us and identifies with us. Creation and history demonstrate, argues Schillebeeckx, the interconnectedness between the mystical and the political, between communion with God, and a commitment to action in the world, a 'political holiness' to which Christians are called.

9.8 Torrance

Thomas F.T. Torrance was Professor of Christian Dogmatics at the University of Edinburgh from 1952 to 1979, and Moderator of the General Assembly of the Church of Scotland. He is best known for his analysis of the correlation between knowledge in theology and in natural sciences. Whilst acknowledging that theology and natural sciences have their own distinct concerns, he maintained that they are inseparable. They both require a scientific method in order for their subject matter to be understood. Whilst the natural sciences tackle our understanding of creation, as their investigation deepens they increasingly have cosmological and epistemological questions forced upon them.

Knowledge, both in theology and in the natural sciences, is acquired, argues Torrance, by allowing reality to make itself known to us and to impose itself on our understanding. For Torrance, reality reveals itself to the sciences by making us capable of understanding. The pursuit of knowledge involves an endeavour to conform our understanding with the reality that is present before us, and to shed those conceptions which we have acquired uncritically or which we have inappropriately forced on to a subject matter from another field of knowledge. Torrance calls both for a 'positive position' towards traditional knowledge and methods and for a process of critical reflection to test these and to discriminate between true advances in knowledge and distortions of knowledge. Torrance describes earlier theories in theological science as 'transparent disclosure models' through which truth in creation as it has come from God 'shines through'. He rejects the position taken by most biblical and historical commentators who see such theories as arising out of culturally determined human efforts to grasp truth. Torrance argues that the theories of the past, present and future need to be collated to create a unified view of truth.

The concern of natural science and theology is to analyse the reality which presents itself to us and to search for its deeper meaning, the interconnectedness within the subject matter. Essential to the task is a trust in reality as it presents itself to us accompanied by an endeavour to permit our thinking to conform to this reality and thereby deepen our understanding of it. Reality actively presents itself to us and we must respond by knowing it in the way it has provided for us in order that our thoughts and language correspond to it.

Torrance's approach to the past and present is evident in his treatment of the Church Fathers, whom he sees as advocating a theology based upon the Word of God as revealed in Scripture. He rejects the humanist explanation of their works as simply a development of human responses and as relative cultural reactions to their own times. For Torrance, the Fathers resisted the harmful and distorting influences of Hellenism and Judaism and were giving voice to the Christian Faith as it was developing its own internal logic.

The human response that is called for is an openness to reality, which Torrance has described as a kind of foreknowledge, or an initial anticipation. Knowledge of reality consists of our reaction to a host of separate and different, often disorganised, experiences, and the reaction required is an intuitive leap by which all the information is fused into an ordered pattern or integrated whole: '... the scientist allows the reality he investigates in its own internal structures to impose itself on his apprehension, so that in his contact with it he is committed to a boundless objectivity beyond himself together with an unceasing obligation to let himself and all his preconceptions be called radically into question'.

For Torrance, the starting point of scientific enquiry is belief, without which the development of scientific knowledge would not be possible. He defines belief as:

'... a prescientific but fundamental act of acknowledgment of some aspect of the nature of things ... without which scientific inquiry would not be possible.'

Belief is thus central to knowledge and is something which is not itself capable of being proved or disproved. Faith is the most basic form of knowledge and forms the basis upon which all rational enquiry proceeds. Torrance maintains that all forms of scientific enquiry start from this basis. Belief in God's Christ is based on a response to God's action, and it is not capable of external validation. Theology's task is not to seek validation but to reveal what it means.

Torrance favoured Michael Polonyi's analysis of beliefs, namely that we carry out our scientific activity within frameworks of values which determine our intuitive response to reality. These frameworks are not fixed but are capable of modifying themselves and expanding in response to reality. We each live in our own different frameworks, and disagreements between those frameworks can only be overcome by persuasion in response to divine truth.

The universe is intelligible, but because its comprehensibility has infinite depth it is also mysterious. It is impossible to reach any full understanding because its comprehensibility extends further than we can comprehend. Hence the development of our understanding rests upon two beliefs – that of an orderly universe and that of a contingent universe – natural science has to proceed on these bases if it is to understand the structures of the universe by thought and experiment. Whilst natural scientific knowledge is unchangeable and intelligible, because it remains mysterious, our understandings of it are relative, not objective.

Torrance argues that his model of scientific understanding of reality reveals a close connection between the objectivity of the natural sciences and the beliefs that sustain it, and the objectivity of the Judaic and Christian traditions and the beliefs which sustain them. Torrance claims that the understanding of the order and contingency of the universe is not an original discovery by natural science itself, but has its origins in the Judaic–Christian theological tradition in which God is depicted as having created a world in which mankind exists as separate from him. God's creation of an ordered world – his relationship to the world – is revealed in the Incarnation which both distinguishes and unifies the divine and the natural. The world is independent from him so that its nature is susceptible to study. The essential difference between the natural sciences and theological science is that natural science is the study of the contingent order of the universe with the goal of understanding its structures, and the latter is the scientific study of the source of the contingent order by means of the self-presentation of the triune God.

Theological knowledge, Torrance argues, occurs when Christians are engaged in the self-knowing of God through and in the natural world, and those who gain knowledge through this presentation can do no more than express their understanding in words and ideas which are to a greater or lesser extent transparent and through which God's truth shines through.

For Torrance, we are engaged in a mission to purify the knowledge available to us by analysing it. His analysis leads to those who have an engagement with the self-presentation of God having a privileged and exclusive position, and whilst they are conduits or transparencies of divine knowledge they are nevertheless in one sense providers of such knowledge.

9.9 Moltmann

Jurgen Moltmann (born **1926**) was appointed to the chair of systematic theology at the university of Tubingen in **1967**. He is best known for his *Theology of Hope* published in 1964, and his emphasis on the power of hope and on God's solidarity with human suffering. He was heavily influenced by Marxist and Jewish thinking.

In his earlier works, Moltmann contrasts the Cross and the Resurrection of Jesus. The Cross is said to represent death and the absence of God, whereas the Resurrection is life and the presence of God. The Cross represents the identification of Jesus with the world as it is now, sinful and suffering, Godless and Godforsaken. The Resurrection is the promise by God of a new era for the whole world. The Cross is interpreted in terms of God's love for the world and his solidarity with mankind, in an attempt to respond to the problem of human suffering and God's failure to prevent it. The Resurrection is seen as representing hope for the destiny of the world. Moltmann's theology is firmly trinitarian: after the Cross and the Resurrection, the Spirit prepares the way for the coming of the Kingdom of God. God's promise is seen as a promise concerning the destiny of the whole of mankind, and his solidarity with the Godless and Godforsaken as demanding a committed response from the Church. The Church's task is to set about the transformation of the world, to cajole the world to move in the direction of the new Kingdom that will come.

A key feature of Moltmann's theology is his recognition that our theological statements are provisional, and that individual theologians may claim only to make a contribution to theological thought. Moltmann argues that theology must be characterised by dialogue; it must be ecumenical and open to input from other disciplines. Theology cannot claim to possess all knowledge – there is yet much that remains to be learnt. Moltmann calls for dialogue, but a critical dialogue from a standpoint rooted in Christ.

Moltmann's approach to history and the destiny of the world was to call for a positive commitment from the Church for change and the will to participate in the transformation of the world in order to direct the world towards the Kingdom of God. The Church's engagement should be spurred on by God's promise in the Resurrection of a fundamentally transformed and new creation in which all the dead are raised to life. The hope that the Resurrection gives us for the future of the world brings with it a deep realisation of the shortcomings of present reality, and the possibility of change. Christianity requires a cynicism towards the status quo and an anticipation of change.

In a theme recalling the work of Schillebeeckx, Moltmann reconciled faith in God in the presence of suffering and evil by arguing that in the Cross, God demonstrated his solidarity with mankind in its suffering; in the Resurrection, God has given a promise of hope that he will overcome evil and suffering; and that in the here-and-now the process of conquering evil and suffering can be commenced through Christians actively participating in the struggle to transform the world. Moltmann's view of mankind's suffering is one characterised not only by the pain of the unnecessary suffering of the innocent, but also the suffering of the sinner in his alienation from God. In the Cross, God, in an act of divine love, suffers in solidarity with mankind. God's love is not passive but participatory, identifying fully with the Godless and the Godforsaken.

The trinitarian nature of the Cross and Resurrection are important themes in Moltmann's work. Christ the Son experiences in himself the alienation of the Godforesaken as demonstrated so vividly in his cry of abandonment on the Cross: 'Eloi, Eloi lema sabachtoni?' Christ suffers the pain of desolation, the Father experiences the pain of witnessing his Son's death. The Cross is the ultimate revelation of God's love for the world. Moltmann acknowledges that God's solidarity does not explain why God permits suffering in the world, but it does offer an understanding of suffering in which God's response is rooted in love, and not merely that of a passive observer.

God's trinitarian nature is to be seen also in Moltmann's concept of the Church. The Church occupies an intermediate state on the journey between the historical Jesus and the transformation of the world that will herald the Kingdom of God. In this journey, the Spirit directs not only the Church but the whole of mankind in its mission to transform. Hence the Church must not close itself to dialogue with other faiths and with secular wisdom. Moltmann is critical of the extent to which Christianity has become a civil religion existing for the mutual benefit of its adherents. He calls for true commitment, active participation and a clear desire to improve and transform the status quo. The Church should not exist for us, rather it must be a community of believers acting out a distinctive commitment to a messianic mission. Moltmann is critical of infant baptism – voluntary discipleship being essential for this commitment. He sees Christian fellowship as a fellowship of equals and hence is critical too of the traditional and particularly the Catholic concept of ministry. His concept of the Church mirrors the Cross – one of solidarity with the poor, not the giving of charitable donations – but solidarity in which the Church actively challenges social injustice and poverty in the world.

Moltmann rejects the traditional concept of God as impassible. God is affected by the world in the sense that his love for the world causes him to suffer in solidarity with it. God experiences the world through his trinitarian nature, that is of three divine persons in a loving relationship with each other, affected by each other and their experience of the world. Moltmann insists on God as possessing a trinitarian nature in which Father, Son and Spirit all relate to each other as equals without hierarchy in a fellowship of love. Moltmann rejects monotheistic descriptions of God, which he argues are used to justify monarchical and imbalanced relationships of power. God as Trinity is a fellowship of love, and his Kingdom is characterised by relationships based on a fellowship of love between equals.

God's solidarity with the poor and the suffering, and the call to the Church to anticipate, plan for and initiate the messianic Kingdom demands, Moltmann maintains, positive and urgent action on the part of Christians. He sees abuses of human rights as an affront to God in whose image we are made and an arena in which Christians can unite with others to progress the world in the direction of the Kingdom.

Moltmann sees God as Spirit dwelling in the world, not just with mankind. Hence his model of fellowship and community extends also to man's relationship to the planet Earth and its resources which we continue to exploit. The destiny of the world, argues Moltmann, is also to be the destiny of mankind, and he calls for humanity to participate in a community with nature, to recognise our solidarity and interdependence with it.

9.10 Kung

Hans Kung, born in 1928 in Switzerland, studied at the Pontifical Gregorian University in Rome, was appointed professor of fundamental theology at the university of Tubingen at the age of 32 and later played an active role in the preparation for the Second Vatican Council. He stands out among twentieth century Roman Catholic theologians as the most widely read and the most controversial. From his early work on Hegel, through his major examination of the problem of God in *Does God Exist?*, to his recent writings on social ethics and globilisation, he has embraced the philosophy, natural theology, dogmatics and ethics of contemporary theology. A recurring theme in Kung's thinking is the importance of dialogue with other faiths and between the different Christian communions. In his early work *Justification: The Doctrine of Karl Barth and a Catholic Reflection* (1957), he sought to analyse the areas where Protestants and Roman Catholics might in fact agree, and whilst expressing critical reservations about aspects of Barth's doctrines, he maintained that there was a broad uniformity. His conclusion encouraged him to consider how the Christian churches, and the Catholic Church in particular, might change to advance the cause of Christian unity.

The Vatican Council (1962–65) prompted many theologians to consider again their understandings of the Church and its structure. For Kung, the priesthood is a priesthood of *all* believers. The believer has no need for a mediator between himself and God. Kung insisted that positions within the Church must be justified by reference to New Testament teachings, and that the New Testament does not support the division between clergy and laity to be found in the Catholic Church, and other Christian communions. Kung did not oppose leadership within the Church, rather he insisted that it should be based on biblical principles: it must be based on the concept of service, and willingness to respond to demands for change which correspond to biblical teachings and good reasoning.

Kung's challenge to the basis of authority within the Church brought him into conflict with the Pope himself following the encyclical *Humanae Vitae* (**1968**), in which Pope Paul VI condemned all forms of artificial birth control. Kung's response was not only to challenge the wisdom of the encyclical, accusing the Church of being inhumane, archaic, legalistic and resistant to Christian renewal, but also to question the doctrine of papal infallibility. He highlighted occasions in the past in which the papacy had been in error, and the particular circumstances in which doctrine came to be drawn up at the First Vatican Council in **1869–70**. Kung's views, set out in detail in *Infallible: An Enquiry* (1970), brought him into sharp conflict with the Church authorities. His refusal to back down led in **1979** to the withdrawal of his right to teach religion and his move to the independent Institute for Ecumenical Research at the University of Tubingen.

An essential requirement for genuine theological debate, Kung stressed, was freedom of thought. The Sacred Congregation for the Doctrine of Faith took a rather different position, declaring in **1979** that he was no longer to be considered a Roman Catholic theologian and stating:

> 'The Church of Christ has received from God the mandate to keep and to safeguard the deposit of faith so that all the faithful, under the guidance of the sacred teaching office through which Christ himself exercises his role as teacher in the Church, may cling without fail to the faith once delivered to the saints, may apply it more thoroughly to life ... It is necessary, therefore, that theological research and teaching should always be illumined with fidelity to the teaching office since no one may rightly act as a theologian except in close union with the mission of teaching truth which is incumbent on the Church itself.'

> 'Kung's theological approach reveals a firm commitment to Scripture as the source and yardstick of Christian theology, and an appreciation of the importance of human experience as a source for theological study. Scripture and human experience both require interpretation, and a process of critical correlation. Where Scripture and experience conflict, it is the gospel which must take precedence.'

In Kung's best known work, *On Being a Christian*, he formulates his doctrine of Christ, setting it in the modern-day context. He discusses what it means to be Christian, and what is required of a Christian *today* in the context of a world in which other religions and humanistic philosophies all claim to offer meaning. In *Does God Exist?* Kung sets out the history of our understanding of God, and the critiques of the main atheist philosphers. His aim is not to demonstrate that God does exist, but rather to establish the rationality of belief in God. He seeks to demonstrate how none of them have succeeded in disproving the existence of God. He emphasises that a belief in God is not a matter only of our reasoning but is bound up with our whole being and hence it is a matter also of our instincts, our values, our traditions – all the historical and social characteristics of humanity that make us who we are. After discussing the Jewish and Christian faith in God, Kung argues that the biblical faith in God 'is in itself coherent, is also rationally justifiable and has proved itself historically over many thousands of years'. Kung sees *all* our thoughts and doubts, our intuitions and reasoning – not just those on which we base a belief in God, as founded on an '*a priori* act of trust'.

In *Christianity and the World Religions*, published in 1984, Kung argues that the boundaries of ecumenical discussion must be extended to include all the world religions. A concomitant of such an objective must be an acknowledgment by Christianity that no religion can be said to have received the whole of truth – rather we are all at different points in pursuit of the same goal. Christians must therefore seek a greater understanding of the traditions of other world religions.

Kung's greatest achievement has been to present Christianity and his own theological perceptions in a language and style which can be understood by the non-theologian, a vital stepping stone to the progress of inter-Christian and global ecumenical discussion.

9.11 Pannenberg

Wolfhart Pannenberg (born **1928**) was professor of systematic theology at the university of Mainz, and later professor at the university of Munich. His years as a student saw a growing academic interest in the theological significance of history for the Christian faith. Pannenberg, together with a number of other students, known as the 'Pannenberg Circle', sought to develop a new understanding of the relationship between faith and history. They caused a storm with the publication of a volume of essays entitled *Revelation and History* which was credited as unveiling a new departure in modern theology. It was in working through the ideas in this work that Pannenberg's theological outlook was to develop and mature.

The central feature of this new departure which Pannenberg was to develop was his understanding that revelation could not be properly interpreted as the revealing of truths about God but had to be comprehended as God's self-revelation. Pannenberg maintained that if there was only one God, then divine self-revelation must mean that there can only be a single unique revelation in which God acts simultaneously as the author and means of that revelation. Pannenberg argued that Scripture demonstrates that God does not reveal himself directly, but only indirectly through participating in history. If revelation is to mean specifically God's self-revelation, then it must mean revelation at the culmination of history, when the whole of history, its meaning and the destiny of the world are revealed.

Pannenberg maintains that the ultimate destiny of the world was anticipated and realised in the resurrection of Jesus. Jewish history, argues Pannenberg, is one of an increasing realisation of God's participation in history, culminating in the

Apocalypse when God's revelation of himself is made complete. As the destiny of the world, and the ultimate divine self-revelation, are inevitably universal, so too is the anticipation and realisation of God's revelation in the resurrection of Jesus.

A crucial feature of Pannenberg's theology is that he insists that it must be based on knowledge which is capable of being rationally established outside faith. With this in mind, Pannenberg seeks to demonstrate who Jesus is – the Christ – from the only concrete starting point – the reality of the historical Jesus. Historical research tells us not only that Jesus was an historical figure but, argues Pannenberg, also confirms Jesus' resurrection as the most likely explanation for the historical events of the Easter story. Accordingly history provides confirmation not only of Christ's divinity, but also of the humanity of Jesus and his role as the fulfilment of human destiny. Pannenberg also points to Jesus' complete obedience to his heavenly Father as confirming him as the Son of God.

Pannenberg maintains that the essence of humanity is not merely an inherent openness to the world, but an openness for God. He sees humanity as predisposed to seek a relationship with God, a predisposition which pervades human culture. Christ's resurrection, as the realisation of human destiny, provides us with hope that we will share in the resurrection and fulfil our true destiny in communion with God in his kingdom, simultaneously enjoying true freedom and participating in humanity's shared destiny. Pannenberg maintains that Jesus' resurrection is the guarantee of our own resurrection and demonstrates God's love for us, the enduring unlimited value of each person and the basis of true freedom in Christ. As God's ultimate destiny for the world is anticipated and realised in the resurrection by giving himself to the world, the eschatological community of humanity in the Kingdom of God is symbolised, represented and anticipated in the Church. The Church's task is to develop the world community of the Kingdom of God and to stand firm against attempts to restrict and deny freedoms. This model of the Kingdom of God provides strong support for the ecumenical movement and exposes the disgrace of divisions within the Church.

Pannenberg defines theology as the science of the hypothesis of God, an hypothesis which he seeks to establish by reason outside faith. God cannot be directly experienced, but is only approachable through our subjective understanding of meaning gained through our experience of the world and which is expressed in the great religions. Accordingly the history of religions is the starting point for an analysis of humanity's experience of God. Christianity thus exists in the context of a number of religions which have in common a history of reflection and contemplation of indirect divine experience. Pannenberg describes the theological claims of religion as hypotheses. These can only be fully confirmed when the ultimate destiny of mankind is realised but, Pannenberg argues, we do possess pointers with which to test these hypotheses. Christian theological hypotheses, he argues, are to be rejected unless they are shown to follow from biblical traditions, are capable of being confirmed by our present experience and in the context of philosophical reflection, and fit in with our previous experience of the area of that hypothesis and with the maturity of modern theological debate.

The key feature of Pannenberg's vision of Christian theology is the role of universal history, with its roots in the people of Israel who gradually came to understand in the Apocalyptic vision of their faith that total reality is history.

Apocalypticism was continued in the Christian faith through the universal eschatological anticipation signified in the destiny of Jesus. The merit of such a theological account of history is that it provides a unity to our perceptions of history and also permits the possibility of the unforeseeable. It is only anthropocentric understandings of history promulgated in the Enlightenment that require history to be interpreted as governed by a uniformity of events, and created only by humanity to the exclusion of a theological interpretation of history. Such a view of history denies the possibility of substantial and authentic change and closes off the possibilities for understanding history as within a context of meaning. Pannenberg's theological interpretation of history permits change and denies any contradiction between faith and history – indeed historical research is a tool with which to demonstrate faith's validity.

Pannenberg insists that faith must be based on knowledge rather than being merely a non-rational or non-reasoned blind decision and, moreover, based on the kind of knowledge which is susceptible to scientific enquiry, rather than available only to those who already believe. Whilst theological knowledge must be susceptible to scientific enquiry, humanity's thirst for knowledge and truth is not, argues Pannenberg, atheological. He sees all knowledge and reason as characterised by anticipation of the future. As we employ knowledge and reason to understand and order our lives, this necessarily involves a vision of the final future. Faith, which Pannenberg argues is inherently compatible with reason, is essentially eschatological in that faith trusts in anticipation of the future – the coming of the Kingdom of God.

Knowledge and truth, Pannenberg argues, are not static but change as history unfolds and are revealed in their entirety only at the end of time. Whilst Pannenberg maintains that the destiny of the world has already been anticipated and actualised in the Resurrection, that does not mean that the future is not open to change and novelty.

Eschatological anticipation is a key to Pannenberg's understanding of God and the 'futurity' of God. Pannenberg recognises force in the argument that it is possible to gain an understanding of human existence without introducing the concept of God at all. He acknowledges that humanity is predisposed to seek out God, but that as revelation remains a *future* event, it is in the future that God will demonstrate his existence, his nature and the truth about history. It is in his future *coming* that the Kingdom of God and his being will be realised. Pannenberg views clearly mark a significant departure from the traditional doctrine of God, and for example of Creation.

Pannenberg has been criticised by some for grounding Christian faith on historical research and abandoning a role for theological reflection as supportive of the truth of Christian faith. Conservative Christians, however, have welcomed his emphasis on revelation as an historical event.

9.12 Jungel

Eberhard Jungel, born in 1934, has been strongly influenced by Karl Barth. He has written widely on many theological issues and his work is heavily influenced by his approach to religious language which, in his earliest publications, he sees as flowing from divine intervention – God's 'coming in speech'. In later works he acknowledges that language about God is not something created by God, but as flowing from an organised human system that can only be understood in relation to the context of the speaker. However, argues Jungel, language has both a regular usage and an extended usage arising out of metaphors and analogies. Thus the parables have references to ordinary worldly stories but simultaneously also refer to the Kingdom of God – God 'comes to speech' in them. Without destroying the ordinary understanding of language – God comes to the world and in doing so adds to and extends it.

Jungel's understanding of the person and work of Christ, his christology, is centred around the idea of God identifying himself with the human person Jesus, and his relation to Jesus's death. The meaning of Christ's death is revealed in the Resurrection, in the identity of God with the crucified man Jesus. The language of the Resurrection explains Jesus' past in that it asserts his divinity without requiring support in any explicit statements by the man Jesus – whose existence is disclosed at the Resurrection to be both human and divine. Our language about the Resurrection explains Jesus' identity.

Jungel's approach to the doctrine of God is heavily influenced by his christological position. Our concept of God arises not from agreement as to the character of divinity, but rather from our dwelling in God's self-identification with the crucified Jesus. Theology creates its appreciation of what God is like from the manner in which he revealed himself, and the fact that he suffers. Jungel sees language about God's suffering and death as providing insights into the modes of being of God. He dislikes language about God which suggests that he cannot suffer, and he sees God as expressing his being on the Cross, rather than denying it. God's autonomy is his freedom to love and give himself in identification with Jesus, through his capacity to suffer death.

God's plan for mankind is revealed only in Jesus Christ whose true humanity is the centre of mankind's story. He sees human existence as arising out of the creative power of God, which provides for greater possibilities for individuals than do our own projects for self-determination. More recently, under the influence of Barth's theology of a covenant of partnership between God and man, Jungel has come to see human existence as initiated by God, but proceeding as a 'correspondence' between God's acts and the human person who responds to an active God.

Jungel is critical of natural theology which attempts to search for God through nature and human reasoning without divine revelation, because not only does it ignore the uniqueness of Christianity, rendering it no more than an example of religious knowledge, but it fails to take into account man's capacity to change in response to revelation. Jungel advocates a concept of natural theology that is not limited in actual human experience or the actuality of nature, but to what is possible for the world through God's self-revelation which does not accept the world as it is.

Bibliography

R. Bauckham, *Moltmann: Messianic Theology in the Making*, Marshall Pickering (1987)

John Bowden, *Edward Schillebeeckx: Portrait of a Theologian*, SCM, London (1983)

Carl E. Braaten and Philip Clayton (Eds), *The Theology of Wolfhart Pannenberg. Twelve American Critiques*, Augsburg Press, Minneapolis (1988)

Ernst Feil, *The Theology of Dietrich Bonhoeffer*, Fortress Press (1985)

Alan G. Galloway, *Wolfhart Pannenberg*, George Allen & Unwin, London (1973)

Herman Haring and Karl-Josef Kuschel (Eds), *Hans Kung, His Work – His Way*, SCM Press (1993)

R.A. Johnson, *Rudolf Bultmann: Interpreting Faith for the Modern Era*, Collins, London (1987)

David Kelsey, *The Fabric of Paul Tillich's Theology*, New Haven, CT (1967)

Hans Kung, *On Being a Christian*, Wallaby, New York (1977)

J. Macquarrie, *The Scope of Demythologising: Bultmann and His Critics*, London (1966)

Gerald A. McCool, *A Rahner Reader*, Seabury, New York (1975)

W. Nichols, *Pelican Guide to Modern Theology*, Pelican, London (1971)

Edward Schillebeeckx, *Ministry: A Case for Change*, Crossroad Publishing Company, New York (1981)

S.W. Sykes (Ed.), *Karl Barth: Studies of His Theological Method*, Oxford University Press (1980)

J.B. Webster, *Eberhard Jungel: An Introduction to His Theology*, Cambridge University Press, Cambridge (1986)

■ ⋈ **10** Modern theology: twentieth century theological movements

10.1 Post-liberal theology

The term 'post-liberal theology' is associated with the ideas emanating from the Yale Divinity School, and in particular with George Lindbeck's work *The Nature of Doctrine* which appeared in 1984. Post-liberal theology has arisen out of an increasing scepticism towards liberal theology. Its proponents reject an analysis of the Bible which treats it as either an historical source or a symbolic account. Post-liberalism rejects claims to religious knowledge which are universal and shared by all mankind, and rejects also the concept of individual religious experiences. The essence of religion, claim post-liberal thinkers, is man's existence within a given tradition. This cultural–linguistic approach insists that there is no religious truth apart from subjective truth within human knowledge and culture. Accordingly, Scripture does not possess authority in any objective or universal sense, but only because the Christian community has chosen to employ it to reinforce its identity.

A significant contributor to the ideas which came to be known as post-liberal theology was **Hans Frei**. In *The Eclipse of Biblical Narrative*, published in 1974, he noted the manner in which until the seventeenth century the Bible was treated as a story about the world, with people attributing meaning to their lives by seeing themselves as part of that story. Frei contrasted this with subsequent centuries in which the Bible account was no longer seen as the real world, but instead had to be incorporated into people's lives by understanding the Bible either in terms of an account of historical events, or as a symbolic narrative which served as a vehicle to illustrate universal truths. Frei rejected both these explanations of Scripture in favour of understanding Scripture as a story *per se* – not like any story but as one which houses the history and destiny of mankind.

Frei dismisses the quest for the historical Jesus and the individual's attempts to experience Christ. He states that these efforts in truth are a rejection of the Gospel which itself contains what we need to know of Christ. The central characteristic of Christ is his resurrection. Scripture tells us this essential trait: Christ 'is the resurrection and the life' and accordingly that he is present with us. Post-liberal theology is of no assistance in a debate with non-Christians – indeed the purpose of theology lies elsewhere in describing and analysing Christian belief within a pre-supposed Christian framework and tradition.

In *The Nature of Doctrine,* Lindbeck describes three accounts of how religious doctrines function:

(i) the *propositionalist* which explains doctrine as passing on objective knowledge;
(ii) the *experiential–expressivist* which understands doctrines as symbolic descriptions of people's feelings and approaches about life;
(iii) the *cultural–linguistic* or *regulative* stance which explains doctrines as a set of the Christian community's regulations governing belief, discussion and conduct.

Lindbeck seeks to undermine the experiential–expressivist position by challenging the idea that religious doctrine describes some universal experience that we can all share. Our concepts of religion are facilitated and limited by our abilities to express ourselves and accordingly are determined, claims Lindbeck, by our cultural and linguistic framework. We cannot stand outside or escape from the cultural and linguistic concrete circumstances in which we are set. Different religions are like different languages. One language may be richer and facilitate ease of expression and widening of understanding, whilst another may be dry, limiting and barren, but it is impossible to determine that one is true and another false. The purpose of theology for Lindbeck is not the pursuit of universal knowledge or experience but the exposition and improving of the Christian community's system of beliefs.

Stanley Hauerwas has also sought to challenge the belief that different world religions are merely manifestations of a universal religious experience, claiming that it is only on becoming part of a Christian community that it is possible to have experiences that would not otherwise be experienced. For Hauerwas, there are no universal ethical rules available to us and hence ethical debates that occupy so much of our energies are pointless if based upon a search for such principles. Difficult moral decisions should not be taken on the basis of such debates, but on a consideration of context and of an understanding gained from cultural tradition. Hauerwas rejects attempts to rationalise ethics in objective terms. To use his words: 'The story that liberalism teaches us is that we have no story'. For Hauerwas, stories which seek to demonstrate good and bad are far more instructive, because they appeal to our sense of right or wrong, a sense which is grounded in our culture and which, because it cannot be analysed and understood, liberals seek to discount. The purpose of moral theology is to provide the Christian community with the material to preserve its moral code, not to seek out some objective moral principles with which to justify or amend it.

Ronald Thiemann has applied similar thinking to the doctrine of revelation. Revelation cannot be the subject of knowledge, an inevitable conclusion based on evidence that can be analysed or from a religious intuition, or bibilical assertion of which we can be truly certain. Thiemann argues that assertions about revelation protect and support the central Christian belief that God's initiative precedes all human action. Theologians should adopt an 'holistic' approach, for once we appreciate how much of Christian life and practice would be lost if we let go of our convictions about God's initiative in the world, and acknowledge that revelation safeguards our convictions about his initiative, we realise the importance of retaining a doctrine of revelation. We can do this, says Thiemann, if we abandon the fruitless search to base the doctrine on self-evident truths.

Revelation is to be treated, Thiemann argues, as part of the doctrine of God, as a promise by him. With this concept of revelation as a promise, belief in God's prior initiative in his relations with mankind is retained, for man cannot respond to a promise until it has been made. Revelation is justified not by an appeal to some indisputable foundation, but to its unity with the rest of Christian life and doctrine.

Critics of post-liberalism frequently accuse it of seeking to avoid the debate about faith and ethics and retreating into a form of Christian ghetto. The validity of Christian theological and ethical claims, say the critics of post-liberalism, must be capable of external analysis and judgement. If theology consists of no more than a debate about the rules which the Christian faithful should adopt in their lives, then Christianity has abandoned any claim to assert objective truths.

10.2 Evangelicalism

The term 'evangelical' is today used to refer to a phenomenon which transcends denominational boundaries and which stresses the authority of the Bible. Evangelicals share a number of common beliefs, the most important being:

(i)   the authority and historical accuracy of Scripture;
(ii) eternal salvation only through faith in Christ;
(iii) the need for personal conversion; and
(iv) the urgent call to evangelise.

Evangelicalism is not peculiar to any one denomination. It is transdenominational. It is a trend within mainstream denominations, including Anglicanism, Presbyterianism, Methodism and Roman Catholicism, as well as house groups and the less-established movements. Not surprisingly, it is strongly ecumenical. Evangelicals of all denominations usually share the same hymns, methods of evangelising, emphasis on Bible study, and even the same pastoral and ecclesiological language, tone and manner.

In the nineteenth century, evangelicals on both sides of the Atlantic established numerous voluntary societies aimed at missionary work, social reform and the circulation of religious tracts.

Its interdenominational character has meant that the evangelical movement has failed to develop its own academic theological tradition. Rather, evangelical theologies have developed within the different denominations, although all have shared the desire for orthodoxy, the belief in Scripture as ultimate authority for the Christian life, and an emphasis on a personal salvation through faith.

In the United States, the emergence of an evangelical theology was preceded by the rise of fundamentalism which centred on the key doctrines of the absolute and literal authority of Scripture, and of the second coming. Fundamentalism was essentially a 'siege mentality' reaction against the advances of secular culture, and the belief that the theological training colleges were under the domination of liberal theologians. The evangelicalism that emerged in the **1960s** and **1970s** was a combination of evangelical enthusiasm and a determination to establish evangelicalism as a theology of the intellect as well as the heart, in contrast to the counter-intellectualist stance of fundamentalists.

Whilst fundamentalism will not countenance any notion of biblical criticism that seeks to question an unwavering literal interpretation of the Bible, evangelicalism acknowledges the principle of a 'reasonable' degree of biblical criticism. Similarly, whilst the two have a common commitment to certain beliefs, such as biblical authority, fundamentalism is far narrower in its outlook and firmly insists on a series of additional doctrines which for evangelicals are of little, if any consequence.

Berkouwer, appointed to a professorship at the Free University of Amsterdam in **1945**, was concerned primarily with the relationship between faith and revelation. He believed that whilst liberal theologians had become preoccupied with subjective human experiencing of revelation, the orthodox position discounted the human experience. For Berkouwer, the divine nature of the Word of God made available to mankind in the Scriptures provided the bridge between the divine and the human, and the correlation between faith and knowledge. Berkouwer's theology is firmly rooted in the absolute authority of the Bible, the divine biblical call to faith and mission, divine judgement and Christ's Gospel of salvation. The purpose of theology, argues Berkouwer, is not to seek a knowledge about those matters which transcend the faith, or to endeavour to 'unravel mysteries', but to call Christians to hear the Word of God, and test Christian beliefs and assertions against the authority recorded in Scripture.

A major contributor to the foundations of evangelical theology was **Helmut Thielicke**, who was professor of systematic theology at the University of Tubingen for twenty years from **1954**. He argued that, first and foremost, theological thought must be guided by the Holy Spirit. Such an approach allowed for God's own authority in theology and his freedom to participate in theological thought. The Incarnation, Thielicke maintained, is the solution to man's alienation from God. God's Word, through the Holy Spirit, provides the means of communion with God, and the benchmark for ethical values and judgements. Through the Incarnation, God expresses his solidarity with mankind, and through the work of the Holy Spirit involves himself with our hopes and troubles.

In the United States, **Carl F.H. Henry** emerged as one of the leading evangelical theologians, noted in particular for his robust defence of the traditional evangelical position on the authority of Scripture in his six-volume work *God, Revelation and Authority*, which he completed in **1983**. Henry was one of a number of young theological scholars in the early post-war years who were keen to disassociate evangelical theology from what was seen as militant and irrational fundamentalism, and to strengthen evangelicalism as a theology within the mainstream Church. The fundamentalists of the far right were seen as too closely associated with the xenophobic forces of anti-Communism, too critical of advanced education and too judgemental of other denominations.

A central element of the evangelical theology which Henry presented was what he termed 'evangelical theism'. He argued that modern man has been won over by relativism, leaving himself deprived of moral absolutes and certain truths. The answer to man's yearning for stability and certain knowledge is God who gives us faith and hope, and the rational justification or authority for our faith and hope is God's own revelation. It is therefore imperative that Christianity responds to this situation by appealing to man's reason. The mission of the theologian is to present the faith in terms of the truth, not simply in terms of a personal relationship with God. The foundation for biblical theism is the pre-supposition that God has revealed the truths underlying all knowledge. For Henry, divine revelation is the origin of all truth, reason is our means of appre-hending it, the Bible is our source of principles for authenticating it, and logic is a means of testing it. The responsibility of a theologian is to present the elements of biblical revelation in a coherent picture.

God has secured our salvation by Christ's atonement, and has given us the Holy Spirit through whom He continues to encourage us in accordance with His divine revelation recorded in Scripture, and by such further knowledge which successfully passes through our process of biblical authentication and rational analysis. Our powers of reasoning and logic were given in order to enable us to test and understand divine revelation.

The major achievement in the post-war years has been the development of evangelical authority free from the chains of fundamentalism, but without abandoning biblical authority as a source of divine revelation. In the future the strength of evangelicalism, both in terms of the evangelical movement generally and in terms of academic theology, is likely to increase owing to the increasing number of pastors and theology academics who having undergone training at the increasing number of evangelical schools established from the **1950s** onwards.

Two issues that currently concern evangelical theology and that have yet to be fully resolved are the nature of biblical revelation, and the social aspects of salva-tion. In relation to the former, if Scripture is not the literal Word of God, how are the two related, and the Word of God ascertained? As to the latter, evangelicalism is criticised for its preoccupation with spiritual salvation, and its apparent lack of concern for the physical needs and earthly aspirations of people, in particular the poor.

10.3   Eastern Orthodox theology

After the fall of Constantinople, the centres of Eastern Orthodoxy shifted to Russia. In the twentieth century the development of thought within Orthodoxy has been predominantly of Russian origin, both before **1917**, and after the dispersion of the Russian intelligentsia, most notably to Paris. The late nine-teenth century had seen a tremendous flourishing of intellectual thought in Russia as within but a few decades it became exposed to three hundred years of Western theological debate. In this era **Vladimir Soloviev** contributed much to Russian Orthodox theology by his adoption of the cosmological figure of 'Sophia' who represented divine wisdom. Sophia, for Soloviev the incarnation of God, brings about the reunification in the Church of man with the cosmos, and liberates man from his limitations and his alienation. This promise of sophianic humanity – of a society that evolves and grows in unity with the cosmos – is far more attuned to orthodoxy that to the legalistic systems of authority characteristic of Roman Catholicism, or the individualism of Protestantism. Soloviev develops ideas of earlier writers such as **Stephanovich Khomyakov (1804–60)** on the concept of *sabernost*, meaning 'catholicity' or a supra-individual consciousness of the Church.

The vitality of the nineteenth century could not be sustained in the face of the institutional repression which once again became the tool of a totalitarian state. The development of the orthodox theological tradition was continued by emigrés such as **Sergei Bulgakov (1871–1944)**, **George Flovosky (1893–1979)** and **Vladimir Losky (1903–58)**. Twentieth century Russian theology has generally consisted of a discussion between those who have accepted the cosmological picture painted by Soloviev and those who reject it in preference to a more traditional approach based on the Church Fathers. Bulgakov saw Sophia as the divine nature – God's own life. Sophia is not a person or a being, but the impulse that seeks harmony and order. When human selfishness shatters the 'sophianic' whole, God as Word and Spirit liberates and enables us to understand the wholeness of things. Bulgakov argued that liberation teaches us to understand the wholeness of things and that we cannot exist alone, but only in communion with others and with the Church – by which he meant the fellowship of the spirit: 'Sophia is the process of becoming'. Bulgakov rejected concentration on an individual relation in Christ or reliance upon a single infallible authority such as the Bible or the Pope, instead the identity of the Church should rest firmly in the common sharing of life in the Spirit. Christ does not 'act' in the Church; rather, Christ is the place where uncreated and created Sophia come together. The divine life of constant selflessness brings about a created life in which alienation is overcome.

Losky and Flovosky both sought to counter the influence of mystique in Russian theology and to call for a return to the Church Fathers. Flovosky maintained that Christian theology must strengthen its commitment to its patristic, Greek and Byzantine roots, and emphasised the importance of history in knowledge. He rejected the concept of objective knowledge, pointing out that each historical source was created from a given perspective, and that in the search for historical knowledge, research itself is carried out and interpreted from a personal perspective. Accordingly, Christianity cannot free itself from the historical past – the starting point for theological debate and for faith and practice is the history of the Church, its language and methods, as handed down from the Church Fathers. It is not possible to have a theological debate outside this context. Flovosky sees the Eucharist as the foundation of genuine *sobernost*, in which fellowship is shared not only between believers but in unison with the 'whole company of heaven'.

The disintegration of the Soviet Union will inevitably lead to the development of home-grown schools of Russian orthodoxy, although the effect of the dispersion of so many of the intelligentsia will mean that Russian emigré theologians will continue as a major influence, particularly in the United States. Greek theological thought had contributed little in the nineteenth century and first half of the twentieth, but has over the last thirty years begun to exercise much greater influence.

10.4 Process theology

Process theology became prominent in the **1960s** in the United States and was a development from the metaphysical system proposed by the philosopher and logician **Alfred Whitehead (1861–1947)**. Whitehead maintained that all entities are to some extent self-creative. He argued that whilst God is the unsurpassably superior form of self-creation, all self-creative beings are necessarily co-creators of the divine reality, at least in relation to those aspects of divinity which are consequent upon the world. Because God is actively involved in creation, he cannot be unaffected by it – he must embrace all the possibilities of change within himself.

Process theologians developed these ideas to construct a new doctrine of God, an alternative theism, in which God has both 'abstract' or 'necessary' attributes, and 'concrete' or 'accidental' attributes, which are those which come into contact with the world and are changed by this encounter. The latter cannot be attributed to God in classical theism as its doctrine of God excludes the possibility of God being relative or changing. Process theology conceives God as supreme relativity and supreme 'becoming' as well as eternal, absolute, necessary and independent. Process theologians argue that orthodox theism is internally contradictory – whilst in orthodox theism everything about God, including his divine will, is necessary, the world in which his will takes effect is contingent.

Process theology asks: how can God know and love the world if he remains unaffected by it? A God who does not, indeed cannot, suffer in solidarity with his suffering people and who does not relate to them, is not worthy of our worship and faith. Process theology claims that divine perfection entails not absoluteness, but rather the power to relate to the world and the power to be changed by it. God's perfection is accompanied by his intimate relatedness with the creaturely realm. God relates to the world and is enriched by it, and in turn he enriches and changes the world. Man, however, can never be superior, as God alone is infinite. This concept was taken up by the theologian **Charles Hartshorne**. He defined God's divine perfection as:

> ' . . . excellence such that rivalry or superiority on the part of other individuals is impossible, but self-superiority is not impossible . . . the perfect is the self-surpassing surpasser of all.'

God remains super-eminent: he includes within his divine experience the temporal dimension of the world, but he is also eternal.

The most assertively Christian theological presentation of process theology is that of **John Cobb** who emphasises the concept of 'creative transformation'. He argues that 'creative transformation' is caused by novelty originating from the divine Logos and that it is Christ that facilitates creative transformation. Christ's presence is the presence of God's love causing creative transformation and generating more love.

Process theology has come under attack from many sides, in particular for its assumption that an inability in God to suffer means that he is not capable of involvement with men in their pain and suffering.

10.5   Liberation theology

The term 'liberation theology' is used to signify the movement which took real root in Latin America in the **1960s** and **1970s**. It arose as a reaction against the history of oppression and colonisation under Spanish and Portuguese rule, of neocolonialism and economic exploitation by Britain and the United States in the twentieth century, and of extreme poverty and repressive military regimes from the **1950s** onwards. It was a reaction not only against deprivation and oppression, but also against the position hitherto taken by the Church itself. From the time of Emperor Constantine, the Church had in large part identified itself with the State and the status quo, and in the New World and the developing world was closely associated with European imperialism.

Liberation theology was also a response to developments within the Roman Catholic and Protestant Churches in the **1950s** and **1960s** on the issues of justice and peace, in particular the position taken by Vatican II on the need for human dignity and change within society. In **1968** the Roman Catholic bishops of Latin America met in Medellin, Colombia, to discuss the lessons to be drawn from Vatican II. This conference marked a turning point in the history of the Church in Latin America: the Church articulated a new vision of faith, centred on an alliance with the poor and dispossessed, and an opposition to the institutionalised violence characteristic of this region.

These developments found support in the political theology of such writers as **Jurgen Moltmann** and **Johann Baptist Metz**. Moltmann, for example, wrote of a vision of a critical Christianity in solidarity with the disadvantaged, and seeking the transformation of society. At the same time, liberation theology drew on Marxist theory as a tool of social analysis revealing the relations of power within society and the means of change, as an aid to the interpretation of history as a struggle between the alienated masses and the small capitalist ruling class, and lastly as pointing in the direction of the kind of political programme required to bring about a just society. Inevitably, liberation theology is highly critical of the structures of capitalism and has identified itself with the ideals of socialism. Whilst criticised by many for its use of the theories of Marxism, liberation theologians were by no means the first to draw on non-Christian writers. Liberation theology, moreover, is not a restatement or a variant of Marxism, rather it seeks the transformation of human beings to realise their full God-given humanity which is not determined by the structures within society.

Liberation theology offers a new understanding of the Christian faith. Sin is no longer a matter only of the morality of the individual's actions, but is to be understood in terms of the structures of society that result in poverty and deprivation. Redemption is linked to the liberation of the poor, and Christ is seen not only as a political rebel, in solidarity with and sharing the sufferings of the poor, but also as a liberator and transformer of mankind. Christianity is then a siding with the poor in solidarity and in pursuit of liberation and transformation. It does not advocate a particular form of political order, nor can it accept Christian separatism, but it does demand a critical assessment of the political order in which we find ourselves, solidarity with the poor and dispossessed, and a relentless pursuit of transformation into the Kingdom of God. Christian faith and love become inextricably merged with a demand for justice.

Two of the most influential of the Latin American liberation theologians are Peruvian **Gustavo Gutierrez**, and the Argentinian **Jose Miguel Bonino**. In his *Theology of Liberation* (1971) and subsequent works, Gutierrez offers an interpretation of the Bible, Christianity and history from the perspective of the poor and alienated. He highlights the social and economic consequences for the poor arising out of the structures of the capitalist developed world and uses the symbolisation of the Exodus and the promised land, and Christ's proclamation of the Gospel to the poor, to urge and predict the liberation of the poor, and the transformation of society. Not only is God present among the poor and sharing their suffering, but his Church is called to be a prophetic witness in Latin America. Gutierrez is highly critical of modern theology which he argues is preoccupied with whether the modern rational 'bourgeois' can still believe without suspending his use of reason. How, Gutierrez asks, can modern theology be so consumed with this question whilst failing to understand and challenge the structures of society which divide human beings and cast aside most of mankind as of no account? Liberation theology is entirely different. Not only is it centred on the poor and God's presence among them, but it identifies the modern rational bourgeois with whom modern theology has been preoccupied as the oppressors of the poor throughout history. True communion with God requires participation in the plight of the poor, not a distanced detachment from them.

Liberation theological thought is dominated by Roman Catholic writers. **Bonino**, a Methodist, is one of the few significant Protestant contributors to this debate. His works illustrate the central role of history in Latin American liberation theology and the importance of the socio–political–economic context in which we live. The Bible, Bonino maintains, is both an account of God acting in the history of the past, and a promise that he will continue to act in the future. Throughout the past, and in the future, God acts to transform and to bring about his kingdom. Thus history is an account of how God is bringing about this transformation, an account in which men cannot be neutral. We all, even by inertia and omission, support a particular political stance, and are thus each responsible for history. A Christian is called upon to assist in God's transformation, and hence has to side with the poor and dispossessed. God acts to bring about his Kingdom, but we are called upon to act also in obedience to his will.

It is this call to action which demands theological thought. Man must endeavour to comprehend God's will by biblical study and by a scrutiny of the signs of the times. A crucial part of this task, however, is to appreciate human limitations: we are all a product of, we are all 'situated' in our own socio–political–economic background and environment, and our theological thought is similarly 'situated'. Whilst theology should engage with other disciplines to analyse and understand the past and the present, it should also seek to understand the direction of God's will and to transform history in accordance with that will.

Whilst theologians have contributed much to the debate within the Latin American Church, liberation theology is essentially a grass roots phenomenon which arose out of reflections upon the lives and faith of the poor. Those reflections inevitably extended to the structures and institutions which bring about

and sustain poverty. This has meant engaging in debate with philosphy, economics, politics and the social sciences.

In the First World, liberation theology has attracted criticism because of its
identification of liberation and salvation, which some see as reducing salvation
to worldly concerns and ignoring the more spiritual aspects and attempting to
ally God with one particular political position. Others see liberation as unbiblical
on the grounds, it is said, that the rich are in some way excluded. In truth, liberation
theology can resist such criticisms – whilst its essence does involve a judgement
against the lifestyles of the oppressors and the structures that perpetuate the
divisions between rich and poor, it does not advocate a particular cause and
equally it does seek to encompass all people in the transformation towards the
Kingdom of God. There is criticism too that liberation theology is primarily political, in contrast to the stance long taken by theologians and churchmen that
matters of politics and religion are unconnected and should remain so. That
criticism attracts the charge of naivety: in the modern world, politics is all pervasive and concerns every aspect of our lives, and Christianity, in calling for transformation and placing demands upon our lives, is inherently political. Indeed
neutrality is impossible, for inaction and inertia reinforce the status quo and
involve their own political judgements and responsibilities. To quote Bonino:
'Theology has to stop explaining the world, and start transforming it'.

Liberation theology has certainly been successful in challenging the Christian
agenda and the traditional Christian concept of sin. For many, their concept of
liberation is no longer limited to their freedom to accept God and freedom from
individual sin. Theological analysis has also undergone significant transformation out of an understanding of the 'situatedness' of our knowledge, of its
dependence on power, class and ideological outlook, and of the need for critical
analysis of how these factors distort our perceptions of the world and mankind.
Liberation theology has been successful too in providing the poor of Latin
America with a new voice and consciousness.

10.6 Feminist theology

The feminist movement is now an integral part of modern Western culture. It
seeks justice for women in terms of emancipation and opportunities, and aims at
the removal of barriers which deny human rights. Feminist theologians have
engaged in debate with traditional religions, taking them to task for the roles that
they allocate to women and the negative way in which women are presented as
imaging God. Feminist theologians seek to analyse religious traditions, symbols
and texts, and to highlight the underlying gender assumptions.

One of the earlier 'pioneers' of feminist theology was **Elizabeth Cady Stanton**,
who in her eighties assisted in the collecting together of biblical texts referring to
women. In this work, *The Women's Bible*, first published in **1895**, she sought to
demonstrate how religion, Church and State sought to persuade and convince
women of their essential inferiority.

In the modern era, the post-war years saw women admitted to an increasing
number of theological colleges and schools of divinity, particularly in the United

States, resulting in a small but growing number of female feminist theologians gaining positions within academia, of whom **Mary Daly** was one of the most influential. Mary Daly has sought to expose and discredit untrue biological and philosophical theories about women, and the abuse of such concepts as 'natural' and 'feminine' which are used to limit and restrain women. In *Beyond God the Father* (1973), she argued that women should abandon Christianity on the grounds that it was incapable of reforming its inherent bias against women derived from its male saviour figure, and its long history of undermining women. In *Gyn/Ecology*, she highlights the exclusion within the Trinity of any female presence in the divine cosmos.

The feminist critique has not been uniformly anti-Christianity. Many feminist scholars, such as **Phyllis Trible**, have sought to uncover and emphasise the positive roles played by women in the Old Testament and in the development of Christianity from the earliest days of the Church. In *God and the Rhetoric of Sexuality*, Trible identifies biblical texts which challenge those texts and translations which seek to subordinate women. She illustrates how biblical scholars are prone to rewrite biblical female imagery. In Deuteronomy 32: 8, for example, the Revised Standard Version '*You were unmindful of the rock that begot you, and you forgot the God who gave you birth*' is recorded in the Jerusalem Bible as: '*You forgot the God who fathered you*'.

A thorough analysis of Jewish history and of early Christianity reveals that women did assume leadership roles and that the history of the Church, until recently exclusively the domain of male theologians, requires reappraisal to take into account, for example, the indispensable part played by women in early missionary activity. Whilst a number of feminist theologians have turned their backs on mainstream Christianity, others such as **Rosemary Radford Ruether** have called for feminists to avoid being stifled by existing Christian institutions, and instead to seek to permeate and influence them and benefit from them in order to advance feminist theology's creativity.

Feminist theology poses a challenge to a number of traditional theological concepts, in particular the maleness of God, the nature of sin and the person of Christ. The persistent descriptions of God as male and the use of male pronouns is criticised as no more logical than describing God as female and employing female pronouns. Rosemary Radford Ruether, in *Sexism and God Talk: Towards a Feminist Theology* (1983), advocates the use of the term 'God/ess' to describe God. **Sallie McFague**, in *Metaphorical Theology* (1982), argues that insufficient appreciation is given to the fact that the description of God as Father is metaphorical – it is not intended to provide an analogy with human relationships. A number of feminist writers maintain that our idea of sin, involving such concepts as pride and ambition, is essentially male orientated as women are prone to experience lack of pride and lack of ambition and self-worth. This point is taken up particularly by **Judith Plaskow**, in *Sex, Sin and Grace* (1980), when she emphasises that descriptions in theology of human experience are frequently descriptions only of male experiences, and that the arguments of theologians such as Tillich concerning experience are not universal.

Rosemary Radford Ruether and others have maintained that the very nature of christology is sexist, with **Elizabeth Johnson**, in *Consider Jesus: Waves of Renewal* *in Christianity* (**1990**), illustrating how the maleness of Jesus has been theologically abused. It is often employed to advance the argument that only men fully image God. Similarly it is often used to justify beliefs concerning humanity – that the female is somehow inferior. Both arguments, of course, are used to support a male-only priesthood.

Feminist theologians respond by making the obvious, but nonetheless powerful point, that to be human Christ had to be male or female and that his maleness is merely a contingent feature of his identity in the same way that he happened to be Jewish. His maleness cannot justify male domination of women any more than his Jewishness would support Jewish superiority over non-Jews, or the superiority of fishermen over tax collectors.

10.7 Black theology

Black theology is concerned with black experience of oppression and discrimination, and issues of justice and liberation. Whilst Latin American liberation theology is focused on how capitalist structures create an alienated underclass of the poor, black theology is centred on the issue of race, for it is race that has allocated the Blacks to a past of slavery and colonialism, and a present of economic dependence, discrimination and powerlessness.

In North America, black theology arose out of the sufferings of slavery which branded Blacks as inferior. Denied the right to practise their native African religion, the slaves were forcibly converted to Christianity. Ironically, from this white religion which preached the virtues of the after-life, the slaves drew a rather different message – that of a Christ who identified with their sufferings. They reinterpreted the Scriptures for themselves, and in the words of the Negro Spirituals laid the foundations of a black theology.

Whilst emancipation came in **1863**, this meant little change for many Blacks, especially in the South where large numbers of Blacks and Coloureds were still deprived of the right to vote as late as the **1960s**. The Christian faith, as in the days of slavery, provided comfort and hope for a better future. Black Christians followed two different paths. Some joined the congregations of the white churches, but others took refuge in independent black churches. The reaction to the continued state of political, economic and social deprivation in which the majority of Blacks have still found themselves has been mixed. Whilst some have advocated patience, diligence and accommodation, others have called for an assertive challenge to the white establishment in the conviction that only by demanding and obtaining rights, whether by force or otherwise, can progress be achieved.

The black theology movement gained prominence in the **1960s**. A major factor was the rise of the civil rights movement in which many black church leaders played a central role. Of importance too was the controversy provoked by the publication in **1964** of **Joseph Washington**'s book *Black Religion*. Whilst emphasising the distinctiveness of black religion in the United States, he called for integration, arguing that it was not possible to develop a genuine philosophy outside mainstream theology. Washington's work influenced the development of a rather different analysis in **Albert Cleage**'s *Black Messiah*. Cleage called for a break from what he described as white theological oppression, claiming that the Gospel was that of a black Messiah, and that Paul had sought to corrupt this to make it more palatable for his European audience. A third important catalyst in the development of black theology was the emergence of the Black Power movement which rejected the non-violent struggle advocated by Martin Luther King in favour of a militant separatist stance.

Initially black theology developed in the second half of the 1960s within the Black-led churches as a response to the issues thrown up by the campaign for civil rights. In 1966, a statement by the National Committee of Black Churchmen placed liberation as the central plank in black theology. In the early years of the next decade, the debates moved also to the seminaries as black theology became a subject for academic study and analysis. In the late 1970s there was a further change as black theology began to enter into discussion with Latin American liberation theology. The Ecumenical Association of Third World Theologians (EATWOT) was formed in 1976, which greatly facilitated debate and the exchange of ideas, not only with liberation theology, but also with black feminism, African theology and the theologies of other parts of the developing world.

Racism is, not surprisingly, the focal point of black theology. The white and the more politically conservative of the black churches are rejected, their preoccupation with spiritual liberation being seen as facilitating the continuation of racism and its fruits. In black theology, God is the god of Exodus, championing the cause of the oppressed. Like liberation theology, black theology speaks of a process of transformation, of a process of creating what Martin Luther describes as the 'beloved community' in obedience to God's call. The burning issue for black theologians is whether God's call to engage in the struggle to bring about this transformation demanded or permitted violence, particularly in the face of violent and aggressive resistance.

The greatest contribution to the black theology debate is generally agreed to be that by **James H. Cone**. In *Black Theology of Liberation* (1970), Cone appealed to the concept of a God committed to and participating in the struggle for liberation – God is seen in the Bible as identifying with the oppressed, and hence in at least once sense 'God is Black'. In a development reminiscent of thinking within liberation theology, Cone emphasised that 'one's social and historical context decides not only the questions we address to God, but also the mode or form of the answers given to the questions'. We are all subject to our own individual 'situatedness'.

In South Africa, black theology has similarly arisen as part of the voice against racial discrimination and economic exploitation. The Afrikaner minority claimed South Africa for itself, believing that they were the chosen people and that South Africa was their promised land over whose native inhabitants they were to rule. The white minority succeeded in imposing structures on South Africa which enabled the white population to grow in prosperity but at the same time restricting the political and economic rights of the non-white majority. The Afrikaners believed in separate existence and, when in 1948 the Afrikaner Nationalist Party came to power, this belief became a central plank of State policy.

Black theology began to develop against the background of popular resistance in the 1970s and the violent government response as exemplified by the handling of the Soweto troubles in 1976. The inter-racial Christian Institute established in

1963 was compelled to close in 1977. However, the University Christian Movement continued to foster debate, which was further fuelled by the break-away grouping from UCM which sought to raise black consciousness, and which in 1977 formed the South African Students Organisation (SASO). Despite repression and the death of some liberation figures such as Steve Biko in 1977, Church leaders such as Archbishop Desmond Tutu, Bishop Buthelezi and the Reverend Allan Boesak continued to condemn apartheid and proved impossible to silence. Indeed, the attempts to curtail Church leaders only served to unite them in their sufferings with their people.

Black theology came to be shared by most of the South African Churches including the independent Churches and the evangelical denominations. It stresses the centrality of reconciliation, of the liberation of black and white. With the dismantling of apartheid, however, black South African Christians are increasingly sharing the concerns of Africans elsewhere and looking to their past tribal, cultural and religious identities.

African theology developed alongside the growth of African nationalism from the 1930s onwards. It was a reaction to the denigration of African culture and traditional religions which had accompanied the evangelising of Africa. The acceptance of Christ was generally expected to be accompanied by the Westernisation of the believer, and the rejection of prior religious beliefs and practices. The adaptation of Christian beliefs and practices to local traditional cultures had been out of the question. In the 1950s a number of African writers were calling for the Africanisation of Christianity, a position which was given some encouragement by the Second Vatican Council and also in the Protestant churches by the foundation in 1963 of the All Africa Council of Churches. Such thinking continued to gain ground in the 1960s and 1970s and led to the formation in 1977 of the Ecumenical Association of African Theologians (EAAT) which became the focal point for debate on African theology.

A major theme in African theology is, not surprisingly, a call for equality and respect for diversity, and a vociferous protest against what is often termed 'anthropological poverty' whereby local traditional culture is dismissed as unworthy, and the self-respect of its constituents destroyed. Black theology asserts that the Christian Church can attain unity without imposing or requiring uniformity. One of the leading African theologians, **John S. Pobee**, claims in *Towards an African Theology* that the Bible itself recognises that God does reveal himself in non-Christian religions and cultures, and that accordingly whilst these other religions and cultures may be largely in error, they can assist in a greater understanding of the Christian faith.

10.8 Asian theology

Theology in Asia, as in other parts of the developing world, has centred around the concept of the God of Justice, and Christ's and the Church's response to severe poverty, social revolution, social changes, ethnic minorities, the development and denigration of third world cultures, other faiths and the divided Church. Not surprisingly, one issue in particular that naturally arises from those themes is the participation in and response to the world order that is associated with such injustices.

In India, there has been a significant Christian community since at least the fourth century, but these indigenous Christian traditions were added to by European attempts at evangelising, particularly from the eighteenth century onwards. Initially, Indian theological thought was little more than an adoption of Western Christian ideas. By the late nineteenth and early twentieth centuries, Indian Christians were asking why they should not be free to draw upon their own cultural philosophical traditions in the same way as earlier Christians had made use of the works of non-Christians such as Aristotle. Indian theologians answered their own question, and a genuine Indian Christian independent theology developed, inevitably fuelled by the movements for political independence.

The present-day debate within Indian theology includes several strands of thought on the issue of the relationship between Christianity and Hinduism:

(i)   Christ encompasses all other religious experiences including Hinduism;
(ii) Christ represents the ultimate goal of the religious quest of Hinduism;
(iii) Hinduism is to be seen as the Indian equivalent of the Old Testament, the Indian pre-Christian account of God's relationship with Indian Christianity;
(iv) Christianity is simply incompatible with Hinduism and necessitates a rejection of Hinduism.

Stanely J. Samartha, one of the leading Indian theologians, has sought to highlight the importance of asserting the context of theology in India. He rejects the necessity or desirability of having to understand Christ through semitic eyes. Indian theology should be free to make use of India's own indigenous philosophers whose different insights can serve to deepen an understanding of the mysteries of the Universe, just as Origen made use of Platonic thought, and Aquinas used the ideas of Aristotle. Samartha has in mind in particular the Vedanta, and the ideas of its proponent Sankara concerning what is known as the 'advaitic' approach to reality. 'Advaita' is a concept of the all-inclusive unity of God, the world and humanity, in which there is no duality. Samartha rejects what he calls 'the crusade approach' and the 'fruit salad' approach to other faiths. He argues that allowing for the advaitic approach to reality does not involve the merging of two faiths in a religious syncretism. He argues that we should consider a larger framework in which we acknowledge 'differentiated interrelatedness'.

The concept of advaita, of unity, of mystery, prepares us for Christ's coming, for in Christ 'history and nature are held together'. Christ cannot be limited, but will one day reveal the mystery to humanity. In the meantime, mankind should engage in religious dialogue to discover what actions the Gospel calls us to perform. Samartha emphasises that Christ is unbound, and that that statement about Christ is itself an initiation, a call to discussions with other faiths. Samartha's position invites the question: where does Christianity stand in relation to other faiths? Is he not guilty of adopting the 'fruit salad' approach that he tells us he rejects? For Samartha, there are indeed different ways of salvation, different ways to respond to the mystery of the 'Ultimate', but in Christ alone the Ultimate became 'intimate with humanity'. The death and resurrection of Christ were the greatest most decisive demonstations of victory over pain and suffering, and a message that Christians are called upon to share, not with an arrogant, boasting exclusivity, but humbly and with the appreciation that other answers to the questions about humanity and human destiny contain their own insight.

Choan-Seng Song, a former Principal of a theological college in Taiwan, who went on to become a Professor of Theology in California, rejects a theology which considers Israel and the Christian Church as the only 'bearers and dispensers of God's saving love'. He speaks of the 'very big theological blunder' of theologians identifying salvation with the history of Israel and the Christian Church. Song argues that a proper understanding of the depth of the spirit, heart and soul of Asian humanity revealed in its faiths and cultures must inevitably lead to the questioning of the exclusivity of the Christian claim to salvation. Song criticises Western theology, asserting that one cannot base theology on the Church alone in a multi-religious world.

A leading Asian theologian from a different cultural background is **Kosuke Koyama**, who was born in Tokyo in **1929**, and whose grandfather was converted to Christianity from Buddhism. Koyama writes of 'Three Modes of Christian Presence', which he describes as stumbling presence, the discomforted presence and the unfree presence. Stumbling because an unshaken house cannot properly bear witness to the earthquake that is happening; discomforted because Christians cannot bear witness to 'the source of all comfort' without involving themselves in Christ's discomfort on the cross; and unfree because Christians must engage in all aspects of life in obedience to Christ's example.

Koyama believes that the central problems in the world are idolatry and greed, which are particularly endemic in modern industrial society. He emphasises how much Buddhist philosophy and approach to life can contribute, particularly to the issue of combating greed. He insists on the need to contextualise, and the insights to be gained from other religions, including Buddhism, for an under-standing of reality. Koyama advances an agenda for Asian theology which, he argues, needs to address four issues in particular: its understanding of neocolon-isation and the effects upon Christianity in Asia since **1945**; Church history and tradition from an Asian perspective; the relationship between East and West, and North and South; and a mutual understanding between different faiths.

Bibliography

T. Balasuriya, *Planetary Theology*, SCM, London (1984)

Philip Berryman, *Liberation Theology*, Tauris, London (1987)

John B. Cobb Jr and David Roy Griffin, *Process Theology: An Introductory Exposition*, West-minster John Knox Press (1999)

Mary Daly, *Beyond God The Father*, The Women's Press, London (1985)

Enrique D. Dussel, *A History of the Church in Latin America: Colonialism to Liberation (1492–1979)* Wm B Eerdmans Publishing Co. (1982)

J.W. de Gruchy, *The Church Struggle in South Africa*, SPCK, London (1979)

Gustavo Gutierrez, *A Theology of Liberation*, SCM, London (1971)

D. Hampson, *Theology and Feminism*, Blackwell, Oxford (1990)

Ann Loades, *Feminist Theology: A Reader*, SPCK, London (1990)

John Macquarrie, *Twentieth Century Religious Thought*, SCM, London (1981)

Dean G. Peerman and Martin E. Marty, *A Handbook of Christian Theologies*, Nashville (1984)

A. Pieris, *An Asian Theology of Liberation*, Continuum International Publishing Group (1988)

Rosemary Radford Ruether, *Liberation Theology*, Paulist Press (1972)

Rosemary Radford Ruether, *Sexism and God-Talk: Towards a Feminist Theology*, Beacon Press (1983)

Stanley Samartha (Ed.), *Living Faiths and the Ecumenical Movement*, Geneva (1971)

Theo Witvliet, *Africa in the Sun: An Introduction to Liberation Theology in the Third World*, London (1985)

■ Ⅴ II Faith in practice

From New Testament times, Christianity has been a faith that not only seeks to teach about God and salvation in Jesus Christ, but also to show how followers of Christ are to conduct their lives, whether corporately or individually. The technical name for this area of study is *ethics*.

Ethics is not just a Christian concern. Whenever anyone making a decision allows himself to be swayed by anything other than naked self-interest, he is making a decision that involves an ethical judgement. Ethics is about deciding the best course of action from a range of alternatives. People make those decisions on the basis of their own particular worldview, whether religious or secular. Ethics may be personal or corporate; it is a concern of individuals but it can also be a concern of people when they act together with others, as Nation States for example, multinational corporations or as institutions within a State such as trade unions, businesses or Churches. Although ethics is theoretically about deciding the best way to behave, it can often become a tool by which one group oppresses another. For example, some feminist thinkers maintain that sexual ethics has not been used to promote a life-enhancing holiness but as a means of ensuring the continued subordination of women. To ensure that ethics is not simply a means by which a powerful group imposes its will upon another, the question 'Who benefits?' must be asked.

Ethics has two main branches: that of clarifying the fundamental principles upon which decisions have to be based (theoretical ethics), and that of outlining how these principles work in specific instances (applied ethics). Underlying all this is the more philosophical question of how we make these decisions at all. What is conscience? What is the basis of authority? What is reason?

In this chapter we shall consider briefly the various sources of Christian ethics, and then move on to look at the discussions that have ranged on ethical matters throughout the history of the Church. We conclude with a survey of twentieth century concerns.

11.1 Sources of Christian ethics

David Cook, in *The Moral Maze*, identifies the sources of Christian Ethics as:

(i) *The Creation*
(a) *Natural law*, i.e. God's law as expressed in mankind and the world around us.
(b) The fact that we are *created in God's image* and answerable to God.

(c) Our *conscience*, described by many as 'the voice of God within us', that gives us an initial awareness of right and wrong. We should let our conscience be our guide.

(d) *God's creation ordinances*, such as the commands to man to be steward over nature, and for men and women to complement each other.

(e) *The Fall* – the account of the Fall suggests that morality cannot be constructed on the basis of Creation alone.

(ii) *The Old Testament*

(a) The *Covenant* that God entered into with his people, and the commandments and law which represent man's side of the bargain.

(b) The *Wisdom Literature* – Proverbs, Job, Ecclesiastes and the Song of Solomon – contain considerable detail on a wide range of practical problems.

(c) The *Prophets*, again a rich source of moral teaching.

(iii) *The New Testament*

(a) God's *Revelation* in Jesus, who died for the redemption of mankind.

(b) *Kingdom ethics*, the hallmark of the Kingdom being love, with Jesus as the ultimate example of how men ought to live.

(c) *Paul's ethics*: whilst Paul was not seeking to present a systematic text on ethics, we can discern ethical principles from his writing. He does set out patterns of moral teaching and offers means of resolving ethical questions.

(d) *Pastoral epistles* – these were written to Christians who found themselves in particular situations, and contain a host of exhortations and condemnations.

(iv) *Traditions*

An examination of tradition enables us to benefit both from lessons that have been learned and mistakes that have been made. They reflect the heritage and experience of the Church. Jesus himself sought to build upon, not destroy, the Law and tradition of the Jewish faith.

(v) *The Spirit*

The New Testament teaches us that God's Holy Spirit rests in our hearts and minds to guide us into the truth. The Spirit was the one who empowered the early Christians at Pentecost. Claims by individuals to be acting on the authority of the Spirit must, however, be probed and tested to establish their authenticity.

(iv) *The Church*

The Church, the community of God's people, is the context in which the Spirit moves, and is the means of checking claims about the Spirit's directions, and of discerning the true will of God.

11.2 Old Testament ethics

At first sight, the early Christians were simply another subset of first century Judaism who appropriated a common tradition in the light of their experience of Jesus and the Holy Spirit. In common with every other group within first century Judaism, it was 'the Law and the Prophets' which provided the background to the young Church's discussion of how it should live. So it is with a consideration of Old Testament ethics that we must start.

In different parts of the Old Testament we see differing stresses. The prophets call constantly for a radical faithfulness to the one God, shown in justice and mercy to others. The Law and the histories enjoin a faithfulness to God, shown in obedience to the cultic and practical demands of the Law. The way of the wisdom writers is common sense verging on natural law, while in the Psalms we glimpse a range of responses: sometimes the King and sometimes the Law seem to be the focus of the people's religious life.

The central feature of the Old Testament is the Sinaitic Covenant. The overriding duty of the people whom God had designated for his own was to live in obedience to that covenant out of fidelity to God. As it is recorded, the history of the people seems to be a constant relearning of what faithfulness to the covenant entailed. Was it cultic or ethical obedience? The two need not be opposed but the lament of the prophets seems often to be that the people rely on their cultic relationship with God and forget the demands of holiness. In the Old Testament, holiness and righteousness lie in the quality of one person's relationship with others. God's righteousness also was demonstrated in relationship with others: in being faithful to the covenant promises, just as the people's lay in the fulfilling of its demands.

11.2.1 Old Testament attitudes to wealth

Biblical sources: Lev 25: 23–34; Deut 15: 1–11; 23: 24–5; 24: 10–15, 17–22; 26: 1–15; 28: 1–14

Possessions and property were seen as God's gifts and were therefore to be enjoyed. There is no hint that to enjoy the results of one's hard work is in anyway sinful, although it is recognised that on their own they do not bring happiness. God, it was felt, would continue to prosper the work of those who kept his commands, although the book of Job shows that this was being increasingly questioned despite the fact that the writer or editor could not refrain from the happy ending!

God's primary gift to the people, family by family, was the land – 'a land flowing with milk and honey'; to enjoy all that it produced was to receive the promise of God to the Patriarchs. There were laws that regulated the selling of land to protect the poor from losing their stake in the land to the rich. Those who bought land from others were supposed to return it at the seventh year, although whether these regulations were ever put into effect is not known. Protection of the poor was enshrined in legislation and lauded by the prophets. While wealth was God's good gift, there are warnings against putting trust in material things; the good things of creation are to be enjoyed, but only God is to be the people's security.

11.2.2 Old Testament attitudes to power

Biblical sources: Ps 2: 6; 132: 11–12; Josua 1: 16–18; Judges 4: 9; I Sam 8: 4–22; Nehemiah 13: 23–7

Where was the ideal locus of power? Different parts of the Old Testament give different answers. The Psalms depict the view that God had given the King in

Jerusalem power to rule, enthroned on Zion, YHWH's holy hill, YHWH's son and his representative on earth. The Deuteronomic histories, on the other hand, reflect the view that the King was a mistake. God wished to rule the people himself through judges and prophets, and only appointed a King because the people desired to be like other nations. In both traditions, power can only be exercised with God's help and wisdom. There was both a naive acceptance of the exercise of authority being one of God's gift to them, and a growing understanding of how this power corrupts. The final fall of Jerusalem and with it the disappearance of the monarchy were a watershed. Israel did not have an independent King again during the Old Testament period. Some groups longed for the Davidic monarchy to be re-established; others, influenced by the writers of the Deuteronomic histories, saw rule by foreigners as God's punishment for the idolatry and disobedience of the Kings. They felt it was the duty of the loyal Jew to follow the Law and submit to those in authority whoever they were, as long as their demands did not entail disobeying the commands of God.

11.2.3 Old Testament attitudes to family life and sexual matters

Biblical sources: Ex 20: 17; 21: 4–12; Num 27: 1–11; 30: 1–16; 36: 1–12; Deut 21: 10–14, 15–17; 22: 13–30; 25 5–10; Judges 4: 1–24; 19

A woman, under the Law, belonged to a man, whether it be her father, her husband, her son or her nearest male relative, called a 'next-of-kin'. She was his responsibility. If a man wished to marry he had to buy his bride from her father or work for her. Concubines were also mentioned and the practice regulated. Having had sex with a woman, a man was not at liberty to sell her to someone else. The children of both wives and concubines were the man's responsibility and they had rights above and beyond the popularity or status of their mothers.

The sexual behaviour of both men and women was regulated, although women's behaviour more strictly so. She had only one partner – her husband or her master. Although a man could have more than one partner, he was supposed to be in an official relationship with her. She had to be his. Sex with another man's wife, betrothed or concubine, was punishable by death. If a man had sex with a woman while she was still her father's responsibility he was obliged to marry her, on payment, if she was free to do so; if she was not, he was punishable by death. If a woman was raped in the countryside she was given the benefit of the doubt; if the attack took place in a town she was punished, since the Law stated that in the town she should have been able to raise the alarm! These regulations are mainly geared to protecting inheritance by controlling the sexual behaviour of women. If a man died childless, his widow was passed to the nearest willing and available male relative to give her a son on his behalf. There is an attempt to protect women from the worst abuses of the system: in the absence of a male heir, women were allowed to inherit but, since what they owned belonged to their husband, they were only allowed to marry within the tribe.

The Law obviously represents the theory of sexual mores – it is the narrative sections of the Old Testament which provide evidence of how matters worked out in practice. This holds even when they relate incidents that did not happen, because they reveal attitudes that were current at the time of writing/composition.

11.2.4 Old Testament attitudes to violence

Biblical sources: Ex 20: 13; 21: 12–27; Deut 19: 1–13

Violence was strictly controlled. The life and safety of the chosen people and those who 'sojourned' among them was to be respected. Every killing or injury had to be atoned for, although in the regulations concerning cities of refuge there was an attempt to differentiate between actions committed with intent, accidents and self-defence. The rules concerning violence were designed to lift society from operating only at the level of blood feud and reprisal. However, as with other aspects of Old Testament ethics, the narrative passages give a clearer picture of practice than the rules themselves, which may or may not have been kept. The rules also only apply to an Israelite or resident alien; foreigners were fair game.

11.3 Jesus' ethical teaching

As Jesus left no writings, the only source we have for his teaching on ethical matters is the New Testament. While the ethical concerns of the Gospel writers inevitably influenced their portrayals of Jesus' teaching, they did give important themes, such as the Kingdom of God, far more prominence than elsewhere in the New Testament. This does suggest that the Gospel writers were recording some traditions that went back to Jesus himself. In evaluating any portrayal of the ethical teaching of Jesus, we must nevertheless ask ourselves: is this the Jesus that the early Christians remember or a Jesus that they have created?

11.3.1 The context of Jesus' ethical teaching

Biblical sources for Jesus' general attitude to ethics:

Proclamation of the Kingdom	Matt 4: 17, 23–5
Attitude to Law	Matt 5: 17–20
Confrontations about points of Law	Matt 5: 31–2; Mark 3: 1–20; 7: 9–13; Luke 6: 1–5; John 5: 6–10; 7: 22–4
Dismissing of outward show	Matt 6: 1–6; Luke 11: 37–44
Teaching on inner attitude	Matt 5: 21–4
Thoughts on what defiles	Matt 5: 43–8; 9: 10–13; Mark 7: 14–23; Luke 10: 30–7; John 3: 8–9

Preaching the good news of the Kingdom was the thread that bound the ministry of Jesus together. His healing and exorcisms demonstrated that people did not have to live in the domain of darkness – he and those he commissioned had come to set them free. But to be in the Kingdom of God meant living God's way.

So while his proclamation of the Kingdom is a proclamation and demonstration of good news for the sick, the demon-possessed and the outcast, it is not without its cost: *'Repent for the kingdom of God is at hand'* (Matt 4: 17).

Jesus' call to repentance was not a call away from the Jewish heritage: *'Do not think that I have come to abolish the Law and the Prophets; I did not come to abolish but to complete'* (Matt 5: 17). Matthew is generally thought to be the most positive of the Gospels towards the Law but the same point is made in Luke: *'It is easier for heaven and earth to come to an end than for one letter of the law to lose its force'* (Luke 16: 17). Jesus rebukes the Pharisees, not because they observe the Law but because their interpretation of it is faulty: *'You pay tithes of mint and dill and cumin; but you have overlooked the weightier demands of the law – justice, mercy and good faith. It is these you should have practised while not neglecting the other'* (Matt 23: 2). Many of his recorded confrontations with the Pharisees show Jesus reproaching them for the way in which the regulations they have formulated contradict the spirit of the Law they wished to uphold. Jesus stands in the prophetic tradition of Israel when he rebukes those who see obeying God as fulfilling the demands of the cult, rather than following the spirit of the Law in their dealings with others. Matthew sums it up when he twice includes a quote from Moses: *'I require mercy not sacrifice'* (Hos 6: 6 at Matt 9: 13 and 12: 7). Both Matthew and Luke include this summing up of the Law: *'Always treat others as you would like them to treat you'* (Matt 7: 12; Luke 6: 31).

There is little general ethical teaching in the sayings of Jesus because he assumed the Law, and when he taught on such matters it was to deepen people's understanding of what keeping the Law really meant. He taught that what was inside a person had to match up with the outside, because God was not impressed with outward show. This often made Jesus' teaching appear hard because he made it clear that outward conformity to regulation was not sufficient. A man may have refrained from committing murder, but if he is angry with his brother he will be subject to judgement (Matt 5: 21–2). A man may have refrained from the act of adultery, but this was nothing to be proud of if he was continually lusting after other women (Matt 5: 27–8). This rigorist strain can be summed up by the verse from the Sermon on the Mount: *'There must be no limit to your goodness as your heavenly Father's goodness knows no bounds'* (Matt 5: 48). This stress on the state of a person's inner being meant that although Jesus' demands were stringent, the physical constraints on those who wished to live a holy life had disappeared. If holiness and right living started from inside, nothing outside could confer impurity or incur God's displeasure.

Jesus taught that ritual observance did not equate to righteousness. Whilst religious leaders of Jesus' day no doubt accepted that to love your neighbour as yourself was to obey the Law, obedience to this command was rendered impossible if touching a dead body, eating with a less observant Jew, or sitting on a chair previously sat on by a menstruating woman were forbidden. If what was outside could not contaminate, then the person seeking God's way was free to go anywhere and mix with anyone, as Jesus himself demonstrated. Even one's enemies had to be treated as neighbours.

Jesus saw his ministry as ushering in the Kingdom of God. It fulfilled what had gone before and presaged what lay ahead. Most scholars believe that Jesus, as the first Christians after him, expected the end to be imminent. There is no evidence that Jesus expected to be the founder of an extra-Jewish community that would last upwards of 2000 years. It is against this background that Jesus' specific pronouncements on what have come to be seen as ethical issues must be judged. His ethical teaching was geared to helping God's people put into practice more effectively the ethical system they already had for the short time that remained.

11.3.2 Jesus' attitude to wealth

Biblical sources: Matt 6: 2–4; 11: 4–5; 19–21, 24, 25–34; 10: 8–10; 13: 22; 19: 16–28; 25: 35–40; Luke 6: 20–1, 24–5, 34–5; 12: 15–21, 32; 16: 19–31

Common throughout the Old Testament was the idea that if you obeyed God, he would cause you to prosper (e.g. Ps 37: 25). The book of Job shows that right- eousness did not guarantee prosperity but few seemed to doubt that material goods were indeed a sign of God's blessing. Jesus was far more ambivalent. While the criticisms made of him that he was a glutton and a drunkard show that he was not ashamed to enjoy the fruits of creation, his attitude towards ownership was harsher. Though he never condemned wealth and its acquisition, Jesus made it clear that it was a hindrance to entry into God's kingdom, because it inculcated a false sense of security and a neglect of the needs of others. God was the only reli- able source of security; the only use of wealth was to lay up treasure in heaven by giving it away. It is an ethic that the Church has wrestled with ever since.

11.3.3 Jesus' attitude to power

Biblical sources: Matt 6: 41; Mark 10: 42–5; Luke 9: 46–8; 20: 22–5; John 18: 8–11

Jesus said very little about worldly power, and nothing to those who exercised it. He criticised those within his own community who abused the religious authority they had, and he used Gentile rulers as examples of how power ought to be exer- cised. Whatever their limitations, Jesus taught that rulers should be given their due by virtue of the office they hold. In the description of his trial before Pilate in John's Gospel, Jesus states that Pilate's authority derives ultimately from God. In teaching how Christians are to exercise authority in the Church, he puts himself forward as a model: the one who wishes to be the greatest must be the servant of all.

11.3.4 Jesus' attitude to family life and sexual matters

Biblical sources: Matt 5: 27–32; 10: 21, 34–7; 12: 46–50; 19: 3–12; Mark 10: 2–12; Luke 16: 18; John 7: 53 – 8: 1

Despite what has seemed like the Christian obsession with sexual morality, there is little teaching of Jesus on the subject. What little there is concerns adultery and divorce. The debates on divorce among the rabbinical schools are the back- ground to the discussion in the Gospel. The Law allowed a man to divorce his wife (Deut 24: 1–4); it did not specify the grounds on which he might do so, and this was accordingly a matter of considerable debate. The disciples of Rabbi

Shammar only allowed divorce on the grounds of a wife's unchastity, whereas the school of Hillel allowed it on almost any grounds. Jesus is being asked to decide. In such a context, the debate has become not so much about the nature of marriage, but the disposability of wives. In a society where women had no independent status, being either the responsibility of their husbands or fathers, brothers-in-law, brothers or sons, such a question was vital to the security of women. Jesus is firm, women cannot simply be disposed of:

> *Moses permitted you to divorce your wives because your hearts were hard. But it was not like this from the beginning. I tell you that anyone who divorces his wife, except for marital unfaithfulness and marries another woman, commits adultery.*
>
> Matthew 19: 8

This is in line with the status he accords to women throughout the Gospels. The complete prohibition we find in Mark is qualified in Matthew, but even so the disciples are recorded as finding this standard impossibly high. Jesus' methodology in ethical debates of this sort is not to get embroiled in points of law, but to return to first principles.

Jesus' attitude to family life was ambivalent. More important were the new relationships inaugurated by the Gospel and an unstinting obedience to the call of God. Celibacy was mentioned in a positive light as a possible response to the message of the Kingdom. Living in imminent expectation of the end, Jesus did not have to reckon with the possibility that marriage might be contemplated after the call to discipleship.

11.3.5 Jesus' attitude towards women

In an era in which women were seen very much as unimportant and subservient, Jesus' attitude to women was radical. This is apparent not only from his teaching on adultery and divorce, but also from his anointing by the 'sinful woman' (Luke 7: 36) and his willingness to teach women (Luke 11: 38).

It is striking that the authors of the Gospels chose to acknowledge the presence of women at the Crucifixion and the Resurrection. John records that it was Jesus' mother, his mother's sister and Mary of Magdalene who stood near the Cross – of the twelve Apostles it was only James who was present at the Crucifixion. Similarly it was Mary of Magdalene and other women to whom Jesus appeared (Matt 28; Mark 16: 9; John 20: 10). In a culture and time when a woman's testimony was given substantially less credence than that of a man, it is noteworthy that the Gospel writers chose to include these accounts.

11.3.6 Jesus' attitude to violence

Biblical sources: Matt 26: 51–4; Luke 6: 27–30

Jesus' opinion on the matter of an individual resorting to violence is clear: if he sees even an enemy as a neighbour whom he has a responsibility to love, violence is prohibited. How this extrapolates to the wider scale has been a matter of debate ever since. The saying 'those who live by the sword die by the sword' in Matthew 26 seems clear, and the early Church certainly remembered Jesus as forbidding Christians to take part in violence of any sort, a prohibition they maintained at least until the third century.

11.3.7 Jesus' attitude towards forgiveness and repentance

It is clear from Jesus' teachings that whilst we are to 'forgive those who trespass against us', this is not the full picture: forgiveness goes hand in hand with acknowledgement of wrongdoing and repentance. In the Parable of the Prodigal Son (Luke 15: 21), the son said to his father:

> *Father, I have sinned against heaven and against you. I am no longer worthy to be your son.*

Whilst in Matthew 5: 38–42, Jesus exhorts us to 'turn the other cheek', elsewhere Jesus again emphasises the importance of acknowledgement of sins and repentance. In Matthew 18: 15, Jesus teaches that if a brother sins against us, we should show him his fault. If that does not work, we should enlist the help of others. If the brother still refuses to listen, he should take the matter to the Church. If the brother remains obdurate, we are told to treat him as a pagan, or a tax collector.

By advocating forgiveness and repentance, Jesus was not seeking to deny the vulnerable access to justice. In the Parable of the Persistent Widow (Luke 18), a widow who repeatedly requests justice from a judge against her adversary, is rewarded for her perseverance.

11.4 Ethical teaching in the New Testament

Biblical sources: Rom 6; 8: 1–4; 12: 1–3; 13: 9–10; I Cor 7: 29–31; Gal 5: 13–25; Jam 2

Just as Jesus was able to assume the ethical standard of the Law, so in the rest of the New Testament the ethical debate does not lie in discussion of what does or does not make for holiness. Not only were the standards of conduct enjoined in the Law assumed, but the highest morality of the 'Gentiles' was seen to concur with it. Discussion lay on how this standard of holiness might be achieved. Paul, whether consciously or not, developed Jesus' idea of holiness coming from the inside. Following the written code leads only to sin; a Christian is one who has died both to sin and to the demands of the Law by identification with Jesus' death in baptism. From the waters of baptism he rises to live a new life, finding that, as he learns to follow the promptings of the Spirit, the demands of the Law will be more than met in the life that ensues. Paul would not have disagreed with the writer to the epistle of James that faith had to show itself in action, but he would have asked how the writer thought it was possible for them to keep the 'law of love'.

Specific ethical debate in the New Testament concerns problems that arise in trying to serve God in pagan cultures. Examples include Paul's discussions of whether or not Christians should eat meat sacrificed to idols, and areas where the new freedom of the Gospel might be seen to clash with Jewish or Gentile codes, such as the behaviour of women. As the immediacy of the Parousia receded, so more detailed instruction on family, church organisation and relationship to the secular authorities was needed. The ethical teaching of the New Testament is concerned with how individuals should behave. The Church has found it sometimes difficult to agree whether and how that can be extrapolated to a wider scale.

11.4.1　New Testament attitudes to wealth

Biblical sources: Acts 2: 43–7; 4: 32 – 5: 11; 6: 1; 10: 1–4

New Testament writers seemed aware of the potential snare of wealth. Acts suggests that in the early years many held goods in common, while throughout the New Testament wealth is seen as something to be shared. The rich were to feel responsible for the poor and the Church was not to accord higher status to the rich. This egalitarianism was not to be used as a cover for idleness; work had a value in and of itself.

11.4.2　New Testament attitudes to power

Biblical sources: Acts 12: 1–5, 21–3; 13: 19–23; 14: 5; 16: 22; Rom 13: 1–7; I Cor 6: 7*ff*; II Cor 13: 10; I Tim 2: 1–3; 3: 1–23; I Pet 2: 13–15; 5: 1–4

Three different New Testament writers are all clear that secular authorities are sanctioned by God and are therefore to be obeyed and prayed for. They are God's instruments for ensuring peace, tranquillity and justice. However, St. Paul rebukes the Corinthian Christians for resorting to the secular courts in internal disputes – Christians are to respect those in power but to govern their own affairs as far as possible.

The Church must respect its teachers and elders, who are to be dedicated to the Church's welfare and the purity of the Gospel tradition. They are to uphold it by their lives and words. The local congregations seemed to have had a system of presbyters/overseers and deacons, and to recognise the authority of the Apostles from the wider Church.

11.4.3　New Testament attitudes to family life and sexual matters

Biblical sources: I Cor 5: 1*ff*; 7: 1*ff*; Eph 5: 21 – 6: 9; Col 3: 18 – 4: 1; Titus 2: 5; I Pet 2: 18 – 3: 7

Although Jesus' own attitude to women was revolutionary, the early Church's insistence that nothing should 'detract' from the impact of the Gospel ensured that the Church did little to mitigate the patriarchy of its time. Wives are still to submit to their husbands, who in turn are to love and care for their wives. Mutual respect and responsibility were encouraged. The standards of behaviour enjoined in the Law were assumed to hold good, and great stress was placed on sexual fidelity. The early Christians seem to have moved away from Jesus' own ambivalent attitude to family life, and codes of behaviour for Christian households are included in a number of New Testament letters.

11.4.4 New Testament attitudes to violence

Biblical sources: Rom 12: 19–20; I Cor 4: 12–13

Little is said directly on the subject of violence, but love is stressed as the principle by which actions are to be judged.

11.4.5 New Testament attitudes to the resolution of disputes

Any suggestion that Paul condemned attempts by an injured party to obtain justice is wholly misconceived. It arises out of a misreading of I Corinthians 6, where he emphasises that believers should have their disputes decided by judges appointed from their own ranks, rather than having their conflicts resolved by non-believers. An injured party is not prevented from obtaining justice, but if the offender is a fellow believer, the dispute should be resolved within the Church. This corresponds to Jesus' position (see section 11.3.7).

11.5 The ethics of the early Church

By **250 CE**, Eusebius, the Church historian, tells us that the Church in Rome supported more than 1500 widows and poor Christians. The Church stressed the importance of putting faith into practice. Ethical guidance was important and had to be defined in greater detail, as the Church increasingly contained those unfamiliar with the ethical standards of the Old Testament Law. Freedom in Christ was in tension with the increasingly authoritarian nature of the Church, whose leaders felt the importance of retaining Christian distinctiveness in a pagan world. The pressure they felt from pagan hedonism, the example of Stoic detachment from material things and ascetic trends in gnosticism, led Christian ethics in an increasingly austere direction. Tertullian distinguishes between 'advice' (such as Paul's admonition to remain 'as he is') and an 'order' (for example, that partners must not separate). By the time of Ambrose, there was a distinction between ordinary duties incumbent upon all, and perfect ones voluntarily taken up by those who wished to be perfect, resulting in a two-tier morality. This applied in particular to the question of whether or not to marry, and it contributed to the falling status of women as they were felt to be more material and less spiritual than men.

At the start of this period, right behaviour consisted of fulfilling the demands of the Law of Moses in a way dictated by the memories of Jesus, and then the Apostles. By the time of Ambrose, the insights of pagan philosophers had also been taken into account in, for example, his account of the cardinal virtues, prudence, temperance, courage and justice, which he took from Cicero, or his borrowing of his 'just war' theory.

11.5.1 Early Church attitudes to wealth

A sense of responsibility towards the poor, taken together with the awareness of the corrupting nature of wealth, meant that Christians were advised to give away what they could and share what remained. Perfection lay in giving away everything but, as this was not practical for all, a two-tier system evolved. Charity, honesty and self-discipline were required of everyone but perfection lay in accepting greater renunciation voluntarily. Giving away was an end in itself but supporting those in need was also important. This did not simply mean charity: those capable of work were found it and those incapable were supported if they had no relatives of their own to depend on.

11.5.2 Early Church attitudes to power

The traditional acceptance of the State as God's instrument was being tempered by a growing awareness of its hostility or potential hostility to the Church. Obedience was still enjoined except in matters that conflicted with conscience when the State was to be resisted, to the point of martyrdom if necessary. Church authorities had to restrain some extremists who provoked confrontation with the State as they regarded martyrdom as the ultimate renunciation to be embraced.

11.5.3 Early Church attitudes to family life and sexual matters

There was little argument about the standards required of those married or the structure of Christian households. Chastity was imperative and obedience to the head of the household, the 'pater familias', assumed. Discussion centred on whether marriage was desirable at all! It was recognised as good because it was one of God's creation ordinances and necessary for producing children. There remained, however, a fundamental suspicion among many of the male Church leaders towards an institution so physical and so bound up with sexuality that they perceived as their moral Achilles' heel. As we have noted, this lead to a lowering of the status of women.

11.5.4 Early Church attitudes to violence

While soldiers who became Christians were allowed to finish their term, Tertullian was vehemently opposed to Christians signing up and Origen did not deny the charge of pacifism. Soldiers were involved in meting out civil punishment as well as in wars, and the Church was implacably opposed to the death penalty. Soldiers were sometimes martyred for refusing to shed blood and the Emperor Diocletian purged the army of all Christians who refused to make sacrifice to the Emperor. In the fourth century, the attitude of some Christians began to change and by the end of the century the Emperor Theodosius was purging the army of pagans. Ambrose christianises Cicero's 'just war' theory but, although Ambrose accepts the need for war as a policy of State, he still feels that Christians and especially priests should be pacifists.

11.6   From Augustine to the Middle Ages

Augustine believed that humanity's chief end was to seek happiness which could only finally be found in God. Loving God is humanity's purpose and this is inseparable from loving one's neighbour, summed up in his famous maxim 'love and do what you will'. He expounded love in terms of the four cardinal virtues that Ambrose had taken over from Cicero. The controversy is known as the Pelagian crisis (see Chapter 5, section 5.15) after the British monk, Pelagius, who felt Augustine's doctrine preached cheap grace and destroyed the moral responsibility of the individual. Theologians continued to debate the nature of the will and human responsibility before God. Anselm disagreed with Augustine that the fall had destroyed the human ability to will the good, but saw it as only a potential until activated by grace. For Aquinas, too, God's grace was necessary to make it possible for a person both to seek and then to follow the good: his prevenient and his co-operative grace. He was aware of the need to defend human responsibility in the face of the sovereignty of God and envisaged God allowing his will to be done through people's chosen decisions.

The dichotomy between what was required of the ordinary Christian and what was taken on voluntarily by those seeking perfection was continued by Augustine. Indeed, it continued to plague Christian ethical teaching until the Reformation. Voluntary renunciation and service became the hallmark of the monastic movement, which started as a response to the perceived worldliness of the Church and became the means by which the two-tier morality became institutionalised. Because of the importance of hard work within the monastic system, many houses became rich and the movement needed continual reform. For the individual, renunciation became an end in itself, irrespective of the good done by what was given. However it was recognised that not everyone could or would renounce the world entirely and so an elaborate system of guidance, consisting mainly of enumerating sins and prescribing penances for specific failings, grew up alongside monasticism for those still 'in the world'. Christianity gradually became more and more external for the majority practising it: there was an upsurge in mysticism, but the inner life was mostly seen as the prerogative of an elite group of monks and nuns. By the end of the Middle Ages, what had begun as a desire to direct people's conduct in any and every matter had ended in sterile observance, which provided the seedbed of the Reformation.

Like Augustine, Aquinas believed that humanity was intended to seek its highest good in God. He believed in divine law in the mind of God, by which he created a moral Universe whose natural law could be discovered by insight and appropriated to specific circumstances by reason working through conscience. But original sin brought uncertainty and doubt, and so God also revealed his Commandments. Aquinas follows the two-tier scheme in which there are precepts for all to follow, which deal with how to live rightly, but also counsels of perfection for those who wish to follow perfection and abandon the world.

11.6.1 Attitudes to wealth

Suspicion of wealth continued throughout this period. Augustine saw private property as part of the fallen world. The ideal would be to hold all things in common, something he thought was only practical for monks and nuns. Those who were rich were to use their wealth for the benefit of others. He realised that a poor person could be equally corrupted by the desire for wealth, as a rich person by possession of wealth. Aquinas, eight hundred years later, also believed that common ownership was original and that theft driven by need was justified because the right to private property was qualified by the duty to share.

11.6.2 Attitudes to power

While Augustine continued to believe that those in authority had their power from God, he was distrustful of the Roman Empire and condemned its immorality and self-seeking. Those in authority did God's will only so far as they submitted to the true God. Christians had a higher duty to obey God if it came to a conflict, because they belonged to the City of God. All people lived with an end in view: either it was to love God or it was to fulfil their own earthly desires. The City of God and the earthly city were not necessarily synonymous with the Church and State, since Augustine recognised that not all the baptised lived for God, just as not all those outside the Church lived only for themselves. When the State allowed itself to be guided by the Church, and promoted justice and the welfare of its citizens, it fulfilled its God-given purpose.

After Augustine, there was a growth in Canon Law and penitential manuals that endeavoured to guide the Christian in any and every circumstance, including the rights and duties of rulers and subjects. That Christian subjects ought to obey and Christian rulers take notice of Church leaders was taken for granted. Aquinas took the social nature of humanity for granted and therefore civil organisation would have been willed by God regardless of the Fall. Government exists to serve the common good and its law should derive from natural law, otherwise the Christian has no obligation to obey it.

11.6.3 Attitudes to family life and sexual matters

Despite the statement by the Council of Nicaea that conjugal intercourse was equivalent to chastity, Augustine's view of original sin (and perhaps his own experience of sexual temptation) led him to believe that every act of sexual intercourse was tainted from one generation to the next. Thus he was bound to see virginity and abstinence as a higher calling than marriage. Few doubted this in the following centuries, just as few denied the rightness of the patriarchal system as it existed. Marriage ceased to be seen as a private option. Aquinas, eight hundred years later, also saw the options for a Christian as a natural life guided by the moral precepts of the Church or the higher calling of virginity and abstinence. In the eleventh century, celibacy was required by the Church in the West of its priests as well as of the religious.

11.6.4 Attitudes to violence

While Augustine was under no misapprehension about the nature of the State, he believed that, in the role God had given it after the Fall as the guarantor of peace and justice, it was right that it should both wield the civil sword and wage war if necessary. The long-standing Christian disapproval of the death sentence had been overturned and, despite its horror to which Christian writers were not blind, war had come to be accepted as a tool of foreign policy. It was Augustine who formulated the 'just war' theory, which he drew from Ambrose and Cicero, and which the Church has used ever since. It averred that the State may wage war if the war is defensive, a means of last resort and declared with adequate warning. It must not be fought for conquest or power, but for a just peace. Only soldiers may be involved and all prisoners taken or those who surrender must be spared. That violence was justified in certain circumstances became so much a part of the Christian consciousness that when the Byzantine Emperor appealed to the Pope for support against the muslims in 1095, the result was the start of the Crusades. Aquinas saw the State's violence as legitimate so long as the cause was just and the intention in waging war 'moral', that is, to secure a just peace, or the restitution of property stolen.

11.7 Ethics in the Reformation and Counter-Reformation

The various theologies that sprang up in this period had differing doctrines of 'man', of sin and of atonement, and therefore had differing accounts of what constituted a good life and how a person was enabled to live it. Luther's 'discovery' of the Pauline doctrine of justification through faith did not make him lax on ethical issues. He believed that when a person had been regenerated they would, by the in-dwelling Spirit, know both what pleased God and how to live it out. In Calvin's scheme, living a disciplined and obedient life of love for God and one's neighbour was the way to show proof of one's election. The Roman Catholic Church, also aware of the need to purge itself of medieval excesses, stressed the importance of an inner spirituality and an outward righteousness. While Francis de Sales encouraged everyone to make a daily personal devotion, Counter-Reformation ethics was geared to giving practical teaching on what constituted a Christian life. Manuals gave guidance on specific issues, a procedure known as 'casuistry', which has fallen into disrepute because of the tortuous nature of some of the reasoning used. It originally meant 'case by case' guidance for the ordinary Christian.

11.7.1 Attitudes to wealth

The reformers abhorred the 'double standard' in Christianity; holiness was as incumbent upon the cobbler as the priest and thus the ultimate ideal was no longer seen as total abstention from the world. However, Luther was still aware that wealth and its acquisition could easily become one's God. He maintained the Catholic Church's implacable opposition to usury, unlike Calvin who saw gaining a moderate interest from the loaning of one's capital to be as legitimate as obtaining rent from the loaning of one's land, so long as the poor were exempted. Calvin saw it as a Christian duty to make the most of one's resources and therefore saw no harm in acquiring money so long as one was moderate in one's consumption, fair in one's means of attaining it and generous to the poor. But giving away had ceased to be an end in itself and indiscriminate charity was thought wrong. For sects like the Anabaptists, on the other hand, all notion of private property was wrong.

For Luther, one's necessary work, however 'secular', became a vocation; for Calvin, physical and mental work even beyond what was necessary were duties. Some argue that this change in attitude facilitated the later rise of capitalism.

11.7.2 Attitudes to power

Luther developed a 'two kingdoms' theory. True Christians did not need the law in any of its forms because the fruit of their faith would be shown in the righteousness of their lives which would far exceed anything demanded by law. Nevertheless, since the majority of people were not Christians, the State was vital for the maintenance of an ordered society. God ruled Christians through the Gospel of Christ, but others God ruled through the civil authorities which, however secular, were divinely ordered. The government, usually exercised by a monarch, had a responsibility to ensure peace, security and justice. Calvin also saw the State as put in place by God to ensure a good ordered society. It was the duty of a Christian to obey the authorities so long as their government was just and in conformity with God's Law. He favoured rule by an aristocracy. He regarded law, which reached its highest expression in the Law of Moses, as a necessary guide for Christians as well as a restraint for others, and the means by which society could be brought into conformity with God's standards.

11.7.3 Attitudes to family life and sexual matters

In disregarding the traditional 'double standard', the reformers rehabilitated marriage as an acceptable way of life for those wishing to obey God, but their inherited distrust of sex could be seen in their counsels to avoid 'excess' even within marriage. This restoration of status to marriage should have enhanced the status of women but the need to submit to those God had put in authority, including husbands and fathers, was taken for granted by all thinkers at this time. So, in practice, by rejecting the monastic life (because of its abuses and its link with the system of two-tier morality), the reformers denied women what had been an independent sphere of authority.

11.7.4 Attitudes to violence

The prohibition against individual violence continued but most Protestant and Catholic thinking saw violence as a legitimate tool in the hands of the secular authorities in their attempt to keep peace and eradicate lawlessness. The death penalty was the ultimate sanction internally and a 'just', defensive war was a necessary weapon against threats from outside. Some fringe Protestant sects like the Anabaptists returned to the pacifism of the early Church and were persecuted accordingly.

11.8 After the Reformation to the end of the nineteenth century

By breaking with the authority of the ecclesiastical powers, the reformed churches had undermined the concept of an authority external to the individual. Subsequent Protestant ethics has been, in part, a search for a moral authority. It has also continued the debate, begun by Augustine, as to the status of human beings as moral agents. From the early seventeenth century, ethics was also being discussed by those who had rejected Christianity, both Protestant and Catholic. **Thomas Hobbes (1588–1679)** thought that our ethical choices were dictated by a social contract that was held together by self-interest. He believed that even seemingly benevolent actions were prompted by a desire to salve one's conscience or an understanding of what it would be like to be oneself in the particular circumstances one was seeking to ameliorate.

Richard Hooker (1554–1600) designated reason as the faculty in human beings which enables them to receive God's revelation. Reason became a key concept, developed by Christian and non-Christian thinkers alike. It was used to supply both a source of authority and a justification for seeing human beings as able to function morally.

Some, such as the Cambridge Platonists and their immediate successors the Latitudinarians, felt that God had created a rational moral Universe and that therefore reason could be used to deduce the timeless moral principles by which our lives should be governed. In their search for a simple faith as a reaction to the dogmatism of the previous age, they stressed the centrality of ethics. For example, **John Tillotson** (Archbishop of Canterbury, **1691–95**) thought that the purpose of Christianity was to reform people's natures. The end of the seventeenth century saw the beginnings of the controversy with the Deists (see Chapter 8, section 8.5) who saw reason not as the handmaid of revelation, as thinkers like **John Locke (1632–1704)** had assumed, but its judge. Thus, in **1696**, **John Toland** argued that reason provided truth which revelation supplemented, and anything in Christianity which did not derive from reason was to be rejected. While laying the foundations for the scepticism and ultimately the nihilism of succeeding centuries, these early rationalists still stressed the importance of ethical behaviour derived from external authority. Locke still believed that the existence of God and an after-life could be derived from reason and that belief in eternal reward or punishment provided the stimulus for ethical behaviour. By the end of the seventeenth century, however, there were those, such as the third **Earl of Shaftesbury**, (1671–1713) who began to hold that ethical choices were a matter of taste: each person did what seemed right to himself or herself, guided by conscience, which was analogous to the aesthetic sense of that person. The moral value of an action lay in the action itself and not in any universal, and could be perceived by a person's conscience. Underlying all these ideas was the belief that human beings are responsible moral agents, capable of both taking and sticking to ethical judgements.

There were, of course, those who continued to hold more traditional Christian beliefs in this period. The Church of Scotland, for example, regulated the morals of the people with particular strictness and vigour, as Calvin had done in Geneva. But those most prominent in their contribution to the discussion of ethics were the Puritans and the Friends. Puritans were found in both the Episcopal and Presbyterian wings of the Church and were characterised by a Calvinistic personal discipline and attention to the needs of others. They believed firmly in the primacy of revelation and disagreed with the prevailing optimistic view of humanity. They held that humanity was totally depraved because of original sin and that even what seemed like good works were abhorrent to God when carried out without God's grace. They were still in reaction to the Catholic belief in the efficacy of good works. Someone was only able to judge and live rightly once regenerated and with the continual help of God. Their authority was neither reason nor the Church but the Scripture interpreted by an enlightened conscience. Their authority was still external: the God who revealed his will through the Bible, but in practice it was appropriated through the individual.

The Friends further developed the idea of the role of the individual. Although they believed in the sin of Adam being transmitted, they thought it was only imputed to a person once that person had sinned, and that therefore human beings are not inherently depraved. The light of Christ working within could set people free from sin and kindle within them an inner guiding light. They saw that reason and conscience could be misled and that the in-dwelling of Christ was vital in trying to live a righteous life. It is this in-dwelling presence and obedience to it that makes a Christian, not church attendance or affiliation. It was an ethic that demanded both personal holiness and action in society.

As we have seen in Chapter 8, the latter part of the seventeenth century saw an increase in scientific understanding which thinkers had to accommodate. The role envisaged for God declined under the pressure of the new discoveries until he became, for the Deists, simply the one who set the world in motion and who now allows it to run its course. Many traditional doctrines were questioned from both inside and outside the Church but the necessity for moral standards was not. For Deists, the aim of religion was to make people virtuous. They may have argued over the status of revelation with the Latitudinarians but they shared a common approach to ethics, some even believing in judgement after death. Both sides believed that humanity's purpose was to live righteously under the guidance of conscience. **Immanuel Kant** raised humanity's feeling of moral compulsion to an epistemological principle in the continuing Protestant search for an ultimate authority, after the scepticism of **Hume** had toppled reason from its throne.

Philosophers in continental Europe, such as **Diderot**, influenced by Hume, moved increasingly from metaphysics to ethics, which were no longer the prerogative of the Church. Indeed, by the end of the century, many non-conformists were influenced by **Bentham**'s utilitarianism, the moral touchstone of which was the greatest good for the greatest number.

Roman Catholic ethics, or moral theology, continued to rely on traditional sources of authority and consist largely of the exposition of specific cases for use in the confessional. Seminaries were dedicated to producing confessors. There were lively debates between tutiorists and probabiliorists. The former believed in the certainty of a literal application of the law in all matters of doubt, whilst the latter believed that while the presumption always favoured a literal application of law, stronger reasons for seeking the good in a different way could not be ruled out *a priori*. Some were beginning to see that a certain freedom of conscience was needed in matters of doubt. The tutiorist position was held by followers of **Jansen** who believed in a very fierce doctrine of double predestination, a view later condemned by the Church which held firmly to the efficacy of the Cross for all people. Later, 'Jansenist' became an umbrella term to cover all types of moral rigorists in the Church. The sterility of these controversies was offset by a growing movement that sought to bring piety out of the cloister (see Chapter 8, section 8.4).

The eighteenth century has been called the golden age of philanthropy, as many charitable institutions and societies were founded and the thrust towards educating the poor began. Anglican Evangelicals also responded to the challenge of personal holiness and social action, the abolition of slavery being a notable success. The nineteenth century saw the continuation of charitable societies and the foundation of new ones by all sections of the Church, although three-quarters of them were Evangelical foundations. Most were concerned with education, health or self-help. The Church as a body, however, remained aloof from politics and was largely opposed to the Reform Law and unheeding of the desperate conditions produced by industrialisation and the Corn Laws. The morality that the eighteenth century thinkers had proclaimed with almost one voice remained an individual concern.

There were exceptions, such as the clerics who formed 'The Christian Socialist movement' of **1848–54**. They believed in the interrelationship of all humanity and the need for the Church to bear witness. Their teaching was little heeded, although the 'rediscovery' of the importance of the concept of the Kingdom of God in the Gospels by theologians such as Ritschi and Harnack, gave such ideas theological credibility. Whatever the Church's shortcomings, the social and economic plight of the majority of British people became the subject of debate and resolution at Church Congresses and Diocesan Synods. In **1895**, the Diocese of Newcastle passed a resolution that stated that the provision of a living wage for its workers was the first call on the profits of an enterprise. **Hugh Price Hughes**, the Methodist leader in the latter part of the nineteenth century, was working similarly to convince his own denomination of the social nature of the Gospel. A number of Catholic clergy in continental Europe were also seeing the social implications of the faith. In the **1840s**, **Fr Adolph Kopling** formed societies of skilled and apprenticed workmen which tried to influence the spiritual and moral outlook of their members, but also worked towards better economic conditions. Social Catholicism was particularly influential in Belgium, whose Catholic government had introduced legislation to protect women and children in the workforce and institute pensions. By the end of the century, Social Catholicism was mirrored in papal encyclicals, such as *Rerum Novarum*.

Among Protestant thinkers, more was written in these centuries about the philosophy and theology of ethical decision-making than about the specifics of ethics itself. Roman Catholic moral theology, however, has always dealt with specific cases. Our consideration of the various themes will be no more than a general sketch.

11.8.1 Attitudes to wealth

The dominant theologians throughout this period accepted the status quo. Whilst they encouraged works of charity and benevolence, it was accepted that the poor would always be with them. They were slow to realise that economic forces could be controlled and were not as immutable as they perceived the laws of nature to be.

From the Puritans of the post-Reformation period, to the Christian Social Union of the late nineteenth century, there were those who tried to apply what they saw as Gospel principles to the question of wealth. The Friends and the Puritans like **Jonathan Edwards** stressed the importance of hard work and saving, not so as to increase one's standard of living beyond what was necessary, but in order to give to those in need. From the middle of the nineteenth century, many Christians were beginning to appreciate the concept of social justice.

11.8.2 Attitudes to power

Until the Glorious Revolution of **1688** installed William and Mary as monarchs of Great Britain by Act of Parliament, the Church of England had espoused the Divine Right of Kings and the necessary obedience of the subject. Those who stood by this doctrine, and therefore felt they could not swear allegiance to another king during James II's lifetime, left the Church. As the period went on, the Anglican Church became increasingly identified with the State.

The Puritans regarded the State as a God-given institution which was to be obeyed so long as it furthered the will of God: whether it did so or not was a matter for individual conscience. Although the Friends did not fully recognise any authority other than the inner light of Christ, they submitted to the State so long as it did not contradict their consciences. Despite papal denunciation of Elizabeth, English Catholics had largely remained loyal and gradually the legally enshrined prejudices against them were revoked. In continental Europe, the power of the rulers over both Church and State was growing, and most Churches had an ethic of obedience. The Catholic Church was by nature conservative but the turmoil of continental politics in this period made consistency difficult: the papacy was a temporal as well as a spiritual institution. As we have seen in Chapter 8, section 8.7, there was controversy between Gallicans who believed in State control of the Church, and Ultramontanes who believed in the control of all Catholics by the Pope.

11.8.3 Attitudes to family life and sexual matters

Through the seventeenth and eighteenth centuries, most wings of the Church accused society of being dissolute and maintained the traditional patriarchal ethic of Christian family life. Male sexuality had been rescued during the Reformation – to be married was no longer second class. As the period wore on, however, 'nice' women were progressively desexed. Intercourse was seen as something men inflicted on their wives. Christians were at the forefront of the campaign to abolish slavery, but the Church actively opposed the enfranchisement of women. The Reformation had deprived women of the separate sphere they had had in the Convent, and industrialisation increasingly marginalised them in the workforce until it became a status symbol for a man to be able to afford to keep his wife at home.

11.8.4 Attitudes to violence

Little new was added to Christian thinking on this matter except by the Friends. They rekindled Christian pacifism, although they accepted that the unenlightened would be unable to live up to it, thus reintroducing the pre-Reformation 'double-standard'.

11.9 The twentieth century

Roman Catholic moral theology has undergone great changes in the twentieth century but the social Catholicism of the nineteenth century has continued. In Vatican II it was recognised that a holy Christian life could be lived outside a religious house. While the Holy See under **John-Paul II** has remained traditional in its morality, Roman Catholic theologians such as **Bernard Haring** have tried to present a moral theology that remains true, both to the best in Catholic tradition and secular thinking. Instead of morality consisting of following a given set of rules, the importance of an informed conscience acting within a personal relationship with God is recognised.

Protestant ethical thinking has still been preoccupied with the search for authority. **Barth** and **Brunner** rejected human morality and ethical systems as attempts by humanity to decide on their own priorities. Barth stressed that knowing what to do cannot be prescribed outside a situation, but only made known in a living relationship with God. Brunner similarly saw ethics as responding to God in a given situation, but his writing tended to make more of humanity as morally capable and morally responsible than did Barth's. Brunner spoke of divine orders, given in creation, which lay the groundwork for obedience to Christ in specific situations. They are general principles, but God-given, not man-made. They cover marriage, family, labour, economic life, the State, culture and the Church. Similarly **Bonhoeffer** spoke of Divine Mandates of labour, marriage, government and Church, even though he also believed in an ethic which consists of individuals living up to their status as disciples of Christ in every situation that confronts them. Unlike Barth, who believed that making the right decision meant obeying God the Commander, Bonhoeffer believed that the individual had to take responsibility for his own actions.

Protestant ethics began to move away from an exclusive concern with individual holiness; ethics was about decisions made in relationships with others. This can be seen too in situation ethics, the most famous exponent of which was **Joseph Fletcher**. He rejected legalism, arguing that the only condition an act had to meet to be ethical was that it produced the greatest love for the greatest number. No commandment or precept could guide one as to what would be the most loving course of action to take in a given situation, and it might be right to break even the most sacred of taboos to fulfil this criterion of love. Whilst the 'situationist' approaches moral decisions armed with the moral code the he has inherited, the code is merely to assist him in understanding the situation he faces – it is reason that is the instrument of moral judgement. As with Bonhoeffer, it is the individual who makes the decision even though Christ is available as his pattern. This invites the question: what is love and how can we know we are being loving? It also involves the problem of determining the boundaries of the situation facing us. What are the limits in the potentially infinite consequences that we are to take into account for each of the potential decisions open to us? Does everyone's happiness rank the same in our calculations?

One of the greatest advances in the study of ethics in the twentieth century is the growth in ecumenical councils in which differing Christian traditions sought to learn from each other and professional experts on various topics. The World Council of Churches produces a wealth of informed papers to promote action. Promising, too, has been the growth of ethical studies of differing professional practice, such as medicine, law and business. The Church needs to ensure that a Christian ethic is represented in these fields.

11.9.1 Attitudes to wealth

One approach to the global problem created by the consumption of the Northern nations has been the movement to 'live more simply so that others may simply live'. Christians were encouraged to reconsider their lifestyles and to consume less and to give more. They were asked to cut down the amount of energy they used and to make more use of second-hand items. Writers such as **Ron Sider** certainly did not ignore the need for political change, or the need for structural change within the Church. However, these aspects of the thinking tended to be less stressed at a wider church level, as people were attracted to what they thought of as a practical and ultimately less threatening response to twentieth century problems. **Michael Paget-Wilkes** argues if the more affluent Christians took up this call to live voluntarily at a lower level of income, it would not only create a climate for wider economic change, but would also bring to an end the Church's traditional links with the status quo. The spur for most who have written along these lines is the call for justice which resonates throughout the Old Testament, Jesus' own ambivalence about ownership, and the model of holding things 'in common' to be found in Acts. The Bible is seen as authoritative but usually to be assessed within its own context. This calling for Christians to live more simply pre-dated the similar calls to people in the North from environmentally aware groups, but fitted in well with the growing awareness of the ecological crisis.

Liberation theology (see Chapter 10, section 10.5 for a fuller discussion of this topic) has led to an increased awareness among Christians of God's 'bias to the poor'. Consideration of the Bible, particularly the prophetic books of the Old Testament, combined with an experience of poverty, has lead thinkers like **Bishop David Sheppard** and **Chris Sugden** to bridge the chasm among twentieth century evangelicals between those who believed in the salvation of souls, and those who believed in the transformation of society. One of the results of the more positive way in which evangelical Christians viewed social action was the setting up of such bodies as Tear Fund and, more radically, Traidcraft. Tear Fund, although a charity in the more conventional sense of the word, saw that what those trapped by poverty needed as much as material help was self-respect and the chance to control their own destinies, even in a small way. Just as Christian Aid was supporting projects initiated by the local churches abroad, so Tear Fund set up Traidcraft to give small producers in the 'two thirds world' a market for their goods in the North. This vision of trade between North and South, conducted without exploitation, was extended by Traidcraft. They sell a wide range of goods from food to clothes and are organised in a way designed not only to give the producers a fair return for their goods and labour, but also to ensure that the maximum amount of the processing involved takes place in the South. Thus goods grown or made are packaged on site. Traidcraft is not a charity, but an organisation that is trying to put fair business practice into action. Justice, rather than charity, has entered the debate. There are those who are beginning to say that if consideration of the way our world economic system functions is to be truly ethical, it must not balk at assessing the assumptions upon which the system is based, as **Rex Ambler** has pointed out.

Virulently anti-Communist, in part because of the vicious persecution Catholics suffered at Communist hands in Russia and Mexico, papal encyclicals in the twentieth century have nevertheless continued to reflect a concern for economic fairness both within and between nations. Catholicism has been equally clear in its general commitment to capitalism and the fundamental right of private property.

11.9.2 Attitudes to power

Since Christianity became the established faith of the Roman Empire under Constantine, the Church has generally supported the right of the State to exercise its God-given control. The twentieth century has seen the growth of theologies that have challenged that basic assumption. From the liberation theologies of Latin America, the black theologies of North America to the feminist theologies of the West, theology is beginning to be approached 'from below' and to be seen as a means of liberating the oppressed. While some of this thinking, both Protestant and Catholic, can be accused of naivety in drawing the line too simply between oppressed and oppressor as sinned against and sinner, nevertheless it represents a vital corrective to the role that the Church has long played in supporting the powers that be. These theologies are examined more closely in Chapter 10.

The attitude of most church bodies remains traditionally supportive of the status quo. With the advent of representative and pluralist democracy, questions of how far individual Christian consciences can legislate Christian standards for all are increasingly being asked. Many Christian groups which seek to impose what they see as a Christian influence, are often more concerned with issues such as what appears on television screens, rather than poverty, prejudice or applying a Christian critique to the role of their democratic society in the world context. Groups like the Sojourners in the United States represent a noble exception to this general pattern. Christians in the former Communist Eastern Europe were in the forefront of the reform movements, which eventually saw the collapse of the metaphorical Iron Curtain and the very real Berlin Wall.

11.9.3 Attitudes to family life and sexual matters

The twentieth century has seen a profound change in sexual mores, family patterns and the rights of women in the West. The push for change has been entirely secular, the Church sometimes accepting change only once it has happened, but often hanging on as long as possible. The main changes have been birth control, easier divorce and the enfranchisement of women. While the general acceptance, outside the Roman Catholic Church, of birth control has undoubtedly given women with access to it control of their fertility, the medical nature of the pill has meant that another area of women's experience has been given into the hands of professionals, often men. In the 1960s the pill became as much a symbol of a woman's availability for men, as a means of her own liberation. In developing countries it has been used as a means of control, and given impetus to a thinking that places a higher value on the fertility of some groups than on others.

The issue of abortion has also been politicised; for those 'pro-choice', abortion is a vital resource in a woman's right to power over her own fertility; for those opposed, the issue is often not only the right of the unborn but the future of family life. With the wider acceptability of abortion many fear that some, such as teenagers or the poor or those with larger families, will find abortion pressed upon them by those who find their pregnancy unacceptable.

The latter half of the nineteenth century has seen a dramatic rise in the numbers of couples openly cohabiting either before or instead of marriage, and a dramatic rise in the divorce rate. While this implies a breakdown of traditional Christian morality, monogamy, albeit serial, is still more acceptable than promiscuity. The Church and society are beginning, in fits and starts, to recognise and discuss homosexuality.

While women can vote and some women have reached positions of prominence, the majority of those in power are male. The Church has little if anything to say on how to improve the economic or political position of women. Despite the endeavours of the World Council of Churches, there are still many in the Church who see no problem in the continuance of existing structures.

In the seventeenth century, moral philosophy, though debating the hows and whys of ethical decision-making, could assume a common moral code. This is no longer the case. Some thinkers see the family as the bulwark of patriarchy and its demise in its present form as liberating for women. Others see the family unit as something to be preserved at all costs. Some see homosexuality as a God-given gift, while others regard it as an illness or deviancy. Often a person's ethical decisions are more a result of their assumptions than their consideration of a particular issue. The Church is just as torn as society at large by varying opinions, and discussion between those who hold differing opinions is made difficult by mutual suspicion. If the Church is to contribute to the ethical debate in society it must learn how to cope with the disparate positions within its own ranks.

11.9.4   Attitudes to violence

With two World Wars, the Holocaust, conflicts in Indo-China, the Cold War, the emergence of nuclear weapons, continuing strife in the Middle East, the rise in terrorism, civil wars in Africa, the rise of militant Islam and the disintegration of the former Yugoslavia, the twentieth century has had plenty of opportunity to ponder the problems of violence. While the West is learning to forego the use of violence as an official political tool, within their own system many governments still use terror for internal political ends. The Churches in Latin America and South Africa have learnt to stand firmly for the dignity of all human life, although how this principle can be applied in specific instances is not always easy to determine.

The Church has always contained a pacifist wing but many have felt that evils such as the Holocaust cannot be prevented from recurring without a legitimate use of force. Before the advent of nuclear weapons, the Church's 'just war' theory was used to try to delineate when force was acceptable. The theory of deterrent, by which it was legitimate to hold a large enough force to deter any potential enemy, has been used subsequently to justify both the obtaining and keeping of nuclear arsenals. Not all found this acceptable, and Christians and non-Christians alike have worked for disarmament.

11.9.5   Attitudes towards medical ethics

The practice of modern medicine throws up many areas that demand ethical consideration. However, unlike in the contemporary discussion of the world's economic system, where it is clear that the Christian responses must be to work against injustice, even though this might be difficult to flesh out in practice, many of the issues arising in medicine defy such simple analysis. Few Christians would argue with the need to preserve an individual's human dignity, but is that dignity helped or hindered by life support techniques when the possibility of regaining independent life is remote? Can such a decision ever be taken in the abstract? Whilst the sheer technicality leads some to feel out of their depth and unwilling to trespass on what they feel is the preserve of the professional, it is unwise and irresponsible to leave such wide-ranging and important decisions entirely to the medical profession. It is important that neither the rapid developments in medical techniques nor the lack of obvious rights and wrongs lead Christian thinkers to shy away from tackling this area.

Techniques of testing unborn children for a wide range of conditions have resulted in the choice of abortion being offered to parents if their unborn child is discovered handicapped or suffering from various genetic conditions. Whatever the compassionate impulse behind this, Christian ethicists must recognise the implications for the rights of handicapped people. There is a fine line between a desire to eliminate suffering and eugenics. Similar difficulties arise in the developing field of genetic engineering.

Fears have been expressed that the treatment of extremely premature or handicapped babies who have little hope of either a reasonable life expectancy or any quality of life verges on the experimental. Should these children be subjected to invasive treatment that serves only to prolong their suffering? Who is to decide what constitutes a decent quality of life? What about the suffering in 'letting them die'? Who is to decide and how?

These questions are similar to those raised by the technology of life support. By what criterion and by whose authority should the system be turned off? Should there be a detailed procedure set out or should each case be considered on its merits? Who will decide between emotional, medical and financial constraints?

In medicine, as in many other areas, the impulse to develop and improve has gone unquestioned and death has too often been seen as a failure. The hospice movement has done a tremendous amount in putting a more positive approach to death into practice. However, some thinkers are worried that, although both vital and healing, facing up to the naturalness of death will become a cloak for those who wish to deprive the elderly of treatment that would improve their condition. Likewise, those who can see a case for allowing euthanasia and the practice of living wills, because it puts the final control back into the hands of the patient, are still worried that in practice it may become a means of applying pressure on the terminally ill or elderly.

Infertility treatments raise concerns not only about the morality of the procedures, but also about their expense. The issue of prioritisation is becoming an increasingly important element in medical ethics. Christians may still stand by the right of all who are sick or needy to treatment but, when choices have to be made, it is important for Christians to make a contribution to the debate.

Technological developments and financial changes are not the only fields in which ethics play a role: some have been working on the ethics of 'normal' medical practice. Rather than the patient being seen as simply the recipient of treatment it is becoming accepted, at least on the surface, that the patient should be seen as a client, and the medical profession as a resource over which he has rights and legitimate expectations. Again, issues of priorities arise.

Medical ethics is one of the most important areas of ethical debate in the twentieth century, since governments are seeking ethical opinions as one strand of evidence when they propose to regulate practice. Ethics in this area epitomises the complexity that characterises twentieth century life. Accepting this complexity is important for anyone who seeks to make a contribution to ethical debates. This must not mean losing hold of the distinctiveness of the Christian tradition. As it has been throughout the centuries, Christian ethics in the twenty-first century will still be a matter of working out what discipleship means for individuals and groups in their own contexts.

Bibliography

W. Barclay, *Ethics in a Permissive Society*, Fontana, London (1971)
David Cook, *The Moral Maze*, SPCK, London (1983)
J. Fletcher, *Situation Ethics*, SCM, London (1997)
B. Hebblethwaite, *The Adequacy of Ethics*, Marshall, Morgan and Scott, Basingstoke (1981)
K. Ward, *Ethics and Christianity*, Allen & Unwin, London (1970)

Glossary

Apocalypse	Revelation, the end of the world.
Apocrypha	The biblical books received by the early Church as part of the Greek version of the Old Testament, but not included in the Hebrew Bible.
Arianism	The belief that the Son of God is neither eternal nor divine.
Canon	The body of books recognised as sacred and genuine, and hence included in the Bible.
Covenant	A solemn agreement made by God with his people.
Diaspora	The dispersion of the Jews, mainly in the eighth to sixth centuries BC.
Docetism	The belief that Jesus only seemed to live and die in the flesh.
Enlightenment	Eighteenth century philosophy emphasising reason and individualism rather than tradition.
Episcopacy	The government of the Church by bishops.
Eschatology	Beliefs about the destiny of mankind and the world, the study of 'last things'.
Gemara	A rabbinical commentary on the Mishnah forming the second part of the Talmud.
Gnosticism	The belief that salvation is attained through a secret knowledge.
Hellenisation	The imitation of Greek culture.
Hermeneutics	The study of how to interpret the Bible to make it relevant to modern times, whilst being true to its original meaning.
Hexateuch	The first six books of the Old Testament.
Iconoclasm	The breaking up of images, for example in the eighth–ninth centuries in the church in the Eastern Roman Empire.
Incarnation	The embodiment of God in Jesus.
Levites	Members of the tribe of Levi from whom priests were chosen until after the Exile.
Masoretic text (MT)	The recognised text of the Old Testament established by Jewish scholars between the sixth and tenth century AD.
Midrashim	An ancient commentary on part of the Hebrew Scriptures attached to the biblical text.
Mishnah	An authoritative collection of explanatory material embodying the oral tradition of the Jewish Law and forming the first part of the Talmud.
Patriarch	The title of the chief bishop, in particular those with authority over the Church in Antioch, Alexandria. Constantinople and formerly in Rome.
Patristic	Relating to the early Christian writers/Church fathers or their works.
Pentateuch	The first five books of the Old Testament.
Pharisee	Member of an ancient Jewish sect. The Pharisees are referred to only by Josephus and in the New Testament. They were not as strict in their interpretation of Mosaic law as the Sadducees, and did believe in Resurrection.
Pseudepigrapha	Jewish writings ascribed to various Old Testament Prophets but written during or just before the early Christian period.
Qumran	Site of caves on the western side of the Dead Sea where the Dead Sea Scrolls were discovered.

Redemption   Man's deliverance from sin and damnation. In the Old Testament this describes what God did for Israel. In the New Testament it refers to Jesus' death on the Cross.

Sadducees   Members of a Jewish sect or part which denied the Resurrection of the Dead, the existence of spirits and the obligations of oral traditions. They accepted only the written Law.

Samaritans   Inhabitants of Samaria. The Samaritans accepted only their own Pentateuch.

Schism   The separation of a Church into two churches, or the secession of a group owing to doctrinal differences.

Septuagint   A Greek version of the Old Testament, including the Apocrypha, made for the Greek-speaking Jews living in Egypt. Its name derives from the tradition that 70 translators, each working separately, translated the whole. Their versions were said to have been identical, thereby demonstrating that their work was divinely inspired. Internal evidence indicates that the work was divided between a number of translators and was carried out over the third to second century BC. It was used by the early Christians who spoke Greek.

Tabernacle   Tent containing the Ark of the Covenant, used as a portable shrine by the Israelites during their wanderings in the wilderness.

Talmud   The Jewish civil and ceremonial law, consisting of the Mishnah and the Gemara, and some other material.

Targum   The various ancient Aramaic interpretations of the Hebrew scriptures made from the first century AD, and possibly earlier, when Hebrew was ceasing to be spoken.

Theodicy   Justification of divine providence in the face of suffering.

Torah   The Pentateuch.

Index